The Maghrib in the New Century

UNIVERSITY PRESS OF FLORIDA

Florida A&M University, Tallahassee
Florida Atlantic University, Boca Raton
Florida Gulf Coast University, Ft. Myers
Florida International University, Miami
Florida State University, Tallahassee
New College of Florida, Sarasota
University of Central Florida, Orlando
University of Florida, Gainesville
University of North Florida, Jacksonville
University of South Florida, Tampa
University of West Florida, Pensacola

The Maghrib in the New Century

Identity, Religion, and Politics

Edited by Bruce Maddy-Weitzman
and Daniel Zisenwine

University Press of Florida
Gainesville/Tallahassee/Tampa/Boca Raton
Pensacola/Orlando/Miami/Jacksonville/Ft. Myers/Sarasota

Copyright 2007 by Bruce Maddy-Weitzman and Daniel Zisenwine
All rights reserved
Printed in the United States of America on acid-free paper

First cloth printing, 2007
First paperback printing, 2013

Library of Congress Cataloging-in-Publication Data
The Maghrib in the new century: identity, religion, and politics/edited by Bruce Maddy-Weitzman and Daniel Zisenwine.
p. cm.
Includes bibliographical references and index.
ISBN 978-0-8130-3142-2 (cloth: alk. paper)
ISBN 978-0-8130-4470-5 (pbk.)
1. Africa, North—Politics and government—20th century. 2. Nationalism—Africa, North. 3. Islam and politics—Africa. 4. Group identity—Africa, North.
I. Maddy-Weitzman, Bruce. II. Zisenwine, Daniel.
DT204.M27 2007
961.059–dc22   2007028886

The University Press of Florida is the scholarly publishing agency for the State University System of Florida, comprising Florida A&M University, Florida Atlantic University, Florida Gulf Coast University, Florida International University, Florida State University, New College of Florida, University of Central Florida, University of Florida, University of North Florida, University of South Florida, and University of West Florida.

University Press of Florida
15 Northwest 15th Street
Gainesville, FL 32611-2079
http://www.upf.com

Contents

List of Tables vii
Preface ix

1. The Maghrib at the Dawn of the Twenty-first Century 1
   Benjamin Stora

Part 1. A Half-Century after Independence: Rethinking Maghribi History, Memory, and Identity 11

2. The (Re)fashioning of Moroccan National Identity 13
   Mickael Bensadoun

3. Algerian Identity and Memory 36
   Robert Mortimer

4. Berber/Amazigh "Memory Work" 50
   Bruce Maddy-Weitzman

Part 2. Regimes and Societies: New Challenges 73

5. Reflections on the Aftermath of Civil Strife: Algeria, 2006 75
   Gideon Gera

6. The Fate of Political Islam in Algeria 103
   Louisa Aït-Hamadouche and Yahia H. Zoubir

7. From Hasan II to Muhammad VI: Plus Ça Change? 132
   Daniel Zisenwine

8. Justice and Development or Justice and Spirituality? The Challenge of Morocco's Nonviolent Islamist Movements 150
   Michael J. Willis

9. Whither the Ben Ali Regime in Tunisia? 175
   Michele Penner Angrist

Part 3. The Economic Dimension 195

10. The Constraints on Economic Development in Morocco and Tunisia 197
    Paul Rivlin

11. Algeria's Economy: Mutations, Performance, and Challenges 217
    Ahmed Aghrout and Michael Hodd

Part 4. The Maghrib and Europe 235
12. The Maghrib Abroad: Immigrant Transpolitics and Cultural Involution in France 237
   Paul A. Silverstein

List of Contributors 265
Index 267

Tables

6.1. Comparing Electoral Results of Islamist and Nationalist Parties   123

10.1. Population in Morocco and Tunisia, 1970–2003   198

10.2. Population Growth in Morocco and Tunisia, 1970–2000   198

10.3. GDP Growth in Morocco, 1981–2003   200

10.4. Morocco: Balance of Payments Indicators   201

10.5. GDP Growth in Tunisia, 1981–2003   207

10.6. Tunisia: Balance of Payments Indicators   211

11.1. Algeria's Macroeconomic Performance, 1950–2006   218

11.2. Credits from the Banking Sector, Selected Years   225

Preface

The United States government's Greater Middle East Initiative, a policy designed to address the root causes of Middle Eastern instability, violence, and anti-Western terrorism, was largely a result of developments originating in the eastern Asian portion of the Greater Middle East—Afghanistan, Iran, and Iraq. Far less attention has been paid to Europe's immediate neighbors just across the Mediterranean Sea and the Straits of Gibraltar—the Maghrib states, headed by Morocco and Algeria (whose combined population of over sixty million constitutes 75 percent of the five-nation Arab Maghrib Union).[1] Yet all of the dire circumstances confronting Middle Eastern states and societies—entrenched authoritarian regimes lacking popular legitimacy, strong Islamic opposition movements and smaller groups that engage in bin Laden–style terrorism, economic systems that have lagged far behind other regions in the increasingly globalized economy, large youthful populations clamoring for jobs or visas to the West and the resulting migration and social pressures on European countries—are present in varying degrees in the Maghrib. At the same time, their societies are increasingly vibrant, being shaped by numerous cross-cultural currents emanating from Berber, Arab-Muslim, African, and European heritages and the ever-expanding links with Europe and, increasingly, with the rest of the developed world. Indeed, Maghribi political and social systems appear more ripe than those in the Arab and Muslim East for the kind of partnership initiatives envisaged by Western policy makers that they hope will be transformative in nature.

Of course, nothing in the realm of human affairs moves in a straight line, and Maghrib states and societies are sure to find themselves on a twisted and intricate road during the coming decade as they strive to cope with the formidable challenges on their collective agendas. The twelve chapters in this volume, written by both veteran and up-and-coming scholars from a variety of disciplines and national origins, seek to elucidate and analyze the various factors and issues confronting Maghribi states and societies, primarily Algeria and Morocco, with reference also to Tunisia, the third core Maghribi state. The focus of the chapters is overwhelmingly from within, against the background of these countries' often tortured recent histories. The main themes are the intertwining of issues centering on identity, religion, and politics half a century after the Maghribi states attained independence from colonial rule. Taken as a whole, the volume continues the work of the important collected studies on Maghribi affairs published between 1993 and 2000 and in 2003.[2] Moreover, it breaks new ground in a number of areas, particularly with regard to the Berber dimension of contemporary North African society and politics, as well as the larger questions of history, memory, and national identity.

The book opens with an introductory essay by Benjamin Stora outlining these themes. It is followed by part 1, which focuses on the intertwining of past and present as regimes seek to relegitimize themselves while social and political forces reopen questions about their countries' history and collective identity. Mickael Bensadoun examines the two competing sociopolitical movements in Morocco that seek to fashion alternative conceptions of Moroccan collective identity—the Islamist movement and its polar opposite, the Amazigh (Berber) culture movement. Robert Mortimer focuses on the important part being played by Algeria's writers and intellectuals in the renewed fashioning of a national self-understanding through their reflections about Algerian identity, the memories that shape it, and the place of religion in it. Bruce Maddy-Weitzman analyzes Berberist efforts to "remember, recover, and invent" their history in both Morocco and Algeria in the face of a state-sponsored hegemonic historical narrative that confirmed their political and social marginalization.

Part 2 of this book examines the contemporary challenges facing the Maghribi states. Gideon Gera elucidates Algerian realities from the perspective of a regime that managed to survive a brutal civil war against a violent Islamist movement. Louisa Aït-Hamadouche and Yahia H. Zoubir analyze Algeria's Islamist movement against the background of its defeat. Daniel Zisenwine examines the degree to which the new Moroccan monarch, Muhammad VI, has moved toward more reformist policy directions, and Michael J. Willis analyzes Morocco's two leading Islamist opposition movements against the background of the burning question being asked throughout the region and beyond: Can Islamist movements be legitimate political actors in a democratizing system, and if so, how? And what is to be their relationship to the newer radical jihadist groups? Michele Penner Angrist focuses on the Tunisian regime, particularly the paradox of its secular and modern social orientation combined with a hidebound authoritarian, repressive political system.

Part 3 examines in detail the economic dimension of the challenges facing the three Maghribi states: Paul Rivlin looks at the issues facing Morocco and Tunisia, and Ahmed Aghrout and Michael Hodd do the same for Algeria.

The varying challenges posed to European states, Maghribi migrants and societies, and interstate relations between the Maghrib and Europe by the phenomenon of large Maghribi immigrant communities in Europe are already monumental and will only grow in the years ahead. In the book's concluding section, Paul A. Silverstein examines the sociopolitical movements and imaginations enacted within the space of transpolitics that links Algeria and France across the Mediterranean, this in light of the Algerian and French "vanguard" roles in the mass migration from the Maghrib to Europe.

The idea for this book came as an outgrowth of a small workshop held by the Maghrib Working Group of the Moshe Dayan Center for Middle Eastern and African Studies, Tel Aviv University, on May 28, 2003. The stimulating discussions that day, spearheaded by two eminent Paris-based Maghribists, Benjamin Stora and Rémy Leveau, made us realize that the time had come for a fresh collected volume on the Maghrib to address the various new issues that had emerged in recent years and revisit more familiar ones. Asher Susser, director of the Dayan Center, was supportive of the idea from the outset and provided important backing for the project. Special thanks are due to Yahia H. Zoubir for his help in advancing the volume. Thanks also to an anonymous reader for the University Press of Florida for instructive comments and suggestions. We are appreciative of the work of indexer Kahel Yurman, copy editor Karin Kaufman, and proofreader Patterson Lamb.

Sadly, Rémy Leveau passed away suddenly in February 2005. His untimely departure deprived us of a friend and mentor, someone whose gracious willingness to share his knowledge of the Maghrib and constructively critique our own helped to lay the groundwork for Maghribi studies at Tel Aviv University.

A word regarding transcription of names and Arabic terms: For simplicity's sake, we have generally adopted the common Maghribi spelling of Arabic terms and names and, apart from a few instances, avoided use of diacritical marks for the Arabic letters *ayn* and *alif*.

Notes

1. The Arab Maghrib Union consists of Morocco, Algeria, Tunisia, Libya, and Mauritania. Founded in 1989 with great fanfare, amid expressed hopes for establishing closer regional ties and a regional economic bloc, it has utterly foundered, primarily on the shoals of continuing Algerian-Moroccan differences over the future of the Western Sahara, and on Algeria's implosion during the 1990s.

2. I. William Zartman and William Mark Habeeb, eds., *Polity and Society in Contemporary North Africa* (Boulder, Colo.: Westview, 1993); John Ruedy, ed., *Islamism and Secularism in North Africa* (New York: St. Martin's Press, 1994); Dirke VandeWalle, *North Africa: Development and Reform in a Changing Global Economy* (Basingstoke, Hampshire: Macmillan, 1996); John P. Entelis, ed., *Islam, Democracy, and the State in North Africa* (Bloomington: Indiana University Press, 1997); Azzedine Layachi, ed., *Economic Crisis and Political Change in North Africa* (Westport, Conn.: Praeger, 1998); Yahia H. Zoubir, ed., *North Africa in Transition* (Gainesville: University Press of Florida, 1999); Ali Abdullatif Ahmida, *Beyond Colonialism and Nationalism in the Maghrib* (New York: Palgrave Macmillan, 2000); James McDougall, ed., *Nation, Society, and Culture in North Africa* (London: Frank Cass, 2003).

1

The Maghrib at the Dawn of the Twenty-first Century

BENJAMIN STORA

Contemporary Maghribi societies face a host of political, social, and economic challenges, which derive from both the flow and ruptures of North African history over the *longue durée* and the ever-accelerating processes spurred by modernity and globalization. Underpinning these challenges are large-scale demographic pressures, with all the expected impact on state-society relations and relations with Europe, the legacy of authoritarianism and violence, both state-sponsored and from opposition movements, and the region's geo-strategic and economic importance.

The Maghrib today, namely, the core countries of Morocco, Algeria, and Tunisia, in addition to Libya and Mauritania, has roughly eighty million inhabitants. With this many people on Europe's threshold, reinforced by the historic links between the northern and southern Mediterranean shores, the European Union (EU) cannot help but take a keen interest in the unfolding of events in the region. Moreover, the Maghrib itself is widely represented in Europe, particularly in France, where the Muslim population, the majority of whom are of North African origin, ranges between four and five million. This population weighs heavily on France's domestic and foreign policies. Indeed, it is impossible to analyze contemporary European politics without referring to Europe's large North African immigrant population in countries such as France, Spain, Holland, Belgium, Italy, and Germany.

With all of the recent focus on demographics and emigration, other features of contemporary Maghrib life are sometimes downplayed. But the horrific, barbaric violence in Algeria during the 1990s, in which over 150,000 people may have lost their lives in the bitter struggle between the Algerian authorities and radical Islamist groups, will not soon be forgotten, either in Algeria or among its neighbors. And the appearance in May 2003 of radical Islamist terrorism in Morocco served as a reminder that local, regional, and global forces may interact to produce a toxic brew in that country as well.

The third focal point of the Maghrib's ongoing importance has to do with location and resources. The region's strategic location along the Mediterranean coast and in close proximity to the straits of Gibraltar, as well as its status as a commercial crossroads, has drawn French, other European, and U.S. attention for many years. Added to that interest in recent years has been the discovery of a vast repository of natural gas under the Saharan sands, the world's largest desert region, thus increasing the Maghrib's value in the world economic system.

With these underpinnings of North African realities in mind, we can now turn to specifics. The primary political challenge in the contemporary Maghrib is the question of state legitimacy half a century after decolonization. For many years following the achievement of independence, leading political forces in the Maghrib—for example, the Moroccan Istiqlal party, the Front de Libération Nationale (FLN) in Algeria, and Habib Bourguiba's Neo-Destour in Tunisia—drew legitimacy from their earlier anticolonial activities against the French, and the nationalist movements provided these countries with leadership up until the 1990s. Their political vocabularies, as well as many of their stances on substantive issues, were related to the legacy of the anticolonial struggle and their identification with wider Arab nationalism. This ideology served as a means of cooperation and liaison between the three nationalist movements and the wider Arab world. But as the tide of Arab nationalism steadily ebbed, the now-aging nationalist movements were forced to discard their ideological tenets and found themselves adrift without an anchor.

The first country to experience this process was Algeria. Algeria's independence was championed by a nationalist movement, one that was populist and opposed to a multiparty system. The nationalists, who purported to speak for "the people," considered political parties a source of weakness dating from the colonial period. They had little interest in establishing a pluralist political system and asserted that their own movement could confidently lead an independent Algeria. But the country's one-party system, led by the FLN, quickly disintegrated into numerous factions and was unable to effectively lead Algeria's citizens.[1] As Algeria dismantled its one-party system in October 1988, the entire FLN-orchestrated structure collapsed.[2] Concurrently, the disintegration of the Soviet bloc, which had previously supported many Arab nationalist regimes, introduced profound uncertainty in many countries. In Algeria, it helped create an acute "legitimacy deficit." Part of the uniqueness of Algeria was that the FLN had been not merely a political party but a hegemonic "state party." Hence, the legitimacy deficit in the wake of the collapse of the status quo was now especially grave. The FLN's swift political demise during 1988–92 was in many ways the state's demise, affecting its political personnel and ideological representations. In other words, the FLN's crisis proved to be a crisis of historical legitimacy for the state.

This void in Algeria's political landscape, fueled by the regional crisis of Arab nationalism and the concurrent absence of a successor political generation within the FLN, was quickly filled by the Islamist movement, which sought to furnish a new political vision, taking advantage of Algeria's sudden and ultimately short-lived democratic opening. Algerian president Chadli Benjedid's decision in 1988 to lift restrictions on political activity and effectively end the FLN's exclusive control over the political system brought new groups and political organizations to the fore. Among them was a coalition of radical Islamists and traditional pious urban groups, which attracted the country's alienated youth. This extraordinary new force in Algerian politics, the Islamic Salvation Front (Front Islamique du Salut, or FIS) scored sweeping successes in the 1990 municipal elections and in the aborted parliamentary elections of December 1991. At the same time, the advent of democracy brought to the fore a number of components of Algeria's nascent civil society, such as trade unions, women's movements, and a newly independent and combative press. These elements quickly found themselves in a bitter struggle with the Islamists, ultimately resulting in the army's intervention and the descent to civil war. The collapse of the Algerian state party and the attempt by the Islamist movement to fill the resulting void may well presage a similar pattern in other Arab countries.

The question of legitimacy overshadows political developments in other North African nations. For example, the bloodless "medical" coup that overthrew Tunisia's president Habib Bourguiba in 1987 did not contest the ideological aspects of Bourguiba's political legacy. His successor, Zayn al-Abidin Ben Ali, placed stability at the heart of his rule, that is, he sought at all costs to avoid repeating the Algerian experience. In doing so, he drew support from large sectors of Tunisian society.

Although Morocco is a monarchy, it was not immune from its own version of the legitimacy crisis, in which the king's omnipotence and combined political and religious leadership was challenged. King Hasan II attempted to avert this crisis during the 1990s by reaching out to established opposition political parties, such as the Union Socialiste des Forces Populaires (USFP), and incorporate them into the decision-making process. The USFP's assumption of leadership of the governing coalition in 1998 culminated a long negotiation process between the party and the monarchy, ensuring the continued, controlled evolution of the Moroccan political system, in stark contrast to the rupture in Algeria.

The political transition of the Maghrib's postindependence nationalist-authoritarian order to a more pluralist, law-based democratic one is only in its early stages. Indeed, the construction of political democracy in the Maghrib, the only type of system that can attain genuine legitimacy from the populace, is one of the region's greatest challenges. To be sure, Tunisia's ossified domestic political climate and sterilized political system leave little possibility for a significant transformation of political life in the short run. But for Algeria and Morocco, the issue is most salient, and the battles for political liberalization rage in full force. They are fought by groups such as Berber activists, women's rights advocates, journalists, and other civil organizations and forums, as well as Islamists.

In spite of its slow pace, the struggle for greater political democracy in North Africa is far more advanced in the Maghrib than in the Arab Middle East. Even in Iraq, which has begun its own journey toward democracy, one must note that this process was spurred by foreign intervention and guidance. By contrast, Algeria and Morocco's democratic initiatives have been spurred from the outset by indigenous forces, underscoring once again North Africa's unique path of political development, setting it apart from the Middle East.

The second major challenge North African countries—indeed, nearly the entire African continent—currently face is the question of emigration. North African societies are particularly affected by the presence of substantial numbers of qualified, educated individuals unable to find proper employment, who thus seek to build new lives in more prosperous settings, mostly in Europe. Unlike previous emigration waves, made up mostly of unskilled laborers, today's Maghribi migrant workers include large numbers of physicians, pharmacists, engineers, and other professionals. With European countries already wrestling with the need to absorb Muslim immigrants and renegotiate their own social contracts, the continued pressure for immigration also has serious ramifications for Maghribi states. For now, European restrictions on entry visas for potential Maghribi immigrants are likely to increase socioeconomic unrest within the Maghrib states. In addition, those who are desperate enough to leave their home countries at any cost often resort to extreme and hazardous ways to enter Europe, adding another challenge to both Maghribi governments and the European Union.

There are several remedies that might help alleviate this problem. One would be a sort of "European Marshall Plan" for North Africa, a large-scale economic and social development program necessitating massive financial investments. But getting such an enterprise off the ground is no simple matter, particularly since European governments are not of one mind regarding the idea. Not surprisingly, countries directly affected by North African immigration tend to favor such an idea, whereas those more removed from the flow of Maghribi migrants do not. Such a plan could also alter the nature of Euro-Maghribi economic relations. North Africa has, for the most part, remained economically dependent on European states in the postindependence period. The Maghrib remains a supplier of fuels and natural resources to Europe and a market for Europe's industrial exports. Its trade with EU countries is uneven and leaves the region far behind the economic and political powerhouse situated on its northern frontier.[3]

Within North Africa, the allure of Europe remains high, particularly among the younger generation. In contrast to previous generations, which viewed education as the stepping stone to an improved social and economic life at home, many of today's young Maghribis consider emigration to be the most effective means of social mobility. This sentiment is compounded by the impact of Western and European consumer goods, as well as satellite television programs that offer actual glimpses of daily life in Europe. These enticing images sharply contrast with the depressing economic reality in which many North Africans exist. In addition, these young Maghribis are affected by a process of individualization, which also plays a part in their decision to emigrate. Whereas earlier waves of North African immigrants to Europe maintained close ties to their families and the communities left behind, today migrants often feel less restricted by familial expectations and community norms. Emigration to Europe has ceased to be a collective endeavor and has now become primarily an individual enterprise, reflecting the social transformations taking place within Maghribi societies. Any type of a Marshall Plan devised for the region would have to address these social changes, requiring the reconstruction of the region's sorely deficient educational infrastructure and professional training facilities.

The third aspect worthy of scrutiny and analysis in North Africa is the rise of alternative, transnational political identities that implicitly pose challenges to the nation-state as presently constituted. Independent Maghribi nation-states inherited their geographical borders from the colonial era. These frontiers often disregarded traditional geographical affiliations and were contested by local residents. To overcome these difficulties, North African states adopted a mix of Arab nationalism—originating, of course, in the Mashriq (Arab East)—and a harsh, centralizing Jacobinism. The resulting authoritarian state was strong enough to repress for two generations any rival political movements or alternative forms of collective identity. However, this is no longer the case. The rise of competing Islamist and Berber movements pose strong challenges not only to the existing political order but also to the very concept of what modern Maghribi states should be.

North African Islamist movements, for example, view the concept of a nation-state as a divisive political form and prefer to emphasize overarching political concepts such as "the Muslim *umma*" (community) as their point of reference. In their minds, the division of the region into territorial states is a reminder of the colonial era and its destructive legacy on the geographical, political, and social composition in the region. Nonetheless, North African Islamist movements focus the bulk of their attention on local developments within their respective countries, suggesting that they are more "local" in character than their ideology might suggest.

The emergence of an articulate movement promoting ethnic Berber culture and identity among Algerian and Morocco's Berbers has also contributed to the growing debate surrounding the viability of Maghribi states as they are presently constituted. The new Berberist ethos, accompanied by demands for political and cultural pluralism, stands in explicit opposition to the tenets of centralized Jacobin-style state authority, as well as to Arab-Muslim Sunni political tradition. The Berber activist groups are devoted to advancing political democracy, in contrast to the Islamists, who desire the implementation of the Shari'a. However, both challenge the nation-state's omnipotent position, implicitly or explicitly. Indeed, the dialectics of these challenges may well result in the emergence over the next few decades of a "Maghrib of regions," transcending existing political borders and forming alternative sociocultural units that share a common dialect, lifestyle, family ties, and even cuisine. Such a reality would contrast sharply with the Maghrib's colonial heritage and mark a symbolic return to the precolonial era. Indeed, regional cooperation along those lines already exists in some fashion between the residents of Oujda, Morocco, and Tlemcen, Algeria. Both communities share similar political and cultural patterns, as well as affiliation with religious brotherhoods, and their disregard of the political border dividing them is evident, even though it has been officially closed for more than ten years.

This type of regionalism also may lead eventually to some type of federal or confederal framework. To be sure, Maghribi nation-states are currently strong enough to resist these undercurrents. But the rise of Berber movements in Algeria and Morocco, which veer between cultural-ethnic demands and subtle, latent expectations of a greater political voice, suggest that such a scenario may very well become a reality in the not-too-distant future.

A fourth challenge facing the Maghrib in the coming years is the silent revolution currently sweeping through the region regarding the status of women. Algeria experienced demonstrations in the early 1980s over the country's proposed family legal code. Resulting legislation institutionalized women's unequal legal status, granting men the right of repudiation and permitting polygamy.[4] Less than a decade later, Algeria's women's movements and activists were thrust into the battle with the violent Islamist opposition and paid a heavy price: Hundreds of women were killed because of their explicit rejection of Islamist norms of behavior and appearance. Morocco, for its part, has been the scene since the early 1990s of a nonviolent culture war of its own over the issue, culminating in King Muhammad VI's scrapping, in October 2003, of the existing personal status code, the Moudawwana, in favor of a new family law granting women a much greater measure of equality.[5] Moreover, behind these visible battles lies a development of utmost importance: the significant decline in the birth rate in both Algeria and Morocco over the last two decades, following in Tunisia's footsteps. This trend underscores the fact that North African women are increasingly less constrained by traditional mores and social expectations regarding the number of children they will bear and are playing an active role in family planning. The reality of families consisting of five to ten children, which was common twenty or thirty years ago, no longer exists, as the average family size has shrunk drastically. Accordingly, the region is witnessing a change in gender relations. Marriage age for many women is much higher today than a generation ago, when it was not uncommon to see girls just entering puberty married. The rise in the marriage age is particularly noticeable among the Maghrib's urban population. This group has experienced significant changes in its lifestyle, traditions, education, and social interactions. The effects of this revolution, still very much a work in progress, have not been measured. But its impact on the nexus of family, society, state, and politics is likely to be significant.

A final challenge, which reveals yet another facet of the contemporary Maghrib, is the question of language. Language serves as one of the foundations of political and national identity the world over. Yet one of North Africa's particular features is the existence of several languages spoken in each country. Although Arabic is the region's official language, Tamazight

(Berber) and French are widely used as well. Paradoxically, Berber dialects are more widely spoken in Morocco than among Algeria's more overtly politicized Berber communities. French, of course, remains the language of commerce and science and is spoken by millions across the region, in spite of the fact that French was often viewed in the initial postcolonial period as an unfortunate relic of the preindependence period.

The rise of Berber culture movements, which unceasingly demand that Tamazight be recognized as an official national language alongside Arabic, adds another dimension to the complicated North African linguistic landscape. Although ruling regimes have advocated comprehensive Arabization policies throughout the independence era, the degree of proficiency of Arabic among Maghribi populations is still uneven. Many North Africans are unfamiliar, wholly or partially, with classical literary Arabic and resort to local spoken dialects that often deviate widely from extant rules of proper Arabic grammar. The promotion of Berber dialects in daily speech and in the educational system, after decades of declining usage, establishes a potential alternative to the use of colloquial Arabic, further complicating the Maghrib's linguistic scene. Of course, the language question must be understood as an additional component of the complex and increasingly fluid relations between state power and Maghribi societies.

North African countries currently face a host of economic and social difficulties. But it is the recent spate of terrorist attacks in the region and the involvement of young Maghribis in jihadist groups abroad that cast a long shadow on the region's future prospects. Although Algeria's decade of internal strife between Islamist militias and government forces is by now well understood (and largely over), the Maghrib has recently been forced to confront significant incidents of terrorism that depart from the realm of the longstanding tensions between local rebellious Islamist parties and militias and the ruling regimes. These attacks, such as the 2002 attack on an ancient synagogue in Jerba, Tunisia, or the May 2003 bombings in Casablanca, were motivated by darker, jihadist forces with a worldwide agenda not necessarily linked to local Maghribi developments. One indication of how radical a departure their actions are from earlier violence was their employment of suicide bombers, a previously unheard-of phenomenon in the Maghrib.

This form of extreme violence not only challenges the Maghrib's security authorities but also forces North Africa's Islamist movements to negotiate, directly or indirectly, with these destructive forces and formulate their own positions vis-à-vis these groups and their actions. As a result, the delicate balance between Islamist movements and state authorities is likely to suffer additional convulsions, especially if these radical groups attempt to carry out additional attacks.

One final note: The combination of political and economic stagnation has resulted in a troublesome phenomenon—the spread of disinterest and detachment throughout Maghribi societies. There are already indications that the region's political classes have distanced themselves from larger elements of society and appear to be only remotely preoccupied with the lives and lots of broader social segments. Such an attitude fuels sentiments of despair and hopelessness, which can be identified especially among large segments of the Maghrib's overwhelmingly youthful population. Disillusioned by grim economic prospects, and inundated with unrealistic promises made by Islamist movements, the fate of the younger generation should be a matter of concern to any party interested in the Maghrib's future. Indeed, restoring political hope to a population numbed by unmatched expectations and unfulfilled promises may very well be the overarching challenge facing the region in the early twenty-first century.

Notes

1. William Quandt, "Algeria's Transition to What?" *Journal of North African Studies* 9, no. 2 (Summer 2004): 82–92.

2. Hugh Roberts, *The Battlefield: Algeria 1988–2002, Studies in a Broken Polity* (London: Verso, 2003).

3. Gregory White, *A Comparative Political Economy of Tunisia and Morocco: On the Outside of Europe Looking In* (Albany: State University of New York Press, 2001), 49–78; George Joffé, "The Euro-Mediterranean Partnership Initiative: Problems and Prospects," *Journal of North African Studies* 3, no. 2 (Summer 1998): 247–67.

4. Mounira M. Charrad, *States and Women's Rights: The Making of Postcolonial Tunisia, Algeria, and Morocco* (Berkeley and Los Angeles: University of California Press, 2001), 195–200.

5. Bruce Maddy-Weitzman, "Women, Islam and the Moroccan State: The Struggle over the Personal Status Law," *Middle East Journal* 59, no. 3 (Summer 2005): 393–410.

1

A Half-Century after Independence

Rethinking Maghribi History, Memory, and Identity

2

The (Re)Fashioning of Moroccan National Identity

MICKAEL BENSADOUN

During the 1990s, the last decade of his life, Morocco's King Hasan II initiated a process of gradual liberalization of the political sphere. One of its important consequences was the emergence of new discourses on national identity. As freedom of expression expanded, social and ethnic groups increasingly sought to redefine aspects of the Moroccan identity, sometimes in opposition to the prevailing narrative. Islamists, the Amazigh movement,[1] feminist groups, and human rights organizations all engaged in this redefinition, which questioned, either implicitly or explicitly, a number of the founding myths of the nation. At the same time, in the face of both internal and external pressures, the monarchy modified elements of the official discourse on national identity while leaving the monarchy's role as the preeminent unifying symbol of the nation untouched.

One consequence of these developments was an interesting dynamic between the dominant discourse and the counterdiscourses. The official discourse began integrating elements of the counterdiscourses to appease the various groups and the challenges they posed. In turn, the pragmatic trends of these various social movements were tempted to accept the monarchy's co-optation. In particular, the monarchy and the two main forces of contestation, the Amazigh movement and the Islamist movement, participated in a lively triangular dialogue. The struggle over the definition of national identity has hence become an important part of the political game, especially since King Muhammad VI succeeded his deceased father in July 1999.

Although the young king has unwaveringly continued to defend the centrality of the monarchy as a national symbol, he has also tolerated the emergence of discourses that may eventually weaken the historic and religious legitimacy of the monarchy. In particular, the new passion for Morocco's recent history risks becoming an act of accusation against monarchic practices instead of promoting national reconciliation. It allows for a profound critique of Hasan II's systematic policies of repression of political dissidents, notwithstanding the fact that the current political system is not fundamentally different.[2] Since ascending to the throne, Muhammad VI has in large part pursued and expanded on processes initiated by his father. For instance, he has employed the time-honored means of *makhzenian* politics, combining co-optation and repression,[3] to deal with the established opposition political parties, the Islamist current, and the Amazigh movement. Like his father, Muhammad VI has promoted a moderate Islam that recognizes the national and religious legitimacy of the king and draws its main references from the Moroccan context. At the same time, he has lent public support to a pro-monarchy Amazigh movement that is likely to serve as an ally against fundamentalism. The triangular political "game" has resulted in important adaptations in the official discourse on national identity. In the negotiation process over the redefinition of national identity, the king plays a dual role. On the one hand, he acts as a mediator between competing groups, but on the other hand, he seeks to redefine the nation in such a way so as to remain a dominant actor of the political sphere.[4]

This chapter explores the emergence of a variety of new definitions of Moroccan identity since the beginning of the 1990s and analyzes their impact on the official discourse, stressing the political factors underlying these evolutions. It focuses on the main discourses of contestation, the Amazigh and the Islamist, against the background of the official discourse.

The Official Version

Although the official discourse on national identity has undergone important changes over the last fifteen years, it has not altered the founding ethos of the nation. Moroccan national identity, as expounded by the regime in the Moroccan Constitution, is based on three pillars.[5] First, the monarchy is the primary national and religious symbol of Morocco. Along with Islam, it is the main unifying factor of the nation. Second, Morocco is a Muslim and Arab country. Third, the territory of western Sahara, adjacent to Morocco's southern border, is an inalienable part of Moroccan territory, notwithstanding the absence of international legitimacy. These principles have remained a constant in the official discourse and are challenged only by radical fringes of the Amazigh and Islamist movements. Without modifying these foundational pillars, the monarchy refashioned the Moroccan national identity, under national and international pressure.

The publication of French journalist Gilles Perrault's book *Notre ami le roi*[6] in September 1990 and the campaign against Morocco's systematic human rights abuses deeply damaged the country's image in the West. The end of the Cold War had led the international community to be much more concerned with the promotion of democracy. Over time, this became a central aspect of U.S. foreign policy. The collapse of the Soviet Union fostered disproportionate expectations best expressed by the American political philosopher Francis Fukuyama: Capitalism and democracy would spread, and the idea of "democratic peace" had become an achievable goal.[7]

In this context, Morocco, a traditionally pro-Western country, could not accept being presented as a brutal autocracy. Therefore, in the beginning of the 1990s, King Hasan II initiated a campaign aimed at improving the international image of Morocco. His new counselor, André Azoulay, a Moroccan Jew from Essaouira (also called Mogador), played a key role in the promotion of this new image. The monarchy developed a new discourse on human rights and democracy. Morocco committed itself to respect for universal values and to the promotion of democracy with the establishment of the Conseil Consultatif des Droits de l'Homme (Consultative Council for Human Rights) on May 8, 1990, and the revision of its constitution on September 4, 1992. From a nation of subjects, Morocco appeared, however haltingly, to be becoming a nation of citizens participating in global processes.

Morocco's official identity discourse has always insisted on the compatibility of Moroccan Islam with democratic values. Moroccan Islam, symbolized by the religious status of the king as "Commander of the Faithful," is presented as a tolerant and modern Islam, respecting and protecting religious minorities.[8] While Algeria struggled with a bloody conflict between the military-dominated regime and radical Islamist opposition groups during the 1990s, Morocco presented itself as a land of peace and stability.

More than ever, the Moroccan authorities delineated their country's identity in opposition to its "brother enemy," Algeria.[9] Algeria became the "significant other" of Morocco despite the numerous similarities between the two countries. Hasan II tried to convince the West that Morocco was immune from Muslim fundamentalism because of the religious legitimacy of the monarchy: Political Islam could not successfully mobilize the population against a traditional monarchy that protected the Muslim identity of the nation.[10] This maxim was mainly intended for consumption in the West, but it also was diffused in the Moroccan media and reinforced by a historical narrative that emphasized the openness of Moroccan Islam to other civilizations and religions. Morocco was presented as a land of exemplary coexistence among peoples of different faiths, with the authorities and society being especially tolerant and protective toward "its Jews." Moroccan Jewish intellectuals, artists, and politicians[11] participated in the dissemination of this idea, publishing a series of books and articles praising Muslim-Jewish entente under a benign and paternal monarchy.[12]

Hasan II liked to claim that for geographic and historic reasons, Morocco's vocation was to build bridges between civilizations, in particular, between Islam and the West.[13] Responding to Samuel Huntington's "clash of civilizations" thesis,[14] the Moroccan official discourse called for dialogue between civilizations. The golden age of Muslim Spain was repeatedly referred to as an ideal model to be followed, with special emphasis placed on the mutual enrichment in Andalusia between Jewish and Muslim intellectuals. Through the use of festivals and other cultural manifestations,[15] Morocco trumpeted the Andalusian golden age in order to show the world that today's Morocco remained a land of tolerance and could serve as a bridge between civilizations.

At the policy level, this vocation found its expression in the supporting role played by Morocco in the promotion of the peace process between Israelis and Palestinians. The active participation of Morocco in the Euro-Mediterranean partnership was another demonstration of the country's ability to foster understanding and cooperation between the three monotheistic religions.

The overarching theme of the official discourse, then, is that Morocco is a Mediterranean country linked to Europe, the Middle East, and Africa, historically, geographically, and culturally.[16] Its history is rich in reciprocal interactions with foreign civilizations and cultures. Thus Moroccan identity, drawing on this rich heritage, is defined as pluralist in nature, culturally, ethnically, and even religiously, and not monolithic. Such a discourse fits in nicely with the postmodern celebration of plural and hybrid identities. Whereas modernity praised the unitary national state, postmodernity values multiculturalism. Hence Morocco's modified official discourse on national identity seems to prove the Moroccan monarchy's ability to adapt to the cultural requirements of the globalization era.[17] Indeed, the legitimacy of the monarchy, drawing on its status as heir to Morocco's long tradition of sharifian rule, is not principally based on Arab nationalism, enabling a flexible management of the country's various social and cultural forces. Contrary to the old established nationalist parties, the monarchy is not committed to the building of a monolithic national identity and to its political expression, a centralized Jacobin state. As a monarchy, the Moroccan state can more easily deal with minority ethnic, cultural, and religious minorities than can other Arab states founded after French and British decolonization. The *makhzen* system is based on the politics of fragmentation, and over time Hasan II adapted the system to deal with cultural and identity challenges.

Hasan II and the Amazigh Movement

King Hasan's response to the emergence of the Amazigh movement was typical of *makhzenian* politics. Born at the end of the 1960s, the Amazigh movement became much more visible at the beginning of the 1990s, taking advantage of the authorities' willingness to allow for greater liberalization in public life and the region-wide crisis of Arab nationalism. As the decade unfolded, the new communication tools, particularly the Internet, reinforced the movement's activities and enabled it to connect with like-minded groups in Algeria and Europe.

On August 5, 1991, the main Moroccan Berber organizations[18] published the Agadir Charter (Charte d'Agadir relative aux droits linguistiques et culturels Amazighs), which demanded the full recognition of Berber identity as part of the country's national identity. The charter did not use the term "Berber," preferring the term "Amazigh," indicating the movement's aspirations to free the identity of berberophones from the shackles of cultural imperialism, be it of Roman, French, or Arab origin. The charter does not deny the "Arab-Muslim" identity of Morocco but stresses the Amazigh ethnic origins of the Moroccan nation.[19]

The document stresses that the Amazigh movement is not separatist. As a democratic movement, it aims at modifying the national identity, which had been hijacked by the unitary central state and its religious ideology, Salafism. The Amazigh movement's natural political and cultural space is the Moroccan nation, and it does not have nationalist/separatist ambitions. The Amazigh movement challenges the dominant definition of Moroccan identity promoted by the nationalist parties, primarily the Istiqlal and, to a lesser extent, the left-leaning Union Socialiste des Forces Populaires (USFP). According to the Amazigh narrative, Morocco is not an Arab nation but an Amazigh (or, at best, an Arab-Amazigh) nation, which suffered from Roman, French, and Arab cultural and political colonization.

Up until the end of the 1990s, the main opponents of the Amazigh movement were not Islamist but nostalgic pan-Arab intellectuals. For example, Muhammad Abd al-Jabri, a leading Moroccan political philosopher of Berber origin recognized throughout the Arab world, considered the Amazigh movement a product of American and Zionist imperialism that threatened the unity of the Arab nation.[20] In the 1990s, the Amazigh movement fashioned its identity mainly in opposition to Arab nationalist ideologies in both their conservative and leftist expressions while refraining from becoming an antimonarchical force.

As far as the monarchy is concerned, the Amazigh movement does not directly threaten it, so long as its religious and political supremacy remains unchallenged, and so long as the movement does not display nationalist/separatist ambitions. Hasan II's response to the rise of the Amazigh movement fit the *makhzenian* mold, constituting a balanced mix of repression, fragmentation, and co-optation. On August 20, 1994, he delivered an important speech that provided official recognition to the Moroccan Berber dialects (there are three main ones in Morocco), characterizing them as part of the country's authentic national identity.[21] Moreover, the king pledged to introduce the teaching of Berber dialects in Morocco's schools. Royal pronouncements almost always carry decisive weight in Morocco. This one was no exception, leading to a flourishing of the movement. A plethora of Amazigh cultural organizations sprung up, and a number of Amazigh publications were founded. True to *makhzenian* form, the king's speech also marked the initiation of a co-optation policy of the Amazigh movement. A moderate, pragmatic trend led by the movement's leading intellectual authority, Mohamed Chafik, agreed to work with the monarchy, whereas a radical trend led by former militants of the far Left, some of whom are from the northern Rif region, refused the regime's overtures. For the movement's pragmatists, common interests with the monarchy took precedence. On the one hand, the monarchy needed the Amazigh movement to weaken its main opposition, the Islamists, and to support its measures of incremental liberalization. On the other hand, the Amazigh movement was understood by the pragmatists as being incapable of refashioning Moroccan national identity without the monarchy's support.

From the beginning of the 1990s, the Amazigh movement has stressed the correlation between the democratization process and the recognition of Berber cultural rights.[22] According to this view, the Amazigh language and culture are marginalized because Morocco is not yet a democracy. Amazigh intellectuals use the Spanish monarchy as an example for the desired management of linguistic pluralism. Because it is a democracy, Spain has granted official recognition to minority languages since 1978. For the Amazigh movement, the Moroccan monarchy cannot claim to be a democracy as long as it does not give full recognition to the "Amazighness" of the nation. Conversely, in this view, the monarchy needs the Amazigh movement, one of the leading democratic forces of the country, to create a civic nation of free citizens in order to rebuff the Islamist challenge.

Islamism, the State, and the West

Although the monarchy claimed that Morocco was immune from fundamentalism, in fact, from the beginning of the 1990s, it became obvious that Islamism constituted the main opposition force in the country. This became even more apparent as the decade wore on, ironically as a consequence of the king's adroit orchestration of a policy of *alternance*, which incorporated Morocco's traditional opposition parties, mainly from the Left, into a power-sharing arrangement.[23] Although the Islamist movement is deeply fragmented, its different trends make use of what it views as Morocco's identity crisis in order to enlist support. For them, Westernization constitutes the main threat to the Muslim identity of Morocco.[24] Globalization is equivalent with Westernization, and, therefore, the monarchy's strategic choice to participate in globalization processes should be fought. They answer to the official discourse stressing Morocco's vocation as a bridge between civilizations with a counterdiscourse stressing the inevitable clash of ideas between Islam and the West.[25] For the Islamists, Morocco can not and should not try to prove that Islam is compatible with Western values, or, to use Huntington's terminology, Morocco, unlike Turkey, should not become a country "torn" between East and West.

The 1991 Gulf War provided Moroccan Islamist groups with an opportunity to demonstrate their political weight. The massive demonstration organized in Rabat on February 3, 1991,[26] to express solidarity with the Iraqi people served as a coming-out party, of sorts, for these groups. The invasion of Iraq was depicted by the Islamists as a new crusade against an Arab and Muslim country. Moroccan secular pan-Arabists and Islamists were united in their condemnation of the war, the West, and the Zionist enemy. The broad popular affinity with this view made the monarchy's pro-Western discourse and foreign policy appear disconnected from public opinion. Civil society's opposition to the Gulf War seemed to suggest that Morocco was culturally and socially an integral part of the Muslim and Arab world. Moroccan society had not reacted differently from other Arab societies despite Morocco's symbolic troop deployment in support of Saudi Arabia (and, by implication, the Western-led coalition) against Iraq.

The country's intellectual elite also contributed to the strengthening of anti-Western feelings in Morocco. If Algeria and Islamic fundamentalism are, according to the official discourse, the primary significant enemy "others" of the Moroccan national identity, for Islamist and pan-Arabist intellectuals, the Judeo-Christian West is Morocco's and Islam's rival "other." Prior to the publication of Huntington's *Clash of Civilizations*, Mehdi el-Manjra used the term "civilizational war" (*guerre civilisationnelle*) to describe the Gulf War.[27] This secular-Left intellectual set the tone for the Moroccan critique of the West, which has only increased since the events of September 11, 2001. Like Moroccan Islamists, El-Manjra considered the war as a new crusade motivated not only by economic interests but also by cultural and religious motivations:

> There should be no doubt in one's mind that the Arabs are but the first guinea pigs for an experiment designed to perpetuate the military, political and economic domination of the Western world as well as the hegemony of its Judeo-Christian values. . . . The deployment of forces was compounded with psychological warfare of unprecedented magnitude, along with a most revealing hysterical campaign by the media of the West—even Goering would appear like a shaky novice if he saw the new masters of the art of communication and information at work. . . . The Gulf War should not be viewed as a regional conflict nor reduced to a simple confrontation between the Judeo-Christian West and the Islamic world. It is a North-South war, a conflict arising from the Judeo-Christian civilization's inherent will to exert hegemony over all other civilizations, whether Arab, Asian or African, that is all other forms of civilization which are different from the Western one.[28]

Since the end of the Cold War, this type of discourse has become dominant in both Islamist and pan-Arab leftist circles. For them, Morocco, as a Muslim country, should define its identity by opposition to the imperialist West and Zionism. Islamists and secular pan-Arab intellectuals defended similar views regarding the subsequent launching of the Israeli-Palestinian peace process. Their common anti-Western and anti-Zionist feelings led intellectuals such as Abd al-Jabri and the veteran pan-Arabist opposition leader Muhammad Faqih al-Basri to propose the establishment of a national union composed of secular pan-Arabists and of Islamists to oppose the "new crusade."[29] By implication, their opposition was directed not only against the West but also the official policies of their own country.

The rejection of Western culture is one of the main elements of Islamist ideology in Morocco and the Muslim world as a whole. The West is perceived as a historical colonial power that continues to dispossess Morocco and the Muslim *umma* from its identity; part of the Islamists' agenda is to re-Islamize Moroccan society.

Sheikh Abdessalam Yassine, the intellectual leader of Moroccan Islamism, often compares corrupt Westernized elites to the good soldiers of God, presenting Moroccan society as divided by an internal "clash of civilizations":

> At the head of the Islamist caravan advancing with assurance on the road towards power and autarchy, you will find no Westernized fellow-travelers given over to the enemy both intellectually and culturally. You will find no friendships or alliances with the enemy. Neither will you find anyone of neat appearance and "position of responsibility," who is in fact a dreary spy and whose life is spent in a succession of apparatchiks' conferences and parties where information about the potential of the country is hawked about in exchange of hard currency. You will find no clients of Hilton hotels, dance halls and other dens of vice or habitués of seminars airing views akin to those of Freemasons, Zionism, capitalism or intelligence agencies. You will find only soldiers of God mobilized to serve the material and economic cause of the community and considering this as an act of worship rewarded by God.[30]

For the Islamists, Morocco has achieved political independence without cultural independence. Moreover, it is undergoing an identity crisis that leads to underdevelopment.[31] The decolonization process remains to be completed since the "occidentalizing" Moroccan elites are culturally Western and attempting to import a foreign model to a Muslim country. The root of the society's problem is cultural alienation; the solution is to return to Muslim fundamentals, that is to say the implementation of the Shariʻa. This ideology attracts a large proportion of young Moroccans educated in Arabic. In a survey conducted at the end of the 1980s, out of four hundred students polled, 75 percent believed the adoption of the Shariʻa as the law of the land to be the only solution to Morocco's problems.[32]

Islamists propose a model of development that is supposed to suit the local culture, but in fact, like the Salafists of the Istiqlal party, they generally oppose the version of traditional Moroccan Islam promoted by brotherhoods (*zawiyat*). Moroccan Islamists defend a cultural model opposed to the Western elites' way of life. They advocate the acceleration of Morocco's decades-old policies of linguistic Arabization and the marginalization of

French, the language of the colonizer.[33] They seek to fashion a hegemonic, allegedly authentic Moroccan identity based on a mythic reconstructed past in order to build a genuine Islamic state. Islamists make a particular point of rejecting Western liberalism and permissiveness, which are perceived as signs of the West's impiety and moral decadence.

At the same time, Islamist movements everywhere are a product of modernization, and they do not reject modernity *en bloc*. To the contrary, they attempt to appropriate modernity and prove that Islam is not incompatible with modern values and technological progress. To use Yassine's expression, they are interested in "Islamizing" modernity instead of modernizing Islam.[34] If they obviously share some values with the West, Moroccan Islamists tend to stress their differences with the "imperialists." They have a Manichean vision of the world, which opposes the Judeo-Christian corrupt West.

Islamist groups imagine the Moroccan nation as a community of Muslims struggling to gain spiritual and cultural independence from the West.[35] Their ideal political framework is the Muslim *umma*, not the Moroccan nation. However, the moderate Islamists groups that have gained legitimacy since the beginning of the 1990s and are currently embodied in the Justice and Development party (PJD)[36] recognize the temporal and religious power of the monarchy, which is a condition for their participation in the official political game.[37] However, like the more radical groups, spearheaded by Sheikh Yassine's Justice and Spirituality movement (al-Adl wal-Ihsan), as well as the smaller jihadist groups that have sprung up in recent years, they are harsh critics of the monarchy's pro-Western foreign policy and of the official discourse portraying Morocco as a country bridging the West and Islam.

State Fundamentalism

Ironically, the monarchy, because it has played an ambiguous game with fundamentalism, is partly responsible for the strengthening of anti-Western feelings in Morocco. A two-level discourse and policy was employed by the authorities, one for the West and one for national politics. Since the 1960s, King Hasan II used Islam as a political weapon, first against the radical Left and then against Moroccan Islamism following the 1979 Islamic Revolution in Iran. According to François Burgat, Hasan developed a fundamentalist state to limit the potential power of Islamism: "Hasan II knew how to anchor the fundamentalist discourse within the heart of the state, reducing the territory left to the fundamentalism of protest. Fundamentalist-inspired measures largely counterbalanced the few secular, modernist or ecumenical 'provocations' made by the regime (First Congress on Birth Control, the welcoming of the Shah of Iran, contacts with the Jewish community and then the State of Israel and a more general reticence to align itself with the more anti-Western positions of the other Arab regimes)."[38]

Hassan II also encouraged the penetration of Wahabbism in mosques and schools to strengthen the religious legitimacy of the monarchy.[39] Moroccan sociologist Mohammed El Ayadi analyzed the effects of this policy on Moroccan young minds, blaming the educational system for diffusing anti-Western and anti-Semitic feelings. For instance, in the Islamic education schoolbooks of the Education Ministry, Muslims are presented as victims of a Judeo-Christian conspiracy aimed at weakening their faith in Islam. The Zionist movement is considered the expression of a Jewish conspiracy against humanity and religions. Schoolbooks for senior-year classes quote an imaginary fourteenth Zionist protocol: "We need to destroy all religious beliefs. The temporary result of this action should be the development of atheism that we should use for the future generations who will listen to the teachings of Moses's religion that requires that we submit all the nations to our power."[40]

After Judaism, the West is considered the second enemy of Islam by schoolbooks because it spreads values and ideologies such as Marxism, orientalism, and secularism to destroy Islam from inside. El Ayadi's study sheds light on the gap between an official discourse praising dialogue between civilizations and a policy strengthening anti-Western feelings. State fundamentalism contributed to the building of a Moroccan identity based on rejection of the West and Judaism while promoting a peaceful discourse.

Muhammad VI, the Moroccan Spring, and the Amazigh Movement

Islamism became even more visible following Hasan II's death, rendering it impossible for the monarchy to ignore. As the young King Muhammad VI accelerated the pace of political liberalization, allowing a degree of freedom of expression unprecedented in independent Morocco, Islamist movements became less reluctant to display their actual strength. However, they did not produce new discourses on the Moroccan nation. In contrast, the human rights movement and the Amazigh movement did take advantage of the so-called Moroccan Spring to produce new discourses on national identity and revisit national history.

The Reopening of the Past

One consequence of the political liberalization has been the growing discussion in the press of some of the darker chapters in the country's recent history, including the televised testimonies of torture experienced by former political prisoners. For human rights activists such as Driss Benzekri, who spent sixteen years in prison for his revolutionary ideas, a democratic Morocco cannot emerge before it deals with the darkest years of Hasan II's reign, *les années de plomb* (years of lead), from 1965 to 1975.[41] Whether or not Morocco is in the process of a kind of therapeutic catharsis that will lay the ground for a real reconciliation between the monarchy and the Moroccan people or, to the contrary, will delegitimize the monarchical institution remains to be seen. In any case, the formation of a new collective memory, or memories, is now under way.

Traumatic events such as the repression of the March 1965 Casablanca riots, the kidnapping and murder of exiled opposition leader Mehdi Ben Barka that same year, and the failed military coups of 1971–72 are now publicly debated in the media and in testimonies. The Forum Justice et Vérité, created in 1998 to shed light on the repressive policies of Hasan II and provide indemnities for the victims of torture and prison, has become increasingly active under the leadership of Benzekri. For example, on June 26, 2000, the forum participated in the International Day in Support of Victims of Torture, presenting new publications on torture in Morocco.[42] On October 7, 2000, it organized a pilgrimage for five thousand human rights activists and journalists to the notorious former prison of Tazmamart, where many political detainees had been held. In the winter of 2000, Ahmed Merzouki published an important testimony on Tazmamart,[43] which became a bestseller in Morocco and France.

This new interest in recent history indicates the loss of the *makhzen*'s monopoly in the writing of national history and the definition of Moroccan identity.[44] The narrative presented in the daily mouthpiece of the palace, *Le Matin du Sahara*, is now challenged by independent media and historians. "The struggle for Morocco's past"[45] is back, with the potential of laying the groundwork for a nation of citizens defending their right to know, write, and remember their own history after a long period of amnesia. Benjamin Stora believes that this process will be fruitful only if the victims' aim is to tell their history, to inform their citizens and not to seek revenge, which can lead to internal conflicts.[46] Moreover, the state's willingness to acknowledge past faults and repair them is a positive sign for democratization and the reconciliation of the citizens with their political institutions. The creation, by the royal *dahir* ("edict") of January 7, 2004, of the Instance Equité et Reconciliation, a state commission presided over by Benzekri and in charge of the identification and indemnification of victims of human rights abuses from 1956 to 1999, was especially noteworthy, particularly because there is no parallel for such a body anywhere in North Africa and the Middle East.[47] In a speech in Agadir announcing creation of the commission, King Muhammad VI proclaimed that "our goal is that all the Moroccans reconcile with themselves and with their history, that they free their energies and that they participate in the edification of democratic and modern society."[48] He also stressed the fact that this process would reinforce the democratic culture of the nation.

This search for historical truth and quest for reconciliation and reparation may or may not lead to the emergence of a civic Moroccan nation identifying with its political institutions. But in the meantime, it encourages Moroccan citizens to public involvement. The success of the "caravans of truth" (*les caravanes de la vérité*) organized by the Forum Justice and Vérité demonstrates the public's appetite for information and civic involvement. Since the first pilgrimage to Tazmamart, the forum has organized four more caravans to different places that became "des lieux de mémoire"[49] of the dark years of state repression: Kalaa M'Gouna, Agdz, Figuig, and Imilchil in the Atlas mountains.

Judging from the number of recent newspaper articles dealing with different political events of an independent Morocco, the interest in the country's postindependence history has only continued to increase. The independent weeklies *Le Journal* and *TelQuel* are the primary producers of "journalistic history," but the official *Le Matin du Sahara* has also provided a public space for publications dealing with recent history, including the history of the Rif, which was considered taboo under Hasan II.[50] In particular, it provides increasing coverage of the major publications of Berber intellectuals, an indication of the newly found importance of the Amazigh movement.

The Amazigh Narrative

Almost from the outset of Mohammed VI's reign, the Amazigh movement has propagated a powerful alternative narrative of Moroccan national history. In addition to its engagement with contemporary and modern history, this narrative also concerns itself with the country's *longue durée* in order to prove Morocco's continued "Amazighness" throughout history.

One underlying purpose of this approach is to repair the political elites' injustices toward the Berbers and, by definition, the whole nation. Indeed, the Amazigh narrative assumes that there is an almost complete congruence between the Moroccan nation and the Berber identity. When the state, represented by the *makhzenian* elites, discriminates against the Imazighen, the whole nation is wounded and humiliated. This point is made very clear in the Amazigh Manifesto of March 1, 2000,[51] which stresses that the Berber rewriting of Morocco's history and the reparation of historic injustices against Berbers serve the whole nation.[52]

For Amazigh movement intellectuals, Morocco is an ancient nation predating the appearance of Islam and the Moroccan sultanate.[53] As an ethnic, Berber-based entity, Morocco existed long before a modern nation-state system emerged to provide political expression to collective identities. The Amazigh narrative contradicts many aspects of the modernist theories of nationalism,[54] which consider the nation as a modern creation intrinsically linked with the emergence of the state. For Rachid Raha, a Rifian intellectual and editor of the monthly *Le Monde Amazigh*, "the history of Morocco from the High Atlas rupestrian engravings of the Neolithic period until today is a continuous history and a fundamentally Amazigh one."[55]

"Consensual" Amazigh intellectuals such as Mohamed Chafik, Hasan Aourid, and Halima Ghazi even suggest there is a continuity between the Berber kings of Roman times and the monarchs of the modern era. For Hasan Aourid, Juba II is "a great Moroccan King of great finesse and knowledge."[56] This implies that the two main pillars of the Moroccan nation are its Berber identity and the monarchy. In an article published in both *Le Matin du Sahara* and *Le Monde Amazigh*, Halima Ghazi, a historian and member of the Administrative Committee of the Institut Royal de la Culture Amazighe (IRCAM; see below), further developed this thesis. Morocco as a political entity, she states, has existed since antiquity. There is continuity between the Berber *aguellids* (Berber kings) and the modern monarchs of Morocco. In opposition to the official historiography, which stresses that only Islam and the monarchy could unify the different tribes coexisting in the Moroccan territory, she claims that the two founding elements of the Morocco nation are the Amazigh identity and the monarchy, which gave the nation its concrete political expression.[57] Chafik, the Amazigh movement's senior authority and a "consensual intellectual" par excellence, shares this historical analysis when he compares the opposition to foreign domination by Sultans Moulay Ismail (1672–1727), Hasan I (1873–94), and Muhammad V (1927–61, who ruled as king of newly independent Morocco from 1956), to the opposition of Amazigh leaders Masinissa, Jugurtha, and Juba I to invaders more than two thousand years ago.[58]

As the above treatment of Moroccan history indicates, the mainstream Moroccan Amazigh movement is pro-monarchy and extends its support to Muhammad VI. The Amazigh-centered narrative provides the monarchy with a historic and national legitimacy independent from its religious legitimacy. Together with the monarchy, the Imazighen are presented as the main opponents to foreign invasions in Morocco's history. Although they accepted the influence of foreign civilizations, such as Judaism, Christianity, and Islam, they always produced a national version of these cultures to survive.[59] Even the building of a modern Muslim state has not destroyed the Berber identity.

At the same time, the Amazigh narrative stresses the modern period and provides its own interpretation of the distinction made by French colonialist sociology between the *bled al-makhzen*, that is, territory under the sultan's authority, and the *bled al-siba*, the "land of dissidence" controlled mainly by Berber tribes.[60] For Chafik, the *siba* is not a form of dissidence but rather of self-defense against the *makhzen*, which reproduces undemocratic behaviors imported from Eastern political culture.[61] Amazigh historians question the official narrative when it claims that the *bled-al-makhzen* was an effective Muslim state. For historian Mohammed Mounib, the *bled al-makhzen* was controlled by oppressive *caids* (governors), whereas the Berber territories were autonomous lands governed by traditionally democratic Berber institutions.[62] The Amazigh Manifesto claims that the anti-Berber policy of the *makhzen* was due to Andalusian domination of the state apparatus after the fall of Grenada in 1492. Indeed, Muslim Andalusian elites who emigrated to Morocco and attained considerable influence with the sultans considered Berber culture despicable and primitive. Tensions between Berbers and Fassis in today's Morocco include this historical dimension.[63]

The dichotomy of *bled al-makhzen/bled al-siba*, however problematic from a historical point of view,[64] is a central theme of the Amazigh narrative. The former was controlled by undemocratic and imported elites, whereas the "real" nation was located in the Berber countryside. The modern political institutions of Morocco are not considered representative of the nation since they marginalize the Imazighen. Morocco, as a nation, is imagined as distinct from the *bled al-makhzen* by the Berber narrative, which stresses the ethnic and political frontiers separating the Berbers from the Moroccan nationalist movement, a movement that paradoxically took its cue from French colonial rule even as it sought to achieve independence from it. The

Amazigh Manifesto insists on the existence of a strong ethnic Moroccan identity prior to the imposition of the French protectorate in 1912, whereas the nationalist narrative claims that a distinct Berber collective identity is merely a creation of "the divide and rule policy" of the French colonial power. Indeed, the Moroccan nationalist movement, influenced by Salafism and Arab nationalism, represented the Berbers as potential allies of the colonialists because of the "French Berber policy." One of the epic moments in the history of Moroccan nationalism, according to the prevailing view, was the May 16, 1930, "Berber *dahir*," an unsuccessful French attempt aimed at providing juridical autonomy to some Berber tribes.[65]

Not surprisingly, Amazigh historians and activists have sought to rewrite this crucial episode, particularly in order to contest the accusation of the Berbers' alliance with France.[66] Hence they reverse the nationalist narrative of the struggle for independence, claiming that the Berber mountains were the real patriotic centers of resistance to French rule, whereas the urban (Arab) elites limited their commitment to political treatises. They highlight the poetry of the time, which attests to the strong patriotic feelings of the Berber tribes, notwithstanding the establishment's efforts to erase it from Morocco's collective memory.[67]

To be sure, the mainstream Berber critical narrative of modern history draws a clear distinction between the legitimate monarchy and the falsified dominant narrative of the nationalist movement. The enemy "other" of the Amazigh movement is not the monarchy but "Arabo-Islamism," an ideology imported from the Near East and therefore deemed incompatible with the national identity of Morocco, the Islamic West.[68] For Hasan Aourid, the modern state dominated by the Istiqlal party's ideology was built in opposition to the Amazigh identity. The state's Arabization policy is a denial of the Amazigh language and culture,[69] and the Istiqal's political elite used imported ideologies to build an Arab national identity that marginalized the natural defenders of the nation, the Berbers. On top of the previous French colonization, the Imazighen and the Moroccan nation as a whole are suffering from a new kind of colonization, an Arab colonization of Eastern origin. Moderate Amazigh intellectuals have constructed the movement's identity in opposition to both the establishment Istiqlal and the newer Islamist parties, all of which are considered to be "amazighophobic." In focusing on manifestations of Arabo-Islam, the Amazigh movement generally refrains from analyzing the complex relationships between the monarchy and the Berbers since independence. For instance, the Amazigh Manifesto does not mention the role of Prince Hasan in the repression of the Rif rebellion in 1958–59 or the 1971 and 1972 attempts at coups d'état by largely Berber elements in the military.[70] Mainstream Amazigh intellectuals do not antagonize the monarchy, which they consider a potential ally, especially after Mohammed VI took a series of symbolic measures satisfying part of the movement's demands.

On October 17, 2001, Muhammad VI, dressed in traditional Berber clothes, recognized the central place of "Amazighness" in Morocco's national identity in a speech delivered in Ajdir (Khenifra), in the Middle Atlas, announcing the creation of the IRCAM. Putting an end to the Arab hegemonic discourse, Muhammad VI described Moroccan national identity as pluralist in nature and declared that the "historic roots" of Morocco are Berber.[71] Reactions were varied. Some Amazigh militants, such as the former Communist Ahmed Adghirni,[72] saw the monarchy's move as an attempt to coopt and weaken the Amazigh movement in order to prevent the emergence of a militant antiregime Amazigh movement, as had happened in Algeria's Kabylian region. However, the predominant thinking among the Moroccan Amazigh activists was that the foundation of the IRCAM, a follow-up decision to teach Tamazight in some primary schools, and the emergence of a new discourse on national identity were positive developments. In contrast, Moroccan Arab nationalist intellectuals and Islamist leaders criticized the official recognition of the Amazigh identity because it endangered the Arab identity of Morocco.

How is one to understand Muhammad VI's actions? Essentially, he has chosen a path familiar to Moroccan rulers, playing the role of arbiter between competing social forces, in this case, the "Arabo-Islamists" and the Amazigh in their contest over the definition of Moroccan national identity. For instance, the issue of the transcription of the Berber language generated an intense debate regarding which script to employ in the teaching of Tamazight: Latin, Arabic, or Tifinagh (a modified version of ancient Berber writing). Most Islamists vociferously advocated the Arabic script, whereas a majority of Amazigh militants and intellectuals preferred the use of Latin letters for both ideological and practical reasons. Royal intervention eventually resulted in a controversial compromise, the adoption of Tifinagh.

For ideological and cultural reasons, the Amazigh movement is deeply opposed to the Islamist movement. This view was sharpened by the May 16, 2003, suicide bombing attacks in Casablanca by jihadists that killed thirty-three innocent people. Amazigh activists and intellectuals, such as the feminist Meryam Demnati and the radical Mohammed Boudhan, reacted by expounding an explicitly secular discourse in opposition to Islamism and the dominant place of Islam in the political system. Others blamed the importation of oriental ideologies to Morocco for the country's sufferings. For Boudhan, Morocco's "irrational attachment to the Arab East" is a great source of stagnation.[73] An "authentic" Amazigh Morocco, on the other hand, would become democratic and hence develop. Mainstream, less radical Amazigh intellectuals such as Ahmed Boukous,[74] Hasan Aourid,[75] and Ahmed Assid also defend a certain level of secularization, or at least an enlightened Islam that they say is compatible with democracy. Although they generally avoid employing a radical anti-Arab and anti-Islamist discourse, they also claim that North African identity is not oriental and not anti-Western but rather Amazigh and Mediterranean. For those who speak in more explicit political terms, federalism is sometimes presented as an appropriate formula. In a related vein, Iraqi Kurds are pointed to as a model of a determined ethnic minority operating in a hostile milieu.[76]

Conclusion

Moroccan national identity is in the midst of a process of contestation and reconstruction. The redefinition of national identity is the result of continuous negotiations between the elites of new movements and the king who seeks to remain a unifying symbol and actor.[77] The monarchy accepts and sometimes even encourages the emergence of new discourses, such as the Amazigh discourse and the moderate Islamist discourse, as long as they do not question the pillars of Moroccan identity, including the religious legitimacy of the monarchy. Although radical streams of both movements contest the foundational pillars of Moroccan identity, the liberalizing monarchy hopes it can tame these movements by integrating them into the official political game. The Islamist Justice and Development party seems to accept the rules of the game by distancing itself from a Wahabbi-type fundamentalist Islam, which the authorities characterize as an imported ideology opposing the values of Moroccan Islam. The mainstream Amazigh movement, for its part, propagates a discourse that stands in total opposition to the Istiqlal party's and Islamists' ideology without antagonizing the monarchy. Whereas the Islamists seem to abandon the nation to look East, the Amazigh movement aims at becoming the last defender of the Moroccan nation threatened by transnational ideologies. This view has even been applied to Morocco's long-running struggle to incorporate the western Sahara into the kingdom. According to Mohamed Chafik, the western Sahara can only be Moroccan because its population is Amazigh in origin and adheres to Moroccan Islam, which was itself born in the Sahara during the golden age of Morocco, creating a Western Islamic culture distinct from Eastern Islam.[78]

Morocco is currently undergoing an internal political and intellectual struggle involving Eastern-oriented ideologies, which maintain that "Islam is the solution" (*Islam huwa al-hal*) to the society's identity and material crisis; Western-oriented ideologies, which defend the establishment of a liberal democracy; and an Amazigh ideology, which stipulates that the way to cope with modernity and globalization is to strengthen the nation's ethnic Berber roots. These ethnic, cultural, religious, and ideological cleavages will continue to influence the nature of the Moroccan political system. One possible positive scenario could be the emergence of a consociational democracy[79] founded on power sharing among Islamists, liberal democrats, and "Amazighists" in which the monarchy would become a benign moderating and unifying actor.

Notes

1. The Amazigh movement is a predominantly urban-based movement that defends the cultural rights of the Berbers, the indigenous people of Morocco. It employs the terms "Amazigh" (plural "Imazighen") for Berber, "Tamazight" for the Berber language, and "Tamazgha" for the Berber homeland. See Bruce Maddy-Weitzman, "Contested Identities: Berbers, 'Berberism' and the State in North Africa," *Journal of North African Studies* 6, no. 3 (Autumn 2001): 23–47.

2. Myriam et Frédéric Vairel Catusse, "Ni tout à fait le même ni tout à fait un autre: Métamorphoses et continuité du régime marocain," *Maghreb-Machrek* 175 (Spring 2003): 73–92.

3. *Makhzen* (lit. "treasury" or "strongbox") is the traditional term for Morocco's ruling monarchichal-military-bureaucratic apparatus. For a classic analysis of the Moroccan political system, see John Waterbury, *The Commander of the Faithful* (New York: Columbia University Press, 1970).

4. Karim Mezran, "Negotiating National Identity in North Africa," *International Negotiation* 6, no. 2 (2001): 147.

5. For the dominant discourse, see, for example, Muhammad Othman Benjelloun, *Projet National et Identité au Maroc* (Casablanca: Eddif, 2002). Also see Terhi Lehtinen, "Beyond the Moroccan State—The Transnational Nation-Building of the Amazigh Cultural Movement," in *Globalization and the State in the Middle East*, edited by Aini Linjakumpu, 93–127 (Tampere, Finland: Tampere Peace Research Institute, 2003).

6. Gilles Perrault, *Notre ami le roi* (Paris: Gallimard, 1990).

7. Francis Fukuyama, *The End of History and the Last Man* (New York: Avon Books, 1992).

8. Benjelloun, *Projet*, 78–81.

9. Benjamin Stora, "Algeria/Morocco: The Passions of the Past Representations of

the Nation that Unite and Divide," *Journal of North African Studies* 8, no. 1 (Autumn 2001): 14–34; Benjamin Stora, *Maroc-Algérie: Histoire parallèle, destins croisés* (Paris: La Maisonneuve et Larose, 2002), 10–11.

10. Hasan II, *Le Génie de la modération* (Paris: Plon, 2000), 29.

11. Edmond Amran El Maleh, Robert Assaraf, and Serge Berdugo, for example.

12. Robert Assaraf, *Mohammed V et les Juifs du Maroc à l'époque de Vichy* (Paris: Plon, 1997); Simon Lévy, *Essais d'histoire et de civilisation judéo-marocaines* (Rabat: Centre Tarik Ibn Zyad, 2001).

13. Hasan II, *Génie de la modération*, 43.

14. Samuel P. Huntington, *The Clash of Civilizations and the Remaking of World Order* (New York: Touchstone, 1996).

15. For example, the Fes Festival of Sacred Music and the Essaouira Festival of Andalousian Atlantics.

16. Hasan II, *Le défi* (Paris: Albin Michel, 1976), 189.

17. Lisa Anderson, "Dynasts and Nationalists: Why Monarchies Survive," in *Middle East Monarchies*, edited by Joseph Kostiner, 53–69 (Boulder, Colo.: Lynne Rienner, 2000).

18. AMREC, ANCAP, l'Université d'Eté, l'Association culturelle Gheris (Tileli), l'Association Ilmas, and l'Association culturelle du Sous.

19. Anthony D. Smith, *The Ethnic Origins of Nations* (Oxford: Blackwell, 1986).

20. Hasan Aourid, "Le substrat culturel des mouvements de contestation au Maroc: Analyse des discours Islamiste et amazighe" (thèse de doctorat d'État, Université Mohammed V, Rabat, 1999), 333.

21. The king used the term "dialect," not "language," displaying a traditional bias toward the "superiority" of Arabic as a "holy" language.

22. For example, Rachid Raha, "Le mouvement amazigh du Maroc exige la réforme de la Constitution," communication à la plénière dédiée aux Berbères au Forum Social Européé, Paris, November 15, 2003, http://www.berberescope.com/revendications_berberes.htm#6-%20Le%20Mouvement%20Amazigh%20du%20Maroc.

23. Fatiha Layadi and Narjis Rerhaye, *Maroc, Chronique d'une démocratie en devenir* (Casablanca: Eddiff, 1998).

24. For example, Mohammed Tozy, "Islamism and Some of Its Perceptions of the West," in *Islam, Modernism and the West*, edited by Gema Martin Munoz, 153–74, and especially 157 (New York: I. B. Tauris, 1999).

25. For an analysis of views of Morocco's leading Islamist on the issue, see Bruce Maddy-Weitzman, "Islamism, Moroccan-Style: The Ideas of Sheikh Yassine," *Middle East Quarterly* 10, no. 1 (Winter 2003): 43–51.

26. Pierre Vermeren, *Histoire du Maroc depuis l'indépendance* (Paris: La Découverte, 2002), 92.

27. Mehdi El-Manjra, *La première guerre civilisationnelle* (Casablanca: Éditions Ouyoun, 1991), http://www.elmandjra.org/Contents.htm.

28. Ibid.

29. Aourid, "Substrat culturel," 54.

30. Abdesslame Yassine, *Sur l'économie, préalables dogmatiques et règles charïques* (Rabat: Imprimeries Horizons, 1996), 20; quoted by Tozy, "Islamism," 170.

31. François Burgat, *L'islamisme en face* (Paris: La Découverte, 1995).

32. Tozy, "Islamism," 157.

33. Pierre Vermeren, *Le Maroc en transition* (Paris: La Découverte Poche, 2002), 53.

34. Abdesslame Yassine, *Islamiser la modernité* (Casablanca: Al Ofok Impressions, 1998).

35. For example, Nadia Yassine, *Toutes Voiles dehors* (Casablanca: Éditions Le Fennec, 2003).

36. See Michael J. Willis's chapter in this volume.

37. Bruce Maddy-Weitzman, "The Islamic Challenge in North Africa," in *Religious Radicalism in the Greater Middle East*, edited by Bruce Maddy-Weitzman and Efraim Inbar, 171–88 (London: Frank Cass, 1997).

38. François Burgat, *The Islamic Movement in North Africa* (Austin: Center for Middle Eastern Studies at the University of Texas, 1993), 168.

39. Mohammed Darif, "Le Wahabbisme face aux Islamistes," *La Gazette du Maroc*, August 17, 2003.

40. Muhammad El Ayadi, "La jeunesse et l'Islam, tentative d'analyse d'un habitus religieux cultivé," in *Les jeunes et les valeurs religieuses*, edited by Rahma Bourquia, M. El Ayadi, M. El Harras, and H. Rachik, 146 (Casablanca: Éditions Eddif, 2000).

41. Driss Benzekri, "Entre l'inquisition et l'amnésie, il y a la mémoire," *La vie economique*, August 7, 2004.

42. Abdlelaziz Mouride, *On affame bien les rats!* (Casablanca/Paris: Tarik Éditions/Paris Méditerranée, 2000); quoted in Vermeren, *Maroc en transition*, 64–65.

43. Ahmed Merzouki, *Tazmamart, cellule 10* (Casablanca/Paris: Tarik Éditions/Paris Méditerranée, 2001).

44. Benjamin Stora, "Maroc, le traitement des histoires proches," *Esprit* 8–9 (September 2000): 88–102.

45. Ernest Gellner, "The Struggle for Morocco's Past," *Middle East Journal* 15, no. 1 (Winter 1961): 79–90.

46. Stora, "Maroc, le traitement des histoires proches," 88–102.

47. Christine Daure-Serfaty, "Le Maroc vers les droits de l'homme à petits pas," *Le Monde*, December 10, 2004.

48. The discourse can be found at the Moroccan Ministry of Communication's website: http://www.mincom.gov.ma/french/generalites/samajeste/mohammedVI/discours/2004/installaequiteetreconciliation.htm.

49. Pierre Nora, *Les Lieux de Mémoire* (Paris: Gallimard, 1997).

50. For example, the article titled "Moulay Muhammad Abdelkrim El Khattabi, l'Emir Guérillero: 'Le Rif et ses héros,'" *Le Matin du Sahara*, June 5, 2003.

51. The Amazigh Manifesto, redacted by Mohamed Chafik and subsequently signed by hundreds of Moroccan Amazigh intellectuals, presented the main demands of the Amazigh movement to the new king and included a new version of Moroccan history. See the "Berber Manifesto" at http://www.mondeberbere.com/societe.

52. For example, the preamble of the manifesto states, "However, the harm inflicted upon the nation by these conflicts—involving shortsighted, ambitious and irresponsible politicians—the dire consequences of which were not taken into consideration, is a harm akin to a severe wound the healing of which we are all contributing to nowadays."

53. Stora, "Algeria/Morocco," 15.

54. For example, Ernest Gellner, *Nations and Nationalism* (Oxford: Blackwell, 1983).

55. Raha, "Mouvement amazigh du Maroc."

56. Hasan Aourid, "Moi, enfant de deux ans je vous interpelle M. Le Ministre des Droits de l'Homme," *Le Journal*, June 15–21, 1998.

57. Halima Ghazi-Ben Maissa, "L'assise historique de l'institution royale au Maroc," *Le Monde Amazigh* 38 (October 2003).

58. "La volonté des rois du Maroc tels Moulay Ismail, Hasan I et Mohammed V à s'opposer à la domination étrangère par la sagesse et la force à la fois trouve ses origines historiques dans des graines semées du temps de Masinissa, Jugurtha, Juba I depuis plus de deux mille ans." (The will of Moroccan kings such as Moulay Ismail, Hasan I and Mohammed V, who opposed foreign domination with wisdom and strength during those times found its historical origins in the seeds which were sown during the times of Masinissa, Jugurtha, Juba I, more than 2,000 years earlier.) Muhammad Chafik, *Esquisse de l'Histoire des Berbères—33 siècles* (Mohammedia: Alkalam, 1989), 111; quoted by Aourid, "Substrat culturel," 271.

59. For example, the fourth century A.D. Donatist movement and the eighth and ninth centuries heretical Barghawata kingdoms are considered by Berberists as the Berber national expressions of Christianity and Islam, respectively.

60. For an analysis of this dichotomy, see Rémy Leveau, *Le Fellah marocain, défenseur du Trône* (Paris: Presses de Sciences Po, 1975), 7–25. Also see Gilles Lafuente, *La politique berbère de la France et le nationalisme marocain* (Paris: L'Harmattan, 1999), 42–53.

61. Aourid, "Substrat culturel," 175.

62. "Le Dahir berbère, Grand Bluff politique au Maroc contemporain," entretien de Moha Mokhlis avec Mohammed Mounib, *Revue Tifinagh*, March 1998, http://www.mondeberbere.com/histoire/dahir.

63. Hasan Ouzzate, interview with author, Rabat, September 16, 2003.

64. Edmund Burke III, "Theorizing the Histories of Colonialism and Nationalism in the Arab Maghrib," in *Beyond Colonialism and Nationalism in the Maghrib*, edited by Ali Abdullatif Ahmida, 17–35 (New York: Palgrave, 2000); Edmund Burke III, "The Image of the Moroccan State in the French Ethnological Literature: A New Look at the Origin of Lyautey's Berber Policy," in *Arabs and Berbers: From Tribe to Nation in North Africa*, edited by Ernest Gellner and Charles Micaud, 175–99 (London: Duckworth, 1972).

65. John P. Halstead, *Rebirth of a Nation: The Origins and Rise of Moroccan Nationalism* (Cambridge: Harvard University Press, 1967).

66. Amazigh/Berber Manifesto; Mustapha El Quadery, "Les Berbères entre Le Mythe Colonial et la Négation Nationale," in *Histoire des Amazighes*, vol. 2, edited by the Association de l'Université d'Été d'Agadir, 7–51 (Rabat: Editions Bouregreg, 2000); Mohammed Boudhan, "Le Dahir berbère, mythe ou réalité?" *Revue Tifinagh*, March 13, 1998 (http://www.mondeberbere.com/civilisation/histoire/dahir/boudhan.htm); Mohammed

Mounib, *Le Dahir berbère: La plus grande supercherie de l'histoire du Maroc* (Rabat: Éditions Bouregreg, 2002).

67. Aourid, "Substrat culturel," 218.

68. For example, Raha, "Mouvement amazigh du Maroc."

69. Hasan Aourid, "Pour un consensus linguistique," *Le Journal,* July 13–19, 1998.

70. Rachid Raha tries to deal with these events but without antagonizing the monarchy. "La monarchie marocaine et les Imazighen," *Le Monde Amazigh* 26 (September 15, 2002).

71. See "Discours à l'occasion du deuxième anniversaire de l'intronisation de Sa Majesté le Roi Mohammed VI," http://www.mincom.gov.ma/french/generalites/samajeste/mohammedVI/discours/2001/discours_trone2001.htm: "Dans la mesure où l'amazighe constitue un élément principal de la culture nationale, et un patrimoine culturel dont la présence est manifestée dans toutes les expressions de l'histoire et de la civilisation marocaine, nous accordons une sollicitude toute particulière à sa promotion dans le cadre de la mise en œuvre de notre projet de société démocratique et moderniste, fondée sur la consolidation de la valorisation de la personnalité marocaine et de ses symboles linguistiques, culturels et civilisationnels. La promotion de l'amazighe est une responsabilité nationale, car aucune culture nationale ne peut renier ses racines historiques." (As Amazigh is a principal element of the national culture, a cultural heritage expressed throughout Morocco's history and civilization, we desire its promotion as part of our plan for a democratic and modern society. [This society will be] based on the consolidation of Morocco's linguistic, cultural, and civilizational symbols. The promotion of Amazigh is a national responsibility, since no national culture can disregard its historical roots.)

72. Adhmed Adghirni, interview with author, September 16, 2003.

73. Mohammed Boudhan, "Quand un intellectuel a peur de son patronyme," *Tawiza*, April 2004.

74. *Libération,* December 27, 1996, quoted by Aourid, "Substrat culturel, 299.

75. Aourid, "Substrat culturel," 8.

76. Abdellatif Agnouche, "L'Amazighité, une Marocanité spoliée d'un Maroc pluriel," *L'Indépendant Magazine*, December 14–16, 2001.

77. Mezran, "Negotiating National Identity," 168.

78. Mohamed Chafik, "Et si on décolonisait pour de bon," *Al Bayane*, October 23–24, 2004; Souad M'hammedi, "Quand le Sahara devint subitement occidental," *Le Matin du Sahara*, November 5, 2004.

79. For a definition of consociational democracy, see Arend Lijphart, "Consociational Democracy," *World Politics* 21, no. 2 (January 1969): 207–25. For Lijphart, consociational democracy fits divided societies such as Belgium, Holland, and Lebanon. Contrary to majoritarian democracies, consociational democracy (also called "consensus democracies") are based on power sharing and the search for consensus. This model could fit Moroccan political culture.

3

Algerian Identity and Memory

ROBERT MORTIMER

In his broadcast sermon of Friday, December 30, 2005, one of Algeria's state-appointed imams urged Algerians not to celebrate the upcoming New Year's Day. This was, he preached, "a tradition that came from elsewhere," not an authentic national holiday.[1] One day later, the nation's president, Abdel Aziz Bouteflika (who had just returned from surgery and a month of convalescence in a Parisian hospital) offered his New Year's wishes to the Algerian people. This disparity between two official messages was a small reminder of the monumental struggle over Algerian identity that has wracked the country since 1990. Partisans of two societal visions—one sacred, one secular—plunged the nation into a brutal civil war that raged for a decade before being contained, albeit not entirely, by the National Popular Army (ANP). Although the armed rebellion has been reduced to such remnants as the Salafist Group for Preaching and Combat (GSPC), the debate over Algeria's cultural identity has not ended, nor is it likely to in the near future.

Indeed, twentieth-century Algerian nationalism was always split between secular and Islamic factions. As organized political movements began to form in the aftermath of World War I (during which many Algerians served and died under the French flag), reformist Muslims such as Sheikh Abdelhamid Ben Badis rivaled secular politicians such as Messali al-Hadj and Ferhat Abbas for leadership of Algerian Muslims both at home and in France. During the Algerian war of 1954–62, the National Liberation Front (FLN) absorbed Ben Badis's Association of Algerian Ulema and succeeded in imposing a dominant, primarily secular notion of national memory and identity defined by participation in the armed struggle for national independence. Yet a more culturally defined conception of Muslim identity continued to operate just below the surface of official ideology.

Under the single-party system that emerged from the national liberation era, the FLN and its military partner governed for roughly a quarter-century, basking in the legacy of the revolution: Presidents Ahmed Ben

Bella, Houari Boumediene, and Chadli Benjedid grounded their legitimacy in their wartime roles. The official name of the state became the Democratic and Popular Algerian Republic (RADP). Although Islam certainly was celebrated as a key component of Algerian culture, the wartime generation defined national identity in primarily secular terms. As a "popular democracy," Algeria pursued a socialist economy, a nonaligned foreign policy emphasizing leadership within the Third World, and a progressive Arab nationalist culture. As the title of Bruno Étienne's 1977 book, *L'Algérie, Cultures et Révolution*, suggested, over the first fifteen years of independence, Algeria's cultural identity was revolutionary because the 1954–62 revolution defined the nation.[2]

This revolutionary cultural identity was definitively set forth in the National Charter drafted by the Boumediene regime in 1976. The charter identified the primary purpose of the state as "the edification of a socialist society."[3] This militantly socialist document went on to declare:

> Socialism, in Algeria, sets itself an essentially threefold objective:
>
> 1. The consolidation of national independence;
> 2. The establishment of a society free from the exploitation of man by man;
> 3. The promotion of man and his free flourishing.[4]

One section of the National Charter, devoted to "Islam and the Socialist Revolution," states that as an "integral component of our national history, Islam provided a powerful rampart" against colonialism, but that Muslims will best fulfill their religious principles and duties by "reinforcing the struggle against imperialism and engaging resolutely in the path of socialism."[5] In the revolutionary vision of the 1970s, therefore, religion was the handmaiden of a secular modernist project born out of the struggle for independence.

The contemporary Algerian political elite still appeals to the historical memory of that era of struggle. Since the death of Boumediene in 1978, however, the country has followed a path considerably at odds with the project of the National Charter. In particular, a much more traditional conception of Islam than the socialist version of the charter has reasserted itself in civil society. Several factors contributed to the reawakening of a more conservative political Islam. One was the political personality of Boumediene's successor, Chadli Benjedid, who simply was not committed to the charter's rigorous ideology. He permitted a much looser system of cronyism and economic profiteering to take hold in the country. Benjedid also gradually shifted his support to a more conservative faction of the ruling FLN that had always favored a more Arabo-nationalist orientation over the scientific socialism proffered by Boumediene's charter. Dubbed by Algerian popular wit as the *barbefelènes*, or "bearded FLN-ers," this wing of the party harked back more to the rhetoric of Ben Badis than of Ben Bella. These internal divisions gradually sapped the authority of the single party.

Perhaps most fundamentally, however, the notorious non-accountability of single-party systems in general weakened the hold of the FLN on the population at large. Ordinary citizens became increasingly disenchanted with the regime's failure to produce the broader prosperity promised by its socialist rhetoric. The riots of October 1988, coming but a year after the celebration of the twenty-fifth anniversary of independence, dealt a severe blow to the revolutionary identity of the regime, opening a breach through which the rising Islamist countercurrent could flow. The 1989 constitutional reform in favor of a multiparty system, the subsequent legalization of the Islamic Salvation Front (FIS), and the FIS's strong showing in the June 1990 local elections, followed by its stunning victory in the first round of the December 1991 parliamentary elections, constituted an unduly hasty and flawed transition from a secular to a religious vision of society and state. The shock of this largely uncharted shift unleashed a decade of great uncertainty about Algerian identity and the relative places of Islam and the memory of 1954–62 in that identity.

The return to power toward the end of the decade of Bouteflika, one of the last remaining members of Boumediene's inner circle, gave new breath to the waning legacy of November 1954 and certain aspects of the Boumediene era. As someone who had been Boumediene's wartime aide and then his prominent foreign minister, Bouteflika worked hard to refurbish Algeria's now-tarnished identity as a leader of the Third World, dating back to the 1960s and 1970s. Through a series of high-profile diplomatic initiatives, President Bouteflika once again projected Algeria onto the world stage from which it had slipped under Benjedid and his successors during the 1990s. At the same time, he implemented a policy of national amnesty (the referendum of September 1999 and reconciliation of September 2005; on both, see the chapter by Gideon Gera in this volume) that acknowledged implicitly the grievances that had given rise to the Islamist insurrection. Although some journalists characterized the 2005 reconciliation as an act of "amnesia," it is better understood as an effort to integrate the memory of the 1990s into a broader collective identity for the Algeria of the twenty-first century.⁶ This is of course an ongoing process, the ultimate contours of which remain indeterminate.

The political process will continue to validate certain memories and conceptions of identity. At the same time, Algeria's writers and intellectuals are likewise playing an important part in the renewed fashioning of a national self-understanding. Two authors who especially have been concerned with these themes are Assia Djebar and Yasmina Khadra. Djebar, the country's best known literary figure, probes both the history of the colonial conquest and that of the anticolonial struggle in her *L'Amour, la fantasia* (*Fantasia: An Algerian Cavalcade*). Khadra, the pen name of a career officer in the Algerian army, focuses on the more recent civil war of the 1990s in *À quoi rêvent les loups* (*Wolf Dreams*). Together these two novels offer much insight into contemporary reflection about Algerian identity, the memories that shape it, and the place of religion in it. As two of Algeria's most prominent public intellectuals, these writers are shaping the debate about Algerian identity. This chapter examines these cultural productions as windows into the current discourse about memory and identity.

* * *

Recently elected as the first North African writer to enter the prestigious Académie Française, Djebar has produced an extraordinary body of work about the Algerian condition. As a woman writing in French, she is aware that her personal identity challenges certain patriarchal and Arab-centered conceptions of Algerian society. Her 1985 novel *L'Amour, la fantasia* marked a major turning point in her literary career as she turned to substantially more politicized themes. The novel deals with three distinct histories—not only the French conquest and the Algerian liberation but also her own personal itinerary via fragments of autobiography that are present in the work. Thus Djebar probes three layers of Algerian memory, all with particular attention to the experience of women in the nation's encounter with the power and culture of Europe.

Djebar treats the invasion of June 1830 as a cataclysm for the Algerian people, an aggression that unleashed a "cavalcade of screams and carnage which . . . fill[ed] the ensuing decades."⁷ The war and the Algerian resistance to the conquest created a legacy of violence that forms an integral part of Algerian memory. She focuses upon two exceptionally cruel atrocities committed against the Algerian population, notably upon women and children. One was a massacre conducted by the troops of Captain Bosquet in October 1840 in their attempt to defeat the emir Abdelkader. The other, contained in a chapter starkly titled "Women, Children, Oxen Dying in Caves," recounts the extermination by fumigation of the Ouled Riah clan, which refused to surrender to Colonel Pélissier in the spring of 1845. These historical memories forever mark the complex relationship between Algeria and France (explaining—if need be—the recent furor in Algiers over the French parliament's passage of a law calling for the national schools to teach the positive side of French colonial history). In recalling these episodes drawn from "memory's subterranean store-house," Djebar exposes an essential component of Algerian identity, a fierce will to resist outside domination and restore the nation's dignity and freedom.

This will is equally manifest in the second chunk of history revealed in the novel. In dealing with the war of liberation, however, Djebar focuses much more directly on the role of women. This part of the work is based upon oral history, collected in a series of interviews conducted by the author with women from her native Mount Chenoua region of the country (near Cherchell).[8] She titles this section of the work (part 3) "Voices from the Past," transcribing the women's Arabic-language accounts into French so that their personal stories may be heard and their voices preserved. These women all participated in the revolution in varying capacities: as nurses, messengers, and providers of various forms of support to the *maquisards*, who were their brothers, husbands, and sons. Some, of course, were widows, recounting the sacrifices that all Algerians had to make for the cause. "Life was never the same again," one such widow recalled. "'France' began to come up the mountain to our place nearly every morning and evening. Eventually they burned the houses, and then the people! Taking the animals away, killing human beings! . . . Can you imagine what would happen when they arrived at a house and found women alone? . . . I began to go to the hills to help other people: we took food, we washed their uniforms, we kneaded bread . . . until the day when, as God had willed, my husband was killed fighting."[9]

One sees that Djebar translates these testimonies literally, as illustrated by the reference to "France" to designate the French soldiers. Each individual account of hardship and personal bravery contributes to the larger story of women's collective contribution to the cause of national liberation.

Djebar's primary attention to women in the revolution is at once an affirmation of the centrality of the wartime era in Algerian identity but also a critique of the postrevolutionary status of women in the independent country. The reader learns that the defiant young heroine Cherifa is "married now to a taciturn widower. . . . She brings up the man's five children. . . . Cherifa, ageing, in poor health, is housebound."[10] Zohra, who hid and fed the *maquisards* and whose four sons all joined the resistance, gets little recognition for her sacrifices. Another widow is denied information about the circumstances of the death of her husband. These vignettes of women's contributions to the national struggle and their subsequent marginalization raise significant questions about the place of women in postindependence Algeria. *Fantasia* constitutes a declaration that women had earned their right to, but have not been accorded, an equal status in the national identity.

The third strand of history in the novel treats issues of identity at the individual level. The opening paragraph foreshadows the bicultural path that Djebar has traveled as an educated Algerian woman: "A little Arab girl going to school for the first time, one autumn morning, walking hand in hand with her father. A tall erect figure in a fez and a European suit, carrying a bag of schoolbooks. He is a teacher at the French primary school. A little Arab girl in a village in the Algerian sahel."[11]

The little girl will, of course, excel in her studies and advance to a secondary boarding school, later to become the first Algerian woman to be admitted to the École Normale Supérieure in Paris. *Fantasia* expresses the contradictions inherent in Djebar's mastery—indeed, love—of the French language and her knowledge of the abuses of the French colonial order. Her personal identity is riven by her dual attachment to national heritage and international education, rather as the very historical relationship between the two countries has been. Reflecting upon the early colonial enterprise, and notably the passion of the invaders to write about the conquest of 1830, she wonders, "But what is the significance behind the urge of so many fighting men to relive in print this month of July 1830? . . . These texts are distributed in the Paris of Louis-Philippe, far from Algerian soil. . . . Their words thrown up by such a cataclysm are for me like a comet's tail, flashing across the sky and leaving it forever riven."[12]

This ambivalent, forever riven connection remains a dimension of the Algerian identity 175 years later. The secular model of Algerian society has undeniable linkages to the cultural framework that accompanied the colonial era. The autobiographical strand of *Fantasia* offers perceptive insight into this dualism, which is part of the struggle over Algerian identity today.

Since 1985, Djebar has continued to write about matters of memory and identity. Her novel, *La femme sans sépulture* (*The Woman without a Sepulchre*) continues her exploration of women's bravery during the Algerian war. *Vaste est la prison* (*Vast Is the Prison*) extends the work begun in *Fantasia* by tracing Algerian memory back to the pre-Islamic era and the Berber resistance under Jugurtha to Roman expansion into North Africa. Yet other works deal with the civil war of the 1990s. Through this extensive corpus, Djebar has provoked critical reflection upon several historical sources of Algerian national identity. Her central themes in *Fantasia*—violence and atrocities of the colonial intrusion, women's courage and resistance during the war of national liberation, and biculturalism emerging out of the Franco-Algerian historical synthesis—all shed light on the complexity of Algerian identity.

* * *

Djebar was nineteen years old when she went to Paris in 1955. Her admission to the École Normale Supérieure was clouded and then eclipsed by the Algerian war. Shortly after entering this elite institution, she joined the strike of Algerian students in France as decreed by the FLN. Indeed, her effective withdrawal from the school gave her the time to write her first novel, *La soif* (*The Craving*), published in 1957. She then left France for Tunisia, where she worked as an aide in camps set up there by the FLN for Algerian refugees. If Djebar therefore came of age during the war, Yasmina Khadra was literally a child of the revolution.

Born Mohammed Moulessehoul in western Algeria in 1955, he grew up in a family disrupted by the war. His father, who had served as a lieutenant in the guerrilla forces during the revolution, believed that the army was the right career for his son, and he enrolled him in a military academy when the boy was only nine years old. The army became his family virtually as much as his eventual profession. The young cadet was imbued with the mystique of the army and its role in the liberation of his country from a tender age. The army embodied the purpose of the nation and was the guarantor of its future. As a military officer, he saw himself as an heir to an inspiring heritage and as a member of a republican institution that formed the backbone of the political system. The events of the 1990s, however, called this conception into question. In the face of a competing conception of Algerian identity, the officer Moulessehoul, who had begun to write mystery novels around 1990 under the name of Yasmina Khadra, turned to more overtly political themes, notably in *À quoi rêvent les loups*, which was published in 1999.[13]

The novel tells the story of Nafa Walid, a young man from the casbah who dreams of becoming an actor. Unable to live off small parts in third-rate movies, he is obliged to take a job as a chauffeur with "one of the most affluent families in the land."[14] Nafa is thus exposed to a world of privilege and excess that he had never imagined—the lifestyle of the elite of Grand-Alger bears no resemblance to the lot of ordinary Algerians. Drawn into the orbit of the rich and corrupt, Nafa loses control of his personal destiny. He realizes that his own world of aspiring artists, musicians, and poets is doomed, as his fellow artist/chauffeur comrade Yahia puts it, by the "mediocrity" of the system of FLN rule. "And I say," Yahia adds, "give me the Islamic Salvation Front."[15] Nafa replies, "I'm not an Islamist . . . I'm neutral," but the train of events has already begun to push the disillusioned actor/chauffeur into the armed insurrection.[16]

Although the abusive Raja family may be seen as a caricature of the disparities of wealth and lifestyle that had emerged in Algeria in the 1980s, Khadra uses them to reveal the shortcomings of a system in decline. He attributes the rise of the FIS to the failure of the FLN to adhere to a larger societal dream. People have come to believe, as one character puts it, that "the big fish are above the law. . . . There is only one absolute law, *and that is the law of silence*."[17] In acknowledging this sentiment of injustice, which he perceived among ordinary Algerians, Khadra was addressing the waning status of the postwar egalitarian identity. The author commented indirectly on this disillusionment in an interview in 2001, in which he recalled the vastly different mood of his early years as a student at the École des Cadets: "There was an immense hope among Algerians and each person, for his part, was striving to add his stone to the edifice 'Algeria.' People were ready to sacrifice everything in order to be worthy of a country which had every chance to be a great nation. This is a very rich country; the Algerian people are very open, very tolerant, extremely intelligent, [and] creative. We had all the ingredients to succeed."[18] In *Wolf Dreams*, Khadra shows that this belief in the potential for Algeria's success has been tarnished, at least for men like Nafa. As Nafa puts it at the end of his conversation with Yahia, "In Algeria, there's no destiny. We're all at the end of the road."[19]

His faith in the system shaken, Nafa becomes susceptible to the appeals of those who see a different destiny for Algeria. Breaking with the corruption and impunity of the Raja family, he finds solace at the mosque. He is befriended by the Imam Younes, who turns out to be a recruiter for the FIS. Inexorably, Nafa is drawn into the Islamist network, first as a driver on harmless errands, then as a participant in a bank robbery to provide funds for the movement, and eventually as an assassin.

Khadra has said that he felt almost a duty as a writer to tell the story of Algeria's slide into civil war. He took up the subject matter of *Wolf Dreams*, he noted, because he "had a very important message to deliver at a moment when people around the world needed to understand what was happening in our country."[20] Although Khadra sprinkles only a few specific historical events into the text—for example, the arrest of FIS leaders Abassi Madani and Ali Benhadj in June 1991, the cancellation of the second round of the parliamentary elections in January 1992, and the presidential election of November 1995—they are sufficient to allow the informed reader to situate the protagonist in the events of the era. The reign of urban terror begins as Nafa is recruited and Khadra tells us that "police, military, journalists, and intellectuals dropped like flies, one after another at dawn, cut down on their doorsteps."[21] This broad allusion to events that especially touched Khadra (as both a military officer and an intellectual) evokes specific incidents for many of his Algerian readers. The author, the reader senses, is appalled at the story of terrorist violence that he must tell, but tell it he must, in order to demonstrate how his country lost its way—and what he believes is its true identity—during the 1990s.

Part 3 of the novel is titled "The Abyss," recounting the downward spiral of the country and the protagonist. Nafa becomes a killer surrounded by fanatics and is forced to participate in the assassination of the filmmaker who gave him his one opportunity as an artist and then in the internecine violence between the FIS and the even more brutal Armed Islamic Group (GIA). Nafa himself plunges deeper and deeper into the abyss, finally to be betrayed and killed by the security forces. This final section alludes to the horrendous massacres of innocent villagers that marked the death throes of the insurgency. Khadra as author does not flinch in describing these terrible episodes of his country's history. At the same time, the book makes it clear that thanks to its fanaticism and nihilism, the Islamist insurgency is a dead end: Nafa and his band are dead, the civil war a hopeless abyss, the violent exploitation of Islam a false path.

Coming from the pen of a loyal military officer, *Wolf Dreams* is a remarkable novel. Although Khadra is scathing in his portrayal of the extremism of the GIA, he nonetheless makes Nafa's choice of terrorism understandable. Nafa is not initially a violent man but, rather, a disillusioned soul, a cast-off of the system. His personal quest for identity as an artist in a secular and egalitarian society foiled, he turns to the Islamist movement. Khadra, who is committed to the promise of the 1954 revolution, seeks to save that identity by critiquing what the system has become.

One might note that the army is barely visible in the novel. It offers an account of how Algeria became engulfed in civil war, but it is not a defense of the army's role in fighting the insurrection. Khadra's artistic purpose in the novel was not served by such an argument. Yet elsewhere he has felt the need to defend the army and the secular nationalist identity for which it has stood. When two books charging the Algerian army with atrocities in its conduct of the war against the Islamists appeared in France, Khadra spoke out on behalf of the institution from which he had only recently retired.

The controversy began with the publication of *Qui a tué à Bentalha? Chronique d'un massacre annoncé* (*Who Killed in Bentalha? Chronicle of a Massacre Foretold*) in October 2000. The book presents an eyewitness account of the massacre of some four hundred people in the little town of Bentalha on the outskirts of Algiers during the night of September 22–23, 1997. The author, Nesroulah Yous, who owned a small shop and residence in Bentalha, recounts the events over several years that led up to the horrendous atrocity committed there. The gist of the argument, especially as amplified in the postface written by the publisher, François Géze, and journalist Salima Mellah, is that the army via its secret services (the Sécurité Militaire) was implicated in the massacres, which had been attributed to the Islamists. A few months later, the same publisher brought out *La sale guerre: Le témoignage d'un ancien officier des forces spéciales de l'armée algérienne, 1992-2000* (*The Dirty War: Testimony of a Former Officer in the Algerian Army's Special Forces, 1992-2000*), by Habib Souaïdia, a former parachutist who sought political asylum in France. *Le Monde* described Souaïdia's book as an "implacable indictment against the [Algerian] military command accused of using the same methods as its 'bearded' adversaries."[22] Both works obviously called the integrity of the army into serious question, and the reputation of the military was central to Khadra's notion of national identity.

Hence Khadra entered the debate over the honor of the army in an opinion piece in *Le Monde* bitterly titled "To Those Who Spit in Our Tears." The text appeared on the same page as a declaration signed by eight prominent Algerian intellectuals calling for an official judicial investigation into the events alleged in Souaïdia's book: "The crimes of which army officers have been accused require the attention of the legal authorities by virtue of the primordial issues of truth and justice at stake. By comparison the charges lodged against the author of the book, announced with great fanfare by the [Algerian] Minister of Justice, seem altogether derisory. It is imperative that such practices as the immunity of the military authorities cease."[23] As a counterpoint, the paper also published a statement by the Algerian ambassador in France calling the book a fraud and a "negation of the heroic daily battle of Algerians against terrorism and in defense of the emergence of a more democratic system." In stepping into this crossfire, Khadra vehemently upheld the reputation of the institution that epitomized the legacy of 1954.

He would not, Khadra began, retract previous statements in support of the army or, for that matter, the dedication of his 1998 novel *L'Automne des chiméres* (*The Autumn of Pipe Dreams*) "to the soldier and policeman of my country." He goes on to declare "solemnly that, during eight years of war, I have never been witness, neither from near or from far, nor have I ever suspected the least massacre of civilians perpetrated by the army." He continues: "The Algerian army is not a collection of barbarians and assassins. It is an institution of the people that is trying to save its country and its soul with what little appropriate means it disposes of.... To present the Algerian soldier as a mercenary or as a legionnaire without faith or conscience is unjust and inhuman." Khadra grants that the civil war shocked and disoriented a military institution reluctant to believe that "the fatherland could be martyred by its own offspring," but he is appalled by the accusations which he considers an indignity to those who risked and lost their lives fighting the insurgency: "We are the children of our country, unwilling warriors, fighting reluctantly ... offering at any moment a bit of our life to preserve a parcel of our land and our dignity." Khadra's tone is one of chagrin and sorrow at Algeria's "nightmare," but it is most fundamentally a defense of the patriotic and republican values of the institution in which he served for thirty-six years. The author of *Wolf Dreams* understands that the republic has fallen short of its revolutionary legacy, but he insists here that the republic's foot soldiers represent its true identity.[24]

Despite—indeed in the face of—the turmoil of the 1990s, the army is for Khadra the repository of the defining events of modern Algeria. It represents the institutionalization of the heroic era and embodies the memory of the aspirations of the Algerian revolution. This theme is equally evident in Khadra's memoir of his youth as a cadet in the military school system.[25] Although this autobiographical work deals largely with his personal ambition to become a writer—hardly the norm in a military academy—it has been described as a "striking homage to the Algerian army ... [and] the most attractive internal view upon an institution as mistakenly venerated as deprecated."[26] As the controversy over the books of Nous and Souaïdia amply demonstrates, the status of the military institution as the guarantor of one interpretation of national identity was sorely tried by the end of the 1990s. Yet Khadra, the soldier/writer, still embraced the identity of the revolutionary era while exposing (in *Wolf Dreams*) the systemic flaws that provoked the national trauma of the era of the civil war.

* * *

It is not a coincidence that both Djebar and Khadra have written in an autobiographical vein, for matters of national identity and memory are intimately bound up with the nature of personal identity. As a woman who seized the pioneering opportunities that opened up before her, Djebar has written works that celebrate women's achievements and sacrifices in the cause of the nation. Her individual story entwines with that of Algerian womanhood, giving voice to women who did not have the same opportunities and laying claim to full recognition of women's rights in Algeria's self-definition of its identity.

Likewise, Khadra has written poignantly of his personal itinerary from youthful cadet to career military officer to pseudonymous and ultimately unmasked artist/writer.[27] Imbued with the memory of the revolution of 1954 from his boyhood, he, like Djebar, construes Algerian identity in terms of a secular rather than an Islamic republic. As an author, however, he is able to step into the personality of an Islamist militant who has lost faith in that project. His insistence in the opinion piece in *Le Monde* upon the integrity of the army is a testimony to the continuing relevance of the legacy of 1954 for him.

Both authors, as is abundantly evident, deal with violence as a recurrent phenomenon in Algerian history: the violence of the colonial takeover, that of the war of independence, that of the 1990s. In this, they join the analysis of one of Algeria's better known social scientists, Luis Martinez. In his *La guerre civile en Algérie, 1990–1998*, Martinez writes that "violence is a virtue in the political imagination of this country."[28] Martinez sees a long history of social promotion via violence (pirates, *caïds*, colonels, emirs—all "political bandits" of one sort or another) in Algeria. Although his concept of political imagination (*l'imaginaire politique*) is not identical to our concept of identity and memory, the two conceptualizations overlap. Thus these three epochs of violence, as treated in the two novels, are a constituent part of Algerian identity. The issue is less the legitimacy of violence than the specification of the sociopolitical model, secular or sacred, on behalf of which violence is exercised.

The resistance of the nineteenth century as evoked by Djebar and the period of national liberation, treated directly in *Fantasia* and indirectly in *Wolf Dreams* and other texts by Khadra, are both central episodes of Algerian memory. The latter memory is also celebrated in Gillo Pontecorvo's classic film *The Battle of Algiers*. It has become customary to show this documentary-like film on Algerian television every year on July 4, the eve of the annual Independence Day holiday. The film is, of course, a document of revolutionary violence and heroism in the cause of Algerian independence. The great majority of Algerians continue to see this era as primary in the definition of national identity. The fratricidal struggle of the 1990s, however, revealed that the cultural content of independence is still at issue. In this regard, Algeria, and the rest of the contemporary Maghrib, for that matter, are part of a larger search for identity in the Arab and Muslim world.

All nations look to their artists and writers for insight into the meaning of their national experience. The works highlighted in this chapter demonstrate how important historical memory is to Algerian identity. One evokes the trauma of the colonial conquest before centering itself upon the era of national liberation and women's crucial role therein. The other treats the severe postcolonial crisis that arose from disillusionment with the unmet promises of that era. The narratives lead to and from this core memory of the wartime era, which still constitutes the central trope of contemporary Algerian identity. The ambiguities of that era contained in competing Muslim and secular nationalist interpretations remain present in today's debates.

Notes

1. *El Watan*, January 2, 2006.
2. Bruno Étienne, *L'Algérie, cultures et révolution* (Paris: Éditions du Seuil, 1977).
3. *La Charte Nationale Algérienne (27 juin 1976)*, notes et études documentaires 4348-4349-4350, December 28, 1976 (Paris: Documentation française, 1976), 27.
4. Ibid., 29.
5. Ibid., 28-29.
6. See, for example, Michael Slackman, "Top Algerians Prefer Amnesia to Accountability," *New York Times*, September 26, 2005. For an analysis for the 1999 referendum, see Abderrahmane Moussaoui, "La concorde civile en Algérie: entre mémoire et histoire," in *Où va l'Algérie*, edited by Ahmed Mahiou and Jean-Robert Henry, 71-92 (Paris: Éditions Karthala and IREMAM, 2001).
7. Assia Djebar, *Fantasia: An Algerian Cavalcade*, translated by Dorothy Blair (Portsmouth, N.H.: Heinemann, 1993), 8.
8. Djebar also directed a film based upon her project of interviewing women about their wartime experience: *La Nouba des femmes de Mont Chenoua* (1979).
9. Djebar, *Fantasia*, 187-88.
10. Ibid., 141.

11. Ibid., 3.

12. Ibid., 45.

13. The novel was published in Paris (Julliard, 1999). The translation by Linda Black appeared as *Wolf Dreams* (New Milford, Conn.: Toby Press, 2003).

14. Khadra, *Wolf Dreams*, 12.

15. Ibid., 49.

16. Ibid., 50–51.

17. Ibid., 70.

18. "Entrevue," May 10, 2001, in Françoise Naudillon, *Les masques de Yasmina* (Ivry-sur-Seine: Éditions Nouvelles du Sud, 2002), 138.

19. Khadra, *Wolf Dreams*, 51.

20. "Entrevue," 147.

21. Khadra, *Wolf Dreams*, 135.

22. *Le Monde*, February 9, 2001. Both books were published in Paris by Éditions La Découverte, Youss's in 2000 and Souaïdia's in 2001.

23. "Justice!" *Le Monde*, March 13, 2001. The signatories were Lahouari Addi, Madjid Benchikh, Mourad Bourboune, El-Hadi Chalabi, Mohammed Harbi, Salima Mellah, Khaled Satour, and Fatiha Talahite.

24. All quotations in this paragraph are from "A ceux qui crachent dans nos larmes," *Le Monde*, March 13, 2001.

25. See Yasmina Khadra, *L'écrivain* (Paris: Julliard, 2001).

26. *Le Matin* (Algiers), March 13, 2001, quoted in Naudillon, 43.

27. Here I allude to the title of Naudillon's study, *Les masques de Yasmina*.

28. Luis Martinez, *La guerre civile en Algérie, 1990–1998* (Paris: Éditions Karthala, 1998), 9; *The Algerian Civil War, 1990–98* (New York: Columbia University Press, 2000).

4

Berber/Amazigh Memory Work

BRUCE MADDY-WEITZMAN

The transnational Berber/Amazigh[1] culture movement that emerged in recent decades has been a multifaceted phenomenon. As is the case with all ethnonational projects, the elaboration and dissemination of modern Berber identity has been accompanied by the fashioning of a "memory community." This involved a search for a useable past and, once found, its enshrinement in new narratives, rituals, and collective commemorations. Shared memory, Anthony Smith tells us, is as essential to the survival of a collective cultural identity as is the sense of a common destiny.[2] It goes without saying that the greater the success of the process of "remembering, recovering and inventing" Berber history,[3] the greater the influence it will have on Algerian and Moroccan societies.[4]

Berber "memory work" is carried out in a variety of ways and on a number of different levels. In its more popular form, the promotion of Berber history and memory involves a considerable degree of myth making and essentializing of the Berber "spirit" (embodied in Jean Amrouche's memorable phrase, "the eternal Jugurtha").[5] In the realms of scholarship and journalism, the reopening of North African history to include the Berbers often poses real challenges to the "official" history propagated by contemporary North African states and the larger Arab-Islamic milieu of which Berbers are a part. Related to but distinct from the work of historians are acts of commemoration, namely, the creation, elaboration, and vigilant protection of "memory sites" (*lieux de memoire*) that enable groups to buttress their identities against the constant push and pull of historical currents that threaten to sweep them away.[6] Musicians, poets, and writers have taken a preeminent role in this regard, and some, such as writer Mouloud Mammeri and singer-poet Lounes Matoub, have become a kind of "memory site" themselves, as either cultural icons, martyrs to the cause, or both.

The task of Berber memory work is formidable. From the beginning of recorded history in North Africa, the Berbers have been depicted as semi-savage outsiders requiring a civilizing hand. They have been especially burdened by the legacy of Islamic history, which provided them with an Eastern and Arab "origin myth" that legitimized their inclusion in the *umma*, albeit as a primitive community requiring the Islamic faith to justify their mission and assumption of power.[7] Part of this *istislam*, or "submission," involved the seemingly natural superiority conferred on the Arabic language, the language through which God's word was transmitted and subsequently interpreted by the doctors of the holy law. Ironically, it was a non-Berber, the premier Maghribi historian Ibn Khaldun, writing nearly seven hundred years after the Islamic conquest of North Africa, who made the Berbers a "great nation" like others in the *umma*, even as he used them to demonstrate historical laws of the rise and decline of societies.

Up until recently, the essentially oral culture of the Berbers and the dearth of written texts in Tamazight placed Berber memory workers at a severe disadvantage. The steady political, social, and cultural marginalization of Berber communities over the last five hundred years made memory work even more difficult. Smith's description of the difficulties confronting demotic and peripheral ethnies seems apt for the Berbers: "Excluded from the instruments of political transmission and bereft of institutional support, and sometimes without a class of specialists and developed codes of communication[,] ... their memories tenuous, their heroes shadowy, and their traditions ... patchy and poorly documented."[8]

Nonetheless, the threats posed to Berber language and identity by newly independent states' policies of centralization and Arabization, coming on top of the massive upheavals generated by European colonialism and imperialism, and topped off by the often pernicious homogenizing effects of globalization processes on local cultures, have also had a salutary effect. The quest for cultural authenticity, perceived as the basis of collective dignity and hence freedom, is a worldwide contemporary phenomenon in which Berber intellectuals and activists actively participate. As Smith says, if "the secret of identity is memory, the ethnic past must be salvaged and re-appropriated, so as to renew the present and build a common future in a world of competing national communities."[9] No wonder, then, that the Amazigh movement places a premium on memory work.

The Premodern Past

Moroccan history, as it appears in the official education curriculum, is explicitly "nationalist/dynastic," incorporating Islamic history into a specific

Moroccan historical experience beginning with the arrival of Islam and continuing through the establishment of the Idrisid dynasty in A.D. 788 by Idris I, a descendant of the family of Ali, the Prophet Muhammad's son-in-law. Although Berbers are subsumed in this history, they at least carry some implicit standing: The Idrisis are known to have married Berber women, and Moroccan dynasties between the eleventh and fourteenth centuries were Berber-based.[10] By contrast, narrative history as taught in independent Algeria's schools has been strikingly lacking in any Algerian-centered orientation. Thus Algeria's Berberity has been consigned to Algeria's distant past or ignored entirely. Moreover, the twentieth-century Algerian Salafi historian Tawfiq al-Madani regarded the Berbers as "noble savages" in a pristine state, a cultural blank page. It was the Islamic conquest, he wrote, that brought about the "perfection" of the Maghribi people through a fusion of Arabs and Berbers into one community.[11] Only recently has this official Salafi reading of Algerian history begun to be questioned, for example, with Mahiedine Djender's representation of Algeria as the product of the interactions of a Mediterranean civilization.[12]

Amazigh memory workers, regardless of their country of origin, specific national/territorial priorities, degree of militancy, or concern with the standards of historical accuracy, are like-minded in their emphasis on the Berbers as having a pre-Islamic past, and one in which they were active agents, not merely voiceless, nameless foot soldiers and illiterate tribesmen and peasants. Illustrated books for children tell the stories of ancient Amazigh heroes, such as Juba, Massinissa, and the Berber queen Dihya/the Kahina. The Kahina holds particularly mythical status among Amazigh memory workers as the heroic leader of Berber resistance to Islamic invaders (for a recent and contested use of the Kahina in Algeria, see below).[13]

Mohamed Chafik, the dean of Moroccan Berberist intellectuals, has consistently sought to redefine Maghribi collective memory, and hence its identity, by rehistoricizing Morocco's pre-Islamic past. Recorded North African history, he emphasizes, dates back to the Romans, Greeks, Carthaginians, and even, at times, Pharoanic Egypt. The native Amazigh-speaking population was part and parcel of this history, according to Chafik, and produced numerous historical figures, such as Terentius (a Carthage-born playwright writing in Greek and Latin during the second century B.C.), Tertullianus (an important Christian writer from Carthage in the late first century–early second century A.D.), Arnobius (another Christian writer, born in a Numidian village in the second half of the third century A.D), and St. Augustine.[14] For Chafik and other Amazigh activists, language is the defining feature of culture and history (notwithstanding the fact that Amazigh heroes during the Roman and Byzantine period had Latinized names and may or may not have been fluent in the Amazigh language). As such, Amazigh history can be traced even further into the past, many hundreds of years before the *barbaroi* began appearing in Greek chronicles. Moroccan-born ethnologist Helene Hagan has written a fascinating monograph on the Amazigh underpinnings of ancient Egyptian civilization based on the etymological roots of its language.[15] The "Libyan" pharoanic dynasty founded by Sheshounk I in 945 B.C. is now commonly referred to by Amazigh memory workers as the moment of entry of the Amazigh people into history. Indeed, the Paris-based Académie Berbère chose to propagate a Berber calendar with the year of Sheshonk's ascent as its starting point. Accordingly, the year A.D. 2005 is equivalent to 2955. Both dates are used on the masthead of the Rabat-based monthly *Le Monde Amazigh* (*al-'Alam al-Amazighi/Amadal Amazigh*).

No less important for Amazigh memory workers, the Islamization of the Amazigh was not the end of history. It did not subordinate their identity per se, nor bring it to a most perfect state. In fact, it was the Amazigh people themselves, Chafik emphasizes, who played an important role in the dissemination of Islam in both Africa and Spain. To that end, Tariq Bin Ziyad, the fabled Berber commander of the Muslim forces that first crossed into Iberia in A.D. 711, very much belongs in the pantheon of Berber heroes, epitomized today by the Rabat center disseminating Berber culture that bears his name.[16] Conversely, and not surprisingly, the destruction wrought in Andalusia in the twelfth century by the troops of the religiously zealous Almohad Berber dynasty founded by Ibn Tumart is conspicuously absent from Berber memory work. Collective memory, as we know, is always selective, as much about forgetting as about remembering.[17]

Chafik laid out his interpretation of Moroccan Amazigh history during the Islamic period starkly, and at times polemically, in the Berber Manifesto, issued in March 2000 and signed by more than two hundred Berber intellectuals. While providing a detailed exposé of the shortcomings of the independence era, the manifesto also places them in a broader historical context, albeit one not commonly found in the history books. Most people, it says, recognize that the imposition of colonialism in 1912 was made possible by the sorry state to which Morocco had sunk. The reason for this was the triumph of the *makhzenian*[18] political tradition of despotism and oppression, accompanied by "haughtiness, ostentation and pomp." This tradition is said to have been inherited from the Ummayad and Abbasid empires, "contrary to the spirit of political consultation prescribed by Islam," and practiced by the Prophet Muhammad and the first four Caliphs. Coincidentally or not, this latter spirit, as defined by the manifesto, was in line with Amazigh political traditions, which were "geared towards managing the affairs of the jamaʿa ('local community') . . . through dialogue and consultation." The *makhzen*, "pursuant to its heavy Heraclian-Khurasan heritage," was steered for centuries by "influential people," those who could "make or break," who preached hatred toward anything Amazigh, while reducing the historical roles played by "Berbers." Occasionally, the manifesto stated, enlightened Sultans made commendable efforts toward the Amazigh population. However, the *makhzenian* circles "taught hatred towards anything Amazigh to generation after generation of their offspring." Their desire to preserve their privileges led them to blindly adhere to political traditions based upon dogmatic and tightly closed religious thinking. The clash between these two worldviews resulted in violence and disorder, rendering the country easy prey for foreign invaders.

Chafik's emphasis on the purity of Muhammad and his immediate successors, the *rashidun* (the "rightly guided" caliphs), is a theme common to Islamic reform currents dating back to the late nineteenth century. In that sense, Chafik's approach is a consensual one, which seeks to incorporate Moroccan Islam into Amazigh identity. To be sure, Chafik seems to be advocating a more thoroughgoing liberal reform of Islam than that of reformers of earlier generations, in line with modern times. Still, even this view is not universally accepted in the Amazigh activist community, which contains many militant secularists, among them the editor and publisher of *Le Monde Amazigh*, which demonstratively does not include the Hijra calendar date on its masthead. Similarly, the state-sponsored Institut Royal de la Culture Amazighe (IRCAM) is not universally viewed with favor among the Moroccan Amazigh community.[19]

On occasion, Chafik's writings have also been criticized for being essentialist and ahistorical and hence unhelpful to the Amazigh cause. Moroccan scholar Rachid Idrissi takes Chafik to task for ignoring history, for stating without proof, for example, that ancient Berber kings sought to unify all of the Berber tribes under one central power, or for trying to forcibly bridge Morocco's pre-Islamic and Islamic eras (for example, by holding up both the Kahina and the twentieth-century Riffian leader Abd al-Krim as Berber heroes and models; for more on the latter, see below). Chafik's declaration that the conquering Arabs were the enemies of the Berbers, like all other conquerors of North Africa from ancient times to modern, and that it was due to them that the Berbers did not write down their own history was simply inaccurate, according to Idrissi. Such a view, he said, ignored the fact that "the Berbers mixed with the Arabs like pure water with wine" (quoting Mokhtar Soussi, a famous Berber Muslim intellectual of the early twentieth century). The Berbers, said Idrissi, began to have a collective memory when they learned to write in Arabic, as part of the Islamic *umma*.[20]

France's Moroccan Protectorate

The Berber Manifesto's critique of "official" Moroccan history during the years of the French protectorate is withering. *Makhzenian* circles, it claims, actually welcomed the French protectorate and were the main beneficiaries of its rule. Together, they were aligned against the "rebellious Berbers," who were militarily subjugated and then consigned to marginalization and nondevelopment. When the time came for national rebellion against the French, it was the Imazighen who willingly provided the necessary manpower. At the same time, the manifesto studiously avoids any mention of the most powerful Berber leader during the protectorate years, Thami al-Glawi, an omission that can only be understood as a willful act. A positive reference to Glawi, whose power rivaled that of the Sultan's, would situate contemporary Berber discourse on the side of the French colonial power and opposed to Moroccan nationalism, not to mention the legitimacy of the monarchy; mere repetition of the dominant national narrative's negative treatment of Glawi would run counter to the manifesto's overall critique of that narrative. Given Glawi's prominent role in Moroccan history during those tumultuous decades, one can perhaps expect that at some point both dispassionate historians and Amazigh activists more militant than those affiliated with the manifesto will take up the subject.[21]

In contrast to the silence on Glawi, the leader of the 1921–26 Rif rebellion against Spanish and French forces, Muhammad bin Abd al-Krim Khattabi, has become a preferred, even revered figure for modern-day Moroccan Berbers engaged in memory work. Abd al-Krim combined charisma, military prowess, education both traditional and modern, and a political agenda that led him to seek to unify the historically feuding tribes of the Rif into a single political unit. In the process, he accumulated the ultimate anti-imperialist credentials, inflicting a crushing defeat on Spanish forces at the battle of Anoual in 1921, an outcome that resonated widely throughout the Middle East and beyond. This triumph also supplies important ammunition to modern-day Berber activists determined to combat the accusations that Berbers too often collaborated with colonial rule and that their assertion of Berber identity is linked to older colonialist projects to divide Berbers from Arabs.

At first glance, appropriating bin Abd al-Krim may not seem like an entirely smooth matter for secular Berberists. He is generally understood by historians to have been a promoter of Islamic reform,[23] in line with wider Islamic currents at the expense of popular religious practice, which Berber activists often recognize as central to their specific heritage. Nor did bin Abd al-Krim emphasize an explicitly Amazigh/Berber identity in his efforts to mobilize fellow Rifians against the foreigner. Hence, in addition to his Islamic reformist credentials, he is often viewed as a premodern type of leader, leading a not-untypical and ultimately futile nativist revolt against the conquerors.

As with all historical personalities, bin Abd al-Krim's actual behavior and views do not completely fit the requirements of an idealized Berber hero. But contemporary Amazigh activists have not been deterred by these caveats. They concentrate on portraying bin Abd al-Krim as a leader who heroically led his people against the occupier, unlike the urban Arab class, which sat on its hands during the Rifian revolt rather than lend a hand against the colonial oppressor. The recovery of the history of bin Abd al-Krim and his short-lived "Rifian Republic" is hence an ongoing project, intimately connected to the themes of marginalization and identity denial that characterize the contemporary Berberist discourse. Only recently, Amazigh activists initiated a campaign to return Abd al-Krim's remains from Cairo, where he died in 1963, and to construct a combination mausoleum-museum-cultural complex in his Ajdir redoubt.[24] In August 1999, the newly crowned King Muhammad VI conferred an important measure of legitimacy on Rifian Amazigh memory work. Aware of the Rif's problematic status, economically, socially, and historically vis-à-vis the Moroccan central authorities, and seeking to bolster his own legitimacy in a region that his father, as crown prince, had bombed and repressed in 1958–59, Muhammad made a high-profile visit to the region, something his father had always avoided. Moreover, his gestures to the Rifian Berbers were not limited to pledges for material improvement but also included a promise that the Ajdir ruins would be reconstructed and a visit with bin Abd al-Krim's son, who came especially from Cairo for the occasion.

Notwithstanding Muhammad VI's gestures, however, he has failed to address a painful episode that highlights the *makhzen*'s historic indifference to the Rifian war, namely, the Spanish military's systematic use of poison gas against Rifian fighters and civilians, with the assistance of French and German manufacturers. It is only in recent years that this matter has come to light, thanks in part to the work of a number of Spanish scholars and British historian Sebastian Balfour,[25] as well as two German journalists, who revealed German involvement in Spain's actions. *Le Monde Amazigh*, which has played a prominent role in recent years in promoting and disseminating the Abd al-Krim story through articles and conferences, has given prominence to this shocking and sorry episode in a number of issues. The battle against marginalization and official indifference extends to the present: Survivors of poison gas attacks and their offspring are said to suffer from numerous health problems, including inordinately high rates of cancer. But up until now, Moroccan authorities have ignored Amazigh demands and been unwilling to raise the matter of possible acknowledgment and compensation for elderly survivors with the Spanish government, fearing that it would adversely affect bilateral ties.[26] In response, one speaker at a conference held in the Rifian city of Tetouan in the spring of 2004 proposed a number of concrete measures, including suing the German and French companies that participated in the manufacture of the toxic gases used by Spain and appealing to the European Court of Human Rights.[27]

Praising bin Abd al-Krim's anticolonial exploits is only part of the Amazigh movement's efforts to debunk the stigma of collaboration with the colonial rulers, which gained currency especially after the issuing of the so-called Berber *dahir* (royal edict) by the French authorities in 1930. France's attempt to institutionalize Berber customary law at the expense of Qur'anic law served as a crucial catalyst in the formation of the nationalist movement. In recent years, some Berber activists have taken another look at the episode. Muhammad Mounib blamed the nationalists for the false "Berber" appellation of the *dahir*, for it implicitly implicated the Berbers in the French project to divide them from the Arabs.[28] Chafik found another way to debunk the myth of Berber collaboration with the Protectorate, emphasizing the importance of transcribing and studying Amazigh poetry as the reservoir of the memory of resistance to the French occupation during 1912–34.[29] Commemorations of battles against the colonizers, such as the one of Bougafer in the Middle Atlas in 1933, are connected by organizers to other historical and contemporary events in different regions, so as to emphasize the supra-tribal, collective nature of Berber identity.[30]

Battling the Istiqlal

The Moroccan Berberist counternarrative has drawn an almost straight line between official indifference to the Rif and the subsequent founding of the state and marginalization of the Berber communities by the Istiqlal-dominated nationalist movement. The failure of the state to officially commemorate the battle of Anoual or other episodes of resistance to the French pacification campaigns, wrote one commentator, contrasted sharply with its attention to events commemorating the Istiqlal.[31] The murder of Rifian Liberation Army leader Abbas M'sa'adi in 1956, apparently on the order of the Istiqlal's Mehdi Ben Barka, has become another subject of discussion in recent years,[32] as has the authorities' forcible repression of the 1958–59 rebellion. Ironically, one of the eighteen demands submitted to the king in November 1958 by a Rifian committee (which included bin Abd al-Krim's son) was for the rapid Arabization of the educational system throughout the country. The context of this demand was the use of French in the former Spanish zone, to which the Rif belonged, which put the local population at a disadvantage relative to the central authorities.[33] Subsequently, of course, Arabization became one of the chief bugaboos of the Amazigh movement, owing to the overt threat it posed to Tamazight and to the already unequal, subordinate social status of its speakers.

As with the Rifian demands for indemnity for the victims of Spain's poison gas attacks, reopening the wounds of 1958 is not just a matter of concern to historians, or even to identity builders. In February 2004, the Committee of Victims of the 1958 Walmas Events was established. The committee demanded not only the revelation of the truth but also indemnity for the survivors of the repression of the mostly Berber Army of Liberation members, from the Walmas tribal grouping, by the "militia" of the Istiqlal party. As is usually the case, the royal family's role in the events was downplayed.[34]

The first Amazigh intellectual to speak out publicly against the falsification of Moroccan history by the Istiqlal-dominated establishment and the systematic ignoring of the Berbers, those who represent the "real culture of the country," was the recently deceased Ali Sidqi Azaykou (d. 2004). Characterizing the historical origins of Morocco's cultural problem as stemming from repeated colonization by outsiders, including Arabs, and publishing his views in Arabic, no less (adding fuel to the fire), he was convicted in 1982 of "disturbing the security of the state" and imprisoned for one year.[35] Beginning in the 1990s, however, the Moroccan authorities began treating such expressions more benignly. By 2001, the Berber Manifesto could address

Morocco's more recent history in an unabashedly revisionist and explicitly political tone. It hammered away at the denial of Morocco's "Amazighness" and the arrogation by professional politicians and most members of Morocco's elites, since 1956, of "monopolistic rights to 'patriotism' and 'political action.'" Even speaking of this monopolization, the manifesto noted, has long been a taboo in Moroccan life.

Little by little, stated the Manifesto, it became clear after independence that none of the extant political forces, whether pro-monarchy or not, were going to give the Amazigh their due and include them in the definition of a modern Morocco. Instead, successive national governments pursued the policy of building an exclusively "Arab Maghrib," led by an Arabized Morocco. In presenting their demands for a reordering of national priorities, the signatories of the manifesto were determined "to combat the *cultural hegemony*" that has been programmed in order to bury a very important part of [Morocco's] civilizational heritage [emphasis in original].[36]

Although the broad dichotomy laid out in the manifesto between the "good" Berbers and the "bad" Istiqlal/*makhzen* may be generally accepted by the Amazigh movement, a more complex reality has begun to be acknowledged. Some Berbers, including former Liberation Army members, joined the Union Nationale des Forces Populaires (UNFP) in 1959, which was formed by Ben Barka as a breakaway from the Istiqlal. They did so, according to veteran activist Muhammad al-Kassimi, in order to stop the injustice caused to authentic "resisters" by the appointment to high positions of "collaborators," e.g., Gen. Muhammad Oufkir, who served in the French army (as did tens of thousands Berber *goums* [tribal irregulars]) and eventually became the king's right-hand man until his ultimate demise in 1972, and "feudalists," a reference to the Berber rural notables who made common cause with the monarchy through the Mouvement Populaire.[37] The state's crackdown on the tribes of the Khenifra region in 1973 followed an attempted uprising in Moulay Bouaza by the UNFP's secret military wing led by Sidi Muhammad Umed, which, according to Kassimi, had won a measure of sympathy among the civilian population. The punishment inflicted on his family, friends and the region in general is now being spoken of openly, along with demands for indemnities. Meanwhile, Umed fled to Algeria, where he had previously resided for twelve years, died during the 1980s, and was buried there with honors. To complicate the picture further, the UNFP itself may have been involved in the unsuccessful coup d'état against King Hassan II the previous year, through Lt. Col. Muhammad Amokrane. This of course was the event that brought Oufkir, held up by

Kassimi as the "collaborator" par excellence during the 1950s, to ruin.[38] The very fact that *Le Monde Amazigh* published the interview with Kassimi while he was being treated in an army hospital at the state's expense for injuries he suffered while in prison, indicates the increasing possibilities of conducting open discussion of formerly repressed episodes of Morocco's recent past. It also signals that at least some within the Amazigh movement are opposed to reductionist, one-dimensional representations of that past.[39]

Subaltern History

Recovering and remembering rural and tribal history is very much part of the Amazigh culture movement's agenda. Here the primary factor in determining identity is not language per se but land, around which society is organized. In Morocco, the authorities, whether French or Moroccan, are depicted as running roughshod over Amazigh communal land rights and traditions. For example, *Le Monde Amazigh* published a long article denouncing the administrative confiscation of the lands belonging to the Zayan tribes in the Khenifra region, pointing to similarities between current policies and those used by the Protectorate authorities, who had bought out one of the leading *caïds*, Mouha U Hamou Zayani. Previously, he had joined with Arab tribes in their fight against the French during their "pacification" campaign. However, in return for his agreement not to fight the French any further, Mouha U Hamou was granted the lands of neighboring tribes.

The confiscation of communal lands also had important negative effects on social and cultural life. For example, a traditional spring holiday gathering of the Zayan tribes, which featured a theatrical performance by tribal notables involving pledges of mutual solidarity and a sharing of the lands, according to Berber customary law, vanished with the transfer of the lands to Mouha U Hamou. The administrative means for doing so were and remain Royal *dahirs*, which do not recognize customary law and view tribal lands as belonging to the state.[40]

The question of the relationship between customary law and Islamic law has been of continuing interest to scholars. The French Protectorate authorities stepped into a minefield when they tried to formally institutionalize customary Berber practices and thus officially place them on an equal footing with the Shari'a. It is generally held that Berber customary law (*izerf*) is not diametrically opposed to the Shari'a and takes it into account. However,

Injaz Abdallah Habibi, in writing about the Zayan tribes, openly questions whether this is the case, indicating a desire to diminish the religious aspects of Berber identity. His emphasis on the positive aspects of communal village customs is part of a broader theme of Amazigh memory work, namely, the essentially democratic nature of village society and, by extension, Berber culture as a whole (as articulated in the Berber Manifesto). The upland village is presented as the repository of deep-rooted Berber traditions, with the traditional art, handicrafts, and household management by women who stood at the center of daily life.[41] Such treatment at times spills over into an idealization of traditional life, reminiscent of the nostalgia-laden presentation of the Eastern European Jewish *shtetl* (village) by writers and publicists keen on promoting and preserving Jewish identity and culture, even as its base was being eroded and then violently eradicated. Another writer even went so far as to describe village society's organizing concept of *jama'a*, which is usually associated with a (negative) tribal mentality, as having the attributes of love, altruism, love of the land and the "other," and hence being not in contradiction with the requirements of modernity but rather in harmony with it.[42] This may seem contrived; however, it may also fit the category of reinterpreting one's history and society in a useful fashion.

Ali Azaykou, for his part, recommended studying Morocco's past via the method of *l'histoire tatouée*, a metaphor for unwritten documents preserved by geography and archaeology, in addition to the oral traditions embodied in the Amazigh collective memory. In addition, one may learn something even from the actual tattoo often engraved on the Berbers' skin. Use of the tattoo metaphor is especially poignant, given the fact that in contemporary Morocco, the tattoo is often seen as an emblem of inferiority inflicted by one's parents, and considerable efforts are made to surreptitiously remove it, often resulting in scarring of the skin.[43]

Algeria's Berbers – Kabyle and Chaoui or Amazigh?

The Berberist reading of the broad historical themes of Amazigh history in both the pre-Islamic and Arab-Islamic periods, as well as the challenges posed by the postcolonial state, cut across contemporary inter-state boundaries. France's aborted efforts to base its rule on a policy of dividing Berbers from Arabs, underpinned by a well-constructed set of origin and character myths,[44] proved a difficult legacy for Berbers in both Morocco and Algeria, who were at pains to demonstrate their patriotic and anticolonial credentials. Regardless of their efforts, contemporary opponents of the Berber culture movement accuse it of promoting colonialism in a new guise. But unlike earlier decades, Berber insistence on their anticolonialist credentials does not deter them from sharply criticizing Arab nationalism, the dominant ideology of all modern states in North Africa. More and more, Arab nationalism appears in Berber discourse as a pernicious foreign import, its fuller appellation being "Arab-Islamic Ba'athism" or, alternately, "Arab-Islamic totalitarianism." In rejecting the Arab nationalist doctrine of a single Arab homeland (*al-Watan al-'Arabi*) from the Atlantic Ocean to the Persian Gulf, Berberists emphasize the existence of a single Amazigh people existing from time immemorial in its homeland (Tamazgha), stretching from the Canary Islands to the Siwa oasis in western Egypt. Efforts to desacralize the Arabic language include labeling the Arabic script "Aramean."[45] Concurrently, a modified version of the ancient Tifinagh script, preserved for usage by the Touareg Berbers of the Sahara, is held up as an important symbol of Berber identity, and its usage is actively promoted. In the realm of commemorative efforts, pan-Berber identity was recently manifested in a petition by the Paris-based Congrès Mondial Amazigh to the UN's Committee for the Elimination of Racial Discrimination (CERD) demanding that France add to its list of officially sanctioned holidays the Amazigh holidays of Yennayer (Amazigh New Year, a traditional agricultural festival), occurring on January 12, and the "Amazigh Spring" (commemorating the events in Algeria in 1980; see below), on April 20.[46]

At the same time, the particular historical experiences and social realities of the berberophone communities have shaped their memory work, resulting in a type of "Berberism in one country," carrying at least a potential tension with the pan-Berberist view. Nowhere is this more evident than with the Kabylians, who make up two-thirds of Algeria's berberophone population. To be sure, Kabylians have played a vanguard role in laying the foundation for the modern Berber culture movement, embodied over the last four decades by the France-based intellectual production of such bodies as the Académie Berbère/Agraw Imazighen, the Group d'Études Berbères de L'Université de Paris-VIII, and the Centre de Recherche Berbère at Institut National des Langues et Civilisations Orientales (INALCO) in Paris. However, the same factors that placed them in the vanguard of "pan-Berberism" also resulted in a sharpening of Kabylian specificity. By contrast, the second largest berberophone group, the Chaouia (from the Aurès Mountains), has historically been less isolated from its Arab surroundings and slower to develop a modern Amazigh identity.

The first manifestations of a modern type of Kabylian-Berber consciousness, expressed through new kinds of cultural expressions such as the poetry of resistance of colonization, were already making their appearance at the end of the nineteenth century. At this point, there was no intermediate reference to an "Algerian" or "Maghribian" community, only the immediate Kabylian identity and the wider Islamic one.[47] Jean Amrouche's *Chants Berbères de Kabylie* (1939) was followed by many other works in the fields of music and poetry (e.g., works by Mouloud Féraoun, Taos Amrouche, Mouloud Mammeri, and Ait Menguillet). Their recovery, transmission, and production of Kabylian cultural artifacts were crucial to the development of modern Kabylian identity. On the more explicitly political level, young radical Kabylian militants who fomented the so-called Berberist crisis in 1948–49, sharpened matters further. According to the analysis of Melha Benbrahim, the texts of these militants are dominated by references to the Berber, and specifically Kabylian, patrimony: the reclaiming of the pre-Islamic historical figures Massinissa and Jugurtha, and the heroic resister to the Arab conquest, the Kahina; the fierce Kabylian resistance to the French forces (1857, 1871); references to the Djurdura and the *montagne/adrar* as a symbol of resistance; the honor of the group; and their fidelity to their ancestors and symbolic heritage. Young Kabylian intellectuals, states Salem Chaker, were thus situated at the intersection of radical nationalism of the modern type (*laïque*) and the specific Berber cultural tradition.[48]

Interest in the "Berberist crisis" is part of the wider interest among Kabylian activists in reopening for scrutiny the events of Algeria's war of independence and its immediate aftermath. Scholars have generally downplayed the specific Berber dimension of the Algerian revolution's internal blood-lettings and political purges, for example, the assassinations of Abane Ramadane and Belkacem Krim and the failure of Hocine Ait Ahmed's opposition to the newly independent authorities in 1962–63.[49] Nonetheless, these episodes, underpinned by the wholesale denial of Kabylian specificity—and any diversity, for that matter—in favor of a stridently uniform and uni-dimensional nationalism, are now increasingly viewed as part of the background to the cultural flourishing and simmering proto-political opposition among the Kabylian community during the 1970s. Politically, Ait Ahmed organized his supporters in 1963 under the banner of the Forces des Front Socialistes. This organization would be joined at the end of the 1980s by the smaller, more militantly secular-Berberist Rassemblement pour la Culture et la Démocratie.[50]

The problematic nature of the Algerian state and its failure to adequately accommodate the Kabylian region generated a confluence of circumstances that led to the now-mythical "Berber Spring" (*Le Printemps Berbère*).[51] According to Benjamin Stora, "The effect of the 'Berber spring' was to produce, for the first time since independence and from within Algeria, a public counter-discourse of real import, in a country operating on the principle of unanimism. In that compact universe, where society and state, private and public mingled together in a single bloc, the blossoming of autonomous popular associations and organizations gave texture to Algerian society. The appearance of cultural, democratic pluralism allowed conflicts existing 'within the people' to be expressed and resolved by political means."[52]

In terms of memory work, the anniversary of the Berber Spring has become a central commemorative event for Amazigh cultural associations in Algeria and the diaspora.[53] Since 2001, it has been joined by *Le Printemps Noir* (Black Spring), the bloody events sparked by the death of a young Kabylian in police custody that resulted in the deaths of over one hundred people, a veritable civil revolt against the authorities and the creation of a new body outside of existing political parties, the *aarouch* (lit. "tribes"), which led an ongoing struggle to change the nature of Kabylian-state relations and, by extension, the nature of the Algerian state itself. The extent to which the *aarouch* constituted a modern, grass-roots organization drawing sustenance from traditional collective village symbols or, alternatively, constituted an unwelcome reversion to factionalized, premodern antidemocratic tribal norms remains to be determined.[54]

The two "Springs" of 1980 and 2001 serve as bookends, of a sort, to the breakdown of the postindependence FLN Algerian state and the descent into horrific violence during the 1990s between the authorities and Islamist opposition forces. These tumultuous times resulted in the creation of Kabylian "martyrs," from the numerous intellectuals and artists slain during the violence of the 1990s,[55] to Guermah Massinissa, the youth whose killing touched off the Black Spring in 2001. Singer and poet Lounes Matoub is perhaps the most prominent martyr of them all. His murder in June 1998, allegedly by Islamist extremists, touched off massive antigovernment demonstrations throughout Kabylia, and his last CD, released posthumously, contains a withering indictment of the postindependence Algerian state, set to the tune of Algeria's national anthem, with the refrain of "Betrayal, Betrayal." The cover of the CD, drawn by Ali Dilem, one of Algeria's leading caricaturists, contains images of dripping blood, the Amazigh flag, Algeria's military and political leaders and leading Islamists, a reference to the Arabization language policy, and a sign that reads "Algeriassic Park." It serves as an almost iconic poster, being used by Berber satellite television (BRTV) broadcasting from Paris, for example. Matoub's death, and those of others, quickly came to serve as a reference point for increased Kabylian militancy. Given the centrality of cultural producers in the fashioning of modern Kabylian/Amazigh identity, it was fitting that a veteran singer/poet/activist, Ferhat Mehenni, has taken the lead in recent years in promoting autonomy for Kabylie, a radical idea indeed.[56] Whatever the course events would take, it was clear that the fears of Mouloud Mammeri, the Kabylian cultural icon of the previous generation, of another "absurd death of the Aztecs" was premature, at the very least.[57]

Although Kabylia has been at the center of the Algerian Amazigh movement's political and cultural ferment, it would be mistaken to assign it exclusivity.[58] Berber memory work in the Aurès region, the site of the fabled Berber resistance to the invading Arab-Muslim forces at the end of the seventh century, has recently reached a new level. In February 2003, L'Association Aurès El-Kahina erected a large statue of the heroic Berber queen in the center of the town of Baghaï, in the wilaya of Khenchela. The statue was designed by a graduate of the École Nationale des Beaux-Arts d'Alger. Of course, such a public commemorative act could not be done in Algeria (except perhaps in Kabylia) without the consent of the authorities. In fact, the ceremony was attended by the president of the republic himself, Abdel Aziz Bouteflika. The president's presence was clearly intended as a gesture to the Amazigh community, with whom the state has been at loggerheads for so many years (though primarily in Kabylia, not in the Aurès); it also indicated a desire to place greater emphasis on specifically Algerian history, albeit a particular reading of it. Indeed, one shouldn't take this too far; his presence at the unveiling of the Kahina statue was ignored entirely by the national press.

Of course, Amazigh activists contest the state's orientation to Berber heritage, whether it involved appropriation or neglect. One Aurès-centered Web site, displaying the picture of the new Kahina statue, added superimposed images of the Amazigh flag on both sides of the Kahina statue's pedestal.[59] Activists bemoan the degradation and official neglect of the archaeological site, which is considered to have been the mountainous redoubt of the Kahina. Some academics have urged that UNESCO be approached to include it on its list of protected World Heritage sites, and that the Ministry of Culture take the lead in promoting its value, as it was inhabited from prehistoric times until the eleventh century Hilalian invasion.[60] According to Chaouia activists, the endangered status of another site poses a threat to their collective memory: the mausoleum of Imadghacen, a cylindrical pedestal eighteen and a half meters high and fifty-nine meters in diameter in the wilaya of Batna, which is among the oldest material evidence of the Massyle Amazigh dynasty, and which under the subsequent rule of Massinissa is considered to have sought to unify the Maghrib into a single entity. A suggestion to rename the Batna airport after Imadghacen (Imedhassen) was rudely rejected, prompting the following rejoinder from the disappointed former governor of Batna, who had been removed by Bouteflika allegedly following the pressure of the "local mafia": "Just as you have negated our origins at this moment, there will come a generation which will negate you."[61] Meanwhile, Chaoui Amazigh activists have begun using the name anyways.[62]

Concluding Thoughts

As Lawrence Rosen has shown in his study of a Moroccan village, day-to-day social boundaries between "Arabs" and "Berbers" are generally fluid and negotiable,[63] belying the all-too-common tendency among pundits and policy makers, past and present, to cast in stone the "Berber-Arab dichotomy." Nonetheless, in light of the social, cultural, and political developments in Morocco over the past thirty years, it would behoove researchers to revisit this relationship, particular as Berber memory work proceeds apace. The same is true regarding neighboring Algeria. In his insightful analysis of "the Berber" as a national signifier in Algerian historiographies, James McDougall warned against the possibility that the development of a Berber counter-narrative to the Algerian state's dominant narrative might harden social boundaries and intolerance in the name of cultural authenticity, a process that would in effect substitute one essential "authenticity" for another.[64] Indeed, one can identify without difficulty this tendency among some Amazigh militants.

At this point, Berber memory work, and the Berber/Amazigh culture movement to which it belongs, is clearly a genie that has been let out of a bottle whose cork was then discarded. Its future course, permutations, and points of emphasis will depend in no small measure on the policies of the Algerian and Moroccan states toward the phenomenon. Will their dominant national narratives be sufficiently modified to include Amazigh elements? Can one imagine, for example, that daily newspapers will include the Amazigh year on their masthead, alongside the year according to the Muslim and Gregorian calendar? (Perhaps this is not so far-fetched; after all, the Moroccan palace's French-language mouthpiece, *Le Matin du Sahara*, includes the date according to the Jewish calendar on its masthead!) Alternatively, will space be made for multiple, even competing narratives? Will Amazigh commemorative efforts be legitimized or repressed? And what may be the impact on the Amazigh movement's memory work of varying state policies? One may only say that the fashioning of Amazigh identity through memory work promises to be an ongoing and ever-increasing enterprise that will surely have an impact on, and interact with, parallel processes currently reshaping the identity of Algerian and Moroccan societies as a whole.

Notes

Note: This study was supported by the Israel Science Foundation (grant no. 525/04–21/5). Special thanks to Samir Ben-Layashi for his assistance in researching this article.

1. For convenience's sake, the terms "Berber" and "Amazigh" will be used interchangeably throughout this chapter.

2. Anthony D. Smith, *Nations and Nationalism in a Global Era* (Cambridge: Polity Press, 1995), 133.

3. Bernard Lewis, *History—Remembered, Recovered, Invented* (Princeton, N.J.: Princeton University Press, 1976).

4. The percentage of berberophones in Algeria is generally deemed to be 20–25 percent, and in Morocco 40–45 percent.

5. Jugurtha was the king of a united Numidia between 156 and 104 B.C. and grandson of Massinissa. He died in a Roman prison. The article is remembered as depicting the Berbers as eternally rebellious; in fact, there was much more to Amrocuhe's 1946 article, which described the duality of Berber culture in response to the "other" and recommended the shedding of (female) cultural characteristics that prevented the Berbers from becoming agents in history. Michael Brett and Elisabeth Fentress, *The Berbers* (London: Blackwell, 1996), 269–70.

6. Pierre Nora, "Between Memory and History: *Les Lieux de Mémoire*," *Representations*, Memory and Counter-Memory special issue, 26 (Spring 1989): 12.

7. Abdelmajid Hannoum, *Colonial Histories, Post-Colonial Memories: The Legend of the Kahina, a North African Heroine* (Portsmouth, N.H.: Heinemann, 2001), 7–9; Brett and Fentress, *Berbers*, 120–32; Michael Brett, "Ibn Khaldun and the Arabisation of North Africa," *Maghreb Review* 4, no. 1 (January–February 1979): 9–16.

8. Smith, *Nations and Nationalism*, 64.

9. Ibid., 146.

10. Maya Shatzmiller, *The Berbers and the Islamic State: The Marinid Experience in Pre-Protectorate Morocco* (Princeton, N.J.: Markus Weiner, 2000).

11. James McDougall, "Myth and Counter-Myth: 'The Berber' as National Signifier in Algerian Historiographies," *Radical History Review* 86 (Spring 2003): 75, 80–81.

12. Ibid., 82.

13. The murkiness of the actual historical record has helped spawn a veritable Kahina industry among just about every myth-seeking group that ever had anything to do with the Maghrib, from French colonialists to Arab nationalists to Jews to feminists, and even brought grudging acknowledgments from more conventional Muslim historians. Hannoum, *Colonial Histories, Post-Colonial Memories*.

14. Mohamed Chafik, *Lamha 'an Thalatha wa-Thalalthun Qarnan min Tarikh Al-Amazighiyyin* (A Look at Thirty-Three Centuries of Amazigh History) (Quneitra, Morocco: Boukeili, 2000), 78–81.

15. Helene Hagan, *The Shining Ones* (Philadelphia: Xlibris Corporation, 2000).

16. Mohamed Chafik, *Min Ajl Magharib Magharibiyya bil-Awlawiyya/Pour un Maghrib d'abord Maghrébin* (in Arabic section) (Rabat: Centre Tarik Ibn Zyad, 2000), 16–17.

17. For a discussion of Ernest Renan's famous remark to this effect, see Benedict Anderson, *Imagined Communities*, 2nd ed. (London: Verso, 1991), 199–201.

18. *Makhzen*, literally "strongbox" or "treasury," is the term commonly used to denote the Moroccan central authorities.

19. Paul A. Silverstein and David Crawford, "Amazigh Activists and the Moroccan State," *Middle East Report* 34, no. 4 (Winter 2004): 44–48.

20. Rashid Idrissi, "Al-Tarikh al-Amazighi: al-Hadath wal-Idiyulujiyya" (Amazigh History: Event and Ideology), *Prologues/Muqaddamat* 27/28 (Summer/Fall 2003): 116–27. His critique is of Chafik's book, *Mafhum al-Tarikh* (Understanding History), published in 1992. Soussi draws considerable interest from Amazigh scholars, owing to his intellectual weight. However, although his Berber origins are considered to be a factor in fashioning his identity, his concern with the wider Moroccan Arab-Islamic milieus is properly and frankly noted. Ahmad Boukous, "Mohammed Mokhtar Soussi, figure emblématique de la différence," *Naqd* 1, *Intellectuels et pouvoir au Maghrib: Itinéraires pluriels* (Printemps 1998): 101–18.

21. Orit Yekutieli, "The Never-Ending Story: Thami al-Glawi and the History of Modern Morocco" (master's thesis, Ben-Gurion University of the Negev, August 2003) (in Hebrew), 78–81.

22. Abd al-Karim Ghallab, *Tarikh al-Haraka al-Wataniyya Bil-Maghrib* (The History of the National Movement in Morocco) (Casablanca: Matba' al-Najah al-Jadida, 2000), 1:30–31, 453–64. Ghallab himself was a member of the Cairo-based committee for Moroccan national liberation, headed by Abd al-Krim, in the late 1940s. Ghallab and the other committee members, he says, were more "realistic" in their views than Abd al-Krim.

23. C. R. Pennell, *A Country with a Government and a Flag: The Rif War in Morocco, 1921–1926* (Wisbech, England: Menas Press, 1986); Jamil Abun-Nasr, *A History of the Maghrib in the Islamic Period* (Cambridge: Cambridge University Press, 1987), 378–82.

24. *Le Monde Amazigh* 55 (December 15, 2004), 4; *Maroc Hebdo International* (December 10–16, 2004), 13.

25. Sebastian Balfour, *Deadly Embrace* (Oxford: Oxford University Press, 2002).

26. "Gaz Toxique Contre Le Rif," *Le Monde Amazigh* 43 (March 2004), 13 (article originally published in *Nador*, February 18, 2004); "Before the Hiroshima and Nagasaki

Bombs, the Rif Resistance was Confronted with the Use of Weapons of Mass Destruction" (in Arabic), report on a conference addressing Spain's use of poison gas in the Rif war, *Le Monde Amazigh* 44 (April 2004), 4.

27. Resumé de l'intervention de Mimoun Charki, "Pour Des Revendications, Aux Fins De Reparations, Pour Les Prejudices Subis Suite a L'Utilisation D'Armes Chimiques De Destructions Massives Dans Le Rif," *Le Monde Amazigh* 44 (April 2004), 4; *Maroc Hebdo International* (December 10–16, 2004), 13.

28. *Tafsut* 35 (October 2002): 5; David M. Hart, "The Berber Dahir of 1930 in Colonial Morocco: Then and Now (1930–1960)," *Journal of North African Studies* 2, no. 4 (Autumn 1997): 11–33.

29. Chafik, *Min Ajl Magharib Magharibiyya*, 93–122. For a sample, see Michael Peyron, "Amazigh Poetry of the Resistance Period (Central Morocco)," *Journal of North African Studies* 3, no. 1 (Spring 2000): 109–20.

30. "Commemorating the Anniversary of the Battle of Bugafer" (in Arabic), *Le Monde Amazigh* 45 (May 2004), 9.

31. Muhammad Zahid, "Anwal: A Way-station Embodying the Existence of Dignity and Freedom" (in Arabic), *Le Monde Amazigh* 36 (July 2003), 9.

32. See the extensive discussions of the subject in *Le Monde Amazigh*: 16 (February, 2002), 4–8; 17–18 (March 2002), 4–7; 46 (June 2004), 6–7.

33. David M. Hart, "The Tribe in Morocco: Two Case Studies," in *Arabs and Berbers*, edited by Ernest Gellner and Charles Micaud, 47 (London: Duckworth, 1973).

34. *Le Monde Amazigh* 46 (June 2004), 4–5.

35. His death on September 10, 2004, occasioned a number of articles in *Le Monde Amazigh* 50 (October 2004), including a reprinting of the original piece that had landed him in jail. His death was ignored by the mainstream Moroccan media. Even the Moroccan TV news bulletin in Tamazight mentioned it only in passing. The Web site www.mondeberbere.com, on the other hand, placed his picture in the center of its home page.

36. See http://www.mondeberbere.com/societe/manifest.htm.

37. Rémy Leveau, *La fellah marocaine: Défenseur du Trône*, 2nd ed. (Paris: Presses de la Fondation Nationale des Sciences Politiques, 1985). The Mouvement Populaire and its offshoot, the Mouvement National Populaire, have proved to be durable political framework for organizing and channeling the interests of pro-monarchy Berber rural notables.

38. In December 2000, two Moroccan weeklies published a 1974 letter from one of the UNFP's former personages, Muhammad Fqih Basri, alleging that the leadership had been a party of Oufkir's plans. For the resulting uproar, see Bruce Maddy-Weitzman, "Morocco," *Middle East Contemporary Survey* (2000), vol. 24, edited by Maddy-Weitzman (Tel Aviv: Moshe Dayan Center for Middle Eastern and African Studies, Tel Aviv University, 2002), 417.

39. *Le Monde Amazigh* 31 (February 2003), 6.

40. Injaz Abdallah Habibi, "Collective Lands from Joint Tribal Ownership to State Administrative Control: An Example from the Zayan Tribes in the Khenifra Region" (in Arabic), *Le Monde Amazigh* 52 (November 2004), 4–5.

41. For a sensitive and loving account of one educated Kabylian's return to his native village and the aesthetics of his mother's housekeeping, see Rabah Seffal, "Remember Me?" *The World & I* (September 1992): 612–23.

42. Muhammad Aswayq, "The Amazigh Value System: Concepts Regarding Thought, History and Modernity" (in Arabic), *Le Monde Amazigh* 52 (November 2004), 12.

43. Ali Sidqi Azaykou, *Tarikh al-Maghrib aw al-Ta'awilat al-Mumkina/Histoire du Maroc ou les Interpretations Possibles* (Arabic section) (Rabat: Centre Tarik Ibn Zyad, 2002), 239–47. The tattoo metaphor and its contemporary meaning among some Amazigh youth was remarked upon to me by Samir Ben-Layashi.

44. Paul A. Silverstein, "France's *Mare Nostrum*: Colonial and Post-Colonial Constructions of the French Mediterranean," *Journal of North African Studies* 7, no. 4 (Winter 2002): 1–22; Edmund Burke III, "The Image of the Moroccan State in French Ethnological Literature: A New Look at the Origin of Lyautey's Berber Policy," in *Arabs and Berbers*, edited by Ernest Gellner and Charles Micaud, 175–99 (London: Duckworth, 1973).

45. The historical basis for such a statement is the decisive influence of the Nabatean Aramaic script on the subsequent Arabic script. Joseph Naveh, *Early History of the Alphabet: An Introduction to West Semitic Epigraphy and Palaeography* (in Hebrew) (Jerusalem: Magnes Press, 1989), 148–56.

46. See the Congrès Mondial Amazigh Web site, http://www.congres-mondialamazigh.org, "France: Discriminations a l'égard des Amazighe."

47. Salem Chaker, *Berbères Aujourd'hui*, 2nd rev. ed. (Paris: L'Harmattan, 1998), 29–30.

48. Ibid., 36–37, quoting Melha Benbrahim, "La poésie kabyle et la résistance à la colonisation de 1830 à 1962" (these de doctorat de 3eme cycle, Paris EHESS).

49. Williams Quandt, "The Berbers in the Algerian Political Elite," *Arabs and Berbers*, edited by Ernest Gellner and Charles Micaud, 285–303 (London: Duckworth, 1973).

50. A stark denial of Berber existence was made by newly independent Algeria's minister of culture, who declared in 1962 that "the Berber . . . is an invention of the Pères Blancs" (a French missionary order). Mohand Tilmitane, "Pouvoir, violence et revendications berbères," *Awal* 18 (1998), 21–38; idem, "Les Oulémas algériens et la question berbère: un document de 1948," *Awal* 15 (1997): 77–90; Amar Ouerdane, "La 'Crise Berberiste' de 1949, Un Confit a Plusieurs Faces," in *Berbères: Une identité en construction*, edited by Salem Chaker, *Revue de l'Occident Musulman et de la Méditerranée* 44 (1987): 35–47; M. Harbi, "Nationalism algérien et identité berbère," *Peuples mediterranée* 11 (1980): 31–37; Bruce Maddy-Weitzman, "The Berber Question in Algeria: Nationalism in the Making?" in *Minorities and the State in the Arab World*, edited by Ofra Bengio and Gabriel Ben-Dor, 38–40 (Boulder, Colo.: Lynne Rienner, 1998).

51. Jane Goodman, "Reinterpreting the Berber Spring: From Rite of Reversal to Site of Convergence," *Journal of North African Studies* 9, no. 3 (Autumn 2004): 60–82.

52. Benjamin Stora, *Algeria 1830–2000: A Short History* (Ithaca, N.Y.: Cornell University Press, 2001), 182.

53. Paul A. Silverstein, *Algeria in France: Transpolitics, Race and Nation* (Bloomington: Indiana University Press, 2004).

54. For a through discussion of the issue, see "Algeria: Unrest and Impasse in Kabylia," *International Crisis Group, Middle East/North Africa Report 15*, June 10, 2003, International Crisis Group Web site http://www.crisisgroup.org/home/index.cfm?id=1415&l=1.

55. Assia Djebar, *Algerian White* (New York: Seven Stories Press, 2000). The book does not just focus on the untimely deaths of intellectuals during the 1990s, nor is it a tract of Kabylian militancy per se. Nonetheless, the author's literary narrative of events sheds much light on the intertwining between Berber/Kabylian specificity and Algeria's broader cross-cultural reality.

56. Ferhat Mehenni, *Algérie: La question Kabyle* (Paris: Éditions Michilon, 2004).

57. McDougall, "Myth and Counter-Myth," 84.

58. A recent diatribe against Salem Chaker for his alleged exclusion of Aurès Berbers in his promotion of the teaching of Tamazight in French schools highlighted tensions and differences within France's Amazigh community. Ammar Negadi, "Collectif Aurèssiens de France," Les Chaouis des Aurès Web site, http://aureschaouia.free.fr.

59. See http://aureschaouia.free.fr. The image has apparently since been removed.

60. *Le Journal des locales*, December 5, 2004.

61. "BATNA: Menaces sur le mausolée d'Imadghacen, menaces sur notre mémoire," http://aureschaouia.free.fr.

62. See http://aureschaouia.free.fr/webgallerie/picture.php?/1611/category/22. The airport is officially named after Mostéfa Ben Boulaïd, a guerilla commander in the region during the war for independence.

63. Lawrence Rosen, "The Social and Conceptual Framework of Arab-Berber Relations in Central Morocco," in *Arabs and Berbers*, edited by Ernest Gellner and Charles Micaud, 173 (London: Duckworth, 1973).

64. McDougall, "Myth and Counter-Myth," 70.

2

Regimes and Societies

New Challenges

5

Reflections on the Aftermath of Civil Strife

Algeria, 2006

GIDEON GERA

On April 8, 2004, Algerian president Abdel Aziz Bouteflika was reelected for a second five-year term by a convincing majority of the voters (85 percent). During his first term, he had successfully consolidated the regime's military triumph over the Islamist insurgency, rehabilitated Algeria's international standing, and regained the country's solvency, sustained by the global rise of oil prices. The reaffirmation of Bouteflika's presidency in 2004 marked the turning of a page in the country's history. What, then, might that "new" page signify for Algeria's dominant order, an Arab "liberal autocracy,"[1] and for the country's efforts to recover from a two-decades-old social and economic crisis?

Formative Conditions

Algeria's recent history, like all historical sequences, has to be understood against a background of constraints, that is, its formative conditions and their corollaries, as well as their contingencies.[2]

Identity

Throughout history, collective identities in the Maghrib have been based on two factors, the tribe and, since the seventh century, Islam. Indeed, over time Maghribi Islam overlaid tribal identities among berberophones and arabophones alike and endowed their centuries-long resistance to foreign rule with a religious/protonational imprint. However, whereas in Morocco and Tunisia specific political entities evolved, precolonial Algeria lacked any indigenous supra-tribal political tradition strong enough over time to form the basis for an "Algerian" entity. This fact constitutes an essential point of departure for the analysis of present-day Algerian politics. Indeed, the thinness of Algerian national identity is demonstrated by the continuing persistence of tribal-like regional loyalties and factionalism within the country's political, military, and intellectual elites. Additional problematic aspects for the Algerian polity that are probably related to the country's tribal heritage are the continuing use of violence for political purposes and the opaqueness of the core of power.[3]

Algerian society has been profoundly fashioned by Islam. The French colonial administration (1830–1962) inadvertently promoted reformist Islam (which in turn spurred the nationalist movement). Thus Algerian nationalism was never secular; independent Algeria has always been self-consciously Muslim, although Islam was proclaimed the state religion only in the 1976 constitution.[4]

Algeria gained its independence from France in 1962, after a violent eight-year war of liberation. Yet the 130 years of colonial rule constituted much more than just repression and resistance; its enduring impact is felt in the realms of contemporary Algerian culture, language, and politics. Professionals, high-ranking officials, and intellectuals have been educated in French, a background that still assures access to many of the most lucrative positions in society. The francophone elite forms the readership of the numerous local French newspapers. Furthermore, the advent of satellite television programing continues to popularize French among younger generations. Repeated attempts to legally impose Arabic as the official language have not succeeded.[5]

The complex and fractious nature of Algerian politics and society re-emerged shortly after independence, compelling the regime to seek a coherent form of national identity in order to strengthen its legitimacy. Basing itself on the well-known slogan "Islam is my religion, Algeria is my country, and Arabic is my language,"[6] it attempted to nationalize Islam, Arabize the educational system, and rewrite Algerian history accordingly. This policy had unforeseen and dire consequences: The cleavages between Arab and Berber (the latter's language was refused official status), between Arab-educated and French-educated sectors, and between Islamist and secular trends have not only persisted but deepened over time.

Hydrocarbons

Algeria's main economic resource is oil and natural gas, providing more than 90 percent of the country's export earnings and 60 percent of government revenue. Consistent with its *étatist*, collectivist, and nationalist ideological foundations ("revolutionary socialism"), the Boumediene regime

(1965–78) nationalized ("decolonized") this essential asset in 1971, putting most of the economic resources of the state into the hands of its rulers. This was the inception of the Algerian *rentier* state. In practical terms, the army-supported regime depends almost exclusively on the rents that oil and gas production provide in order to remain in power. Hence, significant fluctuations in hydrocarbon revenues have had immediate social and political repercussions. Thus the fall in oil prices in the mid-1980s, which deprived Algeria of half of its foreign revenue, caused a deep recession and brought Algeria to the verge of bankruptcy, forming the backdrop to the country's descent into crisis and bloodshed. The recent rise of oil prices endowed it, by contrast, with billions of additional dollars (export revenues increased from $11 billion in 2000 to $16.7 billion in 2003, giving the regime considerable breathing space).[7] One lesson of the crisis of the 1980s was a revision of the hydrocarbon investment law, adopted in late 1991 and reaffirmed in 1993, which facilitated expansive foreign investments in Algeria's oil and gas sector in order to bolster production.

The location of most Algerian oil and gas wells in the southern part of the country, remote from population centers, provided an important advantage for the regime. Cordoning off these regions ensured the continuing production and export of oil and gas, even throughout Algeria's violent era of the 1990s. Alternatively, it has been rumored that the regime achieved a tacit understanding with the main Islamist opposition group, the Front Islamique du Salut (FIS), to keep the oil and gas fields outside of the conflict.[8]

The State

The French bequeathed to Algeria a centralized "Jacobin" state along with a huge bureaucracy, the form of which has been retained in the independence era. On the outside, all the trappings of a modern state are present—national symbols, political and judicial institutions—but inside they have been "hollowed out." French officialdom was replaced by a new, neopatrimonial ruling class in the military, the administration, and the sole (until 1989) legal political party—the Front de Libération Nationale (FLN). The new elite established itself as a *nomenklatura* in the Soviet mold (critics often describe it as a "mafia"), which had uncontrolled political power and enjoyed economic advantages unavailable to most. This half-secret core has ruled opaquely through a rigid chain of command (e.g., within the Sécurité Militaire, the secret police) and an elaborate means of control and communication. Parallel to, or rather beneath, the Jacobin structure, regional affiliations, clan structures, and patron-client networks are continuously active social forces. They include competing military clans and networks. These institutional shells supplied legitimacy and facilitated co-optation of a part of the opposition into Parliament, tying it to the regime yet excluding it from sensitive portfolios.[9]

The Military

The real power in the country since independence in 1962, and unopposed since 1965, has been the Algerian military (Armée Nationale Populaire; ANP) establishment—that is, its High Command and security services, commonly known as the *pouvoir* (lit. "power," "authority") or *decideurs* ("decision makers"). It has been described as "both the royal family and king-maker," and it has always designated the president, starting with Boumediene in 1965. As the central institution of the state, together with its prestige, control of patronage, and material resources, the military *nomenklatura* has emerged as a major status-quo interest group; it has provided its members with economic advantages and watched over the conservation of these privileges. It has developed into a continuous and significant channel of upward social mobility: Neither the degradation of its image nor the extreme violence military personnel endured have dissuaded thousands of secondary school graduates from applying for admission into military academies. At times of economic crisis, being a member of the military offers the possibility of economic solvency.[10] Thus many among recently graduated officer-cadets are from middle-class families, driven by social and economic ambitions.

Nonetheless, Algeria's High Command is comprised of clans, divided according to origin, cultural background (arabophone or francophone, religious or secular), past military service (the most influential generals at present were deserters from the French army during the war of independence; they effectively replaced veterans of the anti-French guerrilla forces), and—according to some observers, most importantly—economic interest.[11]

Corollaries

A Continuing Socioeconomic Crisis

The policies of rapid economic development and industrialization after independence contributed to accelerated population growth rates (the size of Algeria's population has tripled since independence, from ten to thirty-two million), extensive urbanization, increasing shortages of housing and educational and medical services, and the breakdown of infrastructure. After 1986, the provider-state no longer had the means even to minimally satisfy its citizens, who were accustomed to being fully attended by the government. Unemployment became severe, even among university graduates. As a result, an implicit social contract was broken and a mass of newly urbanized youth (70 percent of Algerians are below the age of twenty-five) was alienated from a state that seemed to no longer offer them prospects for the future. Their distress erupted violently in the bloody riots of October 1988 and later fed the civil war. Furthermore, economic liberalization measures since 1981 and accompanying corruption accentuated the gap between haves and have-nots. A short-lived attempt to introduce systemic reforms in 1989–91 was stymied by the ruling elite, which was unwilling to forgo its privileged position. This crisis is a structural one, and it has endured to the present.[12]

Clientelism and Corruption

The distribution of oil-generated wealth by the state became a main tool of social manipulation—for patronage, co-optation, and corruption. To reinforce the stability of his regime, Boumediene established a clientele network, comprised of the military, the bureaucracy, and his connections with the private sector, that developed into centers of urban enrichment.[13] With the ascent of Chadli Benjedid to the presidency in 1979 and the adoption of a macroeconomic policy of economic liberalization, including stimulation of the private business sector, clientelism and corruption increased: On the microeconomic level the regime decided which private enterprises would be granted privileged access to markets, credits, and contracts (especially in the state-controlled import and export sector). To Chadli, selected as a compromise candidate, this was one way to recompense his colleagues. Such patronage enriched only a small group of retired superior officers, high officials, and local capitalists and simultaneously nourished large-scale corruption.[14]

One consequence of this was the evolution of a parallel market, of smuggling and illegal commerce (*trabendo*), which attracted the unemployed and disaffected, especially among Algeria's youth. Evidently, *trabendists* could not operate undisturbed without the connivance of local civil and military authorities. Later, Islamist insurgents joined others (including "mafias") in the parallel market to support themselves. The scope of *trabendo* commerce was huge, estimated at 30–70 percent of the Algerian GDP.[15]

Radical Islamism

A militantly religious element had been continuously present within the Algerian liberation movement and within the postcolonial regime, with varying strength. Two irreconcilable tendencies developed within Algerian Islamism, one conservative, and one radical-revolutionary. The first coexisted, however disapprovingly, with the regime, whereas the latter strove to delegitimize and ultimately replace what it characterized as corrupt, impious, and Westernized rulers.

Four developments fostered the rise of radical Islamism in Algeria (which would contribute decisively to the country's implosion in the early 1990s):

1. The identity-building efforts of the regime included the furthering of Arabic schooling. This required the importation of teachers of modern standard Arabic from Egypt, whose scope was increased during the early 1980s under Chadli. Many of these teachers were at least sympathetic to the Muslim Brotherhood and its violent offshoots and spread their message throughout schools and mosques.
2. There has been no Algerian figure remotely resembling the Ayatollah Khomeini or the Egyptian Islamist ideologue Sayyid Qutb in stature.[16] At the same time, the Khomeini revolution in Iran increased the self-confidence of radical Islamists in Algeria, as it did elsewhere.
3. The struggle against the Soviet invaders of Afghanistan attracted hundreds of Algerian volunteers;[17] upon returning home, these "Afghanis" became the nuclei of the most violent Islamist groups in Algeria.
4. The deteriorating socioeconomic situation during the 1980s provided the emerging "countersociety" of the Islamist movement with a disgruntled population.

Direct Military Involvement

The 1980s witnessed the *embourgeoisement*, namely, the increasing involvement in economic activities of senior military personnel and their clients. Prior to 1988, the military fulfilled mainly the backstage role of guardian of the state, but that year's riots, which it was ordered to forcibly quell, led the military to become more actively involved in public life. The subsequent adoption of a multiparty system, and especially the emergence of a legal and powerful Islamist party, was viewed with consternation by the military High Command, which doubted President Benjedid's ability to manage the reform process. In particular, senior military officers feared that the military's role as protector of the state would be endangered, along with the economic privileges they had accumulated.[18] Furthermore, they questioned whether the state could integrate a major radical Islamist movement into the formal political system, considering the FIS to be a foreign-inspired threat to the country's stability. This view was reinforced by the FIS's strong (and widely popular) support of Iraq in the Persian Gulf War, contrary to official policy.[19]

The Bloody Decade

In January 1992, following a first round of nation-wide parliamentary elections on December 26, 1991, which portended an overwhelming FIS majority in the new Parliament, the military High Command, supported by the secular elements of civil society, who feared the application of religious law (Shari'a), refused to accept the imminent FIS victory and carried out a "preventive takeover." It assumed full powers, annulled the elections, forced the resignation of incumbent President Benjedid, who had previously declared his willingness to "co-habit" with the elected Islamist leaders, and dissolved the FIS. The High Command's actions constituted "a Janissary reflex," stemming from fear that the FIS would endanger their privileges and lives, and a desire to prevent any potential democratization of the regime.[20] The ensuing armed Islamist insurgency against the "heretic" regime, fed partially by the continuing social and economic crisis, was brutally defeated. The human toll was enormous and estimated anywhere between 100,000 and 150,000 fatalities, including civilians, insurgents, and members of the security forces.[21] Briefly, one may distinguish three stages of this struggle.

Islamist violence was initially directed at the security forces, especially against local police, and secular intellectuals. This led to a conjunction of civil society and the military. State institutions continued to function as best they could; the Islamist edict to close schools was generally defied, despite the killing of teachers and the destruction of schools. The military reorganized and reequipped itself. Trusted to protect the supply of natural gas to Europe, and despite, or perhaps because of, the state's dire financial situation, Algerian authorities received generous aid from European states, particularly France, and the International Monetary Fund. This aid eventually allowed Algeria to postpone for a time the implementation of an IMF-imposed structural adjustment plan. Counterinsurgency became a first-priority national enterprise. A special "anti-terrorist corps" was set up in 1993 under the command of future chief of staff Gen. Muhammad Lamari, a well-known "eradicationist" who advocated the merciless quelling of Islamist activity. On the other side, the extremist Groupe Islamique Armé (GIA), formed by bitter opponents of the regime, melded with veterans of the Afghan war and urban criminal gangs. The GIA initiated a murderous campaign against foreigners and civilians of all ages, declaring in April 1993 that not just the regime but also the entire society was apostate, thereby sanctioning the massacre of innocent civilians.

In the second stage of the struggle, the military reestablished its hegemony over the country in three years of bitter fighting, between 1995 and 1998. Lacking sufficient regular forces to contain the insurgents in rural areas, it "privatized" the conflict by militarizing rural society, distributing arms to village "self-defense" guards and other local militias ("patriots," according to the official terminology). Ironically, the authorities were assisted by the continuing wave of atrocities committed by both insurgents and government forces, as well as by the violence that resulted from local vendettas. As a result, the Algerian populace, exhausted from the protracted conflict, was anxious to reestablish peace.

During the struggle's third stage, in the fall of 1997, the army inflicted a strategic defeat on the FIS by attaining a cease-fire with its military arm, the Armée Islamique du Salut (AIS), without conceding to the FIS any renewed political role. The threat of an Islamist regime had been removed. The cease-fire also led to a split in the GIA. Even the operations of its most important offshoot, the Salafi Group for Predication and Combat (GSPC), gradually diminished.[22]

Why did the Islamist insurgency fail?[23] First, it was disunited, riven with personal rivalries and violent scissions, and unprepared for protracted conflict. Second, it lost most of its popular support: It was unable to preserve the alliance between the urban poor and the pious middle-classes, which had served as the base of its support, and alienated rural populations. Its ideology, couched in religious terms, lost its appeal; the population tired of continuing exactions by armed groups and rejected Afghani-style violence, which made daily life a nightmare, affecting all social classes and many villages and families. Third, state institutions held out, thanks in part to foreign financial aid, the military maintained its unity and improved its capabilities, and repression proved effective. Military counterterror operations, reinforced by the "mobilization" of rural populations, became more efficient. Furthermore, the security services increased their ability to penetrate, control, and even co-opt insurgent groups.[24]

The High Command faced two major problems during these years. The first was the need to reinstitutionalize legitimate authority. To that end it carried out a series of tightly controlled electoral exercises, including the election of Gen. Liamine Zeroual to the presidency in 1995, the ratification by plebiscite of an amended constitution in 1996, and parliamentary elections in 1997. Yet none of these actions could solve a major contradiction in the authorities' method: how could the regime be legitimized through the ballot box when the rules of the electoral game were rigged from the start? Moreover, the military leadership was unable to refute repeated allegations of its involvement in the massacres of civilians, which tarnished Algeria's international image.

The second challenge facing the authorities was how to alleviate the deteriorating two-decades-old social and economic crisis without hurting their own interests. The High Command represented the collective material interests of a caste of superior officers (whose number had risen from 20 in 1978 to 140 in 1998),[25] anxious to preserve their exclusive access to rent resources. But doing so was no simple matter, and the rivalries and competition within the military elite threatened to tear them apart. A well-publicized crisis in the High Command, compounded by allegations of corruption and fraud by generals close to President Zeroual, resulted in Zeroual's premature resignation in the fall of 1998. His colleagues then decided to install a civilian president in order to reconstitute their legitimacy. Their choice, or, more accurately, the choice of the security services and one of the military "clans," fell on Bouteflika.[26] With the High Command's open support, he was duly elected in April 1999 as the only candidate, after his six rivals withdrew their candidature on election eve, protesting what they described as massive fraud and intimidation.[27]

Bouteflika's Presidency

The Man and His Vision

Abdel Aziz Bouteflika was by no means a new actor in Algerian politics, but his assuming the office of president constituted the introduction of a new and significant element into the political equation. Bouteflika can only be understood in the framework of the social, cultural, political, and economic structures, formal and informal, in which he has been embedded, and the resulting interests, constraints, obligations, and strategies that underpin his policies.

Bouteflika was born in 1937 in the Moroccan city of Oujda, adjacent to the Algerian-Moroccan border. At a very young age, he joined the Algerian Liberation Front and became an early intimate of its military commander, Houari Boumediene. When Boumediene took over as president (1965), the twenty-eight-year-old Bouteflika was appointed foreign minister. He became internationally known and in 1974 served as chairman of the UN General Assembly. After Boumediene's death in 1978, he was considered (not least by himself) as the natural heir to the presidency. But having neglected internal politics, he was passed over for the succession in 1978 by the High Command, which selected the senior one among them, Chadli Benjedid. Furthermore, Bouteflika was accused of embezzlement, although he was never prosecuted. At the age of forty-two, he chose exile and was excluded from the Central Committee of the FLN. He lived comfortably and discreetly as an advisor in the Gulf Emirates and Switzerland. Among others, he counseled Shaykh Zayid bin Sultan Al Nuhayan, president of the United Arab Emirates. In 1987 he returned to Algeria, and in 1989 he was reintegrated into the FLN's central committee. In 1994 he turned down the military's request to run for the presidency.

Nicknamed "Little Big Man" (he is five feet six inches tall), Bouteflika is an adroit tactician and unscrupulous manipulator with abundant political experience. He considers himself a statesman and thus distinct from his predecessors. Proud of his comeback from years in the political desert, he has been seeking historical revenge. Since assuming the presidency, Bouteflika has been obstinate in his quest for autocratic power and touchy about his personal standing, but also very cautious and aware of existing constraints. His stated role models are Napoleon and Charles de Gaulle. Having agreed to be the military's candidate for the presidency, Bouteflika was aware that they would constrain his ambitions. In order to reduce his dependence on the military High Command, he had to form his own political base. Therefore, he planned his campaign to the smallest detail in advance. His first tasks were to fashion an appropriate image and assemble a team to assist him. He projected a constructive persona of an experienced statesman with a "revolutionary" past who had "returned" to reunite his nation, stabilize the country, and ameliorate its lot. He portrayed himself as supported by the military without him having asked for its backing.[28]

Central to his team was his family; his brother Said became his close counsel. He then rallied old allies of the Boumediene era, such as Nur El-Din "Yazid" Zarhuni, who was with him at Officers' School and served as chief of intelligence under Boumediene. In 2000, he appointed former general Larbi Belkheir, who had headed Benjedid's bureau and later served as his interior minister and was considered to be one of the most powerful officers in Algeria, to again assume the position of director of the president's office. Belkheir was among those who had promoted Bouteflika's candidacy within the High Command and later helped him control his conflict with the military. During his first election campaign, Bouteflika established more than two thousand committees of support, a key part of his efforts to build a loyal grass-roots base of support.[29]

Bouteflika's First Term, 1999–2004

During Bouteflika's first term, Algeria gradually emerged from eight years of civil strife, although violence did not entirely abate. The country's international standing improved, as did its overall economic situation. Following up on the defeat of the Islamist insurgency, Bouteflika fulfilled some of the expectations of his military sponsors. The initial cease-fire agreement concluded in 1997 between the military and the AIS was reinforced, resulting in the gradual reduction of violence. Bouteflika quickly decreed a National Concord, which pardoned all insurgents not guilty of murder or rape, and had the decree endorsed by a national referendum. On the other hand, he accepted the military's insistence on preventing the FIS's return to political activity and supported the continuing campaign against the violent core of the jihadist groups (GIA and GSPC).[30] (For the ambiguities of the National Concord, the continuing struggle against recalcitrant Islamist groups, and Bouteflika's policy dilemmas regarding the Islamist current, see the chapter by Aït-Hamadouche and Zoubir in this volume.)

Rebuilding Algeria's international relations in order to enhance its political and economic standing was also high on Bouteflika's agenda. His vast diplomatic experience stood him in good stead, and his achievements were numerous: gaining a consulting role for Algeria with the G-8 group of rich nations, a seat on the UN Security Council, and the renewal of Algeria's traditional leadership role in Africa through the African Union. During 1999–2003, Bouteflika visited no less than ninety countries in 170 trips.[31] By projecting an acceptable image of the regime, he became indispensable in foreign affairs.

Bouteflika was greatly helped in his endeavors by two partly interrelated developments: the windfall of continuously high oil and gas prices, which filled the coffers of the treasury with billions of dollars (about $40 billion by the end of 2004),[32] and the September 11, 2001, attacks in the United States, which Bouteflika used to cement his relationship with the United

States (and France). In the aftermath of the terrorist attacks, Western interest in the continuing stability of Algeria increased; more than ever, security cooperation and economic aid was in the interest of the EU and the United States. France, in particular, as well as other EU countries, were increasingly concerned about the spread of militancy among its expanding and often alienated Muslim population (see the chapter by Paul A. Silverstein in this volume). Instability in Algeria could not only endanger energy supplies but also lead to an even greater outflow of Algerians seeking refuge and economic security across the Mediterranean and threaten domestic stability in Europe.

However, socioeconomic conditions in Algeria improved only very slowly. The rate of urbanization accelerated, resulting in 60 percent of Algeria's population being classified as living in urban areas in 2004, up from 50 percent in 1987; unemployment rates remained very high (24–30 percent), infrastructure was insufficient, and the social gap increased. Heavy bureaucracy, opaque financial systems, and corruption continued to hinder investments (excluding the oil sector). A severe earthquake in central Algeria in May 2003, which caused 2,200 fatalities and left 150,000 people homeless, exposed the inefficiency of the government. Popular feelings toward the regime turned from hope to disappointment and were poignantly expressed by crowds welcoming the visiting French president in early 2003 with shouts of "Visas, visas."[33] In April 2001, a violent confrontation erupted in Kabiliya (quickly termed the "Black Spring") between the population and the Gendarmerie after the latter's brutal killing of a youth, underscoring the Kabylian Berbers' longstanding economic, social, and political grievances, as well as a more general and widely shared alienation from the regime. The clashes resulted in more than one hundred civilian fatalities and led to a massive protest in Algiers calling for a democratic regime for the country.[34] Fearing an escalation, the government redeployed the Gendarmerie and the region calmed down, but pacification did not entail cooperation, development budgets were cut, and the Kabyles relied largely on the "informal" economy. The radicalization of the Kabyles led the government in 2002 to initiate a dialogue with a new amalgamation of local leaders (*aarch*) and to accede to a major Berber demand: recognition of their language, Tamazight, as a national language. However, this concession did not satisfy the *aarch*, who demanded recognition of Tamazight as an official language on a par with Arabic, as well as the permanent removal of the Gendarmerie and justice for the victims of the violence. As a result, subsequent parliamentary and presidential elections were largely boycotted in Kabiliya (only 17.8

percent of the voters participated in the latter). Seeking to repair the damage, Bouteflika addressed the Kabylian question in his second inauguration speech, calling for continuation of the dialogue with the tribal notables because "Kabiliya could not exist without Algeria and Algeria could not exist without Kabiliya."[35]

Disenchantment with the regime was expressed in other ways as well. For example, in the mountainous, rural areas, GSPC bands found an asylum of sorts (and consequently refrained from attacking villages and even sometimes distributed their "booty" among them).[36]

Relentless in the pursuit of his essential objective—achieving a power base autonomous from the military and then reinforcing and prolonging his rule—Bouteflika was constrained by several policy dilemmas. The foremost of these, a reflection of the country's enduring socioeconomic crisis, has been the necessity of structural economic reforms, which have been consistently advocated by Western governments and international financial institutions, versus the importance of maintaining the status quo. A prerequisite for coherent economic reforms, including the long-proposed privatization of state-owned enterprises, was the elimination of the dominant interest groups (patron-client networks) that control the circuits of rent distribution and thus their profits (through commissions, revenues deriving from lucrative positions, land, or enterprises, diversions of funds, etc.). This, of course, was a politically impossible condition. In denouncing corruption during his 1999 election campaign, Bouteflika alluded to the military by saying that laws had been enacted to enable fifteen people to control the economy. However, once in office, he avoided implementing major economic and social reforms. Instead, he appointed as ministers a small group of reform-minded economists loyal to him, although never endowing them with decisive authority and repeatedly reshuffling his cabinet. Bouteflika thus safeguarded the existing clientelist system—with its enormous income—and the military's (and his own) privileges in it. This system was managed by Belkheir and a number of retired generals. When a leading private financial group (Al-Khalifa) collapsed and the money invested therein (including by the state and the central trade union) was lost, its connections with Belkheir and the president's family became a handicap.[37] On the other side, as the political and social bases of the insurgents contracted, their connections with local "mafias" involved in illicit economic activities, notably *trabendo*, became more pronounced.[38] (For a fuller analysis of the Algerian economy, see the chapter by Ahmed Aghrout and Michael Hodd in this volume.)

Despite these difficulties, Bouteflika succeeded in his main endeavor, the establishment of his supreme authority. In his ongoing tug-of-war with the generals, he was inspired by Charles de Gaulle. He refused to serve, in his words, as "three-quarters" of a president. On one occasion he declared that he was "the incarnation of the Algerian people. Tell the generals [who brought him to power] to swallow me if they can."[39] In an effort to secure his authority, Bouteflika employed what has been described as "guerrilla tactics": weakening the military leaders even while flattering them and protecting their interests and prerogatives. His continuous leverage on them was his indispensability in providing the regime with the semblance of civilian legitimacy, which they were incapable of establishing.[40]

Unable to change the constitution to a presidential regime,[41] Bouteflika assiduously prepared for his reelection campaign. He reinforced his hold on the bureaucracy and internal security services. One person central to this effort was Zarhuni, who had served as his minister of the interior since 1999 (the High Command refused Zarhuni's appointment to the Ministry of Defense).[42] The May 2002 parliamentary elections displayed his hold on power: The FLN, seen as the president's party, gained 199 seats (out of 389), up from 64 in the "rigged" 1997 election, whereas the Rassemblement National Démocratique (RND), Zeroual's creation in early 1997, was reduced from 155 to 48 seats. The Islamist parties also lost seats, probably reflecting their reduced appeal. The FLN presented a rejuvenated (many younger than forty-five years old), well-educated (80 percent with higher education), and pro-reform list, which seemed to appeal to voters.[43]

Bouteflika's efforts to be reelected were marred by a bitter quarrel with his erstwhile friend and prime minister, Ali Benflis.[44] Following the 2002 parliamentary elections, the president apparently began to suspect Benflis of wanting to replace him. When Benflis was received in Paris with the honors of a head of state, relations between the two became tense. In May 2003, Benflis was removed from office in favor of Ahmad Ouyahia, the head of the RND party, former prime minister (1995–98), and an adversary of Benflis. Ouyahia was profiled in the West as "a model of the new generation [he was born in 1952] of politicians formed by the military. . . . An efficient and docile apparatchik."[45]

The Reelection

Bouteflika was the first civilian president of Algeria to successfully complete his five-year tenure (his predecessors as head of state, mainly military officers, either died in office, resigned prematurely, or were deposed). Now aspiring to a second term, Bouteflika faced five competitors in the campaign, but his main opponent was Benflis, who decided to run with the support of the FLN, which duly adopted him as its candidate. Bouteflika reacted furiously, branding Benflis as a traitor, had the courts freeze allocations of party funds to him, and established a "restoration" movement inside the party to combat his influence. Bouteflika's campaign program consisted of the promise to create another million new jobs (claiming that one million had already been created during his first term) and to construct one million homes. He also talked about revising the constitution and the possibility of giving Tamazight official status by a referendum (a gesture toward the restless Kabylie region), after it had been given the status of a national language. Benflis, for his part, portrayed himself as a man of renewal and change compared to Bouteflika, who had "an archaic vision of the world."[46]

How did Bouteflika manage to obtain the support of the military, essential to his reelection? Despite their differences with the president, the generals decided that his reelection was in their best interest (this may have also been pointed out to them by U.S. officials). A "deal" was cut: Bouteflika gained the generals' practical support, thereby outmaneuvering his opponents, in exchange for preserving their interests. Publicly, through statements by Chief of Staff Lamari, the military adopted a neutral position and called on the state administrative apparatus to do likewise. It backed a revised election law that cancelled the special ballots for security personnel, who previously voted in their quarters overseen by their officers, in favor of having them vote alongside other citizens at their original residences. As it was impractical for most security personnel to return to their civilian residences, many simply did not vote.[47]

During the campaign Bouteflika fully exploited state resources: the civil administration under the control of the Ministry of Interior, special funds, and the media, especially state television. His political supporters came from the portion of the FLN loyal to him, the RND of the prime minister, and the moderate Islamists of the Mouvement de la Société pour la Paix (MSP). In an attempt to partially enlist the support of former FIS members, Bouteflika permitted their head, Abbasi Madani, to leave the country for Qatar after serving his prison term (who promptly denounced him from his exile). Bouteflika also enlisted traditional Muslims by gaining the support of the heads of religious orders (*zawiyat*), mainly in the South.[48] Most important, he promised stability to his trouble-weary population. On the other hand, despite negotiations with their leaders, most of the Kabyle population boycotted the elections.[49]

These circumstances facilitated Bouteflika's overwhelming reelection on April 8, 2004. Whatever the allegations of fraud concerning his surprising majority (85 percent of the vote, or ten and a half million, 58 percent, of eighteen million registered voters), no one, including foreign observers would or could deny his victory. His bitter rival Benflis received less than a humiliatingly minuscule 7 percent of the vote (attaining a small percentage even in his home town).[50] Bouteflika had proven himself a more expert manipulator of Algerian politics than his rivals, both civilian and military.

Aftermath

More than two years after Bouteflika's reelection, the political scene in Algeria had calmed down considerably, indicating its limited impact on both the bulk of the population and the "political classes." The main outcome was Bouteflika's consolidation of all levers of power in his hands, although he had to maneuver, even vacillate, on key issues.

His first move was to quickly regain complete control of the FLN. Benflis resigned his party post immediately after the elections. Shortly thereafter, nearly all the 199 FLN members of Parliament renounced their support of Benflis, leading to the replacement of the speaker of Parliament by a Bouteflika ally. Loyalists were appointed to senior party posts and were confirmed by a party congress at the beginning of 2005. At the same time, while ensuring the party's obedience, Bouteflika gradually distanced himself from the FLN.[51] Within the Parliament, Bouteflika relied on the same coalition of parties as in his first term—the FLN, the RND, and the moderate Islamist MSP. These parties supported his national reconciliation project, which later was adopted by referendum as the Charter for Peace and National Reconciliation (see below), but differed on legislation pertaining to Islamic matters. Recent examples have included the bill freezing the import of alcoholic beverages that was successfully passed by conservatives (including FLN members), the MSP demand to terminate the state of emergency decreed in 1992, and the compromise proposal on amending the family law.[52] Bouteflika has always been aware of, and utilized, Muslim sensitivities. Thus his charter implied the possible political rehabilitation of Islamist insurgents once violent Islamism—a program of "deceit" preached by "illiterates on the margin of society"—had been stamped out.[53]

The strength of Algerian Islam (of all currents) was vividly demonstrated by the adoption of a very restricted reform of the Family Code, after years of governmental preparations. The main gain for women under the new code was the recognition of their right to initiate divorce proceedings, as well as the husband's responsibility to provide lodgings for his divorced wife and her children. On the other hand, polygamy, though requiring a judge's consent, remained legal (Tunisia is the sole Arab country that outlaws polygamy), and the legal requirement for guardianship (*wali*) over a woman remained in force (in contrast to Morocco's new family law; see the chapter by Daniel Zisenwine in this volume). Following the adoption of the law, Bouteflika, notwithstanding earlier promises to the contrary, warned Algerian women not to expect more, because of religious limitations.[54]

Aiming to further deepen his legitimacy under the banner of "national reconciliation," Bouteflika argued that the legitimacy of the regime should no longer be based on "revolutionary" credentials, as time and "mentalities" have changed. Furthermore, as a gesture to supporters of former president Ahmad Ben Bella, Bouteflika annulled the national holiday commemorating the overturn of the Ben Bella regime by Houari Boumediene in 1965—in which he himself had played an important part.[55] A further move was tightening the control of the hostile section of the Algerian press by initiating criminal proceedings against journalists and creating financial difficulties for publishers.[56]

More important, Bouteflika reinforced his authority over the military. In July, three months after the elections, he accepted the resignation of the chief of staff, General Lamari, with whom he had a rather ambivalent relationship, and began to revamp and rejuvenate the High Command (as hoped for by younger officers). He appointed a new chief of staff, Gen. Salah Ahmad al-Qaid, who was long beyond retirement age but well known to the president. Given his age—seventy-four—his tenure was likely to be short. In a complementary move, Bouteflika promoted three relatively young and Western-trained generals. In his July 4, 2004, Independence Day speech he directed the military leadership to devote itself to their constitutionally designated missions (i.e., to remain outside of political affairs) and affirmed that the process of modernization and professionalization of the armed forces, "under the authority and responsibility of the president," would continue.[57] To better implement this policy, in his capacity as defense minister, Bouteflika appointed for the first time, on May 1, 2005, a "minister-delegate" at the ministry who would be answerable directly to him, retired general and Lamari's predecessor as chief of staff, Abd al-Malik Guenaiza. [58]

Concomitantly, Bouteflika endorsed a vast procurement program to renew Algeria's obsolescent armaments, especially aircraft (fifty MiG-29s from Russia) and armor (from France), and agreed with France on the extended training of military personnel. These projects also reflected Algeria's post–civil war strategic aims: a role in the Mediterranean (with the EU and NATO) and (at least) deterrence of Morocco. The chief of staff, on his part, repeatedly defined the battle against terrorism as the military's first priority.[59]

During the years following Bouteflika's reelection, violent acts by Islamist insurgents, mainly the GSPC were sporadic and diminished progressively. They were relentlessly pursued by the security forces, who eliminated most of their leaders and also ran programs to encourage the "repentance" of the insurgents (with the aid of their families), which in turn reduced government security costs.[60] On the other hand, the self-defense groups (which call themselves "patriots"), enlisted by the military during the insurgency, resisted efforts to collect the arms issued to them (and discontinue the salaries paid them).[61]

Bouteflika's reelection also improved Algeria's foreign standing. Relations with France, in particular, and the European Union in general, as well as with the United States, were upgraded continuously as the Algerian regime worked to take advantage of what it perceived as a U.S.-French rivalry for influence in the Maghrib. The pursuit and elimination of a GSPC band in the Sahara region in 2004 was related to the United States' Pan-Sahel Initiative to deny sanctuary and recruits to al-Qaʻida in Mali, Niger, Chad, and Mauritania. It was even represented by French sources as a means to attract more U.S. military support.[62]

Bouteflika repeatedly stressed the country's socioeconomic achievements during his first term: Foreign debt was more than halved (from $40 billion in 2000 to $19 billion in 2003) and economic growth per annum rose from 3.2 to 7 percent. However, the improving macroeconomic situation had little impact on the impoverished urban population. Although the unemployment rate was reduced to 17.7 percent in 2004 (down from 30 percent in 2000), this was still a very high figure, translating into 1.7 million jobless people, 73 percent of whom were younger than age thirty. Housing shortages in the region east of Algiers, which had been stricken by an earthquake in early 2003, were especially acute. Consequently there were occasional popular protests that reflected general unrest; an increase in the price of heating gas, for example, provoked violent reactions all over the country, as did the "discriminatory" allocation of governmental housing in the western portion of the country.[63]

Acutely aware of the situation one year after the his reelection, Bouteflika strove to accelerate economic development, using both foreign capital and growing oil revenues to face up to the challenging needs of the young generation (every year three hundred thousand youngsters join the labor force).⁶⁴ In April 2005, he proclaimed a new five-year plan to invest $55 billion of Algerian capital (in addition to $2.5 billion promised by France) in infrastructure and other socioeconomic (housing, education, health, and education) programs. On that occasion, Bouteflika also expressed his dismay at the reluctance of public and private entrepreneurs to invest in developments projects.⁶⁵

However much Bouteflika and his team of reformers really meant to establish a free-market economy, he remained constrained by the structure of his regime, causing him to vacillate (as he did in other essential spheres, such as family-status legislation). Would not fundamental reforms subvert the established privileges of the military and their clients and cause them to resist?⁶⁶ A case in point was the amendment of the Hydrocarbon Law, which aimed at the privatization of the oil and gas industry. Despite previous cabinet agreement on the amendment, Bouteflika had to scale down the intended reform, rejecting privatization but facilitating indispensable foreign investments, mainly from the Persian Gulf and the United States. Only thus was he able to avoid a head-on conflict with some of the generals, who had special interests in the industry, and the resistance of the General Union of Algerian Workers (UGTA). The General Union was reassured of its unique status, and the FLN's "old guard" was assuaged by the president's continuing adherence to socialism (which he referred to as "the philosophy of angels").⁶⁷ Taking another turn, Bouteflika reshuffled his cabinet on May 1, 2005. He appointed market-economy–oriented ministers to key economic posts, emphasizing his commitment to the implementation of the new five-year plan, which included major reforms (most likely to the displeasure of the old guard and the trade unions).⁶⁸

On September 29, 2005, Bouteflika's Charter for Peace and National Reconciliation was overwhelmingly (97 percent of the vote) approved by referendum. Following up on previous presidential steps, it proposed: (1) amnesty for militants who had handed in their weapons, unless guilty of mass-murder, bombing attacks on public installations, or rape; (2) exoneration of the security services for the "disappearance" of more than 6,000 Algerians, implying immunity for the generals responsible for the repression of the Islamist insurgency; and (3) compensation to the families of the dead and disappeared. Implementation of the charter was left to the president's discretion. It was criticized by associations of the victims and by human rights groups and totally rejected by the GSPC, which openly affiliated itself with Al-Qaʿida in 2006.⁶⁹

Well into his second term, Bouteflika had buttressed his rule and probably aimed to prolong his term by an amendment of the constitution. He had done so, in part, by bending to the formative conditions of his country, maintaining the *rentier* state system, based on a profitable hydrocarbon sector, and accepting Islamic restrictions in various spheres. Yet considerable concern in Algeria and beyond was raised by his urgent hospitalization in France at the end of 2005, although he subsequently fully resumed his duties.[70]

Whither Algeria?

One may consider the development of Algeria as an example of the unforeseen consequences of change (alternately "modernization" or "decolonization," depending on one's preference), at least unforeseen by those who proudly declared its independence in 1962 and by those who overestimated their ability to transform Algeria from a dependent and underdeveloped colony to an advanced developed state. Its recovery from the ravages of the civil war and longer-term prospects depend on the skills and resources of its rulers to reform institutions, this in order to avoid being overwhelmed by uncontrolled and far-reaching consequences of social change.

Algeria is a rich country with abundant hydrocarbon resources that has just emerged from a more than a decade of instability and gloom. It is no longer a candidate for state failure.[71] The positive indications to that end include the crushing of the Islamist insurgency, which probably posed the greatest challenge to the legitimacy of what Islamist radicals termed the "impious" regime, not least because of popular rejection of Islamist excesses; the reelection of Bouteflika, with the consent of the ruling generals; the progressive amelioration of the macroeconomic situation and the acceleration of economic activities; and the increasing foreign interest in the country's stability.

Yet Algeria is beset by severe and enduring socioeconomic problems—in microeconomic terms, the crisis is as bad as ever—and is ill-governed. The growing, youthful, and increasingly urban population suffers from an insufficient infrastructure in health, housing, and education, and from massive unemployment.[72] These problems are exacerbated by structural flaws that hinder the development of the country. Algeria is a centralized, "Jacobin," *rentier* state, based on a military elite and its enduring clientelist networks, which have enriched themselves through endemic corruption. Throughout the years and despite personnel changes, the elites have had a common objective: maintaining the existing system, regardless of the means.[73] One result has been the accentuation of the gap between the few haves and the ever growing have-nots. Seen in this light, Bouteflika's reelection has meant continuity of the existing corrupt system of "predatory" networks, with only gradual and partial modifications. These networks—the beneficiaries of disorder and corruption—may eventually trigger their violent eviction from power, although their possible successors and the direction to be taken by them are of course unknown.

To truly succeed, Bouteflika's program of "national reconciliation" and socioeconomic modernization will have to overcome structural barriers. Genuine reform requires not only overcoming violence but also harmonizing the aspirations of the wider society: alienated Kabylians, Islamists and the victims of their violence, the military and the merchants, and the vast numbers of disillusioned, unemployed youth, who do not care about the mythical war of independence ("the revolution"). Algeria's youth are increasingly exposed to global developments, which cause them to yearn for change and to aspire for better prospects, social equality, dignity, and openness to the world.[74] Thus, reintegrating Islamists into society on the one hand, and reforming, however slowly, the Family Code in order to improve women's status, on the other, implies a reconsideration of Islam, a basic component of Algerian society that possesses political power that must be reckoned with. Socioeconomic modernization requires the military's accord.[75]

Algeria has overcome the violent Islamist interlude of the 1990s, but without having addressed the root causes of the upheaval in the first place. The state has not yet entered the era of political modernity; the family, the clan, the village, and the region continue to be the primary focuses of loyalty and affiliation, at the expense of the "nation." This was reflected in the results of the 2002 parliamentary elections: About 90 percent of those elected were new to office, their average age considerably lower than that of the previous Parliament, and many came from new professional groups and engaged in a new discourse on reforms. Yet their subsequent political behavior and choices hardly differed from their predecessors. Like the latter, they had acceded to election lists in the same fashion: Financial transactions and other goods were exchanged or promised, and they were burdened by obligations reinforced by culturally rooted expectations of reciprocity. Furthermore, the social and economic sanctions for noncooperation with the authorities have not changed; dissent within most parties remained taboo (perhaps with the exception of the MSP).[76]

After forty years of independence a generational change appears already to be under way and will undoubtedly accelerate in the years ahead. But although elites will certainly circulate, this could ultimately be a mere change of personnel, not of the regime. Algeria's ruling elites have the decisive advantage of possessing the means of coercion and co-optation. Already some opposition parties have joined governments; unable to unseat the regime, they submit without renouncing their ideology, hoping to influence society. Competent technocrats and members of the business elite are the regime's clients; these individuals have no political base and do not pose a threat to the regime. As to the aging generals, most of whom stem from the 1950s generation, it is unclear if they can or will replicate themselves in an active political role. (However, to that end, they have already shared some of their "feudal" privileges with their younger colleagues.)[77]

The presidential election certainly postponed, albeit temporarily, a generational change at the top. The younger Benflis was perceived as a modern and competent technocrat with reformist inclinations, but he overestimated his ability to challenge Bouteflika. At present, Abdel Aziz Bouteflika—he of autocratic temperament, a survivor of the "revolution" and a member of the clientelist "system," a follower of the cultural consensus, and someone who is hardly candid in public—belongs very much to the tradition of Algerian political life. Is he the man who will veritably turn the page if his health holds? Many observers are doubtful. His regime is robust, the Islamist alternative has little chance at success, and economic liberalization strengthens the regime, as many try to take advantage of it.[78] As George Joffé has written, "Without fundamental institutional reform, improvements on the macroeconomic level will not produce sufficient results in the micro-economic sphere, and the exploitation of the economy through rent-seeking and violence will continue."[79]

Some observers explore the possibilities of democratization but realize that pressures for change may require both the support of the men in power and outside influence.[80] It may be that the necessary transformations will have to wait for a new political (and military) generation to assume leadership roles. Eventually, the country's political future will come into the hands of the next generation. After all, 70 percent of Algerians are under the age of thirty.

Notes

In memoriam Rémy Leveau, friend and mentor.

1. Cf. Daniel Brumberg, "Liberalization versus Democracy: Understanding Arab Political Reform," Carnegie Endowment, *Working Paper* 37 (May 2003): 3.
2. Cf. Michael Shermer, "The Chaos of History," *Nonlinear Science Today* 2, no. 4 (1993): 1–13.
3. Edmund Burke III, "Theorizing the Histories of Colonialism and Nationalism in the Arab Maghrib," *Arab Studies Quarterly* 20, no. 2 (1998): 16; Gideon Gera, *An Islamic Republic of Algeria?* (and sources quoted there) (Washington, D.C.: Washington Institute for Near East Policy, 1995), 2–3; Daho Djerbal, "Les élections legislatives du 5 Juin en Algérie: Enjeux politiques et acteurs," *Monde Arab, Maghreb Machrek (MAMM)* 157 (July–September 1997): 149–61; Luis Martinez, *La Guerre Civile en Algérie* (Paris: Karthela, 1997), 14–15, 294.; Bruno Étienne, "Clientelism in Algeria," in *Patrons and Clients in Mediterranean Societies*, edited by Ernest Gellner and John Waterbury, 294–97 (London: Duckworth, 1977); Séverine Labat, *Les islamists algériens* (Paris, Seuil, 1995), 294; Jean Leca, "Paradoxes de la Démocratisation: L'Algérie au chevet de la science politique," *Pouvoirs* 86 (1998): 15–17; Abderrahmane Moussaoui, "De la violence au Djihad," *Annales HSS* (1994): 131–33. The rhetoric of jihad continues to be employed by the state: The official journal is *Al-Mujahid*; veterans of the war of independence are mujahidin.
4. Gideon Gera, "The Islamist Movement in Algeria," in *Islam and Democracy in the Arab World* (in Hebrew), edited by Meir Litvak, 203–5 (Tel Aviv: Hakibbutz Hameuchad, 1997). Cf. *Le Monde*, September 11, 2004.
5. Cf. *Le Monde*, September 14, 1999; Étienne, "Clientelism in Algeria," 298–300; Mohamed Miliani, "Arabisation of Higher Education in Algeria: Linguistic Centralism vs. Democratisation," *International Journal of Contemporary Sociology* 40, no. 1 (April 2003): 61, 71.
6. Coined in 1930 by the leader of the Algerian *ulama*, Abd al-Hamid Bin Badis.
7. Benjamin Stora, *Histoire de l'Algérie depuis l'Indépendance* (Paris: La Découverte, 1994), 29, 35; John P. Entelis, "Sonatrach: The Political Economy of an Algerian State Institution," *Middle East Journal* 53, no. 1 (Winter 1999): 9–27; Khadija Mohsen-Finan, ed., *L'Algérie: une improbable sortie de crise* (Paris: IFRI, 2002), 53–56, 73–76, 87–88; Paul Rivlin and Shmuel Even, *Political Stability in Arab States: Economic Causes and Consequences* (Tel Aviv: Jaffee Center for Strategic Studies, 2004), 12; Gera, *Islamic Republic of Algeria?* 12. A one-dollar drop/rise in the average price of Algerian crude entails the loss/gain of roughly $500 million in annual export earnings.
8. Cf. Miriam R. Lowi, "Algérie 1992–2002: Une nouvelle économie politique de la violence," *MAMM* 175 (Spring 2003): 66–68. Throughout the civil conflict only a few and isolated acts of sabotage of the pipelines occurred.
9. Martinez, *La Guerre Civile en Algérie*, 20–23; Étienne, "Clientelism in Algeria," 298–300, 304; Gilles Kepel, "Islamists versus the State in Egypt and Algeria," *Daedalus* 124, no. 3 (Summer 1995): 123; George Joffé, "The Role of Violence Within the Algerian Economy," *Journal of North African Studies* 7, no. 1 (Spring 2002): 33. "Algerian power is

one of the most opaque ... we are dealing with this country like 'Kremlinogists' in the old days of the USSR." "'The Algerian Agenda'—Interview with Severine Labat," *Middle East*, June 1998, 15. Cf. Leca, "Paradoxes de la Démocratisation," 19: "management by secret and rumour."

10. Mohsen-Finan, *L'Algérie*, 62, 67. Cf. Rémy Leveau, *Le sabre et le turban: L'avenir du Maghreb* (Paris: François Bourin, 1993), 218–21, 230–32; Rémy Leveau, "Acteurs and Champs de force," *Pouvoirs* 86 (1998): 35.

11. I. William Zartman, "The Military in Politics of Succession: Algeria," in *The Military in African Politics*, edited by John W. Harbeson, 21–22 (New York: Praeger, 1987); Mohsen-Finan, *L'Algérie*, 11–12, 53, 59, 63–69, 71; "Interview with Severine Labat," 15; *Le Monde*, August 3, 2004.

12. For a 2002 economic survey, cf. Mohsen-Finan, *L'Algérie*, 73–103; Lowi, "Algérie 1992–2002"; and Joffé, "Role of Violence"; Omar Benderra, "Les réseaux au pouvoir: Effondrement de l'État et predation," *Confluences* 45 (Spring 2003): 81–94. See also note 72 below.

13. This did not prevent Boumediene from condemning this state of affairs as "the archaic mentality of the Beylic (the Ottoman state)." Martinez, *La Guerre Civile en Algérie*, 18–21, 264.

14. Étienne, "Clientelism in Algeria," 293–95; Mohsen-Finan, *L'Algérie*, 60, 69, 89, 103; Lowi, "Algérie 1992–2002," 57, 70; Joffé, "Role of Violence," 36–37, 42; José Garçon and Pierre Affuzi, "L'Armée Algérienne: Le Pouvoir de l'Ombre," *Pouvoirs* 86 (1998): 21–22, 47; Isabelle Werenfels, "Obstacles to Privatisation of State-Owned Industries in Algeria: The Political Economy of a Distributive Conflict," *Journal of North African Studies* 7, no. 1 (Spring 2002): 2, 13, 17–18. Cf. Thomas Butko, "Unity through Opposition: Islam as an Instrument of Radical Political Change," *Middle East Review of International Affairs Journal* 8, no. 4 (December 2004), at http://meria.idc.ac.il/journal/2004/issue4/jv8no4a4.html.

15. Lowi, "Algérie 1992–2002," 57; Martinez, *Guerre Civile en Algérie*, 49–50; Joffé, "Role of Violence," 43. See also note 38, below.

16. Labat, *Islamists algériens*, 15–17, 88–89. Cf. Gera, *Islamic Republic of Algeria?* 4; Rachid Boudjedra, *FIS de la haine* (Paris: Denoël, 1994), 31–35.

17. According to official Algerian sources, some two thousand to three thousand Algerians joined the Afghani resistance during 1986–89. Lowi, "Algérie 1992–2002," 59.

18. Paragraph 25 of the 1996 constitution states, "The permanent mission of the National Popular Army is the protection of national independence and the defense of national sovereignty. It is charged to defend the unity and territorial integrity of the country." *Annuaire de l'Afrique du Nord* 35 (1996): 449 (Paris: CNRS, 1998).

19. Mohsen-Finan, *L'Algérie*, 60. Cf. Leveau, "Acteurs," 30, 35.

20. Pierre Robert Baduel, ed., *L'Algérie incertaine* (Aix-en-Provence: Edisud, 1994), 91. Cf. Martinez, *Guerre Civile en Algérie*, 21–32.

21. The latter number was given by Bouteflika, who also estimated material losses to be more than $30 billion. *Liberté*, February 24, 2005.

22. There is an expanding literature on the Algerian civil war: Martinez, *La Guerre Civile en Algérie*; Gera, *Islamic Republic of Algeria?* and "Islamist Movement in Algeria";

Labat, *Islamists algériens*; Sylvie Taussig, "La résistance de la société contre les Islamistes en Algérie—Entretien avec Séverine Labat," *Cités*, 17 (January 2004); "Islamism, Violence and Reform in Algeria: Turning the Page (Islamism in North Africa III)" *ICG Middle East Report* 29 (July 30, 2004): 10–12, International Crisis Group Web site, http://www.crisisgroup.org/home/index.cfm?id=2884&l=1; Leveau, "Acteurs," 30–31.

23. As Gilles Kepel has noted, wherever Islamists did try to capture majority support, they failed. Gilles Kepel, *Jihad: The Trail of Political Islam* (Cambridge: Harvard University Press, 2002), 366.

24. Cf. Stora, *Histoire de l'Algérie depuis l'Indépendance*, 334–35; Martinez, *Guerre Civile en Algérie*, 370–72; Kepel, 9, 362, 366; Taussig, "Résistance de la société," 113, –118; ICG. (*Middle East Report* 29) "Islamism, Violence and Reform in Algeria."

25. Leveau, "Acteurs," 34.

26. The High Command had already offered him the presidency in 1994, but he declined, refusing any collegial rule. This was acrimoniously described by the former minister of defense, Gen. Khalid Nezzar. *Liberté*, October 18, 2003. Mohamed Benchicou, *Bouteflika: Une imposture algérienne* (Paris: Jean Picollec, 2004), 18; cf. *Jeune Afrique*, April 6, 1995; Baduel, *L'Algérie incertaine*, 16; *Le Monde*, April 10, 2004.

27. John P. Entelis, introduction to Luis Martinez, *The Algerian Civil War, 1990–1998* (London: Hurst, 2000), xiv; Luis Martinez, "De l'élection présidentielle au referendum: La quête d'une nouvelle légitimité algérienne," *MAMM* 168 (April–June 2000): 41–50; José Garçon, "Algérie: L'impossible restauration," *Politique étrangère* 64, no. 2 (1999): 343–56.

28. *Jeune Afrique*, April 6, 1999; *Le Monde*, April 8, 10, 2004; *Libération*, October 11, 2003; Mohsen-Finan, *L'Algérie*, 12, 38; Garçon, "Algérie"; Benchicou, *Bouteflika*, 204.

29. Meir Litvak, "Algeria," in *Middle East Contemporary Survey* (*MECS*) 23 (1999), edited by Bruce Maddy-Weitzman, 177 (Boulder, Colo.: Westview, 2001), Meir Litvak, "Algeria," in *MECS* 24 (2000), edited by Bruce Maddy-Weitzman, 162 (Tel Aviv: The Moshe Dayan Center for Middle Eastern and African Studies, 2002); Benchicou, *Bouteflika*, 181; Mohsen-Finan, *L'Algérie*, 44, 47; *Libération*, October 11, 2003.

30. Litvak, "Algeria," MECS (1999), 170–72.

31. *Mideast Mirror*, September 25, 2003.

32. *North Africa Journal* 162 (November 15, 2004), http://www.north-africa.com/162.htm.

33. *New York Times*, March 3, 2003. For an economic portrait, see *Arabies*, April 2004, 50–56.

34. The claim of a separate Berber identity developed into a mass demand in the spring of 1980, causing unrest among Kabyle Berbers, aggravated by the Arabization policy of the regime and the repression of Berber culture and language. Cf. Ernest Gellner, *Nations and Nationalism* (Ithaca, N.Y.: Cornell University Press, 1983), 83.

35. *Le Monde*, April 10, 19, 2004.

36. *Liberté*, September 9, 2002, July 29, 2004; *Le Monde*, April 19, June 3, 2004. Cf. Jean-Michel Salgon, *Violences Ambiguës: Aspects du conflit armé en Algérie* (Paris: Centre des Hautes Études sur l'Afrique et l'Asie Modernes, 1999), 56–61.

37. Mahmoud Merhi, "Pouvoir et affairisme: L'Algérie de réseaux," *Confluences* 45

(Spring 2003): 107–14; Benderra, 88–91; *Libération*, November 11, 2003; *Le Monde*, February 9, 2005; Mohsen-Finan, *L'Algérie*, 44.

38. ICG, *(Middle East Report* 29) "Islamism, Violence and Reform in Algeria":17; Martinez, *Guerre Civile en Algérie*, especially 34–37, 189–228, deals extensively with the economic aspects of the insurgency. According to one estimate, 35 percent of all Algerian economic activity is in the "informal" sector, abetted by corrupt customs officials. *Le Monde*, June 2, 2004.

39. Benchicou, *Bouteflika*, 179, quoting French TV1, September 2, 1999; *Libération*, October 18, 2003.

40. Mohsen-Finan, *L'Algérie*, 38–41.

41. Ibid., 45.

42. Ibid., 11–2, 39, 46; Litvak, "Algeria," *MECS* (1999), 177; Hugh Roberts, *The Battlefield: Algeria 1988–2002: Studies in a Broken Polity* (London: Verso, 2003), 281, 361.

43. Roberts, *Battlefield*, 192; *Mideast Mirror*, June 13, 2002; Isabelle Werenfels, "Algerien nach den Parlamentswahlen," *Wissenschaft und Gesellschaft Aktuell* 19 (June 2002) (Berlin: Stiftung für Wissenschaft und Politik). Cf. Roberts, *Battlefield*, 361–62. Indeed, the FLN had already rejuvenated its roster of candidates for the 1997 elections, applying the lesson of its defeat in 1991. Djerbal, "Élections legislatives," 157.

44. Benflis, born in 1944 in Batna into a Berber family from the Aurès, was a respected jurist who had resigned the post of minister of justice in 1991, refusing to sanction detention centers for Islamists. A veteran of the FLN Central Committee, he was instrumental in reinstating Bouteflika to the committee in 1988. He served as the latter's campaign manager in 1999; after the election he was appointed director of the President's Office, and in 2000, prime minister. For a detailed biography, see *Jeune Afrique*, December 12, 2000, December 21, 2003; *Mideast Mirror*, July 25, 2003; *Le Monde*, April 8, 2004.

45. Mohsen-Finan, *L'Algérie*, 39; Roberts, *Battlefield*, 275; *Le Monde*, May 7, 2003.

46. *Liberté*, March 29, 2004. For his election platform, see *Liberté*, March 16, 2004.

47. The chief of staff, General Lamari, stated that no candidate, not even an Islamist, would be obstructed. Yet the opposition considered the professed "neutrality" of the military as tacit support of Bouteflika. After the election, they denounced seeming divergences between the president and the military as "manipulations." *Liberté*, December 28, 2003, February 29, April 11, 2004; *Mideast Mirror*, February 18, 2005; *Economist*, April 17, 2004; *Le Monde*, April 11, 2004. Ironically, General Lamari had likewise declared the neutrality of the military at the height of the previous presidential election campaign, at a time when it vigorously furthered Bouteflika. *Al-Jaish* (the army monthly), February 1999.

48. The *zawiyat*, the electoral influence of which is especially in the South, had for years supported the regime against the Islamist current, whom they denounced as imported "deviations from the Maleki rite." Smaïl Hadj Ali, "Algérie: Le premier séminaire national des zaouïas," *MAMM* 135 (January–March 1992): 53–67.

49. *Liberté*, January 6, 2004; *Mideast Mirror*, March 19, 2004. Cf. *Le Monde*, April 8, 2004; *Economist*, February 14, April 17, 2004; *Jeune Afrique*, April 18, 2004.

50. *Liberté*, April 10, 13, 2004; *Le Monde*, April 11, 16, 2004. As to the "traditional" way

of voting, it should be borne in mind that at least eight hundred thousand people were dependent on the state. Werenfels, "Algerien nach den Parlamentswahlen," 7.12.

51. *Liberté*, February 2, 3, 2005.

52. For example, *Le Monde*, September 11, November 28, 2004.

53. *Liberté*, November 1, December 2, 2004. Later he raised the question whether those who had issued the *fatwa*s "authorizing" outrages should be included in the amnesty. *Liberté*, May 4, 2005.

54. *Liberté*, February 23, 24, March 9, 2005. On women's rights in Algeria before the amendment of the code, see Caroline Sakina Brac de la Perrière, "Algeria," in *Special Report on Women's Rights in the Middle East and North Africa* (Washington, D.C.: Freedom House, May, 2005), http://www.freedomhouse.org/[research] analysis/special reports/menasurvey.

55. This despite protests by Boumediene's family and friends. *Liberté*, December 2, 2004, February 16, 2005.

56. *Jeune Afrique*, July 11, 2004; *Le Monde* July 1, 13, 2004, April 2005; *Liberté*, November 8, 2004.

57. *Le Monde*, August 5, 2004; *Liberté*, July 5, August 4, 7, 2004.

58. *Liberté*, May 2, 5, 2005; *North Africa Journal* 169 (May 3, 2005).

59. *Liberté*, July, 5, 19, August 4, 7, 16, 18, September 20, November 1, 2004; *Le Monde*, August 3, 5, 19, 2004; *Le Figaro*, August 5, 2004; *Jeune Afrique*, July 11, August 8, 2004; *Vremya Novosty*, June 1, 2004.

60. Jean-Noël Ferrié, "Les limites d'une democratization par la sociéte civile en Afrique du Nord," *MAMM* 175 (Spring 2003): 20; *Liberté*, April 2, 2005.

61. *Le Monde*, January 4, 2005; *Liberté*, May 17, 2004, January 3, 13, February 13, 2005.

62. *New York Times*, May 11, 14, 2004; *Mideast Mirror*, July 2, 2004; *Liberté*, April 2, 2005; *Le Monde Diplomatique*, February 2005; for a recent update, see Emily Hunt, Islamist Terrorism in Northwestern Africa (Washington Institute for Near Eastern Policy, February 2007).

63. *North Africa Journal* 164 (December 16, 2004); *Jeune Afrique*, July 11; *Liberté*, September 6, 2004, February 13, April 9, 2005. Cf. *Arabies*, April 2004, 52–56. For a more recent update on unemployment (15.3 percent) see *El-Moudjahid*, December 2, 2005, February 4, 2006.; *Le Monde*, January 27, 2005.

64. *Arabies,* April 2004, 53.

65. *Liberté*, April 6, 9, 2005; *North Africa Journal* 154 (August 3, 2004).

66. A rare reference was made by Prime Minister Ouyahia: "The supporters of the rent who prospered during the difficult years try and will continue to try to block the consolidation of a state of laws." *El-Moudjahid*, May 22, 2005.

67. Mohsen-Finan, *L'Algérie*, 72; *Liberté*, December 2, 2004, February 6, 23, 24, 2005.

68. *Liberté*, November 21, 2004, May 2, 2005; *North African Journal* 169 (May 3, 2005).

69. Text of the charter in *El-Moudjahid*, August 14, 2005. On the referendum and

GSPC rejection, see the *New York Times*, September 30, October 1, 2, 2005. For the affiliation announcement: *Liberté*, September 13, 2006; *Le Monde Diplomatique*, November 2006. Earlier the GSPC publicly approved of the killing of two Algerian diplomats in Baghdad in July 2005 by Iraqi Al-Qa'ida Liberté, July 27, 2005; Hunt, Islamist Terrorism in Northwestern Africa. For the criticism of human rights groups, see the Human Rights Watch Web site, http://www.hrw.org/backgrounder/mena/algeria (September 2005).

70. He underwent emergency gastric surgery. *Middle East Mirror,* January 20, 2006; *Liberté*, November 15, 2006.

71. *Economist*, March 5, 2005. For an informed observer's view in 1994–95 that "Algeria . . . is on the verge of collapse," see Azzedine Layashi, "Algeria: Reinstating the State or Instating a Civil Society," in *Collapsed States: The Disintegration and Restoration of Legitimate Authority*, edited by I. William Zartman, 171 (Boulder, Colo.: Lynne Rienner, 1995).

72. Joffé, "Role of Violence," 36–37. For a recent overview of the Algerian economy by a longtime banker-observer, see William C. Byrd, "Contre-performances économiques et fragilité institutionelle," *Confluences* 45 (Spring 2003): 59–79, esp. 77.

73. "Algerian society was crushed and impoverished for thirty years by a regime which used mediocrity, sycophancy, and cynicism as criteria for advancement." Tahir Djaout, an Algerian intellectual assassinated by Islamists in 1993, quoted in Mahjoub El-Hamel, "Algerie: l'assassinat des 'clercs,'" *MAMM* 141 (July–September 1993), 143; Mohsen-Finan, *L'Algérie*, 71–72; Étienne, "Clientelism in Algeria"; recently these features were described by an Algerian analyst as a gap between political will to modernize and the "multiple resistances to change." *Liberté*, February 7, 2007.

74. Cf. *Mideast Mirror*, April 21, 2005.

75. Compare the analysis of an Algerian sociologist in *Liberté*, December 4, 2004.

76. Isabelle Werenfels, "New Actors and Political System Change: Some Ideas for a Research Agenda," in *Looking Ahead: Challenges for Middle Eastern Politics and Research*, coordinated by Volker Perthes, EuroMesCo Paper 29 (April 2004): 45–46, http://www.euromesco.net. See also Mohammed Hachemaoui, "La Représentation Politique en Algérie entre Médiation Clientélaire et Prédation (1997–2002) in *Revue Française de Science Politique* 53 No. 1 (février 2003), 35–72; *Le Monde*, June 4, 2004.

77. William Quandt, "Algeria's Transition to What?" *Journal of North African Studies* 9, no. 2 (Summer 2004): 89; Ferrié, "Limites d'une democratization," 21, 28–29; Mohsen-Finan, *L'Algérie*, 65–72.

78. For example, Taussig, "Résistance de la société," 120.

79. Joffé, "Role of Violence," 48.

80. Quandt, "Algeria's Transition to What?" 90–91. For a similar argument, see Isabelle Werenfels, "Algeria: System Continuity through Elite Change." In Volker Perthes, ed., *Arab Elites—Negotiating the Politics of Change* (Boulder, Colo.: 2005), esp. 197–200. This source was not available to me at the time of writing.

6

The Fate of Political Islam in Algeria

LOUISA AÏT-HAMADOUCHE AND YAHIA H. ZOUBIR

The origins of the Islamist phenomenon in Algeria are linked to the country's colonial history, which largely explains why politics and religion have always been intertwined. Islam in Algeria cannot be seen simply as the populace's dominant religion because, more than in any other Middle Eastern and North African society, Islam in Algeria constitutes the fundamental basis of identity and culture. Islamic beliefs and practices regulate social behavior and, to a large extent, govern social relations. Neither Islam nor the Islamist phenomenon can be dissociated from Algerian history, for the Islamist movement is one of the belated progeny of 132 years of colonial rule. Although the socioeconomic failure of the 1980s largely explains the emergence of the movement, its doctrinal aspects draw partly from the crisis of identity generated by the French colonial overlord. The brutality of French rule in Algeria, which included large-scale killing, pillaging, and plundering as well as blatant exploitation of the country's human and natural resources, is legendary. The French also undermined the principal local religious institutions: Mosques and religious schools were closed and sometimes turned into churches or even bars, religious lands were expropriated, and Islamic culture was openly held up to be inferior to Christian/Western civilization.

Thus French colonial domination in Algeria went beyond the monopolistic control that French capitalism exerted over commerce, banks, industry, and agriculture. The colonial state engaged in a systematic uprooting of Arab and Islamic culture. The French administration exercised almost full control over the cultural and religious activities of the indigenous Muslim population. The native population lived in poverty and was denied basic religious, cultural, political, and economic rights, which Europeans, albeit a minority in the country, enjoyed. The colonial yoke was such that some Algerians resorted to absurd religious explanations for their plight, similar to the ludicrous accounts often espoused by modern-day Islamists. Indeed, some Algerians were convinced that colonialism was God's punishment and thus no fight against it was possible.

Colonial policies thus left an indelible imprint on the Algerian psyche. Because France resorted to extremely coercive means in order to establish its cultural hegemony, and because French colonialists treated the native population and values with contempt, Algerians had no other recourse but to cling to their religion, Islam. Not surprisingly, Islam became the most salient component of Algerian national identity, and it remains so today. Ironically, the French colonialists reinforced this trend, referring to the natives as "Muslims" or "French Muslims," never as Algerians. Although secular in nature, the nationalist movement, too, used Arab-Islamic values as symbols for popular mobilization against colonialists. Unlike in Morocco and Tunisia, the nationalist, pro-independence movement in Algeria developed primarily from within the peasantry.[1] French-educated intellectuals stayed away from the radical populist-nationalist groupings and created instead political parties such as the Union du Manifeste Algérien (UDMA), which fought for civil rights and integration. Indeed, contemporary Islamists often argue that they are the legitimate heirs of the nationalist movement, insisting that Sheikh Abdelhamid bin Badis, head of the Association of Ulama (Islamic scholars) established in 1931, inspired the war against the occupant through his famous motto: "Islam is our religion; Arabic is our language; Algeria is our motherland," a slogan Algerians are fond of citing. However, Islamists ignore the fact that the bin Badis program was purely cultural and educational, and that the nationalist credentials of the *ulama* were dubious; indeed, they never included in their program support for the armed struggle against France.

Immediately after independence in July 1962, Algerian authorities manipulated Islam for political and ideological purposes. In order to build a modern identity and gain legitimacy, the successive secular regimes sought to integrate what they defined as a modern type of Islam into revolutionary, vanguard perspectives. Thus Islam, understood in an alleged modernized form, was decreed the "religion of the state" in all four of the country's subsequent constitutions. The state elite conceived of Islam as the foundation of identity of Algerian citizens. The role of the state, at least in the so-called socialist era (1962–80) primarily under Houari Boumediene, consisted in not only bestowing upon citizens the material benefits of the modern world (work, education, and all kinds of quasi-free services) but also in promoting Islamic principles and morality, albeit in tandem with secularism and socialism. Thus state-sponsored religious decrees (*fatwas*) discharged industrial workers from fasting during the holy month of Ramadan. The government also accepted the general closure of stores during Friday prayers and the introduction of religious teaching in schools. Despite this implicit alliance between the regime and Islamists, the latter maintained their pressure on the state to institute a social order in conformity with Islamic values. Notwithstanding the considerable concessions that the government made to Islamists, they rejected the centrality of socialism in the 1976 National Charter designed to underpin the country's development, claiming that socialism was "heresy." The authorities were thus placed on the defensive and reduced to claiming that socialism was simply the continuation of the process of national liberation designed to achieve social justice and equality.

Notwithstanding the existence of a welfare state (free medical care, free education, and subsidized prices), Algeria's rigid, repressive authoritarian political system resulted in growing opposition from a variety of quarters. In response, arguing that the single party was the guarantor of a unified state, the ruling Front de Libération National (FLN) used the tactic of "divide and rule," playing off secular, Marxist, and democratic groups, in turn, against Islamists.

The various Islamist opposition groups emerged under complex conditions.[2] The first Islamist association to appear after independence was El-Qiyam al-Islamiyya (Islamic Values), founded in 1963. Owing to the government's wish to divide the opposition and to make compromises with the Islamist challengers, El-Qiyam enjoyed a semilegal existence until 1970. The association demanded the full implementation of the Shari'a, prohibition of the sale of alcohol, exclusion of non-Muslims from public jobs, and the introduction of religious teaching in schools. Those and other demands were again put forth by the more radical Islamist groups that mushroomed in the 1980s and 1990s.

Islamism as a potent social movement first appeared in the late 1970s and early 1980s; its radicalization deepened in the 1980s as the country was plunged into economic and social crisis. The most violent, albeit small, radical Islamist group rallied around Mustapha Bouyali, who founded the Armed Islamic Movement (MIA) in 1982 and served as its emir (commander) until his violent death in 1987. Earlier, Bouyali had created an organization called the Group for the Struggle against the Illicit (Mouvement pour la lutte contre le péché), which had conducted attacks against bars and individuals. It had little if any effect, however, and soon Bouyali felt compelled to resort to armed struggle against the regime. To that end, he created a small, disciplined organization that was able to carry out specific targeted operations, such as political assassinations and acts of sabotage. Bouyali's actions epitomized the impulsive response some Algerians used against the state because of the lack of any democratic channels to express frustrations and disenchantment with economic and social policies and cultural trends. In the 1990s, some members of this organization would join the guerrilla war waged by Islamists against the authorities.

Democratization, the Rise of Islamism, and Civil Strife

Under pressure from the "street" following the October 1988 riots and due to dissension within the regime of President Chadli Benjedid, the authorities decided to open up the political process and initiated a considerable degree of liberalization. In short order, more than sixty political parties were founded, the most important of which was the Islamic Salvation Front (FIS). Established in 1989 and legalized by the authorities the same year, the FIS was made up of a variety of groups and individuals holding opposing views with respect to democracy and a number of other social, economic, and cultural issues but united by their radical opposition to the state and its policies. These internal differences partly explain why the FIS's program remained ambiguous and popular at the same time. The so-called "Arab Afghans"—that is, those who had recently returned from the war against Soviet forces in Afghanistan—constituted an important and extremely radical faction within the FIS. They made clear their opposition to elections, which they viewed as a Western practice standing in complete contradiction to Islamic values. Furthermore, they believed that the *taghut* (infidel oppressors), that is, the state officials, could only be removed through force. Hence all political games and talk about democracy were useless because they are imports from the West and should not be implemented in a Muslim society. However, the dominant forces within the FIS felt that, given the popular support the party enjoyed among the population, elections would demonstrate not only the popularity of the party but also the negligible weight of the secular parties and the obsolescence of the regime.

It should be noted that the FIS did not represent the entire Islamist movement. Indeed, two prominent Islamist figures created their own political parties. The late Mahfoud Nahnah created in 1990 the HAMAS (Movement for an Islamic Society, later renamed Movement for a Peaceful Society, or MSP), and Abdallah Djaballah founded the Ennahda (Renewal) party the same year. These two parties were unequivocally opposed to violence and supportive of the political process. They were, however, dwarfed in size by the FIS during these years.

In June 1990, the government organized nationwide municipal elections, the first pluralist elections in the country since its independence in 1962. The FIS candidates won overwhelmingly, and as a result they felt empowered on the national level. The municipalities that came under the organization's control introduced practices that were in opposition to state policies (for instance, religious writings on the walls of state buildings and the introduction of parallel "Islamic" markets). The following year witnessed steadily increasing political instability and unrest, highlighted by the postponement of parliamentary elections scheduled for June 1991, and the arrest of many of the FIS's leading figures. However, despite the increased Islamist threat felt by the state and secular civil society, the authorities went through with the first round of parliamentary elections in December 1991. The results marked a stunning triumph for the FIS, which garnered an overwhelming number of those seats whose outcome was decided in a single round of voting and stood poised to achieve an absolute majority following the second round scheduled for January 16, 1992. Alarmed by such a prospect, along with threats that some FIS members had made against the military-civilian establishment, powerful elements within the government compelled President Benjedid to resign and cancelled the second round of the legislative elections. The election's cancellation, and the banning of the FIS shortly thereafter—along with the imprisonment of its leaders—resulted in a general crisis of the state. By 1993, the split within the FIS and the absence of leadership made possible the emergence of an armed insurrection carried out by various factions that were hitherto under the FIS umbrella. Some retained affiliation with the FIS under the banner of the Army for Islamic Salvation (AIS). Other smaller, obscure groups were led by self-proclaimed emirs who set up autonomous brigades (*katibat*) to conduct jihad. The merciless battle that ensued pitted the security forces against armed Islamist groups, for which the civilian population paid a heavy price. Between 150,000 and 200,000 people were killed and many more were wounded. The horrible collective massacres of 1997 and 1998 highlighted the Algerian tragedy and the limits of the *tout sécuritaire* (repressive policy) option that so-called *éradicateurs* within the state had pursued throughout the conflict.[3]

Violence and Politics in the Aftermath of the Civil Conflict

The Civil Concord and Its Benefits

By the late 1990s, the Algerian regime had clearly triumphed over the Islamist opposition. Still, violence had not entirely abated. Following the election of Abdel Aziz Bouteflika to the Algerian presidency in April 1999, the concept of "national reconciliation" came to dominate the political discourse in Algeria. Although the meaning of the term appeared straightforward, the substance that the authorities wished to give to it was ambiguous, indicating that this ostensibly clear concept hid a more complex state of affairs.

Preparation for a climate of national reconciliation had already been well under way before Bouteflika's election, that is, under Liamine Zeroual's presidency (1994–99). After more than five years of uninterrupted military campaign against the Islamist guerrillas, the military hierarchy began secret negotiations with some factions of the Islamist movement. This negotiation resulted in 1997 in a secret agreement, never revealed but finalized and legalized through La loi sur la concorde civile (Law on Civil Concord), which was to last from July 7, 1999, to January 13, 2000, but was unofficially extended indefinitely. On the whole, the law was designed to execute a trade-off between the Islamists and the authorities whereby the former would renounce the use of violence in exchange for judicial leniency.

The Law on Civil Concord was directed at "fighters involved in terrorist or subversive actions" who "did not commit or participate in an action, which has caused death, permanent infirmity and rape" or "did not use bombs in public places." This category of criminals, the law stated, could qualify for leniency if "they accept to fight terrorism under the state authority." It should be noted that the law excluded any reference to possible atrocities committed by state-supported armed forces. It exonerated individuals from legal proceedings and reduced the terms of sentence, or suspended them entirely, for those convicted of antistate activities while enabling the annulment of civil rights, all at the discretion of the "authorities." Thus the law provides for a significant easing of judicial punishments for the masterminds of bomb attacks in public places, assassinations, and rapes, and it nullifies capital punishment and life imprisonment.[4]

Nevertheless, Amnesty International criticized the law's application as being without any judicial structure and control. In fact, no information was given publicly about who was being judged and how or about the undeclared extension of the deadline. Since January 2000, hundreds of armed Islamists have surrendered and benefited from these unknown "clemency measures." According to Amnesty International, they were set free. The law granting forgiveness is still in effect. However, although those who surrendered were socially rehabilitated, they have not and probably will never recover their civil rights. The distinction between social rehabilitation and repossession of civil rights explains why many Islamist critics see the law on civil concord as inadequate.[5]

Even as the law was being implemented, the government's counterterrorism campaign continued. The authorities sought the assistance of repentant Islamists to gather information about the networks and logistics of armed groups such as the AIS and LIDD (Islamic League of Daawa and Djihad). They also sought to establish contacts with other armed groups (e.g., Antar Zouabri's Groupe Islamique Armé, or GIA, and Hassan Hattab's Salafist Group for Predication and Combat, or GSPC) which had split off from the GIA in 1998 to try to persuade them of the benefits of the law). It should be noted that Hattab had broken off ties with the GIA allegedly over disagreements regarding targets: Although Hattab professedly avoided attacks on civilians and insisted on attacking security forces only, the GIA leaders believed that no distinction should be made between civilian and military targets. When some of these groups became weaker and more isolated, the authorities increased contact with them and convinced many of them to lay down their arms. This so-called contact operation started, according to press reports, in September 2003, while the Algerian army led a fierce offensive in the Babor mountains and in the eastern province of Jijel. The authorities did not make public any reports on the results obtained, but they certainly accumulated valuable experience in negotiating with the Jijelian armed groups.[6]

According to FIS president Abassi Madani, a number of members of various armed groups took up the regime's offer after "long negotiations," leaving their sanctuaries for camps directed by the Armée Nationale Populaire (ANP). There is general consensus—though no firm evidence—that about three hundred members of the GSPC laid down their arms in ten departments (wilayat). Other contacts were developed with groups based in the Kabylia region (Adekar, Djurdjura, and Yakouren).

The fate of the groups who refused to surrender remained unclear since, officially, the Concord's measures were no longer applicable after January 13, 2000. In practice, however, the amnesty period never expired because the government believed that its tacit extension would allow additional fighters to lay down their weapons, especially when persuaded to do so by mediators or family representatives. At the same time, the military continued to fight the recalcitrant factions. But the treatment of individuals who abandoned their hideaways remained a mystery. The national and international media subsequently reported on families linked to the GSPC who were removed from their homes and brought to camps directed by the ANP as a means of protecting them from retaliation by competing groups.[7] An AIS leader, Madani Mezrag, indirectly acknowledged this development but refused to qualify those people as "repentant," a designation that would allow them to obtain the same status as AIS members, with whom they were at odds.

Because the Law on Civil Concord produced a smaller than anticipated number of surrenders, the subsequent political debate came to revolve around its prolongation as well as a possible general amnesty. Questioned about this possibility during the electoral campaign, Bouteflika declared, "I cannot make such a weighty promise" (*une promesse aussi lourde*). However, it is clear that he, the architect of the Civil Concord, neither excluded this "solution" nor personally rejected it. From Bouteflika's perspective, the decision to declare total amnesty did not depend solely on him. Yet he made it repeatedly clear that his new presidential mandate would enunciate "clemency measures in favor of those who will regain their good sense and participate in nation building and development."

Farouk Ksentini, chairman of the government-sponsored Human Rights Commission, who declared in April 2004 that "all the initiatives are welcome if they have a legal base and facilitate the evacuation of Islamists' hideouts,"[8] corroborated the view that the regime was strongly considering general amnesty as a definitive solution to the lingering terrorism and violence. Assuming that this would be done within a legal framework, the question as to what kind of message the government would be sending to the opposition and to the rest of society would still remain. Such a solution would risk being seen as the state's implicit recognition of the legitimacy of the Islamist uprising. Moreover, declared or undeclared amnesty would mean, some fear, that employing violence was the only effective way to be heard and respected by state authorities. Those who share this view have decried what they call the "betrayal of the innocent victims."

Bouteflika was decisively reelected in April 2004 with 85 percent of the votes. Immediately afterward, he spelled out the regime's security responsibilities and the bodies responsible for their implementation. Thus clemency measures and the fight against terrorism now fell under the control of the high political authority as well as the justice department and the armed forces. The government's mission was to keep state and society mobilized behind Bouteflika's policies. The "global reconciliation" project was defined as an "inescapable choice" that drew from past experiences and thus should "break the taboos" in order to "avoid exclusion and extremism"[9] within Algerian society. The president urged Algerians to change their mentality, to forgive mistakes of the past, and to move forward. However, the content of the new choices Algerians should make remained unclear. In the official celebrations, as well as within Islamic circles, national reconciliation, which was yet to be formulated as a general amnesty, centered on religious (*rahma*, or "mercy"), nationalist (national unity), and political (peace and security) arguments. On September 29, 2005, voters gave overwhelming support—97 percent of the vote—to the National Reconciliation Charter (see the chapter by Gideon Gera in this volume). This inflated figure may have been orchestrated in order to prepare the ground for a change in the Constitution that would allow Bouteflika to run for a third term, which is not possible under the current Constitution. This scenario is plausible, for who would refuse a third term to a president who has been given an overwhelming mandate to save the country and bring about peace and prosperity?

Residual Terrorism

In October 2001, Minister of Interior Yazid Zerhouni estimated the number of active "terrorists" in Algeria to be between seven hundred and eight hundred; in his approximation, about twenty thousand armed individuals had been "eliminated" since 1992.[10] Similar estimates were tendered in 2003: Army spokespersons declared that there remained between six hundred and eight hundred active opposition fighters, divided between the GIA and the GSPC. Maj. Gen. Mohammed Lamari stated that between 1992 and 1995 there had been twenty-seven thousand insurgents killed. Whereas the AIS and the LIDD had agreed to lay down their arms, both the GIA and the GSPC had rejected the state's offer. According to various sources, an estimated four hundred people, mostly security forces and Islamist militants, were killed in 2003. By September 2004, the number of fatalities had again reached close to four hundred. Nonetheless, there are no independent figures regarding the remaining number of armed opposition forces, let alone the number of those who have surrendered or been killed.

The security services revealed that the diehard groups, the GSPC and the GIA, had had success in mobilizing young people between the ages of eighteen and twenty. This is a new, post-FIS generation, over whom the charismatic leaders of the FIS, Ali Benhadj and Abassi Madani, had no influence. Both groups have rejected any compromise with the government. However, their tactics differed. Whereas the GSPC usually targeted the police and the armed forces, the GIA directed its violence indiscriminately against civilians, mostly in remote areas.

In 1999, while the law on civil concord was being promulgated, the leaders of the recently established GSPC published a "charter" in which they explained the "ideology and motivations" of the organization. Two years later, the GSPC declared its war a "just war" and qualified the surrenders as mere "trials." The group described all those who called for reconciliation as apostates and unbelievers. From the GSPC's perspective, the reconciliation project was basically a tactic to "fight Islam and its guardians." In order to legitimize their discourse, the organization's leaders relied on Salafist ideologues such as Abdelmounaïm Mustapha Halima (Abu Bassir), who generally condoned the methods of the GSPC mujahidin (holy warriors). At the same time, he allegedly urged the group not to target civilians or young conscripts. Since 2002, the organization has widened its area of operations and has sought to form alliances with other Islamist groups. Hence the GSPC has extended its operations to the region of Médéa through the Katiba El Khadra (Green Brigade), led by M'hamed Houti, alias Abou Othba. This *katiba* had been part of the GIA until 1996. It was known for its assassinations of civilians, soldiers, and civil servants. Katibat Djounoud Allah (Brigades of God's Soldiers), led by Ahmed Guellila (Abou Hafs) and based in the forests of Aïn Defla, Chlef, and Tissemsilt (midwestern Algeria), also joined the GSPC. In the extreme west (Mascara, Tlemcen, Saïda, and Sidi Bel Abbès), the half-dozen GIA groups created in 2000 an autonomous organization known as the Salafist Group for Combat (GSC). After some negotiating, Yahia Djouadi, alias Yahia Abou Amar, leader of the GSC, decided to join Hassan Hattab's GSPC. Katibat el Islam (Islamic Brigades), which operates in the Relizane region, made a similar move. However, Katibat es Sunna (Sunna Brigades; "Sunna" refers to the sayings and doings of the prophet Muhammad) in Sidi Bel Abbès (also in western Algeria) refused to unite with the GSPC.

International Influence (Al-Qaʻida)

The September 11, 2001, al-Qaʻida attacks and subsequent U.S. war against the Taliban regime in Afghanistan and increasing vigilance by Western security services revealed the proliferation of radical Islamist networks in North America, the African Sahel, and Europe, as well as the involvement of Algerians in them. This in turn raised questions about radical Algerian Islamists' motivations and goals. Analyses that continued to present the crisis in Algeria solely as a dispute between the Islamist opposition and the military government over specific political issues appeared increasingly anachronistic or, at best, only partial. To be sure, the FIS was primarily an Algerian phenomenon. However, the core of the GIA, which carried out some of the worst atrocities of the Algerian civil war during the 1990s, was made up of "Arab Afghan" veterans of the 1980s. With the evolution of al-Qaʿida and internal splits within radical Algerian Islamist groups, analyses that emphasized the increasingly important influence of external factors on Algerian Islamism have gained new credibility. Thus the Algerian case has progressively been integrated by Western governments and independent analysts into the more general "clash of civilizations" paradigm promoted by both Islamist extremists and strident opponents of political Islam in the West. This is also known as the al-Qaʿida phenomenon.

Evidence of an Algerian connection to al-Qaʿida continued to accumulate. For instance, the Muslim fighters imprisoned by the United States at its Guantánamo Bay installation included a number of Algerian nationals. In the UK, several dozen Algerians were arrested between late 2001 and mid-2003 in Leicester, Glasgow, Edinburgh, London, and Manchester. Arrests in London in January 2003 uncovered a cell that had produced the deadly chemical ricin, and in Manchester, one of the Algerian detainees, twenty-seven-year-old Kamel Bourgass, had been responsible for killing a police officer (the first victim in the UK's post–September 11 antiterrorist campaign).[11] French authorities had long criticized the British government for its allegedly lax approach toward Algerian Islamist activists who operated within and in the vicinity of British mosques. Now, however, increased bilateral cooperation between the two governments resulted in the arrest of the group suspected of producing ricin.

The further arrests of Algerians in France, Spain, Italy, and Germany substantiated the existence of direct links between Islamists fighting the regime in Algeria and international terrorist cells. Various investigations revealed that these cells were definitively linked to networks of international crime. Their methods included the use of credit card scams, human trafficking, and false passports and visas in order to provide logistical support to armed Islamist combatants in Algeria. According to Algerian security officials, the GSPC, whose membership includes a great number of Arab Afghans, benefited from bin Laden's support, having come under his influence shortly after the GSPC's split from the GIA in 1998. As indicated by a former member of the organization, bin Laden himself suggested the name "GSPC." All these facts led experts of international terrorism to view the GSPC through new lenses, reinforced by the group's renaming in January 2007 as al-Qaʻida of the Islamic Maghrib. The group has extended its internal struggle against Algeria's military-backed leadership to international targets that coincide with al-Qaʻida's objectives. These objectives are defined in the frame of "the growth of a utopian, 'universalized' Islamist vision not confined to recognizable borders but based on an inspirational urge to create an Islamic order wherever Muslims are oppressed or subjected to western strategic interests."[12]

Undoubtedly, the profile of some of those Algerians arrested for terrorist activities corresponded to the "utopian, universalized Islamist vision." Many of them were born in Europe—or have spent several years there—and have European or dual citizenship. Their introduction into Islamist circles occurred through popular and radical imams,[13] who led them to military training camps in Afghanistan, from which they have returned to their countries of origin or other places in the West.[14]

From the Algerian government's perspective, the inclusion of its own nationals within the framework of al-Qaʻida was a blessing. First, it put a serious dent in the widely held view in the West, which juxtaposed a repressive military regime with a victimized opposition. Up until then, the U.S. and West European governments had periodically criticized Algerian authorities for not seeking a compromise with Islamists that would, by definition, "adhere to their [Algerians'] own religious and constitutional value system." In the United States, for instance, some policy makers were convinced that *le tout sécuritaire* advocated by the *éradicateurs* in Algeria would not end the crisis, that dialogue was the only avenue to resolve the crisis, and that all of the country's political forces, including Islamists who rejected extremism, must participate in the political process. The Clinton administration was dominated by accommodationists such as Assistant Secretary of State for the Middle East Robert Pelletreau, who preferred dialogue with and integration of Islamists, accompanied by economic liberalization and a dismantling of state monopolies.[15] The rationale for such advice was the principle according to which violence is self-perpetuating and provides the breeding ground for more pernicious forms of political radicalism.

Second, the treatment of Algerian terrorism as being an integral part of a global phenomenon reduced considerably the number of Western commentaries that suggested the military's responsibility for perpetuating violence through the infiltration of government agents in GIA cells and committing atrocities that were then falsely attributed to the Islamists. As a result, Algeria deepened its security cooperation with Western countries, which lifted their quasi-embargo on arms sales, making available to Algeria night-vision and airborne surveillance equipment.

Third, the change in perception provided the Algerian government with new legitimacy in terms of security and political experience. Both the United States and European governments officially and publicly recognized the significance of Algeria's "expertise" in the global war on terrorism. Hence they began to see the Algerian military's role more as a guarantee of the country's and region's stability than as an obstacle to democracy. Not surprisingly, they also drew a parallel between the role of the military in Turkey and the role of the military in Algeria.

Integrating Islamists into the Democratic Process

History has shown that religion in and of itself is not necessarily an impediment to a society's transition to democracy or to the existence of a democratic order.[16] Of course, should religious groups use violence to express their beliefs or to impose their own vision of society, democratization will inevitably fail. One can surmise that given the political conditions that existed in the early 1990s in Algeria (superficial multiparty representation, partial liberalization, military domination, and socioeconomic crisis), and regardless of the prevailing religion, failure to achieve a successful democratic transition was well nigh inevitable.

The failure is related to another *problématique* related to the role of religion in the Algerian experience. In Algeria, religion plays a predominant role in the daily life of the population and tends to be assimilated to, or confused with, the local culture and traditions. Religion is present at school, in the butcher's shop, on television, in marriage ceremonies, and at funerals. Thus it would be anomalous for religion to be absent from politics and one should not automatically reject the integration of nonviolent Islamist parties into the political system. The policy of integrating such parties is rational even if it might seem paradoxical. What makes the policy realistic is the incontrovertible presence—as in the rest of the Muslim world—of this ideological tendency within the political scene. In this context, one should point to one of the most important organized and localized Islamist tendencies, the so-called *jaz'ara* ("Algerianist," that is, a trend in the movement that did not import any foreign Islamist ideology, which claims to represent a purely Algerian Islamist thought). To be sure, the *jaz'arists*, apart from Sheikh Ahmed Sahnoun, did not control mosques. However, they created in 1973 the first prayer room at the University of Algiers and spread this practice to universities throughout the country.

In the Algerian political scene, one can observe a paradox at two levels. At the first level, the paradox can be seen within the political system itself. Indeed, it is this system that has, on the one hand, legally and continuously "forbidden the use of religious values for political goals" and, on the other hand, legally and continuously declared Islam to be the religion of the state. In other words, the system integrated the influence of religion without formally recognizing it. This contradiction, which aimed at balancing various interests within the system, exacerbated divisions among the various power groups or cliques. These groups are allied along familial, regional, or material interests against other similar groups (*lutte des clans*);[17] usually feuds between the clans are conducted through the media and political parties. One particularly public confrontation took place in 1996–97 between partisans of a reconciliation policy with Islamists and those radically opposed to such strategy. A different and even more conspicuous confrontation was that in 2003–4 between supporters and opponents of Bouteflika's reelection. In both instances, however, the clans reached a compromise in order to guarantee the stability and survival of the system. The second level of the paradox stems from the system's association with its environment. The quiet attempt to co-opt some of the Islamist groups while suppressing others created a contradiction between the official political discourse and the government's behavior. This has placed the *décideurs*,[18] the real power brokers inside the regime, in a quasi-clandestine status, which at times compels them to negotiate from a weak position. The concessions made in favor of the Islamists are often the result of these internal contradictions. The best illustration of this phenomenon was the arrangement President Bendjedid reached with the Islamists in 1991 against the will of the *décideurs*. Their secretive status also explains why the government not only never revealed the substance of the negotiations with the armed wing of the FIS in 1997 but also refused to even acknowledge that such negotiations ever took place.

Islamist Political Influence

By 2004–5, it had become difficult to evaluate the real influence of the Islamist tendency in Algeria. There were no public opinion polls and no empirical studies concerning this significant phenomenon, unlike in 1990 and 1991, when their clout was demonstrated in the voting booths (see table 6.1). To be sure, there has been an apparent decline in support for the Islamists since then. However, the political and social factors that led large sections of the Algerian youth to embrace the Islamist ideology have not disappeared.[19] Perhaps the first reason for the continued attractiveness of Islamism is the degree of corruption at all levels that plagues Algerian society.[20] By 2002, for instance, the authorities had removed from office 1,050 previously elected officials, and 500 had been arrested and incarcerated. Furthermore, the courts charged 349 mayors (25 percent of the total, representing thirty-four out of the forty-eight provinces (*wilayat*) with insider trading. Of those mayors, 123 were judged and given jail terms.[21]

The second reason for the persistence of Islamism derives from the nature of the political chessboard. Despite the existence of a gamut of political parties, there remains no credible opposition to the regime. The legal parties are more interested in politicking, as seen in the divisions that exist inside Islamist, democratic, and nationalist tendencies alike, rather than in upholding coherent political programs. This state of affairs is particularly evident during electoral campaigns. The Algerian media correctly point out that the opposition is only capable of acting together to denounce the regime, forming a tactical, circumstantial coalition rather than initiating a coherent alternative force. Personal attacks and ambitious rivalries, rather than effective debate, nearly always constitute a substitute for a concrete program. This weakness of the opposition partly explains why citizens are reluctant to vote under such conditions or to be genuinely interested in debating and participating in political issues. No wonder, then, that political apathy best characterizes today's Algerian citizen.

Before elections, Algerians do not wonder who will be the winner; rather, they debate how widespread electoral fraud will be. This situation led analysts to conclude that multipartyism—as designed by the regime—has in fact deepened the crisis of credibility and that the system is not keen on allowing the emergence of a new political class capable of instituting a genuinely democratic regime that would serve as a viable alternative to both the current system and Islamism. In fact, it is apparent that the first objective of virtually all political parties, Islamist parties included, is to participate in power merely to enjoy the privileges that it offers with little regard for the interests of the citizens at large. According to one analyst, the "new political topography did not establish a multiparty system but a multi-single-party system in which crucial internal democratic rules, such as electing party leaders, were missing."[22]

Those who share this opinion believe that the Islamist opposition outside of the two legalized parties is the only credible opposition capable of threatening the regime. The authorities apparently think likewise. Witness (1) the regime's categorical refusal to recognize the Wafa party of Ahmed Taleb Ibrahimi, the former senior minister in a number of Algerian cabinets, and (2) the regime's denial of having conducted negotiations with the Islamist armed groups. In turn, the regime's failure to take steps to incorporate the Islamist trend, or even acknowledge whatever dialogue has taken place, had a negative impact on other non-Islamist political forces. The resulting continued political stagnation explains why well-known non-Islamist opposition political dignitaries, such Ali Yahia Abdennour, Rachid Benyellès, and Hocine Aït Ahmed,[23] rejected the holding of elections, proposing instead that negotiations with *le pouvoir* (the ruling forces), including the military, be held as a way out of the political crisis that has persisted since the early 1990s.

Clearly, the challenge of Islamist political parties is not fundamentally different from that of Algerian political parties as a whole. As a mediating actor, a political party's role consists of integrating the citizen into the political system by transmitting the citizens' demands to the authorities. If the government addresses those demands satisfactorily, the citizen will feel that she or he really participates in public life and enjoys genuine representation. Following introduction of the multiparty system in 1989, the FIS emerged as the most active party and played the role of an actor capable of gathering, expressing, and representing the citizens' frustrations. However, two important shortcomings in Algerian political life soon became apparent: the citizen-state relationship and the degree of rapport between the citizen and the party. The well-known characteristics of such deficiencies include citizen abstention during elections, cyclical urban riots, general depoliticization, civil disobedience, and religious extremism. The result is a double-edged sword: the appearance of an "authoritarian pluralism"[24] and the emergence of hegemonic parties.

This authoritarian pluralism refers to both the FIS supremacy (1990–92) and the once and current ruling party, the FLN. When a political party becomes hegemonic because of large popular support, its members quickly feel that they have unlimited freedom of action. They conclude that they can decide on basically everything without any consultation with, or authorization from, the authorities. This was precisely the case with the FIS during the early 1990s and with the FLN since 2004. In each instance, a simple and logical slogan summed up the hegemonic discourse. The FIS proclaimed that the "state abandoned the people because the government does not venerate God." The FLN also used the religious reference in promoting "reconciliation" and encouraging "forgiveness." The FIS belittled the religious zeal of its adversaries, and the FLN called for people to demonstrate greater devotion. The FIS did not spell out how the FLN had caused the government to commit apostasy, and the FLN did not detail what forgiving implies. In both cases, confusing but nonetheless attractive enough discourses were sufficient for achieving their respective goals: attaining and preserving power.

Participation and Opposition Strategies (MSP versus MRN)

Today, two main tendencies dominate Islamist political militancy. One can be characterized as participatory, the other as oppositionist. The Movement for a Peaceful Society (MSP) and the Ennahda party represent the first tendency, whereas al-Islah (National Reform Movement; MRN), the result of dissidence within Ennahda, represents the second trend.

The Strategy of Participation

The MSP, known until 1997 as HAMAS,[25] epitomizes the double strategy of the venerable Arab-Islamist Egyptian-based Muslim Brotherhood: Islamization from the bottom and participation at the top. Although the charismatic and popular Mahfoud Nahnah formed the political party in December 1990, its effective existence is much older, owing to the activities of a network that eventually coalesced into the Association of Guidance and Reform (Irshad wal-Islah). This ostensibly apolitical organization, active in educational and social welfare issues, was officially born in the framework of the post–October 5, 1988, liberalization. However, its militants were already and secretly active in mosques and schools and through nonprofit associations under the single-party system. Many scholars, businessmen, and traders remain active members of this association. The party's base of recruitment is essentially among members of the urban middle class, who are asked to support the "national immutable foundations" (*constantes nationales*) enunciated in the Constitution and shared by most Algerians. Thus the MSP's strongest advantage is its deep roots in society and its experience on the ground.

A second important asset concerns the distance the party took vis-à-vis the dissolved FIS. Although FIS president Abassi Madani strongly rejected any type of alliance with HAMAS, then headed by Nahnah (d. June 2003), HAMAS activists consistently criticized the FIS for its alleged opportunism and simplistic rhetoric, as well as its more extremist positions. In 1990, Nahnah highlighted three points that marked his party's distance from the local and national politics of the FIS. He spoke about the consolidation of the Islamic solution, the adoption of moderation and dialogue between citizens, and respect for women by permitting them to participate in the achievement of the global Islamic civilizational project. Furthermore, the MSP leaders were always careful to protect the reputation of their movement. In other words, in post–civil strife Algeria, HAMAS/MSP could claim that it had no links with the FIS and that it had never supported violent groups. Even at the peak of the Algerian crisis in 1994–95, when Islamists seemed on the brink of seizing power, HAMAS maintained a moderate position as an actor advocating and engaging in negotiation, compromise, trade-offs and alliance building.

The MSP's third strong point is its international weight. Nahnah was well known and considered a partner in both Western countries and the Muslim world. His charismatic personality and his status within the Muslim Brotherhood were important cards for the Algerian regime, which sought to strengthen its Islamic credentials. The party also drew support from influential powers such as the United States, which had its own traditional relations with conservative Islamist regimes in the Persian Gulf; with France, which was directly involved in the Algerian crisis through the important Algerian community on its territory;[26] and with the United Kingdom, long considered a strategic center of international Islamism.

Weakness of the MSP Strategy of Participation

Critics within the Islamist current, and outside analysts as well, viewed the MSP's creation as a government attempt to divide the FIS. Ironically, the MSP's weakness stemmed from its Islamist base, which frequently criticized its positions and decisions over the years. HAMAS was faulted for not condemning the interruption of the electoral process in January 1992 and for its decision not to join the second round of the Sant'Egidio initiative, which in early January 1995 brought together to Rome the first "conciliators" (*reconciliateurs*), the FIS, the secular and mostly Kabylian Front des Forces Socialistes (FFS), the Workers' Party (PT), and individual members of the FLN, where they agreed on the *Contrat National*, designed to form the basis for an end to the civil strife.[27] HAMAS/MSP's generally poor showing at the polls led analysts to offer two possible explanations. Either the party had a weak following or it had accepted the authorities' manipulation of electoral results, at times to its own advantage, at other times to its detriment. For instance, in October 1997, the MSP won 69 seats in the National Assembly but dropped to 38 seats four years later. Its marginal status was also evident during the local elections in 2002, which saw the party lose 56 seats in the departmental assemblies (APW) and 871 seats in the municipal councils (APC). The kind of compromises that HAMAS/MSP entered into led critics to depict the movement as the regime's third party, after the FLN and the RND (Rassemblement National Démocratique, the party created in February 1997 to put a political gloss on the ruling military-backed regime). However, unlike the FLN and the RND, HAMAS/MSP members never held important ministerial posts, such as education: They had agreed to this arrangement with the authorities as a trade-off for their participation in the government.

The Strategy of Opposition

The FIS was the first party to choose a strategy of opposition and confrontation with the state. Pushing it to extremes, the outcome was a decade of brutal conflict and a decisive defeat for the Islamists. Consequently the proponents of a strategy of opposition now shun any direct confrontation with the authorities while refusing to contract political and tactical alliances with them. Any genuine rapprochement of an Islamist opponent with the regime's allies, even those belonging to the Islamist camp, thus appears implausible for the foreseeable future.

Abdallah Djaballah, former head of Ennahda and current head of the recently constituted MRN, has presented himself, and with some justification, as the sole leader of the legal Islamist opposition. Politically, the 2002 elections confirmed the MRN's relative strength, garnering 7.7 percent of the votes, which translated into 43 seats in the National Popular Assembly, 374 seats in the departmental elections, and 39 seats in the municipal elections. Djaballah thus defeated the MSP and negated Ennahda, which he had only recently left. The MRN's growing political influence was subsequently demonstrated in 2004 by parliament's passage of laws forbidding the import of alcohol and voting inside military garrisons.

At the symbolic level, decision-making centers confirmed the enhanced status of Djaballah's party. Indeed, during the April 2004 presidential electoral campaign, the regime's strongman, Maj. Gen. Mohamed Lamari, himself declared that the army would respect the election results "even if Abdallah Djaballah was the winner."[28] This instance provided the candidate with new weight, designating him as the leader of the Islamist tendency and showcasing him as the guarantee of the army's neutrality. This last point is particularly important, because a national debate has actually been opened and contradictory opinions are being expressed about the role that the military institution should play in political life.[29] For some analysts, the election denoted the end of the politicized army and a step toward a more genuine democratic political system. To the extent that this was in fact the case, it came about as a result of divisions within the higher echelons of the state apparatus, and the emergence of a second "candidate of the system" from within the FLN, former prime minister Ali Benflis, to challenge Bouteflika.

A completely contrary explanation of the 2004 election results holds that Bouteflika's victory did not constitute a setback for the army but indicated the army's new way of governing. Rather than organizing an election in which the military candidate was obvious (as in 1995 and 1999), the *grande muette* (big mute), as the army is called, spoke out like never before, through official channels and by way of retired officers, declaring that "it supports no particular candidate." It is, of course, not clear whether these kinds of declarations were not simply a way of influencing the course of the election or indicated a genuine withdrawal of the army from politics. Regardless, the statements that the armed forces made, the conduct of Bouteflika's campaign, the evolution of the FLN's internal crisis, the openly partisan intervention in the judicial system, the position of economic and religious lobbies, and international reactions to the election represented unmistakable signals of the changes taking place (for more on the elections and on the Algerian *pouvoir*, see the chapter by Gideon Gera in this volume).

Along with these positive points, the presidential election of April 2004 also highlighted the MRN's inability to assume a more central role in Algerian political life. The fact that Abdallah Djaballah obtained a mere 5 percent of the votes meant that the moderate brand of Islam he represented had suffered a defeat. The continuing strength of radical Islamism was reflected by the fact that a significant portion of Islamist sympathizers did not accept some of Djaballah's compromises, such as his fashioning of a tactical alliance with the secular Berberist Rally for Culture and Democracy (RCD). Furthermore, even if the MRN did achieve national recognition, its support was concentrated mainly in the eastern part of the country, in Skikda, Djaballah's native city.

With a potential electoral base of approximately four million voters (the number of people who voted for the FIS, plus Ennahda and HAMAS, in 1990–91), the Islamist current is sorely underrepresented throughout the various levels of Algerian political institutions. To be sure, the legal Islamist parties' inability to mobilize their potential supporters was paralleled by a similar difficulty among other Algerian political parties. An opinion poll conducted in April 2002 aptly illustrated this point. When asked which party they thought could solve Algeria's problems, 48.8 percent responded that

Table 6.1.

Comparing Electoral Results of Islamist and Nationalist Parties.

	1990	1991	1991	1997	1997	1997	1999	2002	2002	2002	2004
	Mun. (% Votes)	Dept. (% Votes)	Leg. (Seats/% Votes)	Leg. (Seats)	Dept. (Seats)	Mun. (Seats)	Pres. (% Votes)	Leg. (Seats)	Dept. (Seats)	Mun. (Seats)	Pres. (% Votes)
FLN	28.13	31.4	16/23.0	64	373	2,864	73.79	199	798	6,680	85.0
FIS	57.44	57.44	188/47.26	–	–	–	–	–	–	–	–
RND				155	986	7,242		47	336	171	
MSP				69	260	890		38	184	19	
MRN				*	*	*		43	374	39	4.84
Ennahda				34	128	290		0			
Wafa							12%**				

Comparing the Legislative Elections of 1997 and 2002 in Algeria

	1997	1997	2002	2002	Difference
	Votes(%)	Seats	Votes(%)	Seats	
RND	33.7	155	8.2	47	-108
MSP	14.8	69	7.0	38	-38
FLN	14.3	64	35.3	199	135
Ennahda	8.7	34	0.7	1	-33
FFS	5.0	19	–	–	–
RCD	4.2	19	–	–	–
Independents	4.4	11	4.9	30	19
PT	1.9	4	3.3	21	17
MRN	–	–	9.5	43	–
FNA	–	–	1.5	8	–
PRP	0.6	3	0.8	0	-3
UDL	0.5	1	0.6	0	-1
PSL	0.4	1	–	–	–
MEN	-0.2	1	–		

Source: Journal Officiel de la République Algérienne 40 (11 June 1997) and 43 (23 June 2002).
*MRN did not yet exist.
**The government has until this date refused to legalize Wafa.
Note: Mun.: municipal; Dept.: departmental; Leg.: legislative; Pres.: presidential; FLN: Front de Libération Nationale (National Liberation Front); FIS: Front Islamique du Salut (Islamic Salvation Front); RND: Rassemblement National Pour la Démocratie (Democratic National Rally); MRN: Mouvement pour la Réforme Nationale (National Reform Movement); MSP: Mouvement Social pour la Paix (Movement for a Peaceful Society); FFS: Front des Forces Socialistes (Socialist Forces Front); RCD: Rassemblement pour la Culture et la Démocratie (Rally for Culture and Democracy); PT: Parti des Travailleurs (Workers' Party); MRN: Mouvement pour la Réforme Nationale (National Reform Movement); FNA Front National Algérien (Algerian National Front); PRP: Parti Populaire Républicain (Republican Popular Party); UDL: Union Démocratique Libérale (Liberal Democratic Union); PSL: Parti Social-Libéral (Social-Liberal Party); MEN: Mouvement pour l'Entente Nationale (Movement for National Harmony).

none of them could do so. This percentage was even higher among young people between ages eighteen and thirty-four: 52.65 percent. The MSP was mentioned by 4.9 percent of those sampled, of which 67.8 percent were between ages eighteen and thirty-four, whereas Ennahda gathered only 1.3 percent (66.5 percent of whom were between ages eighteen and thirty-four). Less than 1 percent of those polled designated the FIS or the Wafa (which has yet to be legalized) as able to solve Algeria's problems.[30]

The Post-conflict FIS

The Islamic Salvation Front was officially dissolved in March 1992. However, it never lost its centrality in the national debate, whether regarding the legitimacy of violence and terrorism or its legitimacy as a political force, this in spite of, or perhaps even owing to, the fact that the FIS was always closer to being a protest movement than a genuine political party. It never had a clear-cut program of action on national problems but only general principles, the specific policy implications of which were unclear.[31] Furthermore, it was seriously divided internally between radicals and moderates, whose views differed sharply over what policies and courses of action to adopt. More than a decade of violence deeply polarized its sympathizers, strengthened radical forces within the FIS, and propagated a number of independent, militant armed groups operating outside of its control. The front splintered into a multitude of armed bands, obeying their own logic and committing barbaric acts against innocent civilians, policemen, and security forces and their families.

In 1999, the banned FIS took its first political position by calling upon its militants to vote in favor of Ahmed Taleb Ibrahimi in the presidential election.[32] This was the first step toward a political comeback. FIS's return was predicated upon the renunciation of two key demands that it had made at the peak of its success: the establishment of a never-defined Islamic state and the definition of Western democracy as *kufr* (blasphemy). The FIS took advantage of the tactical change in the government's policy, which had "passed from exclusion-eradication to negotiation-integration."[33] Nevertheless, FIS's charismatic leaders were closely watched and their actions restrained. Thus Ali Benhadj was arrested and interrogated by the police forces in September 2003 because he was preparing a press conference.[34] Before that he had met with Ali Benhadjar and Madani Mezrag, of the LIDD[35] and AIS, respectively. Internally, Madani and Benhadj's fundamental objective was to prevent the leaders, such as Madani Lazreg and Mustapha Kartali, who had negotiated the truce with the ANP in 1997, from gaining the upper hand.

Meanwhile, in the midst of Bouteflika's first term, in August 2002, a minority, dissident group from the FIS met at the Belgian German border. Dubbed the Congress Abdelkader Hachani, after the former FIS leader assassinated in Algiers in November 1999, the gathering illustrated the complex situation that has long characterized the FIS and its legacy. Rather than unifying the FIS, it accentuated the divergences between leaders of the interior (those who remained inside Algeria) and those based outside (mirroring, ironically, the FLN's historic meeting in Soummam), such as Rabah Kebir, who lived in exile in Germany until 2006. The conflict revolved around the question of legitimacy, namely, who was the true heir of the historic FIS.[36] Attempts at the congress to create a single authority and designate a spokesman for the party failed. Despite the dissolution of two groups that represented the FIS abroad in the early 1990s, the Parliamentary Delegation Overseas and the Council of Coordination,[37] there continued to be two competing groups, the new provisional committee resulting from the congress in Belgium and the *Instance Exécutive du FIS à l'Étranger* (IEFE), the executive authority directed by the Bonn-based Rabah Kebir. In addition, the rift between the historic and military leaders widened. On one side, veteran FIS figures Abdelkader Boukhamkham and Madani Mezrag constituted a base of support for the IEFE's Kebir. On the other side, fellow FIS veteran leaders Kamel Guemazi and Ali Djeddi supported the alliance between the *jaz'ara* and Salafist trends. In addition, the previous primacy of the interior over the exterior was now contested. Following the arrest of Abassi Madani and Ali Benhadj in late June 1991, the Congress of Fidelity (held in July 1991 in the eastern city of Batna) had designated them as the supreme source of legitimacy. Rabah Kebir and his two lieutenants, Abdelkrim Ghemmati and Abdelkrim Ould Adda (Brussels), backed by Abdelkader Boukhamkham and Madani Mazrag (Algeria), now rejected this designation. They felt that Madani's years in prison and, later, under house arrest prevented him from making any sound political judgments. Both Kamel Guemazi and Ali Djeddi recognized "the primacy of the interior over the exterior" but criticized Abassi Madani; they emphasized the collegial structure of the decision making, and designated the Sant'Egidio initiative as the ultimate political reference.[38]

Beyond all these differences and divisions, FIS leaders, with the exception of Rabah Kebir, consistently refrained from defining the movement's own share of responsibility for the country's continuing crisis. Apart from Kebir, none of the leaders in Algeria or in exile acknowledged the incapacity of the party's political leadership to prevent and contain, let alone combat, the degeneration into wanton terrorism. This incapacity was aggravated by the internationalist dimension, involving jihadist movements whose ranks included Islamists from Afghanistan, Bosnia, and Chechnya. This added dimension weakened the position of Algerian Islamists, predicated, as it was, upon their claim of "defending the [electoral] victory obtained in 1991" while strengthening, particularly after the September 11 attacks, the credibility of the government's longstanding insistence that the armed opposition groups were part and parcel of the internationalist Islamist movement's campaign of destabilization and terror.

Given the FLN's decisive comeback, it is interesting to note the common features shared by the historic FLN, which conducted the war of national liberation, and the Islamist movement, as incarnated in the FIS. In terms of psychological outlook and political culture, one can observe that both tend to reject the "foreigner." Historical references, conspiracy theories, and the sanctification of sovereignty peppered the FLN's discourse, whereas the FIS position refers to the binary division of the world according to Islamist radical thinking (believers/unbelievers; *dar al-Islam/dar al-harb*). At the internal level, both employed a populist discourse based on nationalism, authenticity, and reconciliation for the FLN, and radical change, spiritual salvation, and reconciliation for the FIS.

On the structural level, the FIS was organizationally modeled on the FLN under Chadli Benjedid's reign.[39] Also a "front," the FIS was endowed with a congress, which never met, a *majlis al-shura* (consultative council) instead of a central committee, and an executive committee, the counterpart of a political bureau. Abassi Madani, the president of the FIS, was himself a known former FLN cadre. He was even in the National Assembly that voted on May 29, 1984, in favor of the controversial Family Code.[40] This also explains why Chadli was denounced as a *taghut* (tyrant) but not a heretic. In sum, "the success of the FIS (to the extent that one can speak of success at this point) [has been] based on its declared determination to reproduce the FLN, its institutional system, its social compromise, but without the corruption, the arbitrary rule and the incompetence of Chadli's regime."[41]

Conclusion

The great fourteenth-century Maghribi sociologist Abdul Rahman Ibn Khaldun suggested that the stability of a regime depended upon a combination of three factors. First, the ruling group must be cohesive. Second, they must be able to link interests with those of powerful elements in society. Third, that alliance of interests must be expressed in a political idea that makes the power of the rulers legitimate in the eyes of at least a significant part of the society.

In the Algerian case, multiparty politics, terrorism, economic crisis, and reforms have widely contributed to a weakening of the ruling authorities' cohesion, a deepening of social and political schisms, and the aggravation of differences at the pinnacle of power. These schisms are not new; in fact, they date back to the period of the war of independence.[42] However, the last decade has revealed the unmistakable fissures within the Algerian body politic that hitherto had been hidden.

Still, the measures taken to address Algeria's underlying problems did not result in underlying structural changes. For instance, economic liberalization measures did not presuppose only the end of governmental control but also that of the unofficial monopolies held by various interest groups. This, of course, did not happen. With respect to security issues, the management of the FIS question and the counterterrorism campaign had never been part of a policy reached through overall consensus. The interruption of the electoral process in January 1992 had been a serious break with established principles. Ever since Houari Boumediene's military coup d'état in June 1965, the ANP had avoided intervening directly in the political scene, which remained the prerogative of the "visible power." Now the army appeared to be seeking a return to this modus operandi. Only in recent years, after sustained polices of repression and eradication, had a significant portion of the decision makers chosen to add a reconciliation dimension to their policies, marking the beginning of a new, albeit controversial, dynamic involving further divisions and concessions.

The long years of FLN rule had been based on linking together the power of various interests in society. The FLN had encompassed portions of all of Algeria's political and social tendencies, from Ba'thists to Islamists, from liberals to conservatives, capitalists to socialists. Consequently, governing was done through a balancing of power, through which compromises were made in conjunction with other compromises and trade-offs, while some tendencies joined forces against others. Thus Islamists were encouraged in their opposition to Berberists at the universities; Chadli Benjedid's economic program was a response to liberals by putting an end to Boumediene's socialist projects; and conservatives were offered the Family Code. The ultimate goal was the preservation of the status quo acceptable to all forces.

This system has not really changed in the current era of multiparty politics. The power in place, whatever its tendency, relied on Islamists and conciliators through coalitions with the MSP, Ennahda, and the Parti pour le

Renouveau Algérien (PRA). At the same time, it preserved the support of the eradicateurs by integrating the RCD, with Khalida (Messaoudi) Toumi[43] as a symbol.

The current regime's most difficult task has been achieving legitimacy in the eyes of Algerian society. The outcome of the 2004 presidential election suggests that the Islamist current will continue to play a central role in political life, especially after the referendum on the National Reconciliation charter in September 2005. Inside the government, the Islamist current provides a restraining influence against radical secularists. Outside the government, but integrated in the legal political life, the Islamist current confirms the ongoing evolution of Algeria's political scene. Indeed, the present distribution of roles shows a situation in which a "doctrinaire" political party can still play a political role. As for the illegal Islamist current, it constitutes a pole against which all the opponents of violence can be mobilized. For the Algerian regime, so-called residual terrorism still fulfills a political function: legitimizing the restrictions imposed in the framework of the state of emergency and serving as a deterrent against Islamists who would be tempted to follow in the FIS footsteps.

Notes

1. In Morocco and Tunisia, the main actors of the nationalist movement came from the elites and incipient middle classes.

2. Yahia H. Zoubir, "Resilient Authoritarianism, Uncertain Democratization, and Jihadism in Algeria," in *Democratic Development and Political Terrorism: The Global Perspective*, edited by Bill Crotty (Boston: Northeastern University Press, 2005), 280–300.

3. For information on the political and military confrontation between the Islamist movement and the state during the bitter years of civil war in the 1990s, see William B. Quandt, *Between Ballots and Bullets: Algeria's Transition from Authoritarianism* (Washington, D.C.: Brookings Institution Press, 1998); Michael Willis, *The Islamist Challenge in Algeria: A Political History* (New York: New York University Press, 1999); Luis Martinez, *The Algerian Civil War 1990–1998* (New York: Columbia University Press, 2000); Hugh Roberts, *The Battlefield, Algeria 1988–2002: Studies in a Broken Polity* (London: Verso, 2003).

4. Capital punishment was reduced to twelve years' imprisonment, and life imprisonment was reduced to eight years. Yahia H. Zoubir and Louisa Aït Hamadouche, "Penal Reform in Algeria," in *Providing Security for People: Enhancing Security through Police, Justice and Intelligence Reform in Africa*, edited by Christopher Ferguson and Jeffrey Isima, 75–84 (London: Global Facilitation Network for Security Sector Reform, 2004).

5. See Amnesty International, "Algeria: President calls referendum to obliterate crimes of the past" http://www.amnestyusa.org/countries/algeria/document.do?id=ENGMDE280102005.

6. The Algerian government concluded in September 1997 the still-secret agreement with the Madani Mezrag's Islamic Salvation Army (AIS)

7. Kader Hannachi, "Une amnistie générale des éléments du GSPC ne serait pas à l'ordre du jour," *Le Quotidien d'Oran*, April 27, 2004; *Al-Jazeera TV*, April 26, 2004.

8. Interview with Farouk Ksentini, chairman of Human Rights Commission, "L'impunité est contraire à la morale et à la loi," *El Watan*, April 27, 2004. http://www.elwatan.com.

9. Speech of Abdelaziz Bouteflika, May 8, 2004, *El Watan*, May 10, 2004. http://www.elwatan.com.

10. Hassane Zerrouky, "Islamisme: Combien sont-ils encore au maquis?" *Le Matin*, November 21, 2001, http://www.lematin-dz (the newspaper was shut down in 2004).

11. *Strategic Comments* 9, no. 6 (August 2003), International Institute of Strategic Studies, London.

12. See Mohamed Mokeddem, *Les Afghans algériens: De la Djamaâ à la Qa'îda* (Algiers: Editions ANEP, 2002).

13. Abu Hamza and Abu Qutada were active in the UK and well known in the Muslim world.

14. The media generally refer to two cases. The first was that of Ahmed Ressam, an Algerian national, arrested on the U.S.-Canadian border in mid-December 1999. Ressam was planning an attack on Los Angeles International Airport on December 31, 1999. A junior member of the FIS, he had left Algeria in 1992, fleeing to Europe and then Canada, where he was indoctrinated by Islamist circles in Montreal and sent to Afghanistan. Djamel Beghal, a French citizen of Algerian descent, was arrested in France in July 2001 upon his return from Afghanistan. During his interrogation, Beghal confessed to having coordinated an al-Qa'ida cell in the Paris region with the aim of blowing up the U.S. embassy there.

15. Yahia H. Zoubir, "Algeria and US Interests: Containing Radical Islamism and Promoting Democracy," *Middle East Policy* 9, no. 1 (March 2002): 64–81.

16. Amin Saikal and Albrecht Schnabel, eds., *Democratization in the Middle East-Experiences, Struggles, Challenges* (New York: United Nations University Press, 2003), 2.

17. On the notion of clans in the Algerian political system, see Abdelkader Yefsah, *La Question du pouvoir en Algérie*, 2nd ed. (Algiers: ENAP, 1991), esp. 447 ff. In 1995, former prime minister Mouloud Hamrouche insisted that the Algerian political system is based not on the power of one clan but on the exercise of power by a multitude of clans. "Les clans, le pouvoir, l'armée et la crise," interview with Mouloud Hamrouche, *La Nation* (Algiers), August 8–14, 1995.

18. The *décideurs* are the "real power," that is, a small number of generals and powerful government civilian figures, who nominate the "formal power" (president, ministers . . .) and who make the most important decisions.

19. See Mohamed Farid Azzi, "Maghrebi Youth: Between Alienation and Integration," in *North Africa in Transition: State, Society, and Economic Transformation in the 1990s*, edited by Yahia H. Zoubir, 109–26 (Gainesville: University Press of Florida, 1999). For possible psychological and cultural explanations of the Islamists' success, see Liess Boukra, *Algérie: La Terreur sacrée* (Lausanne: Favre, 2002). For a discussion of the ex-

treme diversity of the Islamists' profiles, see Yahia H. Zoubir, "State, Civil Society and the Question of Radical Islamism in Algeria," in *Islamic Fundamentalism*, edited by Ahmad Moussalli, 123–67 (Reading: Ithaca Press, 1998).

20. On this point, see Dilali Hadjadj, "Algeria: A Future Hijacked by Corruption," *Mediterranean Politics* 12, no. 2 (July 2007): 263–77.

21. Lahouari Addi, "Les partis politiques en Algérie et la crise du régime des 'grands électeurs,'" *Le Quotidien d'Oran*, October 12–15, 2003, http://www.quotidien-oran.com/.

22. Hamou Amirouche, "Algeria's Islamist Revolution: The People Versus Democracy?" *Middle East Policy* 5, no. 1 (January 1998), Middle East Policy Council Web site, http://www.mepc.org/journal_vol5/9801_amirouche.asp.

23. Ali Yahia Abdenour is president of the human rights organization, LADDH. Rachid Benyellès is a retired general and former minister. Hocine Aït Ahmed is one of the historic figures of the Algerian revolution, undisputed leader of the Front des Forces Socialistes (FFS) since 1963, and its candidate in the 1999 presidential election.

24. This expression is from Bertrand Badie, cited in Addi, "Partis politiques en Algérie."

25. On Islamist parties in Algeria, see Yahia H. Zoubir, "Islamist Political Parties in Algeria," *Middle East Affairs Journal* 3, nos. 1 and 2 (Winter/Spring 1997–98): 95–122. The authorities compelled HAMAS to change its name to conform to the constitution, which forbids the formation of political parties on the basis of religious, cultural, or linguistic considerations. See Youcef Bouandel and Yahia H. Zoubir, "The Legislative Election of June 1997 and the Future of the Democratic Transition in Algeria," *Representation-Journal of Representative Democracy* 35, nos. 2 and 3 (Spring/Autumn 1998): 168–74.

26. Paul A. Silverstein, *Algeria in France* (Bloomington: Indiana University Press, 2004).

27. Yahia H. Zoubir, "The Algerian Political Crisis: Origins and Prospects for Democracy," *Journal of North African Studies* 3, no. 1 (Spring 1998): 75–100.

28. See Lamari's interview in the Egyptian newspaper *Al-Ahram*, reproduced and commented in Hassane Zerrouky, "Dans une interview à Al Ahram-Lamari répond à Bouteflika, *Le Matin*, June 18, 2003 http://www.lematin-dz (the newspaper was shut down in 2004). Lamari declared, "Je répète que nous saluons tout choix du peuple, même si c'est Abdallah Djaballah, le leader d'El Islah, à condition qu'il respecte les règles du jeu." (I repeat that we respect any choice by the people even if it's Abdallah Djaballah, leader of El Islah, on the condition that he respect the rules of the game.)

29. In October 2003, the authors attended an international conference whose theme was "Qu'est-ce que la Défense Nationale?" (What Is National Defense?). The conference, held in Algiers, was organized by the Algerian parliament's National Defense Commission. Many high-ranking officers, including Maj. Gen. Mohamed Touati, attended the meetings and debated issues concerning the future role of the ANP in the political system.

30. These results were not all that surprising since two years before, another opinion poll had revealed the same phenomenon: 42 percent of those polled thought that no politician could resolve the Algerian crisis. *Algeria Interface*, April 16, 2002.

31. Yahia H. Zoubir, "Stalled Democratization of an Authoritarian Regime: The Case of Algeria," *Democratization* 2, no. 2 (1994–95): 109–39.

32. Ahmed Taleb Ibrahimi was foreign minister and the advisor to former Algerian president Chadli Bendjedid. His position is close to that of the Islamists. He tried in vain to get his party, Wafah, to be approved by the authorities.

33. "L'Algérie après la concorde nationale," *Dossier Maghreb*, Radio broadcasting Le Monde comme il va (Radio Alternantes FM), http://perso.orange.fr/libertaire/archive/2000/226-mar/algerie.htm. Accessed December 25, 2004.

34. Mohamed Issami, "Algérie: Abassi et Benhadj reprennent leur activisme," *Algeria Interface*, September 11, 2003 (site no longer exists). Benhadj has been imprisoned again in 2005 for allegedly inspiring the execution of two Algerian diplomats kidnapped in Iraq by a terrorist group.

35. A member of the *jaz'ara* tendency, Ali Benhadjar founded the LIDD in 1997 and then joined FIDA, the armed wing of the *jaz' ara*. The FIDA targeted politicians and journalists. Its members allegedly assassinated the head of the labor union, Abdelhak Benhamouda. The LIDD accepted the reconciliation law.

36. Mustapha Bey, "Made: Divided and War of Legitimacy," *Algeria Interface*, September 18, 2002.

37. Respectively, the DPFE, directed by Anouar Haddam and operating from the United States, and CCFIS, a gathering in favor of Ahmed Zaoui, a group of Algerianists of Geneva and the DPFE. In late 2006, Anouar Haddam announced in Washington the creation of a new party. He reiterated the existence of such movement "for freedom and democracy" on February 8, 2007, during a seminar on the Maghrib held in Washington, D.C., in which Yahia Zoubir participated.

38. Kamel Guemazi, Ali Djeddi, Abdelkader Boukhamkham, and Abdelkader Omar were the key figures behind the initiative.

39. The multiparty system was established under his presidency, independent Algeria's third. He is accused by his detractors of having allowed the FIS to gain prominence in order to assure his staying in power.

40. The Family Code is an amalgam of religious, traditional, conservative, and patriarchal values. Some of its articles are clearly contrary to women's rights. Nearly all FLN-dominated governments promised to reform the Code, but the promise was forgotten once the electoral campaign was over. Following his reelection, Bouteflika sought to carry out a reform of the Family Code, but ultimately the changes made were only cosmetic.

41. Amirouche, "Algeria's Islamist Revolution."

42. Strategic issues were raised but never resolved: primacy of civilian politics over the military, pluralism, and identity issues (e.g., the Kabyle question).

43. Khalida Toumi joined the government after years of militant opposition against the regime. She is also known for her fight in favor of women's rights. However, the split with her original party (RCD) isolated her from her traditional environment and made her a member of the establishment. On her biography, see Yahia H. Zoubir, "Khalida (Messaoudi) Toumi," in *Encyclopedia of the Modern Middle East and North Africa*, vol. 4, edited by Philip Mattar, 2195 (New York: Macmillan, 2004).

7

From Hasan II to Muhammad VI

Plus Ça Change?

DANIEL ZISENWINE

The smooth accession of Morocco's King Muhammad VI to the throne in July 1999, following the death of his father, Hasan II, was grounded in the protocols and customs of the Moroccan monarchy. These traditional rites of passage facilitated the transition of power in the kingdom, alleviating previous concerns that it would be marked by instability and uncertainty, leading even to the monarchy's collapse. Within hours of his father's death, Muhammad somberly announced the news in a nationally televised address and assumed his official responsibilities and duties as Morocco's new king. He later received the traditional oath of allegiance (*bay'a*) from the kingdom's religious leadership, which recognized his position as the "Commander of the Faithful" (*amir al-mu'minin*), the spiritual and political leader of Moroccan's Muslims.

The new king's first task was to meet with world leaders who traveled to Rabat in order to participate in the late King Hasan's funeral. Apart from the ceremonial aspects, the new king's discussions focused on issues that occupied a prominent place on Morocco's diplomatic agenda, such as the future of the western Sahara and its relations with neighboring Algeria. It was evident that a new era in Morocco's history had begun. Even as the kingdom mourned King Hasan's death, the public by and large optimistically embraced the country's new leader.[1]

King Muhammad was well aware of the high expectations that accompanied his rise to the throne both at home and abroad. Many Moroccans had known no other leader than the late King Hasan, whose reign extended over thirty-eight years.[2] They now pinned their hopes on the new, young monarch. His numerous statements and interviews as crown prince seemed to indicate that he would promote a political agenda centered on strengthening democracy and pluralism. They also hoped that he would aggressively confront the country's chronic economic problems and ameliorate the living conditions of millions of poverty-stricken Moroccans (see the chapter by Paul Rivlin in this volume). Accompanying their hopes were expectations that the new king would introduce a more open style of leadership, appropriate for the twenty-first century, and discard the monarchy's traditional opacity and secrecy. Indeed, the new king's initial actions suggested that he was intent on pursuing such a course, leading some Moroccans to proclaim that their country was on the threshold of sweeping changes.[3]

During his first months on the throne, Muhammad repeatedly declared his intent to transform Morocco's political system and transcend traditional and structural barriers that hindered the move toward greater democracy. Over time, he even instigated an unprecedented examination of the *années de plomb* (lit. "years of lead"), the initial decades of Hasan's reign characterized by the harsh repression of political dissidents. But despite the king's declared intentions, and despite a number of bold initiatives, the country's historical legacy remains largely at odds with the concept of greater democracy and genuine political pluralism and continues to cast its shadow over political life. The monarchy's position in society remains omnipotent and its control of the political system nearly absolute. To be sure, this system has been refashioned under Muhammad, but the monarchy remains the motor of Moroccan politics. The country's parliamentary system, which had begun its own reform process during the later years of Hasan's rule, still lags behind the royal palace's authority and has not emerged as an alternative center of substantial political activity. Moreover, various components of Muhammad's political and economic reforms were actually initiated during his predecessor's reign, suggesting that the new king's course may be far less revolutionary than the perceptions that surrounded them. Muhammad's initiatives may therefore be more about continuity than change and might be viewed more as "old wine in new bottles" rather than a fundamental transformation of Moroccan politics.

Nevertheless, in the eight years since Muhammad's accession, Morocco has experienced considerable political change. Many facets of its domestic political landscape have been significantly altered and are now a far cry from the past. Political acts and deeds that were once unthinkable have now become standard and routine. Many taboos that previously restricted political activity have been lifted. Political figures have become more outspoken in their statements and less timid in their general conduct. New political forces and personalities have come to the fore, and many of the old guard were removed from their powerful posts and receded from the public spotlight. The monarchy has adopted a more open style in its day-to-day activities and has become more accessible to the general public. At the same time, Morocco has had to face unexpected challenges, such as Islamist-related terrorism. Economic reforms have been introduced and promoted at a very slow pace, and economic conditions remain difficult for millions of Muhammad's subjects. Progress in other areas has also been spotty. Moreover, a number of potentially explosive social and political questions still await resolution. For example, although Morocco's highly contested personal status code has been significantly revised (see below), the impact of its practical implementation on Moroccan society and the status of women remains unclear. Similar uncertainties surround debates concerning reforming the country's political system.

This essay will address Muhammad's first eight years on the throne, elucidate the diverse and often contradictory tracks on which he has proceeded, and assess the impact of his policies on Moroccan political life. In situating recent domestic developments in a broader context, I will also discuss whether they indeed mark a departure from earlier political practices, or are primarily a continuation of the slow-paced reform process initiated by the king's father. Teasing out the answers to these questions should help clarify the Moroccan government's current position regarding the process of democratization and liberalization, and the course it is likely to pursue during the next decade.

King Muhammad's Style of Leadership

The beginning of King Muhammad's reign was shrouded in uncertainty regarding the young monarch's ability to promote a reformist political agenda while maintaining social and political control over a complex polity. Although many of Muhammad's political opinions and inclinations were easily discernable, it was unclear whether his initial personal gestures were a harbinger of meaningful changes in the kingdom's political culture or merely cosmetic alterations of traditional royal policies. In the realm of ceremonial pomp and circumstance, it was clear that new king recoiled from the more ostentatious aspects of Moroccan court life, such as his preference for handshakes when meeting his subjects rather than having his hand kissed, according to time-honored custom, and the closing of the royal harem. Beyond such symbolic gestures, the king asserted the need to introduce a "new concept of authority" that would champion ideals of fairness, transparency, and the rule of law in government affairs. But such statements could not be translated into political reality if the new king lacked his own source of legitimacy. Indeed, the skepticism regarding Muhammad's aptitude and ability to shepherd Morocco into a new era compounded the king's need to seek his own imprint on Moroccan politics.

Muhammad's initial activities underscored his intentions. Seeking to shake off the lethargy that had surrounded the palace during Hasan's final years, Muhammad sought to project an image of an energetic, hands-on leader. Accordingly, the king conducted a series of high-profile visits to various parts of the country, including remote provinces that his father had avoided for years, fearing vocal opposition. In each visit, the assembled crowds enthusiastically embraced the new monarch, who would often personally approach and speak with them rather than speed by in a motorcade. The welcoming throngs dubbed Muhammad the "king of the poor," a king who appeared committed to his people's personal welfare. His manner contrasted sharply with that of his late father, whose authoritarian style instilled his subjects with fear and awe.

It seemed that most Moroccans found Muhammad's image of a concerned, caring, and involved monarch appealing. The months following Muhammad's accession were a period of widespread ferment and excitement, as Moroccans became acquainted with the new king's style and noted the removal of many barriers that in the past had overshadowed public life. Seeking to alter the monarchy's opaque image, Muhammad appointed the first-ever spokesperson for the royal palace, Hassan Aourid, who was one of Muhammad's close associates and was assigned to help explain the new king's policies to both domestic and foreign audiences. It was expected that these changes would be complemented by a strengthening of Morocco's parliament.[4]

A further indication of the king's new approach was the unprecedented publicity that accompanied his 2002 marriage. Traditionally, all aspects of the Moroccan royal family's private lives have been kept far from the public's scrutiny. Indeed, when King Hasan passed away, his wife, who had never been seen in public and was hardly ever even mentioned by name, did not publicly participate in the rites of burial and mourning. By contrast, Muhammad's bride, Salma Bennani, appeared in public and held several interviews with the media, along with her husband. These interviews exposed the royal couple's personal life in a manner that was previously unthinkable. She has since taken an active public role and maintains a relatively high profile. Commentators also noted the king's decision to marry an urban woman (from Fez) instead of solidifying political alliances by marrying the daughter of a Berber tribal leader, the traditional Solomonic-like practice.[5]

But the king did not limit his initial actions to highly publicized, symbolically laden public activities and set out to leave his imprint on a host of domestic political and social questions that were considered "sensitive" during Hasan's reign. These included strengthening the representative political system and the parliament's role in public life and revisiting the legal status of women. Doing so was a delicate and problematic undertaking, for it threatened to expose the deep fissures and cleavages within Moroccan society. At times, these fissures even appeared to endanger the country's stability and caused the reform-minded king to pause and reevaluate the impact of his reforms on social and political structures. These periodic pauses were perplexing to many Moroccans, especially during moments of crisis when the public anxiously waited to hear the king's pronouncements on the matters at stake. Consequently, some of the early doubts concerning Muhammad's ability to skillfully lead Morocco into a new era resurfaced.

Such was the case, for example, in the aftermath of the Islamist terrorist attacks in Casablanca on May 16, 2003. The attacks shocked the Moroccan populace, which quickly turned to the king, looking for guidance and reassurance. But Morocco's previously outspoken and visible monarch was curiously absent for weeks from the ensuing debate about the attacks and their impact on Moroccan society. Apart from the king's initial visit to the attacked sites, there were no official statements concerning these events. It seemed that Muhammad and his advisers were uncertain about how to respond. They also may have been waiting to gauge the public's views regarding the appropriate measures to be adopted by the government. Although the government hastily enacted emergency legislation aimed at combating terrorist activity, and cracked down heavily on the perpetrators, supporting networks, and suspected sympathizers, it initially refrained from further reform measures. Indeed, it seemed as if the entire political system was overshadowed by the attacks and their aftermath.[6]

Eventually, however, the king gathered himself together and asserted anew his commitment to shepherding his country into a new political era. In an October 2003 speech to parliament, Muhammad announced a widespread change in Morocco's family law, which had long been a contested topic. Earlier attempts to introduce changes in Morocco's family law had been vehemently opposed by Islamist and other socially conservative groups and thus shelved. Muhammad's decision to adopt the new law was clearly part of his overall response to the May 16 attacks, as he sought to put the Islamist opposition, both legal and extralegal, in its place. The timing was propitious: Most of these groups and their leaders, fearful of state-sponsored repression in the wake of the attacks, were especially careful to toe the line, declaring the king's decision to adopt a new family code a sound interpretation of religious law. Other segments of society warmly welcomed it.

Emboldened by the public response, the king now appeared to be far more determined to confront the burning questions on Morocco's political agenda. But Muhammad's subsequent policies and deeds did not always meet expectations either at home or abroad, raising anew the question, to what degree was the new king really departing from the practices of his predecessors, particularly his father?

Reforming the Political System

Already in 1996, King Hasan had initiated reforms in Morocco's parliamentary system as he sought to improve Morocco's image internationally and prepare the ground for an orderly transition of power to his son. They included the establishment of a bicameral parliament, in which the lower house (Chamber of Deputies) would be elected by a direct ballot for five years, a departure from the previous unicameral parliament in which only two-thirds of the members were elected by direct ballot. The newly established upper chamber (Chamber of Counselors) would be chosen by special bodies drawn from local and regional councils, professional associations, and trade unions. Members would be elected for nine years, with one-third of them to be chosen every three years. The upper house would be able to propose legislation and also dissolve the government with a two-thirds vote.

However, these structural changes did not significantly alter the nature of Morocco's political system, as Hasan and the monarchy remained the dominant force. Moreover, the 1997 parliamentary elections were plagued by doubts surrounding the vote's transparency and fairness. Opposition parties raised numerous complaints of fraud and other abuses, demonstrating anew that achieving genuine democracy in Morocco was to be an arduous road.

The next step in Hasan's political reforms was the formation of an *alternance* government, which he had been promoting for a number of years. After a long period of negotiations, Hasan was able in March 1998 to establish a cabinet based on veteran, mostly left-of-center opposition parties, led by Abderrahman Youssoufi of the Union Socialiste des Forces Populaires (USFP). Greeted with much fanfare, the new government was expected to forcefully address the country's dire socioeconomic situation while repositioning the cabinet's role in the governing of the country. The idea behind the formation of an *alternance* government was to increase the influence of political parties within Morocco's power structure and promote governmental responsibility. Such a development had the potential for a kind of power sharing between the monarchy and the government that would, by definition, modify the monarchy's hegemony over political life. Conversely, the new government's composition affected Morocco's complex power relations between state and society. The participation of opposition parties in the government compelled other players in the political arena to redefine their own often ambivalent positions toward official policies and the political establishment.[7] This was particularly relevant to Islamist groups, which were forced to reconsider their stated preference to refrain from participation in public life. Although some, such as Harakat al-Adl wal-Ihsan (Justice and Spirituality movement), remained outside the formal political system, others, under the rubric of the Party of Justice and Development (PJD), felt compelled to play according to the *makhzen*'s[8] rules (see Michael J. Willis's chapter in this volume).

But Youssoufi's government did not live up to expectations, dashing hopes that Morocco would evolve rapidly toward the establishment of a full-fledged constitutional monarchy. The government's economic programs were considered a far cry from the measures required to improve the lives of most Moroccans. By the time of Muhammad's accession in July 1999, Youssoufi's cabinet had lost much of its public luster. Morocco's *alternance* experiment had also affected its political parties. Ironically, joining the government had eroded the historic opposition's ability to offer a viable alternative. The USFP, in particular, was now perceived as a co-opted, weakened movement. The 2002 parliamentary elections thus seemed to come just in time, offering an opportunity to energize political life. Unlike the 1997 vote, these elections were widely perceived as transparent and fair, bereft of glaring incidents of corruption. But the successful voting process could not eclipse the widening fissures within and between the ranks of political parties, and their inability to play an active role in political life. For example, interparty disagreements over technical voting procedures prior to the elections forced the Interior Ministry to intervene. The public seemed to be generally dissatisfied with political parties and did not view them as important agents of potential change. Instead, many Moroccans affiliated themselves with organizations that were not part of the official political system and viewed them as alternative forums for political involvement. These included Islamist groups and various NGOs.[9]

Many observers noted the need to reinvigorate what appeared to be a lethargic government, whose program for political reform had stalled. The 2002 parliamentary elections thus seemed to come just in time. Unlike the 1997 vote, these elections were widely perceived as transparent and fair, bereft of glaring incidents of corruption.

However, the new government formed after the election was in many ways a disappointment. Instead of appointing a party leader as prime minister, as befitting a genuine parliamentary system, Muhammad appointed Driss Jettou, a nonparty technocrat known as a palace loyalist and a skilled administrator.[10] Some observers viewed Jettou's appointment as a potential opening for the business elite to become more involved in policy making. In that sense, the appointment constituted another step in incorporating new social elements into political affairs. On the other hand, one could argue that the appointment demonstrated that the entire *alternance* experiment had been an insignificant aberration in Moroccan political life, which remained centered on the king's personal political calculations.[11] Indeed, Jettou's surprising nomination signified that Muhammad's support for affording greater responsibilities to political parties did not translate into a willingness to loosen his hold over the government. Hence it remained unclear how Morocco's political parties and parliament would ever be able to obtain the necessary "maturity level" if they continued to be sidelined by the palace.

Morocco's political parties initially reacted with consternation to Jettou's appointment. A USFP official noted that the new cabinet did not reflect election results, and raised doubts over the new cabinet's ability to confront Morocco's challenges. The left-leaning PPS (Parti du Progrès et du Socialisme) also expressed its displeasure over the connotations and implications of Jettou's nomination. Questions were raised about the thinking behind Jettou's nomination and the king's new measures. Other parties, such as the center-right Istiqlal, sought to reinforce their influential position within the new government, and were less apprehensive about endorsing Jettou. It was unclear, however, whether the new cabinet would provide these parties with greater political muscle.[12]

The king's policies and statements in other areas also raised questions about the monarchy's role in political life. Muhammad's social initiatives, novel as they were, did not compromise the palace's longstanding grip on political and economic affairs. Indeed, Muhammad did not significantly alter the established balance between the monarchy and the government. In fact, he established a mechanism that endowed the monarchy with even greater responsibility and power. Shortly after his ascent to the throne, for example, Muhammad announced the establishment of the Hasan II Fund for Development, a major philanthropic organization independent of government supervision, which was given the task of alleviating the social and economic plight of Morocco's legions of poor people.[13] This policy was reminiscent of the Moroccan state's heavy involvement in the construction of civil society in the early 1990s and reflected the historical legacy of a co-opted political system.[14]

The Hasan II Development Fund and a number of other permanent royal commissions charged with treating "strategic" issues have emerged as the central conduits of reform in contemporary Morocco, eclipsing parliament, political parties, and other governmental institutions. The outcome has been a hybrid system, in which royal commissions and governmental institutions are charged with similar tasks. There is no clear division of responsibility between these two poles, but the royal commissions have become the agencies in Muhammad's Morocco that make many decisions later endorsed by the government or approved by parliament. In that sense, the essence of Moroccan politics has not changed under Muhammad. Examples of these new commissions include the Royal Institute of Amazigh Culture, established in 2001 to promote Morocco's Amazigh/Berber identity (see Mickael Bensadoun's chapter in this volume) and the Commission on Equity and Reconciliation, which was given the task of investigating previous human rights abuses (see below). Both were widely viewed as palace-controlled mechanisms. Their establishment was frequently accompanied by the co-option of former regime critics through their appointment to important positions. Hence, the likelihood of genuine public debate on the issues at hand became less likely, leading many to speak of the emergence of a neo-*makhzen*, which includes the king and his close advisers. This neo-*makhzen* is in essence a reproduction of monarchical dominance, suggesting again that the king's underlying modus operandi is more similar to that employed by his forebears than the proponents of reform had hoped would be the case.[15]

Human Rights and Press Freedoms

The oscillation between continuity and change has been particularly evident in the realm of civil liberties, human rights and press freedoms, where the regime has been historically vulnerable to international criticism. Improvements in the regime's human rights record, which began in the last decade of Hasan's rule and accelerated after Muhammad's accession, included greater respect for basic civil and political rights and the expansion of freedom of expression and association and were duly noted by human rights organizations.

More recently, the Moroccan authorities have added an additional element to the picture. In an unprecedented undertaking among Arab countries, the authorities opened up a public revisiting of a dark chapter during Hasan's long reign.[16] As in other instances, it was the monarchy, not other political or social forces, that defined the discourse and parameters of a debate concerning a sensitive and potentially explosive topic.[17] In a speech delivered shortly after his rise to power, Muhammad acknowledged the state's responsibility for the disappearance of dissidents, mostly during the 1970s. Muhammad initially established an "arbitration panel" charged with compensating victims or their surviving heirs. By the time the panel ceased to function, in July 2003, it had settled nearly four thousand claims. Critics argued that the panel offered compensation but did not establish a process to seek either justice or the truth. The accompanying publication of testimonies and memoirs recounting these events including prison experiences further fueled the public's interest in the process.

The task of further investigating these abuses was then assigned to a state-created Commission on Equity and Reconciliation (Instance Equité et Reconciliation, or IER) in January 2004. The IER was hailed by the king as "the last step in a process leading to the definitive closure of a thorny issue," and the commission's mandate was described by regime spokesmen as the most serious effort ever by Moroccan authorities to recognize and make amends for past abuses. Besides investigating and recording testimonies, it was charged with continuing the arbitration panel's work of compensating victims, as well as to produce a historical account of repressive acts during Hasan's rule.

Many doubts were raised regarding the commission's likely effectiveness, due to a number of restrictions in its mandate. For starters, critics noted that the IER was not permitted to prosecute individuals charged with human rights violations, this to the dismay of former victims and Moroccan human rights activists. Nor was it able to compel testimony. The commission's work was thus a far cry from similar investigations in other countries, such as South Africa. Former victims raised doubts whether the commission would end Morocco's cycle of repression, pointing to the enfeebled nature of the country's judicial system, which was unlikely to indict suspects, some of whom continued to hold public office. Indeed, Morocco had retained formal continuity between Hasan's abusive regime and the current monarchy, with the commission itself being beholden to the state. Reports on the commission's work avoided any direct criticism of the deceased monarch's policies and conduct, merely acknowledging that bad advisers were responsible for previous misdeeds and misguided Hasan.

Notwithstanding these shortcomings, the IER's establishment was an important development, underscoring the monarchy's stated quest to initiate a "housecleaning process" by confronting earlier dark chapters in Moroccan history and thus permit Morocco to enter a new era. What remains unclear, however, is whether the commission's proceedings will exorcise the ghosts of the past and be the harbinger of a new era where human rights and civil liberties will be the cornerstone of a revised Moroccan polity. Meanwhile, the renewed repression against Islamist dissidents following the Casablanca bombings in 2003 appeared to mark another swing of the pendulum back toward the modus operandi of the past—arbitrary arrests, abuse of human rights, and torture. A hastily enacted tough antiterrorist law led to widespread arrests and harsh sentences imposed on Islamist activists. What was sauce for the goose was not necessarily sauce for the gander.[18]

A closer look at these actions revealed, however, that these heavy-handed policies were in fact already in place prior to the May attacks. Many radical Islamists had been arrested, unauthorized mosques that served as hotbeds of Islamist activities shut down, and radical Islamist publications banned. These measures did not prevent the Casablanca attacks. Nonetheless, the effect of the government's repressive measures on public life was not as deep as some analysts had argued. The aftermath of the attacks did not dramatically change the regime's orientation and intentions.[19]

Another area of uncertainty regarding Morocco's future path was the degree of freedom to be accorded to the press, which had been heavily restricted during much of Hasan's reign. On the one hand, the new atmosphere occasioned by Muhammad's rise to power was reflected in the print media's unprecedented willingness to address sensitive topics. New publications, such as the popular French-language weekly *TelQuel* transformed the media landscape, treating thorny issues that had never before been addressed in the Moroccan media, such as past incidents of human rights abuses, the status of women, or historically charged questions concerning the collaboration of influential Moroccans with the French colonial government during the nationalist struggle for independence.[20] Although Moroccan journalists enjoyed a higher degree of freedom than ever before, important limitations remained. For example, the authorities refused to abolish long-held red lines related to the king's person, the monarchy's legitimacy and opaque inner workings, and the justness of Morocco's claim on the territory of Western Sahara. Journalists and editors who sought to test the continuing validity of these taboos found themselves embroiled in court proceedings and facing economic penalties and even imprisonment.

The focal point for the authorities' firmness in dealing with misbehaving journalists was the longtime gadfly Ali Lmrabet. In April 2005, Lmrabet was banned from exercising his profession for ten years, and fined a hefty sum to boot, following Lmrabet's seemingly sympathetic comments toward Sahrawi refugees in Algerian camps run by the Polisario movement struggling against the imposition of Moroccan sovereignty in the Western Sahara. The ban followed on the heels of his imprisonment in 2002–3 for publishing satirical cartoons of Moroccan officials and for the more serious offense of publishing data on the royal palace's annual budget. Information concerning the inner workings of the monarchy remains tightly classified in Morocco and is a sensitive topic rarely raised in public. Another journalist, Hamid Naimi, was convicted in March 2005 in several libel cases dating back to 1998, lawsuits that had been reactivated in late 2004 after Naimi published an article about the embezzlement of public funds by a number of officials. Concurrently *TelQuel* was reprimanded by the palace after publishing a report about the daily life of Princess Lalla Salma. The magazine was accused of "meddling in the princess's private life" and warned not to publish any information or news about the private life of members of the royal family.

A more serious case involving the royal family's position and freedom of the press emerged in June 2005. Nadia Yassine, a Moroccan Islamist activist and daughter of Justice and Spirituality head Shaykh Abdessalam Yassine, denounced the Moroccan monarchial regime, noting that it did not suit Morocco, and expressed her preference for a republican form of government. A government spokesperson noted that Yassine's statements violated the Moroccan constitution, and that the press code defining the responsibilities of persons who make such statements, those who publish them, and those who distribute them were perfectly clear. Legal proceedings were thus initiated against her and against two journalists for publishing "anti-monarchy statements." Although Moroccan newspapers criticized Yassine's comments, noting that they were a "deliberate provocation," they were closely following the government's behavior in the unfolding case, seeking to gage the government's "red lines" concerning freedom of the press.[21]

These cases generated criticism from international organizations that regularly monitor the degree of press freedom in Morocco.[22] Overall, the seeming resurgence of curbs placed on press freedom, and the difficulty of journalists in transcending taboos and barriers limiting their work indicated again that Muhammad's policies were more in line with the past than his oft-espoused vision for the future.

The Family Code Reform and Its Implications

The vagaries surrounding Muhammad's policies and his vision of Moroccan life in the twenty-first century eventually vanished from at least one highly contentious arena—the long-running debate over the status of women. Here, one could point to exponential changes, which were likely to have a significant long-term impact on Moroccan society. In light of the vehement opposition that had emerged during the 1990s against any change in the status quo, it had initially been far from clear that the new king would be willing to challenge the traditional normative and legal framework underpinning Moroccan family life. Hence the king's decision in autumn 2003 on the side of far-reaching change caught many by surprise.

The status of women has long served as a bone of contention within Moroccan society. Many advocates of sweeping changes in the laws that governed family life and defined the legal status of women based their calls for reform on Morocco's economic situation, pointing to the high rate of illiteracy among women as one of the reasons for Morocco's dire economic straits. At the same time, women's lives had been substantially altered in a number of important areas during the closing decades of the twentieth century, including accelerated urbanization, declining birth rates, changing social norms, and a rising average marriage age.

Notwithstanding the significance of these changes, many obstacles to the fuller integration of women in society remained. Entrenched social attitudes and norms underpinned the legal status of women, as articulated in the existing Moroccan personal status code, the Moudawwana (completed and officially released in 1959), and were in turn shaped by the code. Women and liberal activists, therefore, had long made the Moudawwana the primary target of their agenda. Beginning in the early 1990s, they campaigned in favor of a new code that would redefine the role of women in the country. Over time, the issue became a touchstone of the broader struggle between tradition and change across Moroccan society, with religious clerics and other conservative factions likening any departure from the religious principles that governed the existing law to apostasy. Although secular left-of-center political parties in Morocco such as the USFP expressed support for changing the law, little action was taken apart from palace-initiated cosmetic alterations, demonstrating anew the impotence of the formal parliamentary system.[23]

A renewed effort to fundamentally alter the Moudawwana got under way in 1999. This time the initiative came from reformist elements from within the *alternance* government, which presented a comprehensive plan to advance the status of women in the legal, economic, and social spheres. But widespread protests against the plan gave the authorities pause, and the king shelved the idea. A year later, he appointed a blue-ribbon commission composed of both secular and religious elements to examine the existing law and recommend modifications, in the spirit of *ijtihad* (lit. the interpretation of the Holy Law to promote human welfare, by qualified individuals, on the basis of reason). By spring 2003, the commission had finished its work and tendered two sets of recommendations to the king, one more narrow in scope and one more far-reaching. The choice, as in so much else in Morocco, would be left up to the monarch.

Although it was not immediately evident, the Casablanca bombings apparently resolved whatever remaining doubts Muhammad had. Clearly seeking to counteract the radical Islamist vision with a more modern and tolerant one combining Islamic precepts with modernity, the king presented his comprehensive plan to the opening of parliament on October 10. Three months later, the new family law was enacted. Among its far-reaching provisions, it equalized of the status of men and women as joint heads of their household, removed the guardianship (*wali*) requirement from women upon reaching the age of eighteen, raised the minimum marriage age to eighteen, expanded women's rights in matters of divorce and child custody while limiting men's ability to repudiate their wives according a simple decree (*talaq*), and placed severe restrictions on the ability of men to contract polygamous marriages.

The king's determination to implement fundamental reform on behalf of Morocco's women reassured the country's liberalizing forces. In addition to the substance of the changes themselves, the fact that Muhammad had forged ahead in the face of vocal opposition marked his boldest assertion of leadership yet. At the same time, although civil society did contribute significantly to the process of discarding the Moudawwana, ultimately the changes came about by royal fiat, not through the actions of representative institutions. Ironically, the king's actions thus affirmed anew that the monarchy remained the country's central political force.

Conclusion

An assessment of Muhammad's policies during his first eight years on the throne reveals ongoing tension between two seemingly conflicting trends, reform and change, on the one hand, and retention of preponderant power by the *makhzen*, on the other. Muhammad often advocated the expansion of democracy and a strengthened role for political parties in public life. It should be noted, though, that these reforms and their guiding ideology were rooted already in the final decade of Hasan's reign, making them as much about continuity as change, with only the pace of the latter being slightly accelerated. Similar examples of continuity lay in some of the king's initiatives, which strengthened the monarchy's grip over public life and often co-opted elements of Morocco's nascent civil society. As a result, Muhammad's reign, contrary to early expectations, has bolstered the monarchy's grip over Moroccan society at the expense of political parties. Concurrently other elements of civil society, while newly stirring, remained heavily dependent on *makhzen* policies. The monarchy has maintained its position as Morocco's preeminent proactive force because at the moment, no other political institution can match its ability to implement widespread reforms. Morocco's political parties, stifled and marginalized during Hasan's reign, lack the leadership and public standing to play a major role in political life, and await new, younger members. Whether a new generation of Moroccans will choose to join and transform these parties into powerful political forces, with the monarchy's support, remains an open question.

In the eight years since Muhammad's rise, Morocco's political landscape has experienced substantial changes toward greater openness. Morocco's foreign friends, namely the United States and the countries of the EU, have continuously voiced their support for reform measures already taken and have urged the Moroccan government to continue with other planned reforms. At the same time they, like the authorities themselves, are keen to preserve social stability, in order to avoid a repetition of Algeria's short-lived experiment with democracy and swift implosion. They therefore remain careful to side with the authorities in their policies of controlled, measured liberalization. As for conservative and Islamist factions, the economic, social, and cultural impact of accelerated globalization and the regime's own steps toward liberalization pose both threats and opportunities to their world views and political and social programs.

In spite of the uncertainties concerning Muhammad's reign and his long-term goals, one should also be cognizant of his country's rich history, and its ability to maintain a sense of cohesiveness notwithstanding its myriad cleavages. If history is any guide, the kingdom is more likely to continue to evolve incrementally, avoiding sudden and far-reaching ruptures while inching its way toward an altered political, social, and economic reality.

Notes

1. Bruce Maddy-Weitzman, "Morocco," in *Middle East Contemporary Survey* (*MECS*) 23 (1999), edited by Bruce Maddy-Weitzman, 424–28 (Boulder, Colo.: Westview, 2001).

2. Rémy Leveau, "The Moroccan Monarchy: A Political System in Quest of a New Equilibrium," in *Middle East Monarchies: The Challenge of Modernity*, edited by Joseph Kostiner 117–30 (Boulder, Colo.: Lynne Rienner, 2000).

3. Maddy-Weitzman, "Morocco" (1999), 429–30.

4. Ibid., 430–31; Bruce Maddy-Weitzman, "Morocco," *MECS* 24 (2000), edited by Bruce Maddy-Weitzman, 415–16 (Tel Aviv: Moshe Dayan Center for Middle Eastern and African Studies, 2002).

5. For two classic studies of the Moroccan monarchy's political and social role, see John Waterbury, *The Commander of the Faithful: The Moroccan Political Elite—A Study of Segmented Politics* (London: Weidenfeld and Nicholson, 1970); Rémy Leveau, *Le fellah marocain: Défenseur du trône* (Paris: Presses de fondation nationale des Sciences Politiques, 1985). On King Muhammad's family life, see Caroline Pigozzi, "Mohammed VI en famille (une interview)," *Paris-Match*, May 13, 2004.

6. François Soudan, "L'ombre du 16 mai," *Jeune Afrique/L'Intelligent*, September 21, 2003.

7. James Sater, "The Dynamics of State and Civil Society in Morocco," *Journal of North African Studies* 7, no. 3 (Autumn 2002): 101–18; Marguerite Rollinde, "L'alternance démocratique au maroc: Une porte entrouverte," *Confluences Méditeranée* 51 (Autumn 2004): 57–67; Hamid Barrada, "Comment Youssoufi a formé son gouvernement?" *Jeune Afrique*, March 17, 1998; Hamid Barrada, "Le printemps marocain-faut-il y croire." *Jeune Afrique*, March 31, 1998.

8. Literally "strongbox" or "treasury," the word is the traditional name for the Moroccan ruling monarchical-military-bureaucratic apparatus.

9. François Soudan, "L'année de tous les espoirs," *Jeune Afrique/L'Intelligent*, Decem-

ber 25, 2001; Ziady Hassan, "Maroc: Le mode de scrutine de la discorde," *Jeune Afrique/ L'Intelligent*, January 8, 2002.

10. Maddy-Weitzman, "Morocco" (1999), 435–36, and idem, "Morocco" (2000), 418–20.

11. Fouad Laroui, "Maroc: La fin de la politique," *Jeune Afrique/L'Intelligent*, November 25, 2002; François Soudan, "Maroc: Pourquoi Jettou?" *Jeune Afrique/L'Intelligent*, October 14, 2002; Driss Benali, "Le gouvernement actuel ou la monteé de l'insignificance," *L'Economiste*, November 27, 2002; Michael J. Willis, "Morocco's Islamists and the Legislative Elections of 2002: The Strange Case of the Party that Did Not Want to Win," *Mediterranean Politics* 9, no. 1 (March 2004): 53–81.

12. Abdelmohsin el-Hassouni, "Jettou; Jugez-moi aux resultants!" *L'Economiste*, December 2, 2002; Abdelmohsin el-Hassouni, "Les instances des parties délèguent leurs pouvoirs," *L'Economiste*, October 21, 2002; Mohamed Chaoui, "Les parties cherchent leurs marques," *L'Economiste*, October 11, 2002; Nadia Lamlili, "Les parties politiques réagissent," *L'Economiste*, October 11, 2002.

13. Maddy-Weitzman, "Morocco" (1999), 431.

14. Sater, "Dynamics of State and Civil Society."

15. Saloua Zerhouni, "Morocco: Reconciling Continuity and Change," in *Arab Elites; Negotiating the Politics of Change*, edited by Volker Perthes, 61–86 (Boulder, Colo.: Lynne Rienner, 2005).

16. See Susan E. Waltz, *Human Rights and Reform: Changing the Face of North African Politics* (Berkeley and Los Angeles: University of California Press, 1995), 10–133; Kevin Dwyer, *Arab Voices: The Human Rights Debate in the Middle East* (London: Routledge, 1991), 110–40.

17. Sater, "Dynamics of State and Civil Society."

18. Younes Alami and Ali Amar, "Morocco: To Tell the Truth," *Le Monde Diplomatique*, April 2005.

19. John P. Entelis, "The Democratic Imperative vs. the Authoritarian Impulse: The Maghreb State between Transition and Terrorism," *Strategic Insights* 4, no. 6 (June 2005). This is an electronic journal, available online at www.ccc.Nps.navy.mil/si.

20. For examples of such reports, see Telquel Online, http://www.telquel-online.com.

21. See ArabicNews.com, http://www.arabicnews.com (June 15, 29, 2005); Karima Rhanem, "The Republic of Nadia Yassine," http://www.moroccotimes.com (June 8, 2005); Mustapha Sehimi, "Nadia Yassine, la 'sans culotte,'" *Maroc-Hebdo International*, June 10, 2005.

22. Statement by Reporters san frontiers, April 14, 2005, as posted on http://www.allafrica.com.

23. For a detailed analysis on the Moudawwana and the efforts to reform it, see Mounira Charrad, *States and Women's Rights: The Making of Post-Colonial Tunisia, Algeria, and Morocco* (Berkeley and Los Angeles: University of California Press, 2001), 158–68; Laurie A. Brand, *Women, the State, and Political Liberalization: Middle Eastern and North African Experiences* (New York: Columbia University Press, 1998), 46–68, 69–91; Alain Rousillon, "Réformer la moudawsana: Statut et conditions des marocains,"

Maghreb-Machrek 179 (Spring 2004): 79–99; Bruce Maddy-Weitzman, "Women, Islam and the Moroccan State: The Struggle over the Personal Status Law," *Middle East Journal* 59, no. 3 (Summer 2005): 393–410. For a study on the positions of Moroccan political parties toward the law, see Mokhtar Benabdllaoui, "Al-Ahzab al-siyasiyya wa masalat islah al-moudawwana" (The Political Parties and the Question of Reforming the Moudawwana), *Prologues: Revue maghrebine du livre*, Hors-série, 3 (2003): 9–22.

8

Justice and Development or Justice and Spirituality?

The Challenge of Morocco's Nonviolent Islamist Movements

MICHAEL J. WILLIS

The absence of a large Islamist movement has long distinguished Morocco from other Arab states. However, events over recent years have altered the widespread perception that Morocco was immune to Islamism. First and most dramatically there was a coordinated series of suicide bomb attacks carried out by militant Islamists in Casablanca, Morocco's largest city, on the night of May 16, 2003. Second, an Islamist political party, the Parti de la Justice et du Développement (PJD), made substantial gains in legislative elections in 2002: It quadrupled its representation and became the third largest party in the national parliament.[1] Third, another Islamist organization—the Justice and Spirituality (al-Adl wal-Ihsan) movement—grew in size and influence. Indeed, it appeared to have greater support than the PJD. Most international media attention was drawn to the small clandestine group involved in the Casablanca bombings. The involvement of Moroccan extremist groups in the bombings in the Spanish capital, Madrid, ten months later on March 11, 2004, resulted in further interest. However, although the groups involved in the Casablanca and Madrid attacks achieved a higher profile, in reality they are much smaller in terms of membership and uninvolved in local political and social affairs and hence have less chance of having an impact on Moroccan politics and society in the longer run than either the PJD or al-Adl wal-Ihsan. Accordingly, this chapter focuses on these two important movements and assesses their influence and importance in Morocco.

A Challenge Contained

The origins of both the PJD and al-Adl wal-Ihsan date back to the late 1960s and early 1970s. Many of the PJD's current leadership were involved in al-Shabiba al-Islamiyya (Islamic Youth), an organization that established itself in Casablanca and was led by a school inspector, Abdelkrim Mouti', who was disillusioned by the secular drift and ineffectiveness of the political process in Morocco. For its part, al-Adl wal-Ihsan's origins are to be found in the writings and ideas of a single individual, Abdessalam Yassine, also a school inspector, who, having spent time in a Sufi order in the 1960s, proceeded to write a series of books and tracts analyzing the kingdom's problems, which he believed were due to the insufficient attention paid by the state to Islam.

Any potential challenge al-Shabiba al-Islamiyya or Yassine might have made to the political status quo through their activities and criticism of the regime was preempted in the mid-1970s, when both were perceived by the authorities to have crossed a red line and were thus repressed. Al-Shabiba al-Islamiyya's development of a militant underground wing parallel to a public structure devoted to educational and strictly religious activities attracted the ire of the authorities. In 1975 they accused the organization of being responsible for the assassination of a leading leftist, Omar Benjelloun, and acted forcefully to break it up.[2] For Yassine, his sending of an open and audacious letter to King Hasan II in 1973 in which he criticized the Sovereign and questioned his attachment to Islam, earned him a place in one of the kingdom's mental hospitals.

The late 1970s and the following decade saw small sporadic activity linked to both former members of al-Shabiba al-Islamiyya and Abdessalam Yassine. Following the killing of Benjelloun, Mouti' fled into exile and his influence declined, attempts to continue to coordinate the organization from abroad notwithstanding. In the early 1980s, a number of former members of al-Shabiba al-Islamiyya formed an informal association that was tolerated by the authorities because of the group's renunciation of most of the more radical and critical positions adopted by Mouti' in the 1970s—notably his criticism of the Moroccan monarchy and his ambivalence regarding the use of violence. Although the group was officially tolerated, its repeated requests to form a legal political party were turned down by the authorities. The fact that Yassine was effectively working alone meant that any potential challenge to the regime he represented was removed once he was imprisoned. Although he was released from the mental hospital after less than four years, Yassine's continued willingness to publicly criticize the regime resulted in further periods of detention before he was consigned in 1989 to a lengthy period of house arrest. From the early 1980s, Yassine had begun to develop a small but dedicated following for his ideas. However, his attempts to obtain legal recognition for his association (which became known as al-Adl wal-Ihsan in 1987) were rejected, and in 1990 most of his closest supporters were also arrested and imprisoned.[3]

Thus it seemed that the Moroccan government would be able to rebuff indefinitely, and without difficulty, whatever putative Islamist challenge might be mustered by any of the kingdom's small Islamist groups and organizations. This stood in marked contrast to the existing situation in most other Arab states. The 1980s had seen Islamist groups grow in strength and influence in Egypt, Lebanon, and the Palestinian territories. Closer to Morocco, Tunisia's Islamists had begun to mount a major political challenge to the state by the late 1980s and in Algeria, the aftermath of the crisis of October 1988 and the introduction of a new multiparty political constitution had seen a mass, populist Islamist political party, the Islamic Salvation Front (FIS), stride to center stage.

The reasons for Morocco's success in containing all Islamist challenges to the system were understood to be multifold. One explanation put forward was Morocco's traditionally more pluralistic complexion, religiously and politically. The existence of a multiparty political system from the onset of Morocco's independence in 1956 was seen as providing an outlet for political protest and opposition that was not afforded in other Arab states, virtually all of which had adopted single party political systems upon attaining independence. As a result, opposition sentiment did not end up becoming channeled, as it did in Tunisia and Algeria, into one single large movement that was almost invariably Islamist in orientation. On the religious front, the strength and persistence of Sufi practices and organizations in the kingdom was seen as providing a bulwark against the spread of Islamist ideas: The mystic and apolitical aspects of Sufism were viewed as undercutting support for the more literalist and political impulses of most Islamist movements. Moreover, it was also argued that the tradition of doctrinal and organizational pluralism also served to inhibit the development of a single unified Islamist movement of the type seen in Algeria and Tunisia. Indeed, al-Shabiba al-Islamiyya and its successor organizations had failed to unite and make common cause with Abdessalam Yassine and his supporters.[4]

Although some explanations for the weakness of Islamist movements stressed the pluralism of religious and political life in Morocco, others emphasized the unity, strength, and resolve of the regime. The regime in Morocco and its supporters have traditionally been unanimous in stressing that the real reason behind the relative weakness of Islamist movements in Morocco is the religious standing of the monarch. It is argued that Moroccan monarchs' claim of descent from the prophet Muhammad, together with the king's official status as *Amir al-Mu'minin* (Commander of the Faithful), give the monarchy a religious authority and legitimacy that effectively undermines the religiously based discourse and criticism of the Islamist groups. Charges of being too secular or of neglecting Islam can be easily made against presidents and regimes that have no clearly religious dimension, but are much harder to promulgate against a relative of the prophet himself and a monarchical institution that has traditionally draped itself in religious imagery and symbolism.

For some observers, the religious dimensions of the Moroccan monarchy's power and control are in reality overstated and have only been given credibility because of the tenacity with which they have been reiterated by state officials. Analysts such as Henry Munson point instead to the much more tangible dimensions of royal power and control to explain the success of the Moroccan state in controlling the expansion of the country's Islamist movements.[5] Under the supervision of King Hasan II, the country developed effective security structures that successfully headed off a number of attempts from the political left in the 1960s and 1970s to marginalize or overthrow the monarchy. These successes left the security services well equipped to deal with the type of challenge that could be potentially posed by the Islamists during the 1970s and 1980s. Indeed, surveillance, infiltration, detention, and periodic repression of these groups were effective in preventing their growth and spread.

A Challenge Renewed

The containment of Moroccan Islamist movements during the 1970s and 1980s contrasted sharply with their subsequent rapid expansion. What had changed? Perhaps the factors that were traditionally advanced to explain the weakness of Morocco's Islamist movements had been altered to the point where they no longer were effective.

The explanations linked to Morocco's established political and religious pluralism do not seem to be very relevant in this regard. To account for an expansion in Islamism one would expect there to have been a reduction in the degree of pluralism during the last fifteen years. In fact, there was a clear *increase* in pluralism. At the political level, not only was there a further significant increase in the number of legal political parties but, more important, the institution of parliament was given (ostensibly) enhanced powers through two sets of constitutional reform. Therefore, theoretically at least, Islamist movements were subject to even greater competition from among political parties seeking to build viable alternatives to the ruling authorities. On the level of religion, support and interest in Sufi ideas and organizations arguably grew in Morocco during this same period, suggesting that support for Islamist ideas should have been further undercut. Among the Islamist organizations themselves there was no great coalescence into a single movement or even an alliance. The two main movements have continued to maintain their distance from each other due to differences over both strategy (al-Adl wal-Ihsan's view has been that the electoral and formal political process is essentially a sham) and ideology (the PJD has taken a much more conservative and uncompromising line on social issues such as the place of women in society than have Yassine's supporters). Moreover, the Islamist field itself became even more diverse and pluralistic during this period, most notably on the more radical and violent fringes, as was demonstrated by the groups involved in the attacks in Casablanca and Madrid. Thus a reduction in pluralism was clearly not behind the expansion in Islamist sentiment.

Changes in the attitude and approach of the Moroccan state provide an alternative explanation for explaining what might have changed. As shown earlier, there are grounds for skepticism regarding the importance of the religious dimension of the Moroccan monarchy's overweening power. Nevertheless, it has been argued that King Muhammad VI, who ascended to the throne following the death of his father, Hasan II, in July 1999, lacked the religious as well as personal authority that had been enjoyed by Hasan, due to a combination of his youth and more reticent character, and also because of the difficulty of succeeding a personality such as Hasan who had established such a powerful presence during thirty-eight years on the throne. However, such an argument would seem to run counter to the official view that the religious dimension of the ruler's authority in Morocco was attached to the institution of the monarchy itself rather than to any individual ruler per se. Moreover, the succession took place only at the end of the 1990s, when it was already clear that the Islamists had been on the rise for several years.

What about the effectiveness of the security forces in dealing with any challenge to the regime? On this point there does seem to be some evidence to suggest that changes that occurred from the 1990s did help facilitate a growth in Islamist activity. As part of a broader policy of political liberalization, there was a scaling back of Morocco's security apparatus, allowing Islamist movements greater freedom to act. It thus seems that this was the largest contributing factor to the growth in overt manifestations of Islamist activism over the last fifteen years.

Political Reform and the Opening to the Islamists

The 1990s in Morocco marked the beginning of a very gradual process of political liberalization that would continue into the following decade. Initiated by King Hasan, this liberalization was prompted by a number of factors. First, the kingdom had experienced turbulent times in preceding decades, notably in the 1970s, when Hasan survived two attempts on his life. By the beginning of the 1990s, however, domestic politics had been put on a more even keel and the regime clearly felt less threatened and more willing to relax its hitherto iron grip on political power. Second, changes at the level of international politics, most notably the end of the Cold War, had seen Europe and the United States put new pressure on states elsewhere to democratize and improve their human rights records: Former Cold War allies in Africa, Asia, and Latin America were no longer able to argue that such reforms might threaten their contribution to the struggle against communism. As a staunchly pro-Western state during the Cold War, Morocco came under pressure to politically liberalize and improve its dubious human rights record. A third factor that contributed to Morocco's impetus to reform was the advancing age and declining health of King Hasan. Aware of his own mortality, the politically astute monarch decided that the best way of avoiding leaving a potentially destabilizing political vacuum when he died and which his son, Muhammad, might struggle to fill, was to broaden the power base of the regime through reform.

The eventual outcome of these pressures for reform and liberalization was a series of measures that began with the release of virtually all of Morocco's political prisoners in the early 1990s, continued with two sets of constitutional reforms in 1992 and 1996 that gave more power to the national parliament, and culminated in 1998 with the formation of a government dominated by parties from the traditional (mainly leftist) opposition. At a more general level, freedom of speech and freedom of the press were both noticeably expanded.

As indicated, a relaxation of control on the country's Islamist movements became part of this broader process. However, there were also more specific motivations for the regime. King Hasan had watched the rise of powerful Islamist movements in neighboring Algeria and Tunisia in the late 1980s with a certain sanguinity. However, two events gave him cause to think that Morocco might itself soon have to face a challenge from the country's Islamists. The first event was the demonstration in May 1990 by some two thousand Islamists outside a court in Rabat following the sentencing of the leadership of al-Adl wal-Ihsan to prison terms. The second was the presence of large numbers of Islamists in the mass demonstration against the Gulf War that occurred in Rabat in February 1991. This show of strength by the kingdom's Islamists convinced Hasan and his advisers of the importance of developing an effective response. In looking for possible examples to follow, Hasan was presented with two very different models: Algeria's unrestricted opening to the Islamists beginning in 1989 and Zayn al-Abidin Ben Ali's initial restricted opening in the late 1980s and then, from 1991 onward, swift and total repression and exclusion of Tunisian Islamists and other opposition groups. Neither model was appealing. The unraveling of Algeria's experiment in the early 1990s and the descent into conflict after a belated attempt by elements in the regime to close the door on the Islamists highlighted the shortcomings of this approach. Tunisia's unswerving repression of all political dissent not only went against Morocco's more pluralistic history and impulses but was arguably also unfeasible in a country that was several times larger in area and had three times the population of Tunisia.

As an alternative, Hasan turned to a middle course of action that had a deep-rooted tradition in Moroccan politics: that of co-option. Since independence, the palace had consistently undermined and defanged opposition to the regime through the selective co-option of certain groups and individuals. The acceptance in 1998 of seats in government by longtime opposition parties was perhaps the final act in the successful taming and co-option of the leftist and nationalist forces that had intermittently contested the complete dominance of the political system by the monarchy since the 1950s. The regime thus resolved to remove the threat posed by the Islamists by attempting to bring them into the political system.

It was clear to the regime that by far the biggest and best organized movement in the country was that of Yassine's al-Adl wal-Ihsan. Support for Yassine and his ideas had steadily grown through the 1980s, particularly among the young and unemployed, a process that accelerated once the movement began to establish structures for itself. Significantly, the movement's growth was not interrupted or inhibited by the imprisonment of the members of its Majlis al-Irshad (Guidance Council) in 1990. As a result, the authorities began to put out feelers to the movement, approaching the members of the

Guidance Council in prison in an attempt to persuade them to reach an accommodation with the regime. According to members of the council, officials offered the movement legal recognition, the right to form a political party and contest elections and even substantial sums of money. The sole eventual condition was that the movement publicly and explicitly recognize the authority and legitimacy of the monarchy.[6] The offer was, however, rejected, not least because al-Adl wal-Ihsan recognized that a significant part of its legitimacy and popularity as a movement was linked to its criticism of the monarchy's legally infallible position. Suspecting that a gesture of goodwill was needed, the authorities released most of the movement's leadership and in December 1995 lifted Yassine's house arrest. However, scarcely veiled criticisms of the monarchy made by Yassine shortly following his release not only earned him an immediate return to house arrest but also convinced the regime that Yassine and al-Adl were not willing to be co-opted.[7]

Having failed in their overtures toward Yassine and al-Adl wal-Ihsan, the authorities decided instead to see if any other Islamist groups were open to co-option.[8] The obvious candidates were the various successor groups of al-Shabiba al-Islamiyya from the 1970s. As explained earlier, a number of former members had regrouped themselves in the early 1980s, rejecting the radicalism of Abdelkrim Mouti', and had requested recognition as an official association and also the right to form a political party. These requests had been consistently denied by the authorities throughout the 1980s and early 1990s. However, following the failure of the attempted opening to al-Adl wal-Ihsan, the regime turned a more sympathetic ear to this group, which now called itself al-Islah wal-Tajdid (Reform and Renewal). Still wary of allowing the movement to form its own political party, the regime gave an effective green light to the members of al-Islah wal-Tajdid to join an existing but effectively moribund political party, the Mouvement Populaire Démocratique et Constitutionnel (MPDC). The fact that this party was led by an old established politician, Abdelkrim Khatib, who had close links with the palace, satisfied the requirements of co-option. To make doubly sure, Khatib stipulated that members of al-Islah, before joining the MPDC, affirmed their renunciation of violence, their acceptance of constitutional and political methods, and—most crucial of all—recognition of the authority and legitimacy of the monarchy. Having publicly endorsed these principles for some years, the members of al-Islah had no problem in making such a commitment. Consequently, they formally entered the political party in a special MPDC Congress in June 1996.[9]

Once inside the MPDC, the Islah activists worked to transform it into an

Islamist one—a task facilitated by the fact that they substantially outnumbered the other members of the party. The party put up a limited number of candidates in the national legislative elections of November 1997 and was rewarded with victories in nine constituencies, mainly in Morocco's big cities. Within a year of the elections, the party changed its name to the Party of Justice and Development (PJD), marking, in effect, recognition of the transformation of the old MPDC. Despite its small size, the PJD soon developed a reputation for industriousness and honesty in parliament, thus raising its national profile. Other small Islamist groupings were also brought on board, and as a result, al-Islah (which retained its identity as a religious association distinct from the MPDC/PJD)[10] renamed itself al-Tawhid wal-Islah (Unity and Reform).[11]

The authorities' motivation in allowing these developments was, as has been said, to successfully co-opt at least part of the Islamist movement into the legal political process and thus hopefully prevent the coalescence of a large radicalized opposition Islamist movement of the sort witnessed in Algeria, Tunisia, and Egypt. A desire to prevent al-Adl wal-Ihsan from assuming such a role was clearly present in the authorities' calculations. Although organizations such as al-Islah wal-Tajdid were far smaller than al-Adl wal-Ihsan, it was hoped that the presence of al-Islah deputies in the national parliament would serve to undercut and siphon off popular support from al-Adl. In spite of this, there was still awareness that al-Adl wal-Ihsan represented a potential challenge, and thus the door to accommodation was kept open by the regime. An opportunity to achieve such an accommodation was presented with the royal succession of 1999. Wishing to present a positive and reforming image for the new king, together with pressure to clear up the few remaining cases of political exiles and detainees, the regime finally and definitively lifted the house arrest on Abdessalam Yassine in May 2000. The now-aging sheikh did not repeat his behavior in 1995, when he criticized King Hasan immediately upon his release. Still, being anxious to demonstrate that he had made no compromises with the regime, in January 2000, prior to his release, he issued a public letter in which he heavily criticized the deceased Hasan and offered advice to his son Muhammad VI.[12] Despite this public challenge, which consciously evoked Yassine's earlier provocative letter to King Hasan in 1973, the authorities proceeded with their plans to release al-Adl wal-Ihsan's leader, perhaps as a means of calling his bluff.

New Challenges

With both al-Adl wal-Ihsan and the PJD working in a much more open and unrestricted environment, the types of the challenges the two organizations presented to the regime changed accordingly. They were also rather different in nature.

The PJD

The PJD's challenge was in the realm of official politics. As a legal political party contesting elections and sitting in the national parliament, it was able to present its positions on issues in public forums. However, the party was acutely aware that it had been afforded access to the legal political arena only on the sufferance of the authorities and was aware it could lose the place it had been given should it be seen to overstep any "red lines." As a result, the party trod a difficult line between being faithful to its Islamist agenda and supporters while being careful to avoid attracting the ire of the authorities. Thus the PJD steered clear of any criticism of the wider political system and the place of the monarchy and focused more on social and moral issues such as corruption, education, and the place of women in society. The party's clear stance on these issues, together with its reputation for hard work and honesty—not least in the local areas in which its members had been elected—contrasted markedly with most of Morocco's other political parties, which were notable for their vague ideologies and often complete lack of contact with the voters between elections. As a result, the party grew in both stature and support. Yet the PJD's leadership acknowledged that if the party grew too quickly, it could provoke unease both inside the regime as well as among Morocco's allies in Europe and the United States, who were wary about the rise of Islamism. Consequently, spokesmen for the PJD were wont to be modest about both the party's achievements and its future prospects. As the party's deputy leader, Saad-Eddine Othmani, explained in 2000, "We are frightened of frightening people."[13]

Such a stance did, however, present a dilemma when it came to contesting elections: The party clearly wanted to increase its representation in local and national government but did not want to be seen as too successful and thus raise the fear of an Islamist-dominated government. In this regard, the experience of neighboring Algeria loomed large in everyone's minds. A strong performance by the Islamist FIS in local and national legislative elections in 1990–91 had prompted elements in Algeria's powerful military to intervene to cancel the elections and ban the FIS in 1992. The violence and chaos this chain of events had unleashed was something that everyone in Morocco, including the PJD, was anxious to avoid. As one senior member of the PJD acknowledged in an interview, "The Algerian scenario is the fear of all Moroccans."[14]

To forestall such a scenario, the PJD voluntarily decided to put limits on the numbers of candidates it fielded in elections. In the 1997 national legislative elections (as the MPDC), it had put forth candidates in only 43 percent of the electoral districts. In the next set of legislative elections in 2002, the party slightly increased its participation to 60 percent of the districts—a lower percentage than most other parties. In spite of these self-imposed restrictions, the party, after having performed respectably in 1997, achieved extremely good results in 2002, winning forty-two seats and becoming the third largest party in the parliament behind the old historic parties of the Union Socialiste des Forces Populaires (USFP) and the Istiqlal.

The reasons behind what the Moroccan press called the "Islamist breakthrough" were varied. The PJD had certainly helped itself through a well-organized and simple campaign that made good use of the party's strong grassroots organization and the high caliber of the candidates it fielded (81 percent of whom held university degrees). It had also been helped by external factors. At the national level, the party encountered little competition from most of the other competing parties, which had no clear ideology, no grassroots organization, and fielded poor quality (and sometimes illiterate) candidates who relied more on patron-client networks and occasionally vote buying to attract votes. The more established and better organized parties such as the USFP and the Istiqlal suffered from a lack of credibility, having been the major partners in the 1998–2002 government, which had disappointed many with its failure to adequately tackle the country's major social and economic problems. At the international level, the international war on terrorism, the pending war on Iraq, and, most important, the continuing violence between the Israelis and the Palestinians had clearly strengthened sentiments of Islamic solidarity that the PJD, as an overtly Islamic party, benefited from.[15] Indeed, it is the emergence of these international factors that undoubtedly helps explain the rise in Islamist sentiment from 2000.

The PJD's performance in the 2002 elections put it in a potentially influential position. The party decided not to join the governing coalition of parties that was assembled after the elections. Instead, it chose to remain in the opposition, becoming the largest opposition party. The size of its parliamentary representation, together with the ineffectiveness of other parties in the opposition, has meant that the PJD has dominated the opposition discourse and activity in the parliament. In this sense the party seems to be presenting itself as an alternative to the existing government, and given the government's continued lack of headway in solving Morocco's socioeconomic problems, the party would normally be well placed to capitalize on this situation in the next legislative elections, due in 2007.

The prognosis of a PJD victory and assumption of power in 2007 has some weighty caveats, however. First of all, on a technical level, a strong electoral performance is highly unlikely to give the party a parliamentary majority. The adoption by Morocco of a proportional representation (PR) party list electoral system effectively precludes the possibility of any single party winning a majority in parliament and thus being able to form a government on its own. Even if the PJD were to emerge as the largest party, it would have to form a coalition with at least one other party, and probably several, given Morocco's highly fragmented party political map. Parallels with the success of the FIS in Algeria, where the party was set to secure a large parliamentary majority for itself following legislative elections in 1991, are not valid. The single member district electoral system used in Algeria had an amplifying effect on the number of seats that the party attained, as such a system traditionally favors larger, dominant parties. If Algeria had employed a PR electoral system of the type used in Morocco in 2002, the FIS would have almost certainly not been able to secure a parliamentary majority on its own. It should also be noted that the FIS's share of the vote (47 percent) in Algeria in 1991 was nearly five times the share of the vote secured by the PJD (10 percent) in Morocco in 2002.

A second, even more important factor that needs to be considered is that the winning of a parliamentary majority is not, unlike in most European parliamentary democracies, the key to securing political power in the state. Despite the constitutional reforms of the 1990s, all meaningful political power in Morocco still remains within the walls of the Royal Palace and in the hands of the king and his advisers. The king retains the constitutional right to appoint whomever he wishes to government, irrespective of whether they have support in the parliament. Indeed, the king's appointment of a nonparty technocrat, Driss Jettou, as prime minister in the wake of the 2002 elections was a powerful reminder to the parties (who were claiming the post for their own nominees) of the preeminence of the royal prerogative.

A third consideration is that the Moroccan authorities may not tolerate a PJD election victory should it occur. Alarm at the prospect of an Islamist-dominated parliament among both Morocco's elite and its allies in Europe and the United States might prompt the regime to either actively prevent the party from performing well in the elections or, alternately, block its way to government should it become the largest party in the parliament. It is a scenario that at least one senior member of the party regards as highly likely.[16] Indeed, there were accusations that the authorities had already pursued such a course of action during the elections of both 1997 and 2002. First of all, it was argued that the MPDC/PJD had been put under official pressure to reduce the number of candidates they fielded in both elections. Second, the authorities may well have interfered in the counting of votes to reduce the number of parliamentary seats won by the party.[17] Surprisingly, the party itself did not make a big issue out of certain irregularities that appeared to reduce its parliamentary representation. Its leaders were, in fact, content to have a more limited presence in the parliament and thus reduce the risk of the sort of backlash that occurred in Algeria against the FIS after its strong electoral performance. Indeed, when pushed in an interview on the issue of manipulation in the elections of 2002, Saad-Eddine Othmani eventually smiled and observed, "For us, the most important thing is the stability of the country."[18]

The validity of the PJD's concerns about the precariousness of its position was underlined in the aftermath of the bomb attacks that occurred in Casablanca on May 16, 2003. Although the party had no links to the group responsible for the attacks and had explicitly rejected the use of violence for political purposes before the bombings and condemned them unequivocally, the PJD nevertheless came under severe political pressure in subsequent weeks. Opponents of the party in the leftist and secularist press and rival political parties accused the PJD of having helped prepare the ground for the attacks through their sustained and intemperate rhetoric against the West and Israel in the party's newspapers and official statements (all the targets of the bombings had been Western or Jewish establishments). The deputy leader of the USFP, Muhammad El Yazghi, called publicly for the PJD to "apologize to the Moroccan people" for their contribution to creating an atmosphere that resulted in the bombings.[19] More ominously for the party, it became clear that there were important elements within the country's security establishment that now wanted to ban and dissolve it.

The PJD was robust in its own defense, highlighting the absence of any link between those responsible for the attacks and the party and pointing out that many other newspapers, including ones on the Left, had been just as antagonistic to the West and Israel in their columns.[20] Nevertheless, the atmosphere was sufficiently hostile to the party to necessitate some self-sacrifice. The authorities made it clear to the PJD that the price the party had to pay to escape a formal ban would be a dramatic reduction in the party's participation in the September 2003 elections for local government. Before May 16, the party had been tipped to make massive gains, particularly in the major cities, gains it intended to use as a launching pad for the 2007 legislative elections. The party bowed to this demand and cut the number of candidates it planned to put up in the main cities by half, but there was more to follow. The Ministry of Interior contacted the party's leadership to demand that Mustapha Ramid, a PJD member of parliament associated with the party's more radical wing, not be elected to the head of the party's parliamentary group. The party eventually agreed to this as well, albeit not without internal dissent. Ramid gave interviews to the press complaining about interference from the Ministry in the internal affairs of the party.[21] He criticized the leadership's failure to stand up to the pressure exerted on it and argued that the regime's targeting of both him and the PJD in general was due to the independence and effectiveness with which both had operated in the parliament. "The State wants the PJD to be a party that doesn't bother anyone," he said.[22]

Dissent within the party over the degree to which it was willing to succumb to pressures from the Moroccan regime suggests that the authorities were trying another well-established technique of control over the party: the promotion of fissures within the party as a means of weakening it. At the party's Fifth Congress, held in April 2004, figures associated with the party's more accommodationist wing were elected to key positions. One of these figures, Saad-Eddine Othmani, was elected to succeed the aging official leader, Abdelkrim Khatib, who retired. The sending of a congratulatory telegram to Othmani by King Muhammad was interpreted by some as a royal sign of approval and even evidence of successful co-option of the party by the palace.[23] By contrast, attempts by Ramid and his supporters to get the issue of constitutional reform debated at the Congress were headed off. This followed an article in a newspaper written by Ramid in the run-up to the Congress that argued for a revision of the Constitution and which, more importantly, questioned the constitutional idea of the monarchy being "sacred."[24] In an unrelated development, several disgruntled members of the party announced their departure to another party, raising the possibility of the creation of an Islamist competitor to the PJD.

From the perspective of mid-2006, any putative challenge for political power from the PJD seems to have been effectively met by the regime. Not only is the party's leadership in the hands of cautious figures willing to make significant concessions to the regime, but the political context in which the party operates is heavily circumscribed and unlikely to provide the party with any significantly greater freedom of maneuver. The party must therefore wait for more auspicious times. In playing the waiting game, however, the PJD risks losing its credibility with the electorate. It may be seen as having been successfully intimidated and co-opted by the regime, and its objective of changing the Moroccan political system may become inverted, with the party structures becoming infected with the blights of corruption, clientalism, and personal politics that plague and debilitate most other Moroccan political parties. In this way, the regime's strategy toward the PJD opens it up to certain dangers. One of the original reasons for letting the PJD into the system in the first place was to undercut support for other more critical and radical Islamist organizations: initially al-Adl wal-Ihsan, but after May 16, violent jihadist groups as well. Therefore, if the PJD were to be seen as too compromised and tame, this would cost the party legitimacy and could well push Islamist sentiment toward more dissident groups.

Al-Adl wal-Ihsan

The challenge presented by al-Adl wal-Ihsan has clearly been of a different order than that of the PJD. Standing apart from the formal mechanisms of politics, such as elections and the parliament, al-Adl wal-Ihsan has had to articulate its message and agenda in different ways. For the last decade and a half, the movement has focused on building its organization and spreading its message. It is now a large, well-constructed and well-supported organization, with a pyramidal structure and branches throughout the country. New members of the organization are inducted in a methodical manner through groups where they study some of the major writings of Abdessalam Yassine.[25]

The focus on the writings and ideas of Yassine is both a strength and potential weakness of the movement. As a personality, Yassine exercises a powerful appeal to those both inside and outside the movement. A substantial part of this appeal is due to Yassine's consistent refusal to bow to pressures from the regime to cease his criticism of the monarchy and the existing political order and his complete unwillingness to be co-opted. In a state where the monarchy wields virtually untrammeled political power and where deference is demanded, the symbolic courage of a single individual willing to go against the grain is striking. As one young Moroccan man declared, "Whether you agree or not with his ideas, no one can deny that Abdessalam Yassine is the only person ever to have said 'no' in Morocco."²⁶ Yassine has indeed said no, and in powerful ways. His open letter to Hasan II in 1973 was stunning in its audacity. He not only addressed the king in familiar terms (*Ya Habibi*, "My beloved one") but also criticized his wealth and his closeness to the West and even questioned the sincerity of his Islamic faith.²⁷ A second open letter, to Muhammad VI in 2000, was no less frank. He criticized the pomp and expense of the royal succession and argued that King Hasan's greed had resulted in huge amounts of money being stolen from the kingdom, money that could be used to pay off Morocco's large international debt.²⁸

Yassine's willingness to criticize the monarchy directly also extended to attacking the very foundations of royal legitimacy. In an interview with the author shortly after his release from house arrest in May 2000, he stated, "You foreign journalists and academics are mistaken when you say that 'the Moroccan Monarchy's legitimacy is based on descent from the Prophet Muhammad.' This is wrong. If you think about it, there must be thousands of people in Morocco, including me, who are blood descendants of the Prophet. Why shouldn't any one of them be king?"²⁹

In challenging the monarchy so directly, Yassine is consciously placing himself in a long tradition in Morocco, which historically has seen lone pious individuals confront the sultan.³⁰ How aware most ordinary Moroccans are of this tradition is uncertain, but Yassine's popularity is undoubtedly tied up with his courage in being willing to break a taboo and directly confront what he sees as the failings of the Moroccan state and the monarchy.

The weakness of having a movement built around the writings and ideas of a single individual is, of course, bound up with the inevitable difficulties that arise when that individual eventually dies. Yassine was already into his seventies by the time of the lifting of his house arrest in 2000 and has suffered from ill health since that date. The surrounding leadership of al-Adl wal-Ihsan is very aware and sensitive to this issue and quick to rebut its implications. They reject the characterization of their movement as a Sufi *zawiya* (brotherhood) in which everything and everybody depends on the sheikh.³¹ They point out that the movement is highly structured, with a Guidance Council and a Majlis al-Shura (Consultative Council), and that the role played by Yassine as the *murshid* (guide) is certainly inspirational but not structurally crucial to the movement. Major decisions are taken by the hundred-plus-strong Majlis al-Shura rather than by Yassine.³² Furthermore, Abdelwahed El Moutawakil, a member of the Guidance Council, argues that everyone is aware of the mortality of Yassine and that the sort of highly educated people who join the movement would not join it if they thought it would collapse and disappear as soon as Yassine died. He points out that the movement actually expanded when Yassine was in prison.[33]

Another dimension to the challenge mounted by al-Adl wal-Ihsan to the status quo in Morocco is that it is a rather different sort of movement than the classic Islamist movements found in most other Arab countries, and of which al-Tawhid wal-Islah and the PJD are fairly typical. The fact that it is constructed around the ideas and writings of a single man is one distinguishing factor. Also unusual is the clear influence of Sufi ideas on the movement. Yassine spent six years in a Sufi order (the Boutchichiyya), and its legacy in his writings and the philosophy of the movement is evident. Much emphasis is placed by al-Adl wal-Ihsan on the inner transformation of the individual—a distinctly Sufi idea. The movement stresses the importance of changing people first before attempting to change society. This stands in contrast to the more legalistic approach of other Islamist movements, which emphasize the importance of law and behavior. Indeed, al-Adl wal-Ihsan is openly hostile to more literalist and genuinely fundamentalist groups and ideas. Nadia Yassine, the daughter of Abdessalam and a prominent spokesperson for the movement, has criticized the PJD for having rigid views and has condemned Wahhabism as a dangerous "virus" in the Muslim world that breeds "violence and exclusion."[34] Mainstream Sufi figures have argued that Yassine's knowledge of Sufism is superficial. However, the Sufi dimensions of the movement do perhaps help explain the relationship between the parallel growth, noted earlier, of both Sufi ideas and Islamist organizations over recent years.

The events of May 16, 2003, also had repercussions for al-Adl wal-Ihsan, although arguably less so than for the PJD, which held a formal place in the political arena that it potentially stood to lose. Nevertheless, the movement complained of increased harassment from the authorities following the attacks. Like the PJD, its spokesmen unequivocally condemned the bombings, and restated the movement's longstanding commitment to nonviolent methods. In common with the PJD, it argued that poverty and exclusion had been the root causes of the bombings and that had it not been for the influence of nonviolent organizations such as al-Adl wal-Ihsan, able to attract the young and disillusioned, the Casablanca bombings might have occurred much earlier. However, unlike the PJD, al-Adl wal-Ihsan alleged that the Moroccan authorities had for a number of years actually been quietly encouraging the sort of extremist groups responsible for the attack as a means of undermining support for al-Adl wal-Ihsan.[35]

A growing debate within al-Adl wal-Ihsan concerns its rejection of formal political processes in Morocco. Excluded from the official arena, the movement has long affected disdain toward these processes. There are, however, voices within al-Adl that argue that the movement should try to become involved in formal politics should it eventually be offered the chance to form a political party. Many, particularly younger figures, worry that the movement risks marginalization if it continues to stand on the political sidelines. There is also, perhaps, an awareness that the Moroccan regime is unwilling to make such an offer while Yassine is still alive but may well consider doing so once the symbolic figure of the sheikh has gone.

Agendas and Objectives

What do the two movements want, how likely are they to achieve their aims, and if they are at all successful, what are the likely implications for the political status quo and the monarchy in Morocco?

The PJD has publicly set itself the objective of becoming an accepted party within the legal political landscape. It has an agenda that aims at reapplying Islamic values and terms of reference in public life. Such an agenda, the party has declared, will be pursued through constitutional and political means, including debates and elections and in the parliament, where it will seek to persuade other political parties and forces and the public at large of the wisdom of their policies. In this way, the party wants to present itself as similar to any other political party. Significantly, one member of the PJD has made comparisons between the role played by the PJD and that played by Christian Democrat parties in Europe and religious parties in Israel.[36] This acceptance of a place in a pluralistic political system, where policies are pursued by persuasion rather than force and in which the presence of other ideas and agendas is accepted, is the desired end game of all those observers of Islamism who are optimistic about the positive evolution of Islamist movements. The example of Turkey's Justice and Development party (AKP), which won a parliamentary majority in November 2002, is presented as a powerful illustration of how a party with Islamist origins can form a moderate and inclusive government.[37] By contrast, there are many in Morocco who feel that this scenario is unlikely to occur, and that in reality the PJD is a Trojan horse for radical and extreme Islamist ideas. According to this view, the PJD has been allowed into the political system and will bide its time for an appropriate moment of instability to seize power and impose its vision of an Islamic state. The statements and positions of more radical figures in the party, such as Mustapha Ramid, are seen as revealing the true face of the organization.[38] Whatever the truth, the PJD has not attempted to hide its eventual ambition to wield political power. Saad-Eddine Othmani stated, even before becoming party leader, that "a party exists to govern."[39]

Al-Adl wal-Ihsan's objectives are at once more substantial and more diffuse. In the short term, the movement calls for the creation of a "National Dialogue" of all the political and social groups and forces in the kingdom to seek a way out of the impasse in which it believes Morocco to be stranded. In the longer term, regarding the sort of political system the movement wishes to see established, some form of Caliphate is favored in Yassine's writings. But the movement's leaders are quick to assert that this would not mean a simple recreation of the traditional Caliphate established immediately after the death of the Prophet, but one appropriate for the modern day. At the same time, Abdessalam Yassine has also expressed admiration for most of the main aspects and mechanisms of Western liberal democracy, and Abdelwahed El Moutawakil, who heads the movement's political circle, has argued that al-Adl members "have no complex about learning from the Western world."[40] Indeed, almost to emphasize this, El Moutawakil himself completed a master's degree in politics at Warwick University in Britain in 2003. Yassine, however, remains hostile to the secularism inherent in the tenets of most functioning liberal democracies. Moreover, the movement stresses the importance of the education and transformation of society along Islamic lines at the individual level prior to the establishment of an ideal political system. This implied reluctance to trust the judgment of an "unreformed" public does raise the question as to whether al-Adl wal-Ihsan would see the need for a "guiding" and "educating" government based on Islamic principles with all the authoritarian implications that such a government might have.[41]

A Further Radicalization?

The extent to which the broader ideological agendas and strategic objectives of the PJD and al-Adl wal-Ihsan are shared and understood by both the wider Moroccan population and, indeed, the actual supporters of the two movements themselves is debatable. The nuances of these debates arguably bypass most of the followers of both these groups. It seems clear that in common with most opposition political movements, the rank and file is significantly more radical than the leaderships. This distinction is perhaps most marked in the case of al-Adl wal-Ihsan, where a cerebral, thoughtful and fairly moderate leadership is attempting to build a mass movement from a society with fairly modest levels of education. Al-Adl wal-Ihsan has emphasized that all of its members are carefully inducted, that all are aware of the main tenets of the movement through its system of discussion and study groups, thus allowing for the weeding out of more extremist elements and ideas. Nevertheless, such a process must be difficult, and there is some evidence of membership fluctuation between al-Adl, the PJD, and more extremist groupings. The distinctions are even less clear to those outside the movements. One Moroccan newspaper found people in one of the poor districts of Casablanca that had produced some of the suicide bombers of May 16, 2003, expressing the view that al-Adl wal-Ihsan had been involved in the attacks.[42]

The fact that many of the members and supporters of the PJD and al-Adl wal-Ihsan have views that are substantively more radical than the leadership is significant. Nevertheless, the two movements' contention in the wake of the May 2003 attacks that they had exercised a restraining influence on the extremists is not to be discounted. The ultimate failure of this influence to prevent the attacks is put down by both organizations to the failure of the state to adequately address problems of poverty and marginalization that are beyond their own resources and capabilities. This raises the question as to whether continued radicalization of certain segments of the Moroccan population will mean that the PJD's and al-Adl wal-Ihsan's influence will continue to decline in favor of more extremist Islamist groups. The next question, therefore, will be whether the two organizations will attempt to shift their own agendas in a more radical direction to avoid being outflanked by the extremists.

Whether views will continue to radicalize certainly depends, as the profiles of the May 16 bombers indicated, on issues of poverty and marginalization. However, it also depends on events beyond Morocco. A significant contributory factor to the rise of Islamist sentiment in Morocco over recent years has been a series of developments at the international level. As already argued, the attacks on the United States of September 11, 2001, and the resulting war on terror, the conflict in Iraq, and, most important of all, the upsurge in Israeli-Palestinian violence following the collapse of the peace process in the fall of 2000, have served to radicalize large segments of the Moroccan population. These events persuaded them of the essential thesis, shared by all Islamist groupings of whatever coloring, that the Muslim world is engaged in a struggle against the influences and encroachments of the Western world in general and the United States in particular, and that only greater overt attachment to Islamic values and practices can hope to stop these encroachments. The massive expansion in both satellite television ownership and the channels available has meant that ordinary Moroccans are able to have a constant stream of images and commentary coming from Palestine, Iraq, and Afghanistan, with commentaries that invariably emphasize the view of the West as a threat. Indeed, data taken from opinion surveys has shown that popular views of the United States, in particular, have become increasingly negative since 2000.[43] How enduring such views are, and the extent to which they feed into support for both nonviolent and more extremist Islamist organizations, remains to be seen, but there is clearly an important link with events outside the kingdom.

The exact strength and influence of the more violent and extreme Islamist groups and organizations remain difficult to gauge. By nature shadowy and opaque, the huge wave of detentions that followed the attacks of May 2003 has forced them even further from the public view. Several thousand individuals were arrested, and more than two thousand were eventually convicted in the framework of the investigation into the attacks. Most of the membership and support of the amorphous and fragmented extremist groups has traditionally been drawn from the poor and sprawling shantytowns (*bidonvilles*) that ring many of Morocco's largest cities, most notably Casablanca, which supplied all of the May 16 suicide bombers.[44] The lack of any state presence in these areas in terms of public services and transport, schools, and even policing contributed not only to the radicalizing alienation of these areas but also to official ignorance of events and developments there during the preceding years. There was considerable press criticism that after initial police sweeps the areas returned to their original state. However, the government has now launched a well-publicized initiative to combat poverty in these and other downtrodden urban areas. Any success this initiative achieves will arguably go further in reducing popular support for extremism than political or security-oriented measures.

Conclusion

The overall challenge that the mainstream, nonviolent Islamist organizations present to the political order in Morocco is not one that is immediate. There will be no Iranian-style popular revolution, nor armed uprising of the type witnessed in the 1990s in Algeria, thanks to Morocco's highly conservative political culture and its attendant fear of rapid change. Consensus among Islamists, the regime, and the general public on the need to avoid the path taken by Algeria and the violence and chaos it unleashed is a further powerful incentive to pursue more gradualist options for political change and evolution. The attacks of May 16, 2003, though demonstrating that consensus on this issue was not absolute, provided the country with a taste of what the alternatives to gradual change could be. The very real horror and revulsion that was expressed across the social and political spectrum in the wake of the attacks may lead to a reduction in support for extremist groups, but whether there is a corresponding drop in support for organizations such as the PJD and al-Adl wal-Ihsan—which many see as "fellow travelers" of the extremists—remains to be seen.[45] Gilles Kepel, the French observer of Islamist movements, has argued that the resort to violence by more radical elements in Islamist movements in other states (notably Egypt and Algeria) has alienated more mainstream supporters of Islamist organizations (particularly those Kepel calls the "pious bourgeoisie") and that this has substantially weakened Islamist movements in those countries.[46]

In any event, it seems certain that both the PJD and al-Adl wal-Ihsan will continue their work, seeing their objectives as things to be achieved in the longer rather than shorter term. Their critique of the social, political, and economic shortcomings of Morocco will remain both potent and persuasive as long as the authorities fail to adequately address such problems, and as long as no other political or social force is able to articulate a more constructive critique or alternative. If Morocco continues on its current path of gradual, if halting, reform, the likelihood is that dissident voices and opinions will—as in Turkey—become integrated into the political mainstream and will no longer threaten the stability of the state. The PJD is already arguably part of this process. For al-Adl wal-Ihsan to be integrated there needs to be some compromise achieved on the issue of the constitutional role and powers of the monarchy. The fact that this hitherto taboo subject is now being discussed in sections of the press is a positive indication that the monarchy, for its part, may be willing to contemplate this.[47]

The preference in Morocco for slow and gradual political change may also help explain the rise in support for Islamist organizations over recent years. It may simply be that Morocco is to some extent a "late developer" with regard to Islamism. It is possible that, compared to most other Arab states, Morocco's relatively late urbanization (the percentage of urban dwellers topped 50 percent only in 1993–94) and more drawn out, less sudden socioeconomic crisis has meant that conditions that were traditionally favorable to the growth in Islamism elsewhere did not emerge in Morocco until the late 1990s. It therefore could be argued that Morocco is today at the same stage that Tunisia, Algeria, and Egypt were in the early to mid-1990s.

It now remains to be seen whether Kepel's thesis concerning the global decline in Islamism will be borne out by developments over the next decade in Morocco.

Notes

1. Its showing in the municipal elections in 2003 was markedly weaker.

2. Members of al-Shabiba al-Islamiyya have always denied being behind the assassination of Benjelloun. There are persistent suggestions that the Moroccan authorities were behind the killing in order to rid themselves of a troublesome leftist while providing an excuse to crack down on al-Shabiba al-Islamiyya.

3. For full treatment of the early activism of al-Shabiba al-Islamiyya and Abdessalam Yassine, see Emad Eldin Shahin, *Political Ascent: Contemporary Islamic Movements in North Africa* (Boulder, Colo.: Westview, 1997), 181–88; 193–95; Henry Munson, *Religion and Power in Morocco* (New Haven: Yale University Press, 1993), 159–73.

4. Shahin, *Political Ascent*, 172. According to al-Adl wal-Ihsan, Abdelkrim Mouti', who had had regular contacts with Yassine in the 1950s and 1960s, had approached Yassine early on to form a political party but the latter had replied that he did not feel spiritually ready. Nadia Yassine, daughter and spokesperson for Abdessalam Yassine, interview with author, Salé, July 5, 2001.

5. Munson, *Religion and Power in Morocco*, 115–48.

6. Abdelwahed El Moutawakil, member of al-Adl wal-Ihsan's Majlis al-Irshad (Guidance Council), interview with author, Rabat, June 28, 2002.

7. Specifically, Yassine made a reference to enemies being punished through illness at the very time when King Hasan was recovering from an attack of ill health. Muhammad Tozy, *Monarchie et Islam Politique au Maroc* (Paris: Presses de Sciences Po, 1999), 244n2.

8. Ibid., 243–44.

9. For full details of this, see Michael J. Willis, "Between *Alternance* and the *Makhzen*: At-Tawhid wa Al-Islah's Entry into Moroccan Politics," *Journal of North African Studies* 4, no. 3 (Autumn 1999): 46–49. Al-Islah had significantly eased official misgivings about their stance on the monarchy by a statement made by one of the senior figures in the movement, Muhammad Yatim, in which he argued that the movement did not seek to establish an Islamic state because one already existed "theoretically and constitutionally" in Morocco under the monarchy. Shahin, *Political Ascent*, 190–91.

10. Al-Islah wal-Tajdid/Al-Tawhid wal-Islah was kept organizationally distinct from the PJD to allow the movement to retain a legal organization if the authorities ever decided to ban the PJD as a political party.

11. Willis, "Between *Alternance* and the *Makhzen*," 50–59.

12. For an analysis of the interview, see Bruce Maddy-Weitzman, "Morocco," in *Middle East Contemporary Survey, Vol. XXIV, 2000*, edited by Maddy-Weitzman (Tel Aviv: Moshe Dayan Center, Tel Aviv University, 2002), 422–24. When interviewed by the author soon after his release about why he had not criticized the monarchy on his release

as he had done more than four years earlier, Yassine replied, "I am not a broken record." Abdessalam Yassine, interview with author, Salé, June 22, 2000.

13. Saad-Eddine Othmani, deputy secretary general of the PJD (1998–2004), secretary-general from 2004, interview with author, Rabat, June 7, 2000.

14. Interview with Abdelilah Benkirane in *Le Figaro*, September 30, 2002.

15. For a full account of the PJD's participation in the 2002 legislative elections, see Michael J. Willis, "Morocco's Islamists and the Legislative Elections of 2002: The Strange Case of the Party that Did Not Want to Win," *Mediterranean Politics* 9, no. 1 (Spring 2004): 53–81.

16. Mustapha Ramid, interview with author, Rabat, April 13, 2005.

17. For details of these allegations, see Willis, "Between *Alternance* and the *Makhzen*," 50–56, and Willis, "Morocco's Islamists," 68–70.

18. Saad-Eddine Othmani, interview with author, Rabat, July 23, 2003.

19. *La Gazette du Maroc*, June 9, 2003.

20. Othmani interview, July 23, 2003.

21. Interview with Mustapha Ramid, *Le Journal*, December 13, 2003.

22. Ramid interview, April 13, 2005.

23. When interviewed by the author in 2001, Khatib clearly indicated his preference for Othmani as his successor. Abdelkrim Khatib, secretary-general of the PJD (1998–2004), interview with author, Rabat, July 6, 2001.

24. *Assahifa*, April 7, 2004. Significantly, though, comments made to a newspaper one year earlier by the head of al-Tawhid wal-Islah, Ahmed Raissouni, appearing to question whether Muhammad VI had sufficient background to act as *Amir al-Mu'minin,* led to Raissouni's forced resignation. *Aujourd'hui Le Maroc*, May 12, 2003.

25. Tozy, *Monarchie et Islam Politique*, 198–99.

26. Young Moroccan to author, Casablanca, September 1997.

27. See Munson, *Religion and Power in Morocco*, 163–71.

28. Abdessalam Yassine, "Memorandum: To Him Who Is Concerned," http://www.yassine.net//letters/english.htm.

29. Abdessalam Yassine interview. Al-Adl wal-Ihsan's position on the monarchy is that although the Prophet Muhammad asked people to love his descendants, this should not equate to giving them exclusive political power. Nadia Yassine, interview with author, Salé, July 24, 2003.

30. For an excellent account of this tradition and these individuals, see Munson, *Religion and Power in Morocco*.

31. For such a characterization, and a prediction that the movement will split after Yassine's death, see Muhammad Tozy, "Les Pronostics de Muhammad: 'Les Islamzites ne peuvent pas gagner,'" *Arabies*, February 2001.

32. Nadia Yassine interview, July 5, 2001.

33. El Moutawakil interview, June 28, 2002.

34. Nadia Yassine, interviews with author, Salé, June 9, 2000 and June 27, 2002.

35. Fathallah Arslane, spokesman for al-Adl wal-Ihsan, interview with author, Rabat, July 22, 2003.

36. Tozy, *Monarchie et Islam Politique*, 245.

37. For comparisons between the AKP in Turkey and the PJD in Morocco, see Willis, "Morocco's Islamists," 78–79.

38. For controversies surrounding Ramid's views at the time of the 2002 elections, see ibid., 66.

39. Saad-Eddine Othmani, interview with author, Rabat, June 26, 2002.

40. Abdelwahed El Moutawakil, interview with author, Rabat, April 7, 2005.

41. For examples and discussion in English of Abdessalam Yassine's views on politics and democracy, see Abdessalam Yassine, *Winning the Modern World for Islam* (Iowa City, Iowa: Justice and Spirituality Publishing, 2000); Emad Eldin Shahin, "Secularism and Nationalism: The Political Discourse of Abd al-Salam Yassin," in *Islamism and Secularism in North Africa*, edited by John Ruedy (London: MacMillan, 1994); Muhammad Taha El Wardi, "Islamists and the Outside World: The Case of Abdessalam Yassine and al-Adl wal-Ihssan," *Research Papers Series* 19 (Ifrane: Al Akhawayn University, 2003); Bruce Maddy-Weitzman, "Islamism, Moroccan Style: The Ideas of Sheikh Yassine," *Middle East Quarterly* 10, no. 1 (Winter 2003): 43–51.

42. *Le Journal*, May 15, 2004.

43. Pew Research Center, "A Year After Iraq War: Mistrust of America in Europe Ever Higher, Muslim Anger Persists." Morocco was one of the countries surveyed. See the Pew Research Center for the People and the Press, http://www.people-press.org/reports/display.php3?ReportID=206.

44. For a good account of the attacks of May 16, 2003, see Jack Kalpakian, "Building the Human Bomb: The Case of the 16 May 2003 Attacks in Casablanca," *Studies in Conflict and Terrorism* 28, no. 2 (March/April 2005): 113–27.

45. In the local elections of September 2003, the overall vote for the PJD fell significantly in comparison to the legislative elections of the previous year. However, this fall was almost entirely due to the reduced number of candidates the party had been allowed to field in the aftermath of the Casablanca bombings. In areas where the party was able to field candidates, the PJD continued to score well.

46. Gilles Kepel, *Jihad: The Trail of Political Islam* (London: I. B. Tauris, 2002).

47. The francophone newspapers *TelQuel* and *Le Journal* have been particularly notable in their discussion of this issue.

9

Whither the Ben Ali Regime in Tunisia?

MICHELE PENNER ANGRIST

Since its birth as an independent state in 1956, Tunisia has been ruled by a hegemonic political party, the Neo-Destour, currently known as the RCD (Rassemblement Constitutionelle Démocratique), which was the product of a decades-long struggle against the French protectorate. The ending of the Institutional Revolutionary Party's monopoly on executive power in Mexico in 2000 has left Tunisia's as one of the world's oldest authoritarian one-party regimes. Although many have argued that this has been a fortuitous outcome because political stability has spared Tunisia from replicating Algeria's civil war–torn fate, this stability has come at enormous cost to political and civil rights. The public sphere has been deadened and Tunisians have been obliged to pay public homage to President Zayn al-Abidin Ben Ali's cult of personality. A prime political challenge for Tunisia, then, is to democratize while avoiding the instability many fear would be associated with democratization. As Tunisia enters the new millennium, it is worth considering what the future likely holds with respect to the shape of the Tunisian political system. Will the RCD maintain its monopoly in the near to medium term (i.e., the next ten to fifteen years)? Or will it be compelled to loosen the reins and share power with other groups?

This chapter analyzes the prospects for democratization in Tunisia and considers the strengths and preferences of key domestic social forces and civic and political organizations external to the RCD that might be expected to press for democracy. It then discusses the prospects that the regime's international backers might demand democratization and that rifts within the regime might create an opening for democratization. The upshot of this analysis is that political continuity, as opposed to change, will characterize the near to medium term. Recent political developments chronicle the intensification and consolidation rather than the softening of dictatorship in Tunisia. No social group or civic or political organization has the power and preference to challenge the status quo, and although Tunisia's external supporters may temper their positions, these are not likely to be altered dramatically, given the U.S.-declared global war on terrorism. Instead, Ben Ali's assumption and consolidation of power represented substantial regime change in its own right; his transformation of the bases of presidential power has produced a new system that looks viable for the foreseeable future.

Tunisian Politics Heading into the New Millennium

The 1994 parliamentary elections were the first in Tunisian history to see opposition party candidates gaining seats. The combination of the ruling party's preponderant political position and electoral rules that confer advantage on large parties has meant that the RCD has always monopolized the legislature. Tunisian opposition parties entered the legislature in 1994 thanks to a new electoral law that set aside for them 19 of 163 seats (12 percent) to be distributed proportionally to the parties' relative national vote-getting success.[1] Prior to the 1999 elections, the regime increased to 20 percent the percentage of seats that would be held by members of the legal opposition. In the current parliament, constituted by the October 2004 elections, opposition party members hold 37 of 189 seats.

The political impact of the presence of opposition candidates in parliament is minimal, however, as parliament is a distinctly subordinate political institution. It does not initiate legislation and cannot hold the executive branch—the seat of real power—accountable. In addition, with the partial exception of one (harassed) branch of one of the legal opposition parties, these parties on the whole are weak, without substantial roots or popularity in civil society, and severely constrained in their ability to raise funds and use media outlets to get their messages out. The reality of weak opposition parties holding a small minority of seats in a weak legislative institution, therefore, does not add up to serious advances in political pluralism.[2]

The 1999 presidential elections were the first in Tunisian history in which more than one candidate competed. The Popular Unity Party's Mohamed Belhaj Amor and the Unionist Democratic Union's Abderrahmane Tlili "ran" against the incumbent, who is also the leader of the RCD. This was far from a competitive election, however. Ben Ali essentially hand-picked his opponents, engineering the passage of a constitutional amendment in June 1999 that allowed these two minor party leaders to contest the election. In the words of one analyst, "Neither man volunteered his candidacy."[3] Tlili made no pretense of offering Tunisians a real electoral alternative, telling the *Economist* that "he would not change any of the president's policies if elected, just implement them with even greater gusto" and that "the president is a better candidate than he is."[4] Belhaj Amor was more critical, differentiating himself from the president along policy lines. In the end his candidacy too was futile, in part because the government allowed almost no coverage of his campaign on television and radio. Ben Ali officially received 99.4 percent of votes cast, with Belhaj Amor and Tlili receiving 0.3 percent and 0.2 percent respectively. The landslide nature of Ben Ali's victory indicates that this presidential election was less about setting precedents for the toleration of contestation and more about making a very public showing of Ben Ali's political predominance. The same dynamic unfolded in the October 2004 presidential election: Ben Ali officially attained 94 percent of votes cast, while his three challengers each garnered between 1 and 4 percent.

A further indication of the president's unwillingness to relinquish power is seen in developments concerning limits on his term in office. After taking power in 1987, Ben Ali placed term limits for the Tunisian president in the constitution, thus correcting the excesses of his predecessor, Habib Bourguiba, who had made himself "President for Life" in 1974. The new provision stated presidents could serve a maximum of three five-year terms. Yet in May 2002, the government drafted a constitutional amendment that permits Ben Ali to remain in office at least until 2014—a stint in power that would represent more than five terms. The amendment abolished term limits and raised the age limit for presidential candidates to seventy-five.[5] The referendum held to pass this amendment suggested that voter approval of a Ben Ali life presidency was a command performance: "Although voters stood behind a black curtain to cast their ballots, secrecy was virtually impossible. 'Yes' ballots were white; 'no' ballots were black and could clearly be seen through the thin envelopes. Even if attendants couldn't see, they reportedly asked for the unused ballots back."[6]

The regime recently has made efforts to improve its political image by moving legislation through parliament that ostensibly is designed to liberalize Tunisia's press code. Among other things, the amendments removed "defaming public order" as a charge under which journalists could be tried, required the professionalization of the ranks of media outlet personnel, and eliminated prison sentences for journalistic transgressions (replacing them with fines). However, other methods of constraining the press continue to be operative. Publications rely heavily on advertising revenue, and the regime can pressure businesses and institutions into withholding their advertising business from those that are out of favor. Tellingly, between 1998 and 2001 the Committee to Protect Journalists (CPJ, a U.S.-based nongovernmental organization, or NGO) annually named Ben Ali to its list of the "10 Worst Enemies of the Press." In 2001 the CPJ called attention to and condemned a drive-by shooting aimed against Tunisian journalist and government critic Riad Ben Fadhel, calling the incident an assassination attempt.

In short, despite superficial positive changes, a repressive status quo continues in Tunisia. A multiparty parliament notwithstanding, there is no toleration for the expression of political dissent, and the regime impinges on the civil liberties of those who are willing to defy this norm. International human rights activists have been barred from entering the country or detained after arrival, and opponents of the regime have been imprisoned without trial for long periods of time. International human rights NGOs such as Amnesty International and Human Rights Watch continue to be very critical of the RCD regime.[7]

How Firm Is the RCD's Grip on Power?

The authoritarian status quo in Tunisia is as surprising as it is disappointing. Tunisia possesses a large number of characteristics that scholars believe are conducive to democratization. Tunisians are ethnically and religiously homogeneous and have a "protracted experience of political identity long predating the era of colonial mapmaking."[8] After independence, Bourguiba charted a modernizing, Westernizing political path in which he firmly entrenched the notion of civilian rule. His legislative record vis-à-vis women's rights was unmatched in the Arab world, and although he did pursue statist economic development policies during the 1960s, that path was abandoned for a more liberal approach relatively early for the region (the 1970s). The result has been the development of a substantial private capitalist sector and hence the "space for the development of autonomous sources of economic power that might imaginably countervail [the state] one day."[9] Today Tunisia is a relatively prosperous nation with a GDP per capita (purchasing power parity) of around U.S. $8,600, a low poverty rate (6.7 percent of households in 1990),[10] a large middle class, and high education and literacy rates for the developing world. Although all of these factors should bode well for the establishment of political pluralism, that prospect seems out of reach at the present juncture.

The opposite was true in 1987, when then–prime minister Ben Ali eased Bourguiba out of power. As is well known, Ben Ali's opening moves as president raised hopes that Tunisia would head down a democratic political path. He freed political prisoners, legalized opposition parties, convened a dialogue with a wide variety of groups that culminated in the signing of a National Pact in 1988, and asserted that Tunisia's citizenry had reached political maturity and no longer needed the guidance of a hegemonic single party. By the early 1990s, however, it was clear that Ben Ali had either changed his mind or been disingenuous from the outset. At that point, the force of the regime's security apparatus came down not only on his Islamist opponents but also on the secular opposition, human rights groups, and anyone else who criticized what appeared to be a return with a vengeance to the old authoritarian status quo. A critical question therefore, is whether there are actors or dynamics in play today that might undermine that status quo.

Potential for Domestic Challenges to the Regime

Social Forces

According to conventional wisdom, a number of social forces might have been expected to press for enhanced political pluralism, due to the fact that, since the mid-1980s, Tunisia has pursued market reforms that are integrating it into the globalizing world economy.[11] Prior to these reforms, the state played a substantial role in the economy, intervening by establishing tariffs and other import-restricting mechanisms, distributing subsidized credit, and manipulating exchange rates in ways that were pivotal to the success of domestic manufacturing. Because a sizable number of economic actors were beholden to the state and the ruling party for their well-being, both capitalists and workers were reluctant to challenge the rules of the political game for fear that retribution from the authorities would spell material disaster. Thus when the Tunisian state began to allow market forces rather than politicians' decisions to determine the allocation of resources and the fate of domestic businesses in an increasingly competitive world economy, many believed that democratization would follow. Why? Key class actors should have been less reluctant to challenge the status quo if they were no longer dependent on state goodwill for their operations. Moreover, as exposure to the global economy brought deleterious consequences to many, there would be new motive, it was thought, to press for more voice in national decision-making processes.

None of this has come to pass. Consider first the fact that key urban social forces have not organized to challenge the authoritarian status quo. Private industrialists were aloof as Ben Ali appeared to be opening up the political system in 1987; they assented when he ratcheted authoritarianism back up in the 1990s.[12] Instead of mobilizing in the face of reforms that jeopardized their futures, many manufacturers chose to shut down uncompetitive operations and switch to more profitable endeavors; if they came to the regime with concerns, complaints, or demands, they did so on an individual rather than an organized basis.[13] Organized labor, too, was politically aloof during the years of opening under Ben Ali and then publicly supported his campaign for reelection in 1994.

Several factors explain capital's behavior. First, "Tunisia had marginal protectionist elites, which did not enjoy especially privileged linkages to the state, and the early creation of an offshore zone created a substantial class of exporters who were largely unfazed by trade liberalization."[14] As the regime faces relatively few big "losers" in the face of globalization, economic reform is not as politically inflammatory a proposition as it has been elsewhere. Bellin identifies three additional dynamics that explain capital's passivity.[15] The state has not yet fully exited the market and thus business is still somewhat beholden to the state's good graces. The government helps uncompetitive firms to restructure in order to compete in the global market. This assistance is granted on a discretionary basis, however, and everyone assumes that political "troublemakers" would not benefit. In addition, because the state generally has acted in a manner that benefits private capitalists, and because it regularly consults with them, the latter have concluded that democratization would hurt their interests because it would oblige the regime to respond to a much wider array of interest groups, therefore diminishing capitalists' relatively privileged access to state policy-making processes. Finally, Tunisia's capitalists have backed Ben Ali out of fear that, given the presence of a powerful Islamist movement, the professed democratic intentions of which many question, competitive elections would lead to instability or civil war.[16] Business owners require order to ensure the profitability of investments; in Tunisia they have preferred stability under dictatorship to the risks they associate with democracy.[17]

Given the downward wage pressures associated with globalization, that phenomenon should have little upside for organized labor (it does, by contrast, offer opportunities to competitive capitalists). Still, Tunisia's labor union, the Union Générale des Travailleurs Tunisiens (UGTT), has not chosen an oppositional path.[18] Although the state-labor relationship has been confrontational in the past, Ben Ali has established a productive relationship with the UGTT that brings benefits to both parties. The UGTT does not challenge the political status quo and instead organizes worker support for the regime, which Ben Ali sees as a critical counterweight to his Islamist foes. In return, under Ben Ali, the state has intervened in wage negotiations, securing for organized labor wage levels substantially higher than what pure market logic would dictate. Thanks in part to this quid pro quo, organized labor's material status is appreciably higher than that of workers in the informal and agricultural sectors, not to mention the unemployed. These categories represent a majority of Tunisian workers and would likely compete with organized labor for state largesse were democratization to occur. In many respects, therefore, for organized labor to confront the state would be irrational.

Much the same story can be told about rural social forces in Tunisia.[19] In the late 1980s and 1990s, the government privatized state-run agricultural collectives. Although in theory such reforms should free up rural actors—no longer ensconced in state-dominated economic activity—for political activism, in practice this has not occurred. The state pursued decollectivization in a manner that benefited large landowners almost exclusively. They were the primary acquirers of these lands, they continue to benefit from state policies that subsidize credit and other inputs, and are, as a result, stalwart supporters of Ben Ali's regime. Decollectivization did not benefit middle and small peasants, by contrast. Indeed, reform harmed the latter because increasing mechanization of large-scale farming reduced the demand for their labor. Although there is thus much discontent among middle and small peasants, it does not threaten the regime because it is not organized. Middle and small peasants have abandoned farmers' unions, which are now dominated by large landowners and function increasingly sporadically. In addition, party officials draw on Islamic charity norms to pressure large landowners into redistributing sufficient wealth at harvest time and on major religious holidays in order to sustain social peace. Thus prodemocratic movements originating from the countryside are not imminent: large landholders are not interested, and poorer rural actors are hamstrung by poverty, lack of organization, and their dependence on large landowner patrons for their annual subsistence needs.

Mention should be made of one final social group that sees its interests aligned with regime continuity: urban middle-class women. In the 1980s, these actors worried that they would experience a substantial status reduction were Tunisia's Islamists to come to power—either through the ballot box or civil war. As a result they have, by and large, thrown their support behind Ben Ali. Describing the run-up to the presidential election of 1994, Murphy writes, "'L'effet Ben Ali' has become the term used to describe the positive imagery associated with a president who has 'saved' the nation—not least its feminine components, the middle-class elements of which are all too aware of what might have awaited them had the Islamists come to power. Ben Ali has made great media efforts to demonstrate his commitment to the progressive and liberal status of women in Tunisia, and has equally striven to lay emphasis on the reactionary agendas of Islamic political competition."[20] Although this sector of society is neither numerically large nor materially pivotal, the president has nonetheless seen fit to cultivate it.

Antiregime activism thus runs counter to the interests of most social forces. Humbler rural landholders might benefit from political change but cannot effect it. What about the poor, and those who have suffered in the face of market reforms? Here too the regime has acted strategically and thereby manages to retain the upper hand. Spending more than half of its budget on social and developmental programs,[21] it has effectively portrayed itself as a solicitous "provider" to the poor.[22] The state has had to lay off workers and remove subsidies on staple goods and services to comply with standard economic reform practices, and this has been a blow to both the middle class and the poor. The state has sought to cushion the blow to the latter, however, by carrying out carefully targeted transfers of wealth, prioritizing rural development and urban housing projects, and tending quite successfully to job creation.[23] A militant challenge to the regime from this sector therefore also seems remote.

Civic and Political Organizations

In the near to medium term, civil society cannot be expected to help push back the grip of the authoritarian state in Tunisia. Since independence, the single-party regime has fostered the development of civic associations in which its citizens could develop a sense of public spiritedness and participate in national development. However, both Bourguiba and Ben Ali have carefully regulated and circumscribed those associations—including via outright repression—to prevent them from becoming nodes of autonomous power capable of undermining the regime.[24] Civil society finds itself in particularly dire straits under Ben Ali. Bourguiba maintained his position by playing RCD elites off one another as they competed for government appointments and a concomitant ability to service their respective clienteles; protest from civil society was "turned on and off by these elites and by Bourguiba as it suited their political game-playing."[25] Moving into the presidency from outside the party, Ben Ali lacked the resources to play this game. He has worked assiduously to neutralize Bourguiba-era party barons resentful of his ascent to power, feels acutely threatened by their connections to civic organizations, and has either co-opted or repressed civil society to the extent that protest is never tolerated.[26] The result has been that Tunisia's "traditionally vigorous civil society [is] adrift."[27]

There is likewise no possibility that the seven legal, secular opposition parties in the Tunisian political arena can weaken the Ben Ali regime. Their liabilities are numerous and typical of organizations of their ilk throughout the Arab world.[28] They have scant financial resources, a significant portion of which comes from government subsidies. None have substantial grassroots organizations or mass support. This circumstance is the result of several factors, including the lack of social forces interested in and/or capable of backing them, financial limitations, government repression,[29] the fact that policy-wise these parties do not represent sharp alternatives to the RCD, and "the gulf that still separates the educated elite from the rest of the population in the Arab world."[30] As well, these opposition parties have not loomed as principled and politically courageous entities; they stood by as Ben Ali cracked down mercilessly on Islamists in the early 1990s (see below), and in 1994 and 1999, they agreed to occupy the parliamentary seats Ben Ali made available to them. The impression they generated, therefore, was of a co-opted and weak-willed bunch.

Events surrounding the 2004 elections leave much the same impression. At a June 2004 rally held under the slogan "No to a life presidency," a group of opposition parties called on Tunisians to boycott the upcoming presidential election in October, arguing that the outcome was not in doubt.[31] Indeed, boycotts designed to delegitimize electoral outcomes are one of the few weapons weak opposition parties potentially wield in authoritarian settings.[32] Yet three of Tunisia's seven legal opposition parties fielded presidential candidates in 2004, and only two boycotted the concurrent legislative poll. A unified boycott thus was impossible to pull off, and for the five legal opposition parties that gained parliamentary seats in 2004, the impression of co-optation remains because the parliamentary seats set aside for them were a "gift" from Ben Ali that afforded them no real power while putting a more palatable face on dictatorship.

The Tunisian party that did mobilize large numbers of the populace, develop significant grassroots support, and represent a potential counterweight to the regime was en-Nahda (renaissance). Tracing its origins to the Islamic Tendency Movement (Mouvement de la tendance islamique; MTI), which emerged in the late 1970s with a socioeconomic and cultural critique of Bourguiba's regime, en-Nahda garnered at least 15 percent of the vote in the 1989 legislative elections, even though, as the regime had refused to legalize it, it had to run for office wholly via independent candidacies. This evidence of its potential power, combined with en-Nahda leader Rachid al-Ghannouchi's pro-Iraq stance in the Persian Gulf War (a position that resonated widely among the public), moved Ben Ali to crack down on that organization between 1990 and 1992. His efforts effectively destroyed en-Nahda as a political force inside of Tunisia.[33] En-Nahda today probably has about one thousand militants in Tunisian jails, plus one thousand residing in Europe, making it the main Tunisian political movement in exile.[34] Still, en-Nahda has not given up its struggle, engaging in fund-raising activities and operating a trilingual Web site as well as a satellite television station (Ezzeitouna TV). Ghannouchi regularly appears on Arab satellite television; according to Camau and Geisser, Tunisia's streets tend to empty out when he does—an indication that the group's message still resonates.[35]

That message appears to have moderated of late. In the late 1980s and early 1990s, despite indications that en-Nahda would play by democratic rules, the words and deeds of some in the party convinced many that their true goal was the pursuit of a monopoly on power, through violence if necessary, in order to build an Islamic state.[36] After the crackdown, en-Nahda suffered numerous defections of both exiled high-level leaders and base activists who criticized the party and/or Ghannouchi for rhetoric and behavior that was extreme and too confrontational, and as a result politically disastrous for the movement.[37] Many of these defectors have altered their ideologies: although they still seek a society that publicly values and reinforces Arabo-Muslim culture, they are willing to operate in a secular republican political environment. These defections, en-Nahda's impotence in exile, and its hopes of gaining legal recognition as a political party and winning amnesty for its jailed militants all appear to have made Ghannouchi and other top leaders more consistent in their moderation and prodemocratic actions and rhetoric and less reluctant to silence militant voices in the party.

To this end, Ghannouchi and en-Nahda have refused to climb on the radical international Islamist bandwagon that is sympathetic to Osama bin Laden. Ghannouchi has said that this movement does not serve Muslims' interests; he denounced terrorism after the September 11, 2001, attacks on the United States and he has worked with the party to try to prevent en-Nahda members from succumbing to temptations to violence. In addition, "this process of normalization has translated into a renunciation by Nahda of its monopolistic vision—the Islamist party-state as an alternative to the Destourian single party—and a willingness to locate itself now in oppositional milieus, in so doing becoming 'a party like the others' and, more and more, a 'party among the others.'" Today en-Nahda is calling for the formation of a democratic front guided by a coordination committee in which it would be no more than one of the components. Quoting Ghannouchi, "This collaboration between Tunisian Islamists and the secularist opposition is a unique experience in the Arab world. Tunisia could create a model of democracy and coexistence in the Arab world."[38] Not surprisingly, observers remain divided between those who believe en-Nahda has undergone a strategic transformation and indeed seeks a plural polity and those who believe that moderation remains purely a tactic designed to facilitate its rise to power.

Despite skeptics' lingering concerns, en-Nahda's apparent moderation looks to be facilitating a warming of relations between it and Ben Ali's secular opponents. Concerned about the policy consequences if en-Nahda came to power in Tunisia, the latter generally either stood by or assisted the regime as it suppressed en-Nahda in 1990–1992.[39] They were, however, dismayed when, beginning in the mid-1990s, the regime set its sights on them. According to Murphy, the perception grew among secular oppositionists that "the president was becoming personally authoritarian. The security forces began taking new initiatives which, while supposedly directed at defending state security from the instabilities rife in neighboring Algeria, were considered by many to be more aimed at self-consolidation and absolute social control. The message to the legal opposition [was] increasingly one of intolerance of criticism and preparedness to use sanctions to enforce silence."[40] Alarm at this development also promoted rapprochement with en-Nahda, as does the fact that, realistically, the secular opposition will need the assistance of en-Nahda and its partisans on the ground if it is going to put meaningful pressure on the regime. Meanwhile, Yaroslav Trofimov argues that the receding threat of an Islamist takeover in Algeria and elsewhere reassures secularists that reaching out to their Islamist counterparts will not lead to disaster.

What are the signs of rapprochement? There is the story of Mokhtar Yahyaoui. As a prosecutor in the early 1990s he helped crack down on Islamists; in 2001 he was dismissed from his job as a magistrate after publicly criticizing the lack of judicial independence in Tunisia. Today he is "openly cooperating with the Islamists he once dispatched to jail."[41] Camau and Geisser report that in Paris, where the bulk of exiled Tunisian oppositionists reside, there are substantial networks and regular meetings between Islamists and secularists. Tunisian leftist activists have appeared on Ezzeitouna TV, and in 2001, "en-Nahda organized an *iftar* dinner during Ramadan to which most of the political personalities among Tunisian exiles in Paris were invited."[42] Secular oppositionists evidently are responding to en-Nahda overtures: "Nahda has largely succeeded in getting itself repatriated into the Tunisian opposition scene including in the milieus that used to be most hostile to it. Personalities that used to be hardline anti-Islamist (sometimes called 'eradicators') now admit the principle of legalizing a political party of religious inspiration, at the same time continuing to push a functionally anti-Islamist discourse."[43]

In his 2004 book, prominent secular opposition figure Moncef Marzouki reports on a three-day meeting held in Aix-en-Provence, France, in May 2003 at which around thirty representatives of various Tunisian opposition political currents (including en-Nahda) negotiated and signed a document that set out mutually held understandings and end goals: "Non-dogmatic democrats, including representatives of the extreme Left, recognized Tunisians' right to their national and religious identity, enlightened Islamists recognized Tunisians' right to a democratic regime and its basic principles including complete equality, notably between the two sexes. The text says the state will be democratic, recognizing the liberties, pluralism, *alternance*, and sexual equality."[44]

The Upshot

Despite evidence of increasing unity among the ranks of those opposed to Ben Ali's regime, realistically there is little chance that they will be able to pry concessions from it, let alone force it into remission. En-Nahda and its newfound friends in exile are cut off from direct contact with the domestic arena. Secular opposition parties and civil society organizations on the ground are impotent politically, in no small part due to the security dragnet that represses dissent. And no significant social force has the motive and the means to effect change. There is ample reason for discontent: corruption, unemployment, rising prices, and increasing income disparities in the economic sphere in the context of repression in the political sphere. There is, too, evidence of such discontent. The government was disappointed at the turnout for the referendum that extended Ben Ali's term in office.[45] The crowds that gathered upon Bourguiba's death turned "subversive" against his successor.[46] Individual dissenters have resorted to hunger strikes with increasing frequency.[47] Yet without effective organization, discontent cannot translate into pressure for change. If regime change is to occur in the near to medium term, it will have to come from within the regime itself, accompanied, most likely, by a change in the stance of its external backers.

Other Possible Sources of Regime Weakening

The Policies of External Backers

A key force bolstering Ben Ali's regime are his external backers, primarily the United States and France. Both have turned a diplomatic blind eye toward the intensification of Tunisian authoritarianism under Ben Ali. The United States values the Tunisian regime for its firm stance on Islamism, its support for the Israeli-Palestinian peace process, and for its decision to pursue standard IMF policy prescriptions for growth (which appear to be working).[48] The latter is particularly important to the French, who are concerned about the rising tide of North African immigration, much of it driven by the search for economic opportunity. Thus, for example, the referendum extending Ben Ali's term as president passed "without a hint of protest by the U.S. or other Western governments."[49] This type of international support for authoritarian regimes in the Middle East and how they choose to deploy their coercive apparatuses has been identified as a crucial explanation for their comparative longevity in global terms.[50]

Shifts in U.S. geo-strategic calculations in the wake of the September 11 attacks mean that there is reason to question the extent to which the United States will continue to back Ben Ali. Arguing that terrorism emanates in part from closed political climates in the region, President George W. Bush has publicly questioned longstanding U.S. policies supporting the dictatorial status quo for stability's sake and has made democracy promotion in the region a plank in his policy platform. Accordingly, there have been new departures from the administration vis-à-vis Ben Ali. Secretary of State Colin Powell visited Tunisia in December 2003, praising Ben Ali for his policies on education and women and inviting him to the White House, but that visit (in February 2004) entailed both constraints and criticism. Symbolically it included neither a joint news conference nor a state dinner. Substantively, President Bush told reporters he was looking forward to discussing with Ben Ali "the need to have a press corps that is vibrant and free, as well as an open political process. . . ." Although the words might sound mild, human rights advocates say they marked a watershed. It appeared to be the first time Bush has issued a face-to-face challenge on human rights to an Arab leader who has been an ally in the administration's declared war on terrorism."[51]

It is too soon to tell just how much new political pressure the United States will exert on Ben Ali and other allies in the Middle East. One may reasonably speculate, however, that because the Tunisian regime supports so many U.S. policy objectives (toward Islamists, Israel, and Libya, in economic affairs and the war on terrorism, etc.), the United States will take no actions that it believes will seriously undermine regime stability. It probably will limit itself to demanding liberalizing reforms. In this vein we might expect to see a further expanded opposition presence in parliament, reduced press censorship, and fewer human rights abuses. But anticipating a change in U.S. policy dramatic enough to seriously buffet Ben Ali seems wrongheaded.

Cracks within the Regime?

During Bourguiba's tenure as president, the ruling party represented the core structure and support of the regime. As noted above, Bourguiba maintained his leadership by pitting party elites against one another as they competed for his favor and for patronage with which to service their clients. Influential party barons cycled in and out of "grace" according to his signals; they focused their energies therefore on internecine competition and intrigue rather than joining forces to unseat him. Bourguiba also used the party's mass organization to distribute patronage to society in a manner that kept it relatively politically content. The regime possessed a modest security apparatus which it used to quell occasional manifestations of dissent. During the 1970s and early 1980s, however, this apparatus increasingly was not up to this task, and the Tunisian army, which until that point had remained politically marginal due to Bourguiba's policies,[52] had to be called in on a number of occasions to maintain order.[53]

When Ben Ali assumed the presidency, he altered the nature of Tunisia's one-party regime. Having built a career in the army and the Interior Ministry, the president assumed the role of party leader with no power base within it. To secure his position, he filled top party positions with technocrats who either had no prior political experience or were not well connected within the party and were, therefore, personally loyal to him; he routinely rotates them from position to position to prevent them from developing individual power bases.[54] The party is an important organizational sinew of the president's rule,[55] but it now "serves" the regime, whereas it "ruled" in Bourguiba's time.[56] Today the core structural supports of the regime are the business sector, especially that portion profiting from economic reforms, the security apparatus, and the army.[57] The security forces quadrupled in size[58] and became increasingly professionalized under Ben Ali,[59] who steers larger portions of the national budget in this direction than Bourguiba had.[60] The army now has representation on the Council for National Security,[61] and although it functions outside politics, it represents a "dormant force" whose loyalty Ben Ali requires to stay in power.[62] As Ben Ali rose to power from a military career, he should be well positioned to maintain that loyalty. The political profile of both the security forces and the military is enhanced because Ben Ali has placed allies from the Interior Ministry and the military in top party and state positions as well.[63]

These represent substantial shifts in what undergirds Tunisia's one-party regime—shifts that earned Ben Ali the resentment and hostility of many party barons. They not only had lost the succession game to Ben Ali but also found themselves newly politically marginalized. What's more, many objected to the liberalizing economic policies Ben Ali and his technocrats were implementing.[64] Such policies reduced the amount of state patronage party elites could distribute to clienteles—a core dynamic of regime life under Bourguiba. Resentment between conservative Bourguiba-era party barons on the one hand and Ben Ali and his courtiers on the other constituted an important element of tension in the regime and the largest potential for a rift that might have led to substantial regime change. Disaffected party barons and their client cadres could have chosen to break away from the ruling party and found a new party, in effect pluralizing the Tunisian political arena from above.

Such a turn of events did not come to pass—and now that Ben Ali has been in power for seventeen years, it is not likely to. Conservative party barons accustomed to competing with one another for Bourguiba's favor would have had to cooperate as never before to found a breakaway party. Meanwhile, Ben Ali has proven to be a shrewd, able politician. He controls the coercive arms of the regime and has demonstrated his willingness to deploy them without hesitation against political rivals.[65] These facts deter dissenting activity from within the party's ranks. In addition, Bourguiba-era party barons, though no doubt unhappy about their status change, still likely calculate that they are better off serving the status quo than they would be under a pluralizing scenario, for the latter would almost certainly bring a diminution in their political roles. In part for this reason, political scientists have shown that one-party regimes are particularly resilient forms: their average "shelf life" is far longer than military or personalist regimes, for instance. [66] In this respect, party barons are indebted to Ben Ali. The ruling party's health and longevity are key to the preservation of their status as political elites, and Ben Ali's initiatives upon assuming power revitalized and enlarged an organization that had been adrift in the 1980s while Bourguiba's health deteriorated.[67]

In sum, then, we are not likely to see substantial regime change in Tunisia in the next ten to fifteen years. The current balance of forces is too skewed in Ben Ali's favor for such a scenario to unfold. This projection of stasis needs to be understood, however, in light of the fact that the nature and supports of the regime did evolve significantly in the 1990s. Ben Ali has personalized the regime, and in so doing he has laid the foundations for its survival for the foreseeable future.

Notes

Note: I thank Laura Butterfield for her excellent research assistance. An earlier version of this work was presented at the Annual Meeting of the Middle East Studies Association, San Francisco, November 2001.

1. The regime has legally recognized seven secular opposition parties: the Movement of Democratic Socialists, Ettajdid, the Unionist Democratic Union, the Popular Unity Party, the Liberal Social Party, the Progressive Democratic Party, and the Democratic Forum for Work and Freedom.

2. For a more detailed discussion, see Michele Penner Angrist, "Parties, Parliament and Political Dissent in Tunisia," *Journal of North African Studies* 4, no. 4 (Winter 1999): 89–104.

3. Larbi Sadiki, "The Search for Citizenship in Bin Ali's Tunisia: Democracy Versus Unity," *Political Studies* 50 (2002): 506. Sadiki notes that "those who did [run for the presidency] in the past, such as Human Rights activist Moncef al-Marzouqi and Abd al-Rahman al-Hani, a known lawyer, were both prevented from standing."

4. "Bad Movie," *Economist*, October 23, 1999.

5. The amendment also protects Ben Ali from prosecution for life should he live long enough to surrender power.

6. Michael Slackman, "Tunisia's 2 Faces of Progress," *Los Angeles Times*, June 10, 2002.

7. See, for example, "Tunisia: The Cycle of Injustice," *Amnesty International*, June 10, 2003, http://web.amnesty.org./library.

8. Eva Bellin, "Civil Society in Formation: Tunisia," in *Civil Society in the Middle East*, vol. 1, edited by Augustus Richard Norton, 124 (Leiden: E. J. Brill, 1995).

9. Ibid., 124.

10. Emma C. Murphy, *Economic and Political Change in Tunisia: From Bourguiba to Ben Ali* (New York: St. Martins, 1999), 128, https://www.cia.gov/cia/publications/factbook/geos/ts.html#Econ.

11. Tunisia commenced serious trade reforms in 1987, further committing itself to this course in the 1990s by joining the World Trade Organization and by signing bilateral trade agreements with the European Union that, if fully implemented, should result in

the "near total liberalization" of the Tunisian trade regime. On this point see Melani Cammett, "Fat Cats and Self-Made Men: Globalization and the Paradoxes of Collective Action," *Comparative Politics* 37, no. 4 (July 2005): 386. Emma Murphy catalogues multiple external acknowledgments of the extent to which Tunisia has pursued such reforms. Emma Murphy, "Ten Years On—Ben Ali's Tunisia," *Mediterranean Politics* 2, no. 3 (Winter 1997): 115.

12. Eva Bellin, *Stalled Democracy: Capital, Labor, and the Paradox of State-Sponsored Development* (Ithaca: Cornell University Press, 2002). The observation in the paragraph's last sentence regarding labor also comes from Bellin.

13. Cammett, "Fat Cats and Self-Made Men," 21–22.

14. Ibid., 31.

15. Bellin, *Stalled Democracy*, 149–50.

16. Murphy, *Economic and Political Change*, 213.

17. Bellin, *Stalled Democracy*, 150.

18. The remainder of this paragraph summarizes Bellin, *Stalled Democracy*, 151–52.

19. This paragraph summarizes arguments made by Stephen J. King, in *Liberalization Against Democracy: The Local Politics of Economic Reform in Tunisia* (Bloomington: Indiana University Press, 2003).

20. Murphy, *Economic and Political Change*, 214.

21. Slackman.

22. See "Be Happy, and Shut Up," *Economist*, January 31, 1998; Murphy, *Economic and Political Change*, 225.

23. Murphy, "Ten Years On," 115.

24. The regime's repertoire of control tactics include requiring associations to procure Interior Ministry permission to function legally; subsidizing groups so as to undercut their political autonomy; infiltrating potentially threatening organizations with party loyalists in order to control them "from within"; and founding duplicate organizations that dilute their counterparts' influence. Bellin, "Civil Society in Formation," 139–41.

25. Christopher Alexander, "Back from the Democratic Brink: Authoritarianism and Civil Society in Tunisia," *Middle East Report* 205 (October–December 1997): 36.

26. The plight of human rights organizations is a case in point. Both the Tunisian Human Rights League and the National Council on Liberties in Tunisia have experienced marked repression. The regime has closed down the former on more than one occasion and blocked portions of its funding; the government refuses to grant the latter legal status. Activists from both have been harassed and imprisoned.

27. Alexander, "Back from the Democratic Brink," 38.

28. Vickie Langohr, "Too Much Civil Society, Too Little Politics: Egypt and Liberalizing Arab Regimes," *Comparative Politics* 36, no. 2 (January 2004): 188–91.

29. The opposition parties do not have meaningful access to television, radio, or press media. Government agents have prevented some from physically meeting. The generalized climate of fear and forced depoliticization generated by the ubiquitous security service presence also dissuades citizens from openly supporting opposition organizations.

30. Marina Ottaway, "Democracy and Constituencies in the Arab World," *Carnegie Papers/Middle East Series/Democracy and the Rule of Law Project* 48 (July 2004): 8.

31. "Tunisia Opposition Calls on Voters to Boycott Presidential Election," Agence France Presse, June 24, 2004.

32. Marsha Pripstein Posusney, "Multi-Party Elections in the Arab World: Institutional Engineering and Oppositional Strategies," *Studies in Comparative International Development* 36, no. 4 (Winter 2002): 48–49.

33. Murphy, *Economic and Political Change*, 199–201.

34. See Michel Camau and Vincent Geisser, *Le syndrome autoritaire: Politique en Tunisie De Bourguiba à Ben Ali* (Mayenne, France: Presse de Sciences, 2003), 304–13.

35. Camau and Geisser, *Syndrome autoritaire*, 309.

36. For discussions of what is known about Ghannouchi's political beliefs and en-Nahda's blueprint for rule, as well as skeptics' reactions to this blueprint, see Mohammed Elihachmi Hamdi, *The Politicization of Islam: A Case Study of Tunisia* (Boulder, Colo.: Westview Press, 1998), 101–35; Azzam S. Tamimi, *Rachid Ghannouchi: A Democrat Within Islamism* (New York: Oxford University Press, 2001), passim.

37. Unless otherwise indicated, the material in the remainder of this paragraph, as well as the next, is taken from Camau and Geisser, *Syndrome autoritaire*, 306–13.

38. Ibid., 310 (all translations are the author's).

39. See Jonathan G. Farley, "Tunisia—Forty Years On from Independence," *Contemporary Review* 270, 1574 (March 1997): 125–31; Yaroslav Trofimov, "How the West Loses Its Natural Allies—Secularists in Arab World Should Be in Bush's Camp but Are Being Alienated," *Wall Street Journal*, June 26, 2002.

40. Murphy, *Economic and Political Change*, 215.

41. Trofimov.

42. Camau and Geisser, *Syndrome autoritaire*, 305.

43. Ibid., 311.

44. Moncef Marzouki, *Le mal arabe: Entre dictatures et integrismes, la democratie interdite* (Paris: Harmattan, 2004). Quoted excerpt distributed via email by en-Nahda (nahda@ezzeitouna.org), July 6, 2004.

45. Slackman.

46. "Under the Shadow," *Economist*, April 15, 2000.

47. Evan Osnos, "In Tunisia, Starvation Is a Weapon," *Chicago Tribune*, April 13, 2004.

48. In addition, "Washington also credits [Ben Ali] with encouraging Libya's leader, Col. Muʻammar al-Qaddafi, to abandon his unconventional weapons programs." See "Undemocratic Tunisia," *New York Times* editorial, February 18, 2004.

49. Trofimov.

50. Eva Bellin, "The Robustness of Authoritarianism in the Middle East: Exceptionalism in Comparative Perspective," *Comparative Politics* 36, no. 2 (January 2004): 144–48.

51. Maura Reynolds, "Bush Pushes Tunisia for Press Freedom," *Los Angeles Times*, February 19, 2004.

52. Murphy, *Economic and Political Change*, 164–65.

53. Camau and Geisser, *Syndrome autoritaire*, 203.

54. Alexander, "Back from the Democratic Brink," 37.

55. For details, see Camau and Geisser, *Syndrome autoritaire*, 217–20.
56. Murphy, *Economic and Political Change*, 231.
57. Camau and Geisser, *Syndrome autoritaire*, 192.
58. "Behind the Beaches," *Economist*, January 13, 1996.
59. Camau and Geisser, *Syndrome autoritaire*, 203.
60. Alexander, "Back from the Democratic Brink," 35–36; Murphy, *Economic and Political Change*, 200.
61. The charge to this council, established in 1987, is "to collect, analyze and assess information on domestic, foreign, and defense policies with the aim of safeguarding internal and external state security." Quoted in Murphy, *Economic and Political Change*, 185–86.
62. Camau and Geisser, *Syndrome autoritaire*, 208.
63. Murphy, "Ten Years On," 119; Murphy, *Economic and Political Change*, 171.
64. Murphy, *Economic and Political Change*, 232.
65. Ibid.
66. See Barbara Geddes, "Authoritarian Breakdown: Empirical Test of a Game Theoretic Argument," paper prepared for presentation at the annual meeting of the American Political Science Association, Atlanta, September 1999.
67. Murphy, *Economic and Political Change*, 231.

3

The Economic Dimension

10

The Constraints on Economic Development in Morocco and Tunisia

PAUL RIVLIN

This chapter compares and contrasts the performance of the Moroccan and Tunisian economies in recent years. It shows that although they have introduced many of the reforms recommended by the International Monetary Fund (IMF), they have not benefited from economic growth either fast enough or consistently enough to solve serious socioeconomic problems. The reasons include problems in agriculture, the unfavorable international economic environment, and the relationship between the private business sector and the state.

Morocco and Tunisia have the most impressive demographic trends in the Arab world. Between 1980 and 1985 and 1995 and 2000, Morocco's population growth rate fell from 2.53 to 1.62 percent a year, whereas Tunisia's declined from 2.57 to 1.23 percent. These figures compare favorably with Egypt's growth rate (the decline was from 2.46 to 1.90 percent) and that of Syria (from 3.68 to 2.53 percent).[1] (See tables 10.1 and 10.2.) As a result, the absolute annual addition to the population was smaller than it would otherwise have been. Nonetheless, population growth in previous years meant that the base was higher than in the past and thus the absolute increase was too. In 2003, the Moroccan population was 30.6 million and Tunisia's was 9.8 million.[2] It will take years for Morocco to reach a situation in which the annual increase does not place a burden on social services, the housing market, and, ultimately, the labor market. Tunisia, with a smaller and more slowly growing population faces a less daunting challenge in this respect.

The growth of the labor force is determined by the number of young people starting to look for work each year minus the number of those retiring from work. The number of those entering the labor market is a function of how many young people there are, educational opportunities and military service that delay their entry into the labor force, and the participation rate. In both countries, the female participation rate has increased while the

Table 10.1. Population in Morocco and Tunisia, 1970–2003 (millions)

	Morocco	Tunisia
1970	15.310	5.127
1975	17.305	5.668
1980	19.382	6.469
1985	21.995	7.357
1990	24.564	8.207
1995	26.839	8.950
2000	29.108	9.519
2003	30.566	9.832

Source: UN Population Division, "World Population Prospects: The 2003 Revision Population Database," http://www.esa.un.org.

Table 10.2. Population Growth in Morocco and Tunisia, 1970–2000 (% per year)

	Morocco	Tunisia
1970–75	2.45	2.01
1975–80	2.27	2.65
1980–85	2.53	2.57
1985–90	2.21	2.19
1990–95	1.77	1.73
1995–2000	1.62	1.23

Source: UN Population Division, "World Population Prospects: The 2002 Revision Population Database," http://www.esa.un.org.

male rate has declined slightly, the net effect being a rise in the total rate. In recent years the Moroccan labor force has been growing by 2.5 percent a year, which means that an additional 300,000 people enter the labor market every year. In Tunisia the rate of increase has been higher, although the absolute rise has been smaller, about 110,000 annually.[3] These are the numbers of jobs that have to be created every year if unemployment is not to rise in both countries. But in fact, unemployment among young people is one of the most serious problems in North Africa.

Morocco

Economic Reforms and Their Effects

Morocco has followed the stabilization and structural change programs recommended by the IMF and the World Bank since the 1980s. The policy was to reduce large budget deficits and the expansion of inflationary credit used to finance them. Emphasis was placed on cutting public spending, and so stabilization programs reduced both total demand and that of the public sector. The IMF also advocated raising interest rates to real levels (i.e., above the rate of inflation) in order to encourage savings and reverse capital flight, and urged restrictions on domestic credit and money creation. All these measures were also designed to strengthen the balance of payments. In addition, the IMF and the World Bank placed emphasis on the liberalization of foreign trade and the need to devalue the exchange rate in order to encourage exports and discourage imports.

Structural adjustment usually referred to changes in relative prices and in institutions. These included changes in exchange rates and interest rates and thus overlapped with stabilization measures. Structural adjustment was a medium- and long-term policy designed to increase the efficiency of the economy so that it could attain sustained growth with less government intervention than in the past. It included tax reforms, reforms in the ownership, control, and operation of the financial sector, and deregulation of the economy, designed to encourage private sector activity and privatization. This was defined as the sale of assets by the public sector to the private sector or their transfer from the former to the latter.

The economic reforms introduced in the 1980s resulted in much greater economic and financial stability than was experienced in the 1970s, but the rate of growth has been neither fast nor stable. (See table 10.3.) In the period 1986–91, the economy grew by an average annual growth rate of 4.4 percent, but in 1991–98 the rate of growth fell to 1.9 percent. As the population grew by 1.7 percent a year, this meant that GDP per capita increased by only 0.2 percent a year. Morocco went from being one of the best economic performers in the Middle East to being one of the worst. The slowdown in the rate of growth was largely caused by a fall in agricultural value added (these were years of severe drought) and the failure of the non-agricultural sector—industry and services—to compensate. Another reason was that between 1990 and 2000 stabilization policies resulted in a 20 percent real overvaluation of the dirham. This rendered Moroccan exports more expensive on foreign markets and imports. As a result the economy grew more slowly than it would otherwise have done. In 2001, there was a corrective devaluation that helped to restore some of the competitiveness that the economy had lost. There has been an improvement in recent years, as a result of better harvests, and in the period 1999–2003, GDP growth averaged 3.2 percent. In 2003, GDP came to $44.5 billion and GDP per capita equaled $1,478.[4]

One of the main aims of reforms in the 1980s was to reduce the economy's

Table 10.3. GDP Growth in Morocco, 1981–2003 (annual %)

1981	-2.7
1982	9.5
1983	-0.6
1984	4.3
1985	6.4
1986	8.3
1987	-2.6
1988	10.5
1989	2.3
1990	2.2
1991	8.8
1992	-4.0
1993	-1.0
1994	10.4
1995	-6.6
1996	12.2
1997	-2.2
1998	7.3
1999	0.9
2000	0.9
2001	6.5
2002	5.6
2003	3.7

Source: Calculated from IMF, *International Financial Statistics Yearbook, 2002*, and *International Financial Statistics, July 2004*.

reliance on phosphates, thus making the composition of exports less reliant on volatile international commodity markets. In this respect there was a significant improvement. Manufacturing output rose by an annual average of 4.1 percent in the 1980s, which was a considerable achievement given that this was the decade of restructuring, and it compared well with other countries undergoing similar processes.[5] Between 1992 and 2002, industrial output rose by a total of 32.7 percent, significantly more slowly than in the 1980s. But the composition of output barely changed. In 1992, only 9.6 percent of industrial production came from the modern sectors of machinery, transport equipment, electronics, and office, measuring, and optical equipment. In 2002, this had hardly changed and constituted a major failure.[6]

During the 1980s and 1990s, the share of total investment in GDP fell. In 1976–80, it was 27.4 percent; in 1980–93, 25.6 percent; in 1984–87, 24 percent; in 1988–92, 23.2 percent; in 1992, 22.4 percent; and in 1996, 20.2 percent. In 2002, investment accounted for 21.2 percent of GDP. The aim

Table 10.4. Morocco: Balance of Payments Indicators, Annual Averages ($m)

	1986–1993	1996–2003
Current account	-239	484
Trade balance	-907	-2,812
Tourism revenues	1,744	2,163
Foreign direct investment	197	1,048
Workers' remittances	1,719	2,490

Source: IMF, *Balance of Payments Yearbook*, 1994 and 2004.

of the reforms was to encourage private sector investment, and this was partially successful. The share of private sector investment in GDP doubled between 1976 and 2000, but it has fallen since then. Noncentral government investment, which was mainly accounted for by that of the private sector, rose from 10.8 percent of GDP in 1976–80, to 13.8 percent in 1980–83, 15.7 percent in 1984–87, and 19.4 percent in 1988–91. In 1992 it came to 19.2 percent and in 1996 to 16.9 percent. In 2002, 18.5 percent was carried out by the private sector, a fall from 20 percent in 1999–2000.[7]

Areas of success were the reduction in inflation and the improvement in the balance of payments and the reduction of the external debt. In the period 1980–83, the consumer price index rose by an annual average of 9.7 percent. In 1984–87 it rose by 7.9 percent, and in 1988–92 it rose by 6.6 percent. In 1993–95 it averaged 5.4 percent, and in 1996–97, 2.0 percent. Inflation was even lower in 1999–2003, averaging 1.4 percent a year.[8] Table 10.4 shows how the balance of payments strengthened between the periods 1986–93 and 1996–2003. It shows that although the merchandise trade deficit grew, the current account moved from deficit into surplus. This was due to an improvement in the services and income accounts and from a reduction in interest payments on the foreign debt.

As a result of the economic reforms of the 1980s, debt rescheduling, and slow economic growth, in the 1990s, Morocco's foreign debt fell. In consequence, total debt service as a share of exports of goods and services (one of the main indicators of the burden of foreign debt) fell from 33.4 percent in 1980 to 23.5 percent in 2003.[9]

Although the reforms made it possible to borrow abroad with greater ease and on more favorable terms, they also reduced the amount of government investment that was financed by foreign borrowing. The other main change was the increase in manufacturing exports that occurred as a result of the removal of many distortions in the economy. These reforms also attracted remittances and there was a strong increase in tourism revenues in the 1980s. The diversification of exports and sources of foreign finance helped to insulate the economy from the effects of fluctuating phosphate prices and those of droughts. There was, therefore, an improvement in the current and capital accounts, at least until 1995.

The rest of the economy has not compensated for agricultural failures. Manufacturing and manufacturing exports have been particularly weak.[10] This meant that job creation was limited, and Morocco (and to a lesser extent Tunisia) largely missed out on the boom in Third World manufacturing exports that transformed the economies of South Korea, Taiwan, Mexico, China, and, to some extent, India. Although the rate of economic growth was well above that of the population, it was not fast enough to generate new jobs at a rate that would reduce high unemployment rates. Other macroeconomic issues remain: In recent years, the fiscal deficit has equaled 5–6 percent of GDP, which has led to the expansion of government debt. The balance of payments is threatened by the reliance on food imports and by the slow growth of exports.

The economy also remains dangerously reliant on the level of rainfall, because in 2002 only 16 percent of arable land was irrigated, a meager 3 percent increase over a period of more than twenty years.[11] As so little land was irrigated, changes in the amount of rain had major direct effects on the level of agricultural production and thus on GDP. It directly and indirectly affected rural income and employment levels, the number of migrants to the towns, and those levels of urban unemployment. Agriculture has suffered from not only fluctuations in output levels but also a growth of output that has failed to keep up with the growth of the population. In 2000–2003, the average level of agricultural output per capita was 83.8 compared with 100 in 1989–1991.[12] This meant that increasing volumes of food had to be imported. Between 1992 and 2000, the quantity of food, beverages, and tobacco imports rose by 70 percent; those of wheat alone rose by 39 percent. The costs rose by 100 percent and 125 percent respectively.[13] In 1992, food accounted for 13.3 percent of the value of imports. In 1995 this rose to a peak of 17.6 percent, and in 2002 it declined to 12.6 percent.[14] Between 1993 and 2003, food production rose by 50.4 percent while the population increased by 44 percent. This meant that food production per capita rose by less than 0.5 percent a year.

Unemployment

The failure to achieve fast and stable economic growth has resulted in chronically high unemployment. In 2001, the unemployment rate was officially estimated at 12.5 percent. In urban areas it was 19.5 percent, in rural areas 4.5 percent. (Most of those unemployed in rural areas went to the towns in search of work and those who did not find it became urban unemployed.) In the greater Casablanca region, unemployment was 21.4 percent. Among those fifteen to twenty-four years old, the national unemployment rate was 18.9 percent, and among males in urban areas it was 35.4 percent.[15] Unofficially, the rates were deemed to be significantly higher.

Poverty

The number of people living in poverty increased from 3.4 million in 1991 (13 percent of the population) to 5.3 million in 1998–99 (19 percent). Poverty was defined as living below a minimum level of consumption per head, equivalent to $2.50 per head on a national level (in 1993 purchasing power parity terms). The economically vulnerable population, whose consumption levels were at or below 150 percent of the poverty level, increased from 9 million (35 percent of the population) to 12 million (44 percent).[16]

In the 1990s, 84 percent of the increase in poverty was due to the slowdown in economic growth, the rest being due to changes in the distribution of income. Economic growth was much slower in the 1990s than in the 1980s. In the period 1986–91, GDP increased by an annual average of 4.1 percent. In 1991–98 the average was only 1.9 percent. In urban areas, changes in the distribution of income among the poor dampened the effects of the slowdown in economic growth. In rural areas, the lack of growth combined with greater inequality in income distribution resulted in rising poverty. As a result, in 1999, 66 percent of Morocco's poor lived in rural areas that contained 44 percent of the total population. A total of 34 percent lived in urban areas that accounted for 56 percent of the total population. Another key measurement of human welfare—nutrition—showed a serious deterioration in the late 1990s. In 1990–95, an annual average of 1.5 percent of the population was undernourished. In 1999–2001, the share was 2.1 percent, or some six hundred thousand people.[17]

The Private Sector and the State

Although Morocco never experienced a socialist phase such as that experienced by Tunisia and many other Arab countries, the public sector plays a dominant role in the economy, accounting for at least 50 percent of GDP.[18] King Hasan II (d. 1999) expanded the role of the state by buying into the private sector during the period of ostensible economic liberalization in the 1980s.[19] Through his holdings in Omnium Nord African (ONA) he acquired interests throughout the Moroccan economy, including shares in privatized companies. The private sector maintains very close links with the royal court on an individual basis and through organizations such as chambers of commerce.[20] As a result of ONA shareholdings in major banks, the court has gained much control in the banking sector (including placing its people in key positions) and can allocate credit in return for political support. All this limits the socioeconomic status and independence of the business community and the political elite.[21]

The International Economic Environment

Morocco's Association Agreement with the European Union (EU) came into force in 2000 and will be fully implemented by 2012. In 2004 the United States and Morocco signed a free-trade agreement covering industrial and agricultural goods as well as services, government procurement, e-commerce, and intellectual property protection. The agreement provides for the immediate ending of 95 percent of tariffs with the remaining 5 percent to be removed over nine years.[22] These agreements provide duty free access to Moroccan markets for EU and U.S. goods with significant consequences for local producers and government revenues.[23] In 2003, the EU accounted for 75 percent of Morocco's exports and 64 percent of its imports. The United States took 4 percent of exports and supplied 4.1 percent of imports.

The neighboring countries of Algeria, Libya, and Tunisia took only 1.4 percent of exports and supplied only 2.2 percent of Moroccan imports.[24] This pattern of trade, in which most is conducted with the EU and very little with other North African states, has been called a "hub and spoke" pattern. The EU is the hub and it has agreements with different spokes, in this case Morocco and Tunisia. The pattern of trade is the result of preferences given in trade agreements (the bilateral agreements with the EU are much stronger than the bilateral and multilateral agreements within the Maghrib region, notwithstanding the formal existence of the Arab Maghrib Union framework), historical connections, and other factors. In the extreme case, spokes have less market access than the hub as the latter enjoys preferential access to all spokes but a spoke has preferential access to the hub only. A spoke country can avoid this by becoming a hub in its own right by entering into its own set of bilateral or regional trade agreements. This partly explains the signing of such agreements in many parts of the world. There have been numerous initiatives in the Middle East and North Africa, but they have not yet proved effective and the very low level of intraregional trade is the consequence.

Despite the reforms, in 2003 Morocco had an unweighted average import tariff of 36 percent. The average for lower-middle-income countries worldwide was 15 percent.[25] High rates of taxes on imports mean that the loss of revenues when they are cut will be considerable. In so far as they are high, they provide protection for domestic industry. Their removal will have positive effects on efficiency and negative effects on employment and output, at least in the short term. This process is, of course, already under way. In 1999–2000, taxes on imports equaled 19.6 percent of total taxation. In 2003, they accounted for 13.3 percent.[26]

Another major issue in Morocco is emigration. Mass unemployment has meant that many Moroccans want to leave for Europe where they believe that there are jobs and the possibility of higher earnings. Legal emigration to the European Union has been limited to the category of family reunion since the 1970s. As a result, illegal emigration has become a much more significant phenomenon. In 1995, there were 1.27 million Moroccans and 336,000 Tunisians estimated to be living in the main European countries and 105,000 Moroccans and 70,000 Tunisians in Libya and the Gulf states.[27] In 2003, there were reported to be 2.5 million Moroccans living abroad, the vast majority in Europe.[28] Although the latter figure should be treated with caution, most observers agree that the number has increased significantly in recent years. Following illegal attempts to reach Spain by boat, Moroccans regularly drowned and others were arrested and returned, and this phenomenon remains an issue of contention in Morocco's relations with the EU.

As shown in table 10.4, foreign direct investment (FDI) has played an increasing role in the Moroccan economy. The privatization of the sector and the selling of mobile phone licenses boosted the volume of FDI and was one of the main factors why it rose from an annual average of just under $200 million in 1986–93 to an annual average of just over $1 billion in 1996–2003.[29] Bureaucracy, uncertainty about taxes, licenses, regulations, and other government controls have restricted foreign investment in other sectors. As a result, manufacturing output, exports, and the creation of new jobs have been limited, as has the country's integration into the international economy. Morocco, like all Arab countries, largely missed out on the international boom in FDI that led to the creation of millions of jobs in manufacturing in East and Southeast Asia.

Tunisia

Tunisia is a small country both geographically (101,438.2 square miles, just over one-third the size of Morocco) and demographically (9.8 million inhabitants), compared to most other Middle Eastern and Arab states, including its neighbors. Its population is relatively homogenous, both ethnically and linguistically, and its distribution of income is one of the most equal in the region.[30] The number of its citizens living in poverty (defined as living below a minimum consumption expenditure level) fell from 800,000 (8 percent) in 1995 to 400,000 (4 percent) in 2000. The economically vulnerable (defined using a wider definition) fell from 17 to 10 percent.[31]

Tunisia has suffered little political instability in recent years, partly the result of vigorous and successful attempts by the government to root out opposition. Like Morocco, it has followed a liberal economic policy that has reduced budget deficits, cut inflation, and opened the economy to foreign trade. It has very close links with the European Union, which dominates its exports and imports. In many ways Tunisia is the model Arab economy, and given that it has only very limited oil and gas resources (or perhaps because of that), living standards are relatively high. For many years, the Tunisian model was one that other Arab states could follow to advantage, but today problems are apparent.

Economic Developments

Between 1976 and 1985, the economy grew by 11 percent a year; between 1986 and 1996, growth averaged 4.3 percent a year.[32] The slowdown was due to a number of factors. In 1990–91, the Persian Gulf crisis affected the level of economic activity throughout the Middle East; in 1992–93 there was a recession in Western Europe, Tunisia's largest market; and in 1993–95 there were three bad harvests due to drought. In addition, the investment/GDP ratio declined due to uncertainties over reforms in the investment code and the elimination of duties on capital imports. Between 1998 and 2003, the economy grew by 4.6 percent, well in excess of the rate of growth of population. In 2003, GDP came to $23.5 billion, and GDP per capita equaled $2,364.[33] Tunisia, like Morocco, experienced slower growth in the 1990s than in the 1980s, but unlike Morocco, it suffered only two years of negative growth. (See table 10.5.)

Structural change as well as growth is a feature of economic development. Development means that the share of output coming from different sectors changes. Ideally this should be because growth accelerates in more modern

Table 10.5. GDP Growth in Tunisia, 1981–2003 (annual %)

1981	5.6
1982	-0.5
1983	4.7
1984	6.3
1985	3.1
1986	-2.0
1987	5.0
1988	1.6
1989	3.5
1990	7.0
1991	6.4
1992	5.3
1993	2.3
1994	3.2
1995	2.4
1996	7.1
1997	5.6
1998	4.8
1999	5.9
2000	4.7
2001	4.9
2002	1.6
2003	5.5

Source: Calculated from IMF, *International Financial Statistics Yearbook, 2002*, and *International Financial Statistics, July 2004*.

sectors rather than just because traditional sectors decline. The latter should be relative rather than absolute. The modernizing sector is the manufacturing sector and its share in GDP, after increasing from 14.2 percent in 1983 to 17.1 percent in 1993, virtually stagnated and only reached 18.3 percent in 2003.[34] Within manufacturing, however, the mechanical engineering and electronics sector did well. Between 1990 and 2003, its output increased by 107 percent, compared with 90 percent for manufacturing as a whole. Output in the other leading export sectors (textiles, clothing, and leather) increased by 134 percent.[35]

The Tunisian economy faces four major problems. The first is its reliance on agriculture, which in turn is dependent on fluctuating levels of rainfall. The second is the weakness of the private sector, and the third is the unfavorable international economic environment. Finally, and as a result of the first three problems, it suffers from chronic high levels of unemployment, especially among the young.

Agriculture

Tunisia, like Morocco, remains heavily dependent on agriculture despite the fact that its share in GDP declined from 19 percent in 1965–73 to 14 percent in 1997–99. The effect of a change in agricultural output was stronger when agricultural production contracted than when it expanded. Hence a 1 percent fall in agricultural production caused a 0.25 percent fall in GDP, a much larger fall than its share in GDP. A 1 percent rise in agricultural output caused GDP to rise by only 0.17 percent. The difference is due to the fact that as drought was anticipated, activity in agricultural-related industries and services slowed down, with consequent effects on GDP. When good rains were forecast, it was hard to calculate how much that rain would increase agricultural production. Caution was thus built into the upswing, and investments did not increase commensurately. As a result, the effect of change in agricultural production on the economy was asymmetric. This was also true on the demand side: Declining agricultural incomes affected households' consumption more than increasing incomes did.[36]

The share of arable land that is irrigated is low; in 2002 it was 13.7 percent, up from 10 percent in 1990.[37] As a result, fluctuations in rainfall affect the level of agricultural production and thus the rate of growth of national income.[38] Six out of the last eight contractions in the level of business occurred in periods of agricultural contraction. In 1988, when there was a severe drought, agricultural output fell by 30 percent and, as a result, GDP growth was zero. In 1990, when there were good rains, agricultural output rose by 32.2 percent and GDP by 7.3 percent.[39] Average agricultural production per head in 2000–2002 was 18 percent lower than in 1989–91.[40] Between 1993 and 2003, food production declined by 21.2 percent. The population grew by 14.3 percent during that period, which meant that food output per capita declined by 31 percent.[41]

The Weakness of the Private Sector

Compared to other high-growth developing economies, Tunisia suffers from a lack of private investment. Despite satisfactory macroeconomic conditions and structural reforms, growth has relied on public investment and private investment remains low, at around 14 percent of GDP. This is even a lower rate than in the 1980s and early 1990s. One reason for the low private investment ratio is the limited openness of services, markets, and network industries, particularly in IT and transport. This kept the cost of key services high, hindered competitiveness, and deprived Tunisia from significant opportunities for private investment. Another reason was the uncertainty of the business environment, reflecting the risks in Tunisia's international economic environment. But these factors only partly explain the large private investment gap. The World Bank provides a further explanation. Large-scale government interference was often arbitrary and favored those who had personal connections to officials. All this limited competition, efficiency, investment, and production.[42]

The private sector faces government-imposed limitations. First, privatization of the telecommunications, transport, and other sectors has been limited. In other developing countries, including Arab ones, these sectors have attracted substantial private capital and foreign investment. Partly because these sectors remain publicly owned or dominated, competition is limited and so costs and prices are high. This is closely related to weaknesses in the regulatory environment. Government officials retain a high degree of discretion in regulating economic activity. The arbitrary powers used by government officials reflected the state of play in government-private sector relations. Although the government has long recognized its limitations as an entrepreneur and financier, it has not been willing to share power with the private sector. One of the ways in which it maintains control is to act arbitrarily and unpredictably and limit transparency and clarity, especially in the granting of government contracts.[43]

The weakness of the private sector (notwithstanding the fact that it is more developed than in most other Arab countries) has meant that total investment, as a share of GDP, was lower after the economic reforms of 1986 than before. In 1988, it fell to its lowest level, as a share of GDP, since 1960.[44] From 1988 until 1993, there was an increase in investment from 22 percent of GDP to 31 percent. Although these were higher levels than in many Arab states, they were lower than those experienced in the 1960s and 1970s. The share of private sector investment in GDP rose in the 1970s from 11–12 to 15–16 percent. In the 1990s it fell, reaching 12–13 percent in 1995–99.

Tunisia has a large public sector that provides the regime with opportunities for patronage and control. The domestic economy is small and with limited external rents (foreign aid and emigrants' remittances) and so it has been forced to develop manufactured exports so as to provide foreign exchange. The export sector has not, however, been integrated into the rest of the economy and it has not developed enough to gain any form of economic or political independence of the state. In this it is quite different from Morocco.[45] Privatization has been limited: Between 1987 and 1998, assets worth $950 million were privatized, and nearly half of this came from the sale of two cement factories in 1998.[46]

Unemployment

Although the population is growing at only 1.2 percent a year, the labor force is increasing by 2.5 percent a year. Despite its relatively good growth record, unemployment in Tunisia is very high; in 2000, it was estimated at 15–16 percent. The economy has not grown fast enough or in the right way to reduce this rate. The labor force has become more educated and the number of women looking for employment outside the home has increased as a result of successful programs to improve and expand women's education. The demand for highly skilled workers has, however, declined, and this seems to be resulting in a rise in unemployment among the better educated. This phenomenon, which has been detected in other Arab countries, is very worrying because it puts a question mark over one of the most important tools that have been used to bring about economic development. Another reason unemployment is high among the better educated is that they are educated in the wrong things. Tunisians in higher education tend to study nontechnological subjects that yield lower economic returns than those subjects studied by students in countries such as South Korea and Jordan.

The International Environment

The implementation of the Association Agreement with the European Union (AAEU) by 2008 and the phasing out of the Multi-fiber Agreement (MFA) in 2004, which consisted of bilateral agreements establishing quotas to protect domestic textile industries, pose competitive challenges for Tunisia. Over 40 percent of Tunisia's total exports are concentrated in clothing, and 75 percent of total exports go the EU countries. Between 1991 and 1995 the manufacturing export growth rate averaged 12.9 percent per annum, but between 1996 and 2002, export performance worsened and the growth rate of manufactured exports decreased to 3.7 percent.[47] Like Morocco, most of Tunisia's external trade is with the EU. In 2003, the EU took 73 percent of its exports, 0.6 percent went to the United States, and 6.4 percent went to Algeria, Libya, and Tunisia. In that year, the EU supplied 62 percent of its imports, the United States 2.5 percent, and the neighboring North African countries 4.8 percent.[48]

Tunisia suffers from a chronic trade deficit, which averaged $1.4 billion a year between 1986 and 1993 and grew to $2.2 billion in 1996–2003. (See table

Table 10.6. Tunisia: Balance of Payments Indicators, Annual Averages ($m)

	1986–1993	1996–2003
Current account	-426	-656
Trade balance	-1,372	-2,128
Tourism revenues	976	1,563
Foreign direct investment	137	515
Workers' remittances	528	868

Source: IMF, *Balance of Payments Yearbook*, 1994 and 2004.

10.6.) This is despite the fact that since 1993 food imports have accounted for a decreasing share of total imports; in 1993 they took 14 percent, in 2003 they accounted for only 6.7 percent.[49] The trade deficit was partly financed by tourism revenues and by the remittances of Tunisian workers abroad. There was also a deficit on the service account, and the volume of transfers did not cover the deficit. As a result, the current account of the balance of payments was in deficit throughout the period. Tunisia's foreign debt increased from 1970 to 2003, from $600 million to $15.5 billion, but total debt servicing as a share of exports of goods and services fell from a peak of 24.5 percent in 1990 to 13 percent in 2003.[50]

In 2003, the European Union accounted for 79 percent of Tunisian exports and 74 percent of its imports. Its exports have been heavily concentrated: Clothing and textiles accounted for 48 percent of exports. A total of 82 percent of Tunisia's tourism revenues came from the EU.[51] Its share of European markets for manufactured goods has failed to grow at anything like the rate of its South and East Asian competitors in that market. Furthermore, its position in the EU market for textiles and clothing will deteriorate with the end of the MFA.

The agreements that have been signed with the European Union mean that Tunisia will reduce its taxes on imports. This will expose the economy to increased competition from EU goods and, at the same time, government revenues will decline. Like other Arab states, Tunisia is under great pressure to make its economy more efficient. If they cannot cope with the competition, then firms will close and jobs will be lost. This could prove disastrous, given current high levels of unemployment.

There has been a lack of integration of the offshore export sector that produced clothing and textiles for the EU and the domestic sector. European companies invested in Tunisian plants producing textiles and clothing for the European market. These plants did not have free access to the domestic market that remains protected. In 2003, Tunisia had an unweighted average import tariff of 30 percent, double that for lower-middle-income countries worldwide.[52] As a result, a dual system developed, one for export and another for the domestic market. Due to the protection offered to producers for the domestic market and restriction on entry into the domestic market placed on exporters, their technologies, cost, and efficiency levels varied. Although manufacturing has been fairly dynamic, the sector remains small compared with that in other developing countries that have achieved fast income growth. Textiles and mechanical/electrical equipment have performed well as export sectors but have only made a modest contribution to GDP. This is explained by the fact that both these groups of industries rely on imports and add little value to inputs before they are exported.

Finally, Tunisia's tourism revenues have been affected by the recession in Europe and by the terrorist attack in April 2002 on the El Ghriba synagogue on the island of Jerba, which resulted in the death of fifteen foreign tourists and six Tunisians.

Human Development Indices for Morocco and Tunisia

The UN's human development index (HDI) combines information on life expectancy, adult literacy, school enrollment, and GDP per capita. Morocco has one of the lowest indexes in the Middle East, despite the fact that it has improved gradually over time. In 1990 it was 0.54, and in 2002 it was 0.62, an improvement of nearly 15 percent. In 2002, Morocco ranked 125th in the world. Tunisia's 2002 HDI was 0.745, ranking it 92nd in the world. One element in the HDI is adult literacy, and here Morocco's failings are apparent. In 2002, 62 percent of Moroccan women over the age of fifteen years were illiterate, as were 37 percent of Moroccan men. In Tunisia illiteracy was much lower: 37 percent among women and 17 percent among men.[53]

The alternative human development index added data on lifelong knowledge acquisition, especially regarding information technology, women's access to societal power, and measures of human freedom. When these additional criteria were added to the index, in 2002 Morocco was ranked seventy-ninth in the world whereas Tunisia dropped even lower, to ninety-third place. Morocco's political freedom score was a low 0.35, and Tunisia's was 0.18.[54] This reflects the fact that in the 1990s and the early 2000s, Tunisia had become a much more repressive society, whereas Morocco had become less so. According to the World Bank, the UN Development Fund, and others, Tunisia's lack of democracy is, or will be, a factor that retards its economy over time. Morocco's greater openness helps, or will help, its economy. At the time of writing, there is evidence that Tunisia is being held back by a lack of freedom, but Morocco has even more problems than a lack of democracy. It suffers massive socioeconomic deprivation, which its relatively liberal regime is finding very difficult to change.

Conclusion

There are differences and similarities in the economic situations facing Morocco and Tunisia. Both face a very tough international environment that fails to complement the structural changes that they have made at home. When the IMF and the World Bank call on developing countries to make their economies more competitive both internally and externally, the assumption is that they will be given fair access to foreign markets, especially those with which they do the vast majority of their trade. This has not happened. Their major trading partner, the EU, has restricted their exports of one of the main categories of goods in which they have a comparative advantage: agricultural products. Furthermore, through its common agricultural policy, the EU subsidizes exports of its own agricultural production, something that Morocco and Tunisia, at the behest of the IMF and the World Bank, have largely stopped doing. They could never afford the level of subsidy that the EU offers its producers. As a result they have incentives to import artificially cheap agricultural goods (mainly food), with all the negative consequences for employment and the balance of payments. Both countries have mass unemployment, especially of the young, and this is a key indicator of economic failure.

There are also differences. The political evolution of the two has been different, with Tunisia being a more homogenous and centralized state and, now, being more repressive than Morocco. In socioeconomic terms, Morocco's situation is much worse than that of Tunisia. It has large-scale and rising poverty, even malnutrition. Average incomes are significantly lower than in Tunisia.

Agriculture was the Achilles heel of these economies. The failure to increase output meant that imports were greater than would have otherwise been and that agricultural employment was lower. The causes were internal and external: There were not enough incentives to increase output operating in the economy and the Common Agricultural Policy of the European Union discouraged or limited agricultural exports.

Although it has perhaps the best performing economy in the Arab world, Tunisia's private sector is weak and follows the government's guidance. In

Morocco, the late King Hasan outflanked private sector independence as he consolidated his power. The net effect in both countries was that economic liberalization yielded limited benefits, and the inability to cope with foreign competition threatens the future when EU agreements come into full force and import taxes have to be cut.

In Morocco and Tunisia, the state has tried to convince foreign firms to invest, and foreign governments and international organizations to extend aid. Implicit (and perhaps explicit) in these efforts has been the warning that without foreign inflows, the socioeconomic and thus political situation will deteriorate dangerously. The paradox in this situation is that as the state derives its legitimacy from its role as interlocutor in the international economy, the inequality associated with its foreign relations (e.g., implementing IMF stabilization programs) provides fuel for the opposition.[55]

Notes

1. United Nations, Department of Economic and and Social Affairs Population Division, "World Population Prospects: The 2002 Revision, Population Database," http://www.esa.un.org.

2. UN Population Division, "World Population Prospects: The 2003 Revision, Population Database," http://www.esa.un.org.

3. World Bank, *World Development Indicators, 2004* (Washington, D.C.: World Bank, 2004), 43–44.

4. International Monetary Fund (IMF), *International Financial Statistics Yearbook, 2002* (Washington, D.C.: IMF, 2002); *International Financial Statistics,* May 2004 (Washington D.C., International Monetary Fund, 2004); World Bank, *Memorandum of the President of the International Bank for Reconstruction and Development and the International Finance Corporation to the Executive Directors of the World Bank Group for the Kingdom of Morocco,* 1994 (Washington, D.C.: 1994), 5; World Bank, *Kingdom of Morocco: Poverty Update, 2001,* Report no. 21506–MOR, 1:16; World Bank, "Morocco: Country Data Profile," http://www.worldbank.org.

5. Alan Richards and John Waterbury, *A Political Economy of the Middle East* (Boulder, Colo.: Westview, 1996), 238.

6. IMF, *Morocco: Statistical Appendix, 2004,* Country Report no. 04/163, 20, IMF Web site, http://www.imf.org.

7. Ibid., 6.

8. Calculated from IMF, *International Financial Statistics,* August 1998 (Washington, D.C.: International Monetary Fund, 1998) and IMF, *Morocco: Statistical Appendix, 2004,* 11.

9. World Bank, *Global Development Finance, 2005,* vol. 2 (Washington D.C.: World Bank, 2005).

10. World Bank, *Kingdom of Morocco: Poverty Update, 2001,* 1:16.

11. Food and Agriculture Organization of the United Nations (FAO), Food and Agriculture Statistics (FAOSTAT), http://www.fao.org.

12. FAO, *Bulletin of Statistics* 4, no. 1 (2003).

13. *Annuaire Statistique du Maroc* (Rabat: Premier Ministre, Département de la Prévision Économique et du Plan, Direction de la Statistique), 1997: 495; 2000: 630; 2002: 612–14.

14. IMF, *Morocco: Statistical Appendix, 1998*, Country Report no. 98/42, 52, IMF Web site, http://www.imf.org; IMF, *Morocco: Statistical Appendix, 2004*, 16.

15. *Annuaire Statistique du Maroc*, 2002, 496–504.

16. World Bank, *Kingdom of Morocco: Poverty Update, 2001* 1:5–6.

17. Ibid.

18. Fadel Chalak, "Challenges to the Economy and State in the Middle East," in *Looking Ahead: Challenges for Middle East Politics and Research*, coordinated by Volker Perthes, EuroMeSco Paper no. 29 (April 2004): 35, http://www.euromesco.net.

19. Clement M. Henry and Robert Springborg, *Globalization and the Politics of Development in the Middle East* (Cambridge: Cambridge University Press, 2001), 172–73.

20. Bradford Dillman, "Facing the Market," *Middle East Journal* 55, no. 2 (Spring 2001): 198–215.

21. Clement M. Henry, *The Mediterranean Debt Crescent* (Gainesville: University Press of Florida, 1996), 158–59.

22. U.S. State Department, http://www.state.gov/r/ei/bgn/5431.htm.

23. European Union, Europa—The European Union Online Web site, "EU Trade Issues," http://www.europa.eu.int.

24. IMF, *Directions of Trade Yearbook, 2004* (Washington, D.C.: IMF, 2004).

25. World Bank, *Trade, Investment and Development in the Middle East and North Africa* (2003), 136, http://www.worldbank.org.

26. IMF, *Morocco: Statistical Appendix, 2004*, 16.

27. Nadji Safir, "Emigration Dynamics in the Maghreb," in *Emigration Dynamics in Developing Countries*, vol. 4, *The Arab Region*, edited by Reginald Appleyard (Aldershot: Ashgate Publishing, for the UN Population Fund and the International Organization for Migration, 1999), 104.

28. Ninna Nybery Sorensen, *Migrant Remittances as a Development Tool: The Case of Morocco*, International Organization for Migration (IOM) Working Papers Series, no. 2 (June 2004): 5.

29. IMF, *Balance of Payments Yearbook, 1994* (Washington, D.C.: IMF, 1994); IMF, *Balance of Payments Yearbook, 2004* (Washington, D.C.: IMF, 2004).

30. Christian Morrisson and Bechir Talbi, *Long-Term Growth in Tunisia* (Paris: OECD Development Center, 1996), 136.

31. Plaoma Arios Casero and Aristenomne Varoudikis, *Growth, Private Investment and the Cost of Doing Business in Tunisia: A Comparative Perspective* (Washington, D.C.: World Bank, 2004), 4.

32. IMF, *International Financial Statistics Yearbook, 1997* (Washington, D.C.: IMF, 1997), and IMF, *International Financial Statistics*, August 1998.

33. IMF, *International Financial Statistics Yearbook, 2002*; IMF, *International Finan-*

cial Statistics, May 2004; World Bank, "Tunisia: Country Data Profile," January 13, 2005, World Bank Web site, http://www.worldbank.org.

34. World Bank, *Country Assistance Strategy for the Republic of Tunisia, 2004* (Washington, D.C.: World Bank, 2004), 77.

35. *Annuaire de la Tunisie, 2001* (Tunis: République Tunisienne, Ministère du Developpement et de la Cooperation International, Institut National de la Statistique, 2001), 44:129–30.

36. Auguste T. Kouame, *Achieving Faster Economic Growth in Tunisia* (Washington, D.C.: World Bank, 1996), 4.

37. FAO, FAOSTAT, http://www.fao.org.

38. Kouame, *Achieving Faster Economic Growth,* 46.

39. World Bank, *Tunisia's Global Integration and Sustainable Development* 4, no. 1 (2003).

40. FAO, *Bulletin Working Paper* 20 (December 2000): 2–5.

41. FAO, FAOSTAT, http://www.fao.org.

42. World Bank, *Country Assistance Strategy for Tunisia, 2004,* 7–8.

43. Casero and Varoudakis, *Growth,* 11.

44. UN, *World Economic and Social Survey 1996* (New York: United Nations, 1996) 163.

45. Henry and Springborg, *Globalization,* 136.

46. Dillman, "Facing the Market."

47. World Bank, Press Release no. 2004/465/MNA, 2004.

48. IMF, *Directions of Trade 2004* (Washington, D.C.: International Monetary Fund, 2004).

49. World Bank, *Country Assistance Strategy for Tunisia, 2004,* 78.

50. World Bank, *Global Finance Development 2005* (Washington, D.C.: World Bank, 2005), vol. 11.

51. European Union, "EU Trade Issues."

52. World Bank, *Trade, Investment and Development in the Middle East and North Africa* (Washington, D.C.: 2003), 136.

53. United Nations Development Program, *Arab Human Development Report, 2002* (New York: UN, 2002).

54. World Bank, *World Development Indicators, 2004,* 85–86.

55. Gregory W. White, "The Mexico of Europe," in *North Africa: Development and Reform in a Changing Global Economy,* edited by Dirk Vandewalle, 127 (Basingstoke: Macmillan, 1996).

11

Algeria's Economy

Mutations, Performance, and Challenges

AHMED AGHROUT AND MICHAEL HODD

For years the Algerian economy has not performed as well as expected. Despite substantial oil revenues and a significant investment effort, the economy has not produced the increases in output that might be expected. This is mainly due to the predominance of inefficient state-owned enterprises, a lack of openness to trade and foreign direct investment, a climate of regulation that is unhelpful to business and the market economy, and a reluctance to reform the financial sector.

This chapter begins with a relatively long-term perspective that reviews Algeria's macroeconomic situation. In light of the unsatisfactory economic performance, there have been moves in recent years to reform the Algerian economy. The nature and progress of these reforms are the subject of this chapter's second section.

Finally, this chapter looks at the broad challenges ahead for the Algerian economy, including the need to accelerate the process of privatization, the reforms required in the financial sector, adjustment to a more open economy, and management of the oil sector. Careful planning will be required to avoid the hardships and social unrest that economic reform invariably brings in its wake.

Recent Macroeconomic Indicators

The current situation and the impact of the recent economic reforms need to be assessed in the light of what has gone on before.[1] The data on Algeria's economic performance since 1950 are summarized in table 11.1.

Population growth is steadily declining, reflecting the influence of a steady increase in the urbanization of the population, some modest improvements in living standards, and better educational and employment

Table 11.1. Algeria's Macroeconomic Performance, 1950–2006

	1 Population Growth Rate (% per year)	2 Real GDP Growth Rate (% per year)	3 Real GDP/ Head Growth Rate (% per year)	4 Consumer Price Inflation (% per year)	5 Investment to GDP Ratio (%)	6 Annual Output per $1 of Investment (¢)
1950–59	1.9	8.4	6.3	4.8	21.2	40
1960–69	3.5	0.5	-2.8	4.2	21.6	2
1970–79	3.2	5.1	1.9	8.6	39.9	13
1980–89	3.0	3.1	0.1	9.0	32.4	10
1990–99	2.1	1.4	-1.1	19.4	26.4	5
2000–6	1.6	4.4	2.8	2.5	23.3*	19*

Sources: IMF, *International Financial Statistics Yearbook (1972, 1982, 2005)*; World Bank, *World Tables* Washington DC; World Bank, *World Development Report* Washington DC; Economic Intelligence Unit, *Country Report: Algeria*.
Notes: *For the period 2000–2005. Figures in column 6 were derived from column 2 divided by column 5 then multiplied by 100.

opportunities for females. Lower population growth rates will eventually ease the problem of providing employment for new entrants to the labor force, and lowering the proportion of the population below the age of fifteen will reduce the cost of education as a percentage of national income. Both of these developments help in the task of improving living standards.

GDP growth rates have varied over the decades, running very high in the 1950s then falling in the 1960s, with the conflict leading up to independence mainly responsible for the decline. Good growth rates were achieved in the 1970s and 1980s, mostly as a result of the massive increase in investment made possible by the rise in oil prices. With the end of the oil boom and the outbreak of horrific civil strife, the growth rate fell in the 1990s. However, growth rates are currently showing an excellent recovery in the early years of the new century, with rates averaging 4.4 percent for 2000–6.

The high population growth rates up to the end of the 1980s and poor GDP growth rates in the 1960s, 1980s, and 1990s have resulted in only modest improvements in output per head since 1950. GDP per head has risen at around 1.2 percent per year over the fifty-five-year period. The changes in GDP per head are a good indicator of what has happened to average living standards, as the share of GDP going to consumption is much the same in 2005 as it was in 1950. Estimates suggest that average living standards have risen perhaps 40 percent since 1950. More tellingly, however, average living standards are still below the peak level achieved in 1959, after having doubled in the 1950s. Although economic progress was in some respects hampered by the nationalist struggle in the 1950s, this was more than offset by the general boom conditions in the world economy and the financial impact of French troops and military expenditures in Algeria.

Consumer price inflation has been modest, with rates below 5 percent a year in the 1950s and 1960s and then rates approaching 10 percent a year in the following two decades, with a peak in the 1990s of almost 20 percent a year. Since then inflation has come under control, averaging below 3 percent in the years after 2000.

The considerable increases in the investment rate in the 1970s and 1980s were not reflected in comparable increases in output. In the 1950s, as column 6 of table 11.1 shows, one dollar of investment generated an increased flow of income of forty cents a year. Capital productivity fell dramatically in the 1960s to two cents for every one dollar invested, improved somewhat to thirteen cents and ten cents in the 1970s and 1980s, respectively, but fell again in the 1990s to five cents. There was an improvement to nineteen cents in 2000–2005. Although this is still poor by international comparisons—South Asia manages twenty-two cents per one dollar of investment, and East Asia generates twenty-four cents—overall it is clear that the reforms that Algeria began to introduce in the late 1990s have begun to generate some relatively significant improvements.

The Reform Stages

What marked Algeria's development until the final years of the 1970s was the extensive intervention of the state in the economic sector. The state-led economic policy, supported by large-scale public investment and financed by means of revenues from oil exports and foreign borrowing, sought to promote an ambitious program of economic and social development. The end result was the emergence of a large public sector represented for the most part by heavy industries and big farming units. In parallel with this, high levels of public spending had also targeted human development through the provision of a wide range of social services.

By the early 1980s, many of the economic activities in the public sector started to encounter mounting difficulties. Their deficiencies became manifest, and the size of investment required to support economic growth could not be sustained as in the past. Faced with a looming crisis, the decision makers, after spelling out the inadequacy of their predecessors' development policy, introduced some economic reforms that were fundamentally concerned with the restructuring of publicly owned enterprises and the state agricultural sector. As a matter of fact, the change of leadership after the death of President Houari Boumediene in 1979 ushered in a quite different vision of how the country's economic affairs were to be conducted. The new political elite, in its evaluation of the previous strategy of economic and social development, contended that "the conduct of our development was accompanied by grave distortions and profound imbalances both on the economic and social planes and even certain deviations which may compromise dangerously the construction and consolidation of our development."[2] The process entailed reducing these companies' size to functional enterprises with a view to transforming them into manageable small entities and making easy their supervision.[3] The state farming sector, consisting of the self-managed farms and the agrarian reform production cooperatives, was also reorganized into large public units, the Domaines Agricoles Socialistes. But by reason of their limited magnitude, these reforms did not have any noteworthy effect on the performance and direction of the country's economy in general.

The collapse in oil prices in the mid-1980s laid bare the vulnerability of the Algerian economy. As the socioeconomic situation started deteriorating—the yearly average GDP growth rate of less than 1 percent during the period 1986–98 was a case in point—waves of social discontent started to come out in the open in various parts of the country. The culminating point was the uprising of October 1988, the most violent social disturbance since independence, and an event that revealed the dwindling ability to satisfy the needs of the society in a context marked by the dismal performance of the economy, predominantly under state management and control. It would seem that this had impelled Algeria to commit itself to a program of political reform and economic liberalization. A first phase of what was labeled "self-imposed" reforms occurred during the government of Mouloud Hamrouche in the late 1980s. The series of legislative measures enacted were concerned with, among other things, the ending of state monopoly over external trade, liberalization of prices, granting autonomy to public enterprises and subjecting them to marketplace discipline, establishing the independence of the central bank, and opening the financial sector to private investment. This phase could have enabled Algeria to be "the first emerging country to implement a policy of structural adjustment without the assistance of the IMF."[4] Much to the chagrin of Hamrouche's government, the course that political events were to take after the short-lived experience of multipartism and the cancellation of elections in the early years of the 1990s brought to a halt this first liberalization attempt and weakened its prospects.

By 1993, Algeria's economy was in the grip of a severe financial crisis that left the authorities with no other alternative than the inevitable rescheduling of the external debt and the undertaking of comprehensive economic reforms. With the debt service reaching more than $9 billion—representing about three-fourths of the value of exported goods and services—Algeria found it difficult to honor its debt commitments. This was to pave the way for the second phase of reforms, this time under the patronage of the International Monetary Fund (IMF). A standby agreement was concluded with this institution in April 1994. Other arrangements with the Paris and London Clubs enabled Algeria to reschedule a significant part of its foreign debt. Under its Extended Fund Facility, the IMF agreed to a $1.8 billion structural reform credit for a three-year period, 1995–98.[5] The package of reforms, composed of a combination of macroeconomic stabilization and medium-term structural adjustment measures introduced from 1994, sought to attain the following goals:

- Restoring sustainable economic growth and reducing unemployment;
- Bringing inflation down to reasonable levels;
- Improving the balance of payments situation;
- Attenuating the impact of the reforms on the most vulnerable sections of the society.

A number of policy measures, some of which already had been formulated during the time of Hamrouche's premiership, were adopted with a view to achieving the reform program targets. Their principal aspects consisted of the following:

- The realignment of relative prices, including the exchange rate, through rapid and progressive liberalization;
- A tight monetary policy to reduce inflationary pressures and encourage domestic savings through the promotion of positive real interest rates, while ensuring sufficient credit to the productive sector;
- A strong fiscal adjustment aimed at ensuring a tight demand management by reforming the tax system and tightly controlling government expenditure, including the control of personnel expenditure, the elimination of subsidies, and the reduction of public investment;
- The liberalization of the trade and payments systems;
- The liberalization of the exchange regime;

- The restructuring of public enterprises and banks, including the implementation of a privatization program;
- Ensuring a more manageable debt profile through rescheduling and prudent debt management;
- The strengthening of the social safety net and the establishment of an unemployment insurance scheme.[6]

The international agencies, particularly the World Bank and the IMF, have on a number of instances complimented the Algerian authorities for their commitment to economic reforms and the progress they have made in this respect. Assessing the outcome of the four-year phase of stabilization and structural adjustment (1994–98), the IMF considered that "despite the fact that the reform program was launched ... in a difficult social and political environment, it has been remarkably successful in restoring financial stability and establishing the building blocks for a market economy."[7] Although these accomplishments have to be appreciated, one must also admit that the immediate post-adjustment era has not been followed by a strong and sustained economic recovery, which would have enabled the country to address the unemployment problem and the worsening living standards of large sections of the population. It is within this context of poor growth performance and growing social demands that the government, helped by the availability of financial resources, launched two successive economic recovery support plans (PSRE and PCSRE) for the periods 2001–4 and 2005–9.[8]

The $7 billion allocated to the PSRE was aimed at favoring spending in areas such as the modernization of infrastructure and services, the restructuring of public enterprises, the development of human capital, and the raising of living conditions. Without doubt, this plan has induced some improvement in terms of growth and job creation, but its long-term effect in this regard is not quite clear.[9] And the government was quick to point out that, taken as a whole, the PSRE's goal was "to attenuate the negative effects of a deep crisis and create the conditions propitious for a genuine long-lasting development strategy."[10] In other words, the authorities, mindful of the mixed results, drew up a more ambitious, successive five-year plan to consolidate and even enhance those results. In 2005, the PCSRE was earmarked the initial sum of $60 billion, the greater part of which was intended to improve living conditions and develop infrastructure.[11] All things considered, it is what this public investment program will deliver—that is, attaining its objectives—that matters most, something that will hinge on not only how rigorously the program is carried out but also how efficient the structures involved in its implementation are.

A recent study looked at the impact of economic reforms over the 1977–97 period.[12] Financial liberalization appears to have improved the savings rate, and there is some evidence that investment is showing greater response to real interest rates. With fewer administered prices, the economy shows signs of an improved response of inflation to monetary policy, and the exchange rate is responding more effectively to changes in purchasing power parity. However, in production, although there is a tentative indication that reforms have improved labor productivity, they appear to have had no discernable effect on capital productivity. In the labor market there is no evidence of an improved response of employment to the gap between actual and potential output.

Overall there are signs of efficiency-enhancing or growth-supporting improvements in four of the six areas of the economy examined. These results are similar to observations in other reforming economies, where liberalizing key financial variables such as interest rates, the exchange rate, and commodity prices have a prompt and significant effect. The production process, labor markets in the presence of large state-owned sectors, and financial institutions are more difficult to reform. These results tend to reinforce the view that improvements in productive efficiency through further privatization, and improvements in the effectiveness of the financial sector, are the areas where Algeria must look for further economic improvements.

The Critical Issues Ahead

It is clear that the reform program Algeria has embarked upon has enabled the country to make some progress toward a market economy. But the transitional phase is also bringing to light other important issues in the reform agenda that need to be seriously addressed. Delays and slow pace have marked the conduct and implementation of structural reforms. This is mainly true regarding the privatization process and the reform of the financial sector. To put it briefly, policy reform in Algeria is faced with the challenge of integrating the country into the world economy as a strong and competitive partner, and that of dealing with current domestic economic and social difficulties.

Speeding Up Structural Reforms

The privatization of publicly owned enterprises was launched more than a decade ago as a major component of the broad structural reform arrangement with the IMF.[13] It started with a liquidation-privatization operation that saw the bulk of local public enterprises and other state-owned big import and distribution agencies dissolved and the transfer of assets of some of these to employees. This was followed by a limited number of more or less important transactions, such as the opening up of the capital of three public sector enterprises (Eriad in the agro-food, Saidal in the pharmaceuticals, and the El-Aurassi Hotel) on the Algiers Stock Exchange and the establishment of joint ventures with foreign companies in the area of steel industry, chemicals, and telecommunications. Apart from this, it seems that the privatization process has lacked the necessary momentum behind it, not least because it has been subject to fluctuating policy priorities. Even after the revamping of the legal and institutional framework in 2001, there has been no significant headway in terms of actual implementation, partly because of resistance from some stakeholders—for instance, the bureaucracy managing the public enterprises and the trade unions—who believe their interests may be threatened in this process. As some observers have pertinently put it, "For most developing countries, the plans for privatization greatly outweighed their implementation."[14] Such observation is valid in the case of Algeria, where the privatization policy has, until very recently, not moved beyond the stage of stated intentions and lists of public enterprises to be privatized being periodically announced.

Yet the government seems determined to privatize virtually all existing public enterprises.[15] In the most recent assessment of the situation, the minister in charge, Abdelhamid Temmar, expressed his overall satisfaction with the way the privatization program is being handled. According to him, 400 public enterprises had already been privatized and some 300 more enterprises were in the process of being privatized. At this point it is not easy to judge how the process relating to the remaining companies will proceed. However, for this process to advance, it has to be consistent with a program that is clearly defined and properly adhered to. Furthermore, the authorities have been advised by the IMF that "subjecting privatization to the maintenance of employment and activity hinders a successful privatization programme."[16] In other words, the authorities' insistence on preserving the original activity and existing levels of jobs in the enterprises after privatization are considered as serious hurdles, and the Bretton Woods institution

Table 11.2. Credits from the Banking Sector, Selected Years (in billion Algerian dinars)

	2002	2003	2004	2005
Credits to public sector	715.834	791.694	859.657	895.831
Public banks	715.834	791.495	856.976	895.490
Private banks	N/A	0.199	2.681	0.341
Credit to private sector	550.208	587.780	674.731	881.616
Public banks	368.956	487.780	568.605	750.463
Private banks	181.252	100.040	106.126	131.153
Total credit disbursed	1,266.042	1,379.474	1,534.388	1,777.447
Share/public banks	85.7	92.7	92.9	92.6
Share/private banks	14.3	7.3	7.1	7.4

Source: Bank of Algeria, Rapport 2005: Evolution Economique et Monétaire en Algérie (Algiers: Bank of Algeria, 2006).

has suggested their replacement with safety nets to accompany the program in question. Another obstacle to privatization, raised this time by one of the private sector organizations in Algeria, Le Forum des Chefs d'Entreprises (FCE), is the insufficiency of financing from the banking system.[17] The FCE contends that the banks continue to play a marginal role in the privatization process, and more generally in the provision of credit despite the excess of liquidity, estimated at $10 billion in 2005. For years the banks have been lending mainly to the public sector; a trend which seems to be gradually changing as more than 42 percent of credit went to the private sector in 2005 (see table 11.2).[18]

Until recently, the banking sector was entirely under state control.[19] The role of public banks has chiefly consisted of financing public sector enterprises, something that, over the years, has adversely affected their performance. In their provision of directed credit, these banks have, according to some sources, accumulated sizable losses, averaging over 4 percent of GDP per year during the period 1991–2002.[20] Thus a first step toward financial reform has been concerned with addressing the massive nonperforming loans to the country's many loss-making public enterprises. The banks saw a large influx of liquidity as the government implemented recapitalization and debt takeover measures at high cost to the treasury, having reached some $25 billion in the last fifteen-year period.[21]

Measures have also been taken to boost competition and improve the financial sector's performance, especially by permitting the establishment of new private banks and the gradual entry of foreign banks into the domestic market. Since the end of the 1990s, several local and foreign private banks have started their operations. In a similar vein, the opening of the capital of existing state-owned banks to private participation has been encouraged, but no tangible progress has been made so far.[22] It is not surprising, then, to see that the public banks still account for almost 92 percent of the Algerian financial system assets.[23]

The scandal associated with the collapse of Khalifa Bank and Banque Commerciale et Industrielle d'Algérie in 2003 has very much damaged public confidence in the private sector banks.[24] Fraud and money laundering were ostensibly the main reasons behind the authorities' decision to withdraw these banks' licenses to operate and put them into administrative receivership in May and August 2003, respectively. This drew attention to the need for cautious and strict bank licensing and rigorous monitoring of their activities. To remedy these regulatory and supervision gaps, a new legislative bill on money and credit was adopted in 2003, and with the technical assistance of the IMF, the Bank of Algeria is now developing its supervisory capabilities.[25] However, one must admit that bringing the banking sector up to international standards is a long-term goal. The modernization process to improve the system's overall operational capacity continues to face bureaucratic hindrance, yet the introduction of major changes to the sector is now one of the authorities' main priorities. The president himself was reported to have said, "I expect the banks' managers to speed up banking reforms in order to provide our economy with a framework that is favourable to growth and investment. . . . For this reason, the delay in the banking reforms is not tolerated any more."[26] Reforms to allow for a greater role for the private sector in the banking system, especially through the quick selling of one healthy public bank to a reputable foreign one, had also been recommended by the IMF analysts who considered that this "would be important for its demonstration effect, including by transferring know-how to the sector, and would help contain the cost of restructuring other public banks."[27] The modernization of the payments system and the privatization of one state-owned bank are at the moment in progress. In a nutshell, developing a modern and competitive banking system hinges on how effective the reforms affect its role and capacity in financing investment and growth.

Managing the Opening Up to the Global Economy

For numerous developing countries, the 1980s was marked by the undertaking of significant trade liberalization with a view to furthering their integration into the world economy. Having already made substantial inroads into reforming its external trade regime, Algeria is now in the process of pressing ahead with its commitment to regional and multilateral liberalization. Like other southern Mediterranean countries, it concluded an association agreement in 2002 with the EU aimed at, among other things, the gradual phasing in of a free-trade area over a twelve-year period, starting in 2005.[28] In addition to this, Algeria's negotiations to join the World Trade Organization are currently at an advanced stage, and its membership could likely be finalized in 2007. However, it is worth noting that the initiative to establish a U.S.–North African Economic Partnership, engineered in 1998 by U.S. Undersecretary of State for Economic, Business and Agricultural Affairs, Stuart Eizenstat, proved to be an abortive undertaking, especially in its attempt to bolster regional integration between the three countries (Algeria, Morocco, and Tunisia), mostly for reasons related to the unresolved Western Sahara issue. Instead, progress has been achieved in the area of trade and investment between the United States and the individual countries of this region in recent years.

It should be noted that the potential impact of this opening up on the Algerian economy has still not been properly probed. A range of studies conducted on individual and/or groups of developing countries have come up with different conclusions regarding the potential benefits and costs associated with trade liberalization. In the case of Algeria, there is no doubt that this will, at least in the short and medium term, prove disruptive to its economy, especially in sectors such as industry and agriculture, and may well prompt a displacement of a portion of the labor force. As the ongoing course of liberalization seems irreversible, assuaging its adverse effects requires considerable adjustment efforts. The evidence is not convincing that freer trade would, in all circumstances, result in efficiency and growth. For a country like Algeria, the almost exclusive reliance on the export of primary commodities (hydrocarbons), the existence of an underperforming and uncompetitive industrial sector, and a services sector still in very early development cannot guarantee a smooth and less damaging transition. Thus there is a strong rationale for the restructuring of a wide range of economic sectors with the aim of improving productivity and enhancing greater international competitiveness. In this regard, it is too early to judge whether the recent elaboration of a new strategy to boost the development of the country's troubled industrial sector can be seen as a step toward this aim.[29]

Diversifying Away from hydrocarbons

The hydrocarbons sector is indeed the mainstay of the Algerian economy. By way of illustration, it accounted for nearly 98 percent of all export earnings, around 71 percent of government revenues and 38 percent of GDP in 2004.[33] The preponderance of this sector in the country's economy means that prospects for growth remain dependent on fluctuating oil prices in the international market. Even though the IMF predictions show a more or less steady level of hydrocarbons revenue—an average of around $39 billion over the period 2005–2009—it is not immediately obvious that the world energy market conditions would remain favorable to secure such levels of export earnings.[31] This vulnerability was candidly echoed by an official who stated, "Our economy is based too much on hydrocarbons. We must diversify our economy. If not, Algeria will become lost in the global marketplace."[32]

In principle, Algeria would be expected to benefit from trade openness on condition that it shift its export base away from the high level of dependence on hydrocarbons. It is now a fact that its neighbors (Morocco and Tunisia) are moving away from being categorized as primarily commodity economies. Both countries have made fairly significant strides in their efforts to diversify their export structures, with the shares of manufactured goods and services rapidly growing (see chapter 10 in this volume). Altering the prevailing external trade orientation and "rent-seeking" entails accelerating the structural reforms and improving the business environment. In particular, Algeria needs to maintain a level of exchange rate that is competitive enough to enable domestic production to compete with imports and allow non-oil exporters to compete on world markets. With the rising of its international reserve levels—favored by world energy prices in recent years and estimated to have reached about $80 billion as of December 2006—Algeria could use part of these resources to create the conditions that would foster both the development and competitiveness of its manufacturing and services sectors.[33] Only an efficient economy with a diversified export base can cushion the possible adverse effects of exposure to the global economy and ensure a successful participation in the world markets.

Tackling Social Problems

It is clear that the transitional phase of reform Algeria is going through has and will continue to have wider social implications. The restructuring and privatization-liquidation of state-owned enterprises has meant cutting employment, which is part of a process aimed at reducing or even eliminating labor hoarding. The decline in the rate of labor absorption within the public sector and the increasing numbers of first-time job seekers entering the labor market exacerbated unemployment, which, according to official sources stood at approximately 30 percent in 1999.[34] Such a high level of unemployment has, to a great extent, been responsible for the deterioration in living conditions, with poverty having become in recent years a salient feature in society, predominantly in rural areas.[35] The rural population represented 41 percent of the whole population (32.4 million) in 2004.[36] It should be noted that the abolition of subsidies, the devaluation of the local currency, and the state's deficit in the provision of public services are among the factors that have also taken their toll on the purchasing power of large sections of the population. An accurate picture about the extent of poverty cannot be provided due to the variety of indicators used to measure it. Using the poverty line of two dollars per capita a day, UN sources have estimated the Algerian population living below this line to be an average of 15.1 percent over the period 1990–2004.[37] But according to a more recent Algerian source (Centre National d'Études et d'Analyses pour la Population et le Développement), the level of poverty (population living on one dollar a day) was 12.1 percent in 2000 and dropped to 5.7 percent in 2005.[38] Similarly, the unemployment rate fell to 12.3 percent in 2006 compared to 15.3 percent the previous year and 17.7 percent in 2004. In addition to the doubt expressed over these figures, it is worth mentioning that youth unemployment remains a serious problem, representing more than 70 percent of the unemployed. In spite of that the authorities insist that social conditions have improved, which they consider being largely due to the positive impact of the PSRE, that is, the generation of more jobs, increased social transfers, and boosted incomes.

The persistence of social tensions is nonetheless indicative of the limited impact the government program has had on easing many of the pressures experienced by large sections of the society. It is the case that in the last couple of years growth has taken place, but it remains to be seen whether it can be boosted to ensure sustained levels of job creation, at least to bring the unemployment rate down to a more acceptable level. The current economic recovery plan has devoted almost 50 percent of its resources to address social problems (health, education, water, housing, and so forth), twelve times more than what was allocated during the first plan, the PSRE.[39] This, of course, is part of what is known as the "human side" of the adjustment programs, which entail measures to maintain and improve the delivery of public services, particularly for the benefit of the poor. Investing in the social sector is, indeed, a requirement for development. In the final analysis, it is the extent of economic recovery and its sustainability that are of prime importance to any improvement in social conditions. Thus, economic growth is the key vehicle for faster human development, which in turn helps maintain social peace and strengthen social cohesion. Recent data from the UN Development Program show that Algeria has been experiencing some improvement in its human development, though at a moderate pace. Its human development index—an indicator measuring average achievement in three basic dimensions of human development, that is, long and healthy life, knowledge, and a decent standard of living—increased from 0.650 in 1990 to 0.728 in 2004.[40] Obviously, the decade-long instability and violence that plagued the country did nothing to advance the pace of social progress.

Conclusion

Algeria has made some progress over the past decade, and is currently witnessing an encouraging economic performance. Above all, Algeria must persevere with the political process that has seen the beginnings of a return to peace and stability. Without a secure environment, economic progress is impossible.

The key reforms now on the agenda are the privatization of the still-substantial number of state-owned enterprises and the restructuring of the financial sector to include the introduction of international banks. Looking ahead, Algeria must prepare for the impact of a more open economy and the restructuring of production that this will involve. The privatization process needs to be carefully designed to maximize the revenues to the government (which, hopefully, will use these revenues in a socially productive manner) and to avoid the excessive private sector windfall gains of the kinds resulting from the sell-off of state assets in Russia. It must also plan for less reliance on oil, which is notoriously unstable as a source of revenue and unsustainable as deposits are eventually exhausted. The current high oil prices are generating a substantial windfall gain, a gain that can best be used to reinforce the impetus for reform by investing in socially desirable projects that can be constructed by labor-intensive methods (such as housing) and by providing a cushion against the social hardships arising from economic reforms.

It is now clear that economic growth reduces poverty while improving incomes at all levels in society.[41] In the long term, Algeria must look to a liberalized market economy—stimulated by competition from international trade and boosted by foreign investment—to generate improved living standards for its citizens.

Notes

1. Michael Hodd, "Algeria: Economic Structure, Performance and Policy, 1950–2001," in *Algeria in Transition: Reforms and Development Prospects*, edited by Ahmed Aghrout, with Redha M. Bougherira, 35–57 (London: RoutledgeCurzon, 2004).

2. Mahfoud Bennoune, *The Making of Contemporary Algeria, 1830–1987: Colonial Upheavals and Post-Independence Development* (Cambridge: Cambridge University Press, 1988), 263.

3. Ibid.

4. Omar Akala, "L'économie algérienne, de l'ère des réformes (1989–1991) à celle de l'adjustement structurel (1994–1998)," in *Où va l'Algérie*, edited by Ahmed Mahiou and Jean-Robert Henry, 166 (Paris: Éditions Karthala, 2001).

5. IMF, "IMF Approves Credit under Extended Fund Facility for Algeria," press release, 95/31, May 22, 1995.

6. Abdelouahab Keramane, "Algeria: Present Economic Situation and Prospects," *Euro-Mediterranean Partnership* 2 (1997): 27. For more details on the policies adopted, see Karim A. Nashashibi, Patricia Alonso-Gamo, Stefania Bazzoni, Alain Feler, Nicole Laframboise, and Sebastian Paris Horvitz, "Algeria: Stabilization and Transition to the Market," *IMF Occasional Paper* 165 (August 6, 1998): 1–69; Brahim Guendouzi and Khelifa Kadri, "Les retombées de l'adjustement structurel sur le développement local en Algérie," *Les Cahiers du Cread* 46–47 (1998): 135–52.

7. Martha Bonilla, "Algeria's Reform Program Promotes Economic Growth and Transition to the Market," *IMF Survey* 27, no. 17 (August 31, 1998): 277.

8. The abbreviations stand for Programme de Soutien à la Relance Économique (PSRE) and Programme Complémentaire de Soutien à la Relance Économique (PCSRE).

9. According to the government, the PSRE generated 728,666 new jobs between September 2001 and December 2003. Quoted in "Plans de Relance Economique (PSRE et PCSRE)—Dans l'attente de résultats concrets," *El-Watan*, April 11, 2005, 2.

10. Ibid.

11. About 45.4 percent will go to raising living standards, 40.5 percent for the development of infrastructure, and the remaining is to be spent on support for economic restructuring, modernization in the public sector, and developing the use of information and communication technology. With the inclusion of two new programs intended for the country's southern and Haut Plateau regions, the financial package was increased to $144 billions. See Algerian Embassy in France web site, http://www.amb-algerie.fr/Economique/eco_p1.htm (February 8, 2007).

12. Michael Hodd, "Impact of Economic Reforms in Algeria," *Revue des Sciences Économiques et de Gestion* 1, no. 1 (2002): 17–33.

13. For a detailed account on the privatization process, see Ahmed Aghrout, Mohamed Bouhezza, and Khaled Sadaoui, "Restructuring and Privatisation in Algeria," in *Algeria in Transition: Reforms and Development Prospects*, edited by Ahmed Aghrout, with Redha M. Bougherira, 120–35 (London: RoutledgeCurzon, 2004).

14. Paul Cook and Colin Kirkpatrick, "Privatisation Policy and Performance," in *Privatisation Policy and Performance—International Perspectives*, edited by Paul Cook and Colin Kirkpatrick, 5 (Hertfordshire: Prentice Hall/Harvester Wheatsheaf, 1995).

15. Considered "strategic" public enterprises, Sonatrach (hydrocarbons), Sonelgaz (gas and electricity), and SNTF (railway transport) are not concerned.

16. IMF, "Algeria: Staff Report for the 2005 Article IV Consultation," Country Report no. 06/93, March 2006, 19.

17. Oxford Business Group, "Focus on Privatisation—Algeria," Oxford Business Group Web site, http://www.oxfordbusinessgroup.com/weekly01.asp?id=1260 (March 24, 2005).

18. This figure was reported to have been mentioned by President Abdelaziz Bouteflika in his speech delivered on April 7, 2005. See "Bouteflika accable les banques," *El-Watan*, April 9, 2005, 1 and 4.

19. It was the Law no. 90–10 of April 14, 1990, on Money and Credit that, for the first time, allowed for the establishment of private banks.

20. IMF, "Financial System Stability Assessment," Country Report no. 04/138 (May 2004).

21. See interview given by Abderrahmane Hadj Nacer, former governor of the Bank of Algeria, to *El-Watan*, October 28, 2006, 6.

22. For the time being, the authorities have agreed to the first privatization of a publicly owned bank, by approving the sale of a 51 percent stake in Crédit Populaire d'Algérie.

23. Speech by Mohammed Laksaci, governor of the Bank of Algeria, delivered to the Assemblée Populaire Nationale in November 2005, Bank of Algeria Web site, http://www.bank-of-algeria.dz/communicat.htm (February 10, 2007).

24. The collapse of Khalifa Bank is believed to have caused the Algerian government a loss of $1.5 billion. Algeria Interface, http://www.algeria-interface.com/new/article.php?article_id=738 (April 3, 2005).

25. Ordinance no. 03–11, August 26, 2003.

26. Algerian Presidency Web site, http://www.el-mouradia.dz/francais/president/activites/PresidentActi.htm (April 9, 2005).

27. Jules J. De Vrijer, "New Roles for Banks in Algeria," International Monetary Fund Web site, http://www.imf.org/external/np/speeches/2005/020305.htm (February 22, 2005).

28. Ahmed Aghrout, *From Preferential Status to Partnership: The Euro-Maghreb Relationship* (Aldershot: Ashgate Publishing, 2000).

29. For further details see, "Stratégies et politiques de relance et de développement industriels," *El-Moudjahid*, December 20, 2006, 3.

30. Figures cited in IMF, "Algeria: Staff Report for the 2005 Article IV Consultation," 12.

31. IMF, "Financial System Stability Assessment," 27.

32. Speech delivered by Abdelhamid Temmar, ministre des participations et de la promotion des investissements, in a meeting with finance and trade leaders in Washington on December 5, 2004, http://www.bilaterals.org/article.php3?id_article=1016 (March 25, 2005).

33. "Situation financière du pays_:Réserves en hausse, dette en baisse," *Liberté*, January 25, 2007.

34. See statement made by Djamel Ould-Abbes, minister in charge of national solidarity and employment, during the first meeting of the National Observatory for Employment and Fight against Poverty on February 28, 2005, cited in *Le Soir d'Algérie*, March 1, 2005.

35. World Bank, "New Business Plan for Algeria to Focus on Fighting Poverty, Supporting Reform Program," News Release, 2003/417/MENA, June 12, 2003. See also "World Bank Loan to Fight Poverty in Rural Algeria with Job Creation," News Release, 2003/314/MENA, April 29, 2003.

36. World Bank, *World Development Indicators, 2006* (Washington, D.C.: World Bank, 2006), World Bank Web site, http://devdata.worldbank.org/wdi2006/contents/Section3.htm (February 14, 2007).

37. United Nations Development Program, *Human Development Report, 2006* (New York: United Nations, 2006), 293.

38. "La pauvreté et l'inégalité en baisse," *El-Watan*, October 10, 2006, 1 and 6.

39. From 155 billion Algerian dinars in the PSRE to more than 1,900 billion Algerian dinars under current PCSRE.

40. United Nations Development Program, *Human Development Report*, 2006, 289.

41. See David Dollar and Aart Kraay, *Growth Is Good for the Poor* (Washington, D.C.: Development Research Group, World Bank, March 2000); Shaohua Chen and Martin Ravallion, *How Have the World's Poor Fared since the Early 1980s?* (Washington, D.C.: Development Research Group, World Bank, 2004).

4

The Maghrib and Europe

12

The Maghrib Abroad

Immigrant Transpolitics and Cultural Involution in France

PAUL A. SILVERSTEIN

Although exact figures are impossible to come by, an estimated twelve to fifteen million people of Muslim background now inhabit the countries of the European Union. France is the home of the single largest Muslim population in Europe, numbering anywhere between five and seven million, the vast majority being of Algerian or Moroccan descent and a lesser, though sizable, number being of Tunisian ancestry. The Algerian portion of the population is not only the largest but also the one with the longest history in France, spearheading, as it were, the postindependence, large-scale Maghribi migration to the northern shores of the Mediterranean—France, Spain, and Italy—and beyond, particularly to the Netherlands, Belgium, and Germany. The impact of this mass migration on the host states, the immigrant populations themselves, their links to Maghribi societies, and the relations between Maghrib and European states have already been substantial. It is sure to be even more far-reaching in the coming decades.

In light of the Algerian and French "vanguard" roles in the mass migration from the Maghrib to Europe, this chapter focuses on sociopolitical movements and imaginations enacted within the space of transpolitics that links Algeria and France across the Mediterranean. It investigates the simultaneous rise of Islamist and Berberist movements, which have connected marginalized groups in Algeria to second-generation Algerian immigrants in France. These movements have created new spheres for political engagement, which have provided Algerians with effective means of locally contesting state authority in both France and Algeria. The reciprocal flows of people, goods, and information throughout the 1990s that kept Algeria and France closely tied resulted, to a great extent, in the transfer of the political divides of the Algerian civil war onto French soil.

The sphere of political engagement of immigrant actors of various generations has not been solely limited to the Algerian context but also has drawn on new spheres of transpolitics opened up by the European Union's ideological and financial support for regional and minority rights. As Riva Kastoryano and Yasemin Soysal have argued, the institutional architecture of the new Europe has altered the political landscape of immigrant politics, encouraging an effective homogenization of the parameters for the recognition of cultural difference that has aligned national narratives and immigrant claims.[1] However, although this chapter touches on such co-evolution, it is primarily concerned with the cultural involution that Algerian immigrant cultural politics has undergone, with the inward turn to and objectification of ethnic and religious identity diacritics enacted as a response to the assimilatory efforts of late French and Algerian nationalist ideologies.[2] In other words, contemporary claims of "Berber," "Muslim," and "Beur" distinctiveness, largely based in the reappropriation of colonial and early nationalist narratives rejected by postindependence Algeria and Fifth Republic France, have challenged the monopoly on the ideological bundling of people, political power, and territory ideally held by the French and Algerian nation-states. In the pages that follow, I will outline several ways in which Algerian immigrant political projects based in a transnational social imagination have been articulated and contested in France.

Immigrant Politicization

As a number of scholars have demonstrated, Algerian emigration began at the end of the nineteenth century, as Berber-speaking men from Kabylia were recruited to work in the farms of colonial settlers, in the mines in Tunisia, and, later, in the mines, agricultural concerns, and growing manufacturing centers in France.[3] This labor recruitment expanded during and immediately after World War I to provide manpower for the war effort and overcome the manpower shortfalls of the subsequent "lost generation," contracted during the depression of the 1930s and the wartime years of Nazi occupation and the Vichy regime in France, and rebounded during the postwar period of rebuilding and economic expansion known as the "Thirty Glorious Years" (*Trente Glorieuses*). By the beginning of the Algerian war of national liberation, more than six hundred thousand Algerian men labored in France, mostly on renewable short-term labor contracts that allowed for seasonal trips to Algeria. They lived primarily alongside other Algerians (and often co-villagers) in workers' dormitories near work sites, in shared apartments in the working-class areas of major urban areas, or in the growing shantytowns on the peripheries of Paris and Lyon. Although the "community" as such had no representative institutions, "Arab cafés" served as sites for the exchange of information regarding affairs in Algeria or necessities in France, as well as meeting places for expatriate village assemblies (*tajmaâts*), which maintained communal funds for aiding new immigrants, repatriating immigrant corpses, and contributing to village improvement projects.

During the Algerian war and in the years that followed, the Algerian presence in France began to take on more of a permanent character. Wartime and immediate postwar instability in Algeria interrupted normal travel and called into question the rotational system of labor that had been in operation. Increasingly, Algerian men in France began to take advantage of family reunification opportunities and bring their wives and children to join them. By the time France closed the door to future economic migrants in 1974, following the economic slowdown that accompanied the Arab oil embargo in the wake of the October 1973 Arab-Israeli war, nearly one million people of Algerian origin lived in France, both berberophones and arabophones, men, women, and children. They inhabited for the most part an expanding public housing system that consisted of large estates (*cités*) within Marseille and on the outskirts of Paris and Lyon. These *cités* included their own local public schools, which explicitly were constructed to transform the children of immigrants into Frenchmen but implicitly resulted in the reproduction of an immigrant underclass, with immigrant children often tracked to vocational diplomas that qualified them for jobs that were in increasingly short supply. By the turn of the twenty-first century, the *cités* had become sites of racial and class marginalization, subject to disproportionate rates of unemployment, physical dilapidation, a strong underground economy (including a healthy drug trade), and an expanding police presence that provoked occasional outbreaks of communal violence (as occurred most notably in October–November 2005).[4]

Although French integration policies have sought to maintain immigrants as politically quiescent subjects, and although the most recent violence has more often been a reaction to marginalization and a general expression of "hate" of the system rather than a reflection of any particular political ideology, France has nonetheless proven to be a key site of Algerian transpolitics. It was in France, among immigrant workers, that the first Algerian nationalist party, the Étoile Nord-Africaine (ENA) was formed in the 1920s. Likewise, it was there, under the direction of Messali al-Hadj, that the ENA, banned in 1936, was reborn as the Parti du Peuple Algérien

(PPA). Also banned, the PPA survived underground before acquiring a legal, electoralist cover organization, the Mouvement pour la Triomphe des Libértés Démocratiques (MTLD), in 1946. The PPA/MTLD would later (in 1953–54) split into the FLN and the Mouvement National Algérien (MNA), the latter under the direction of Hadj. During the war, France functioned for both of these revolutionary parties as a space of recruitment, logistics, and fund raising. France was structured as the "seventh *wilaya* (province)" in the FLN's operational cartography, and the Fédération de France acted as the de facto French wing of the party.[5] The latter organized demonstrations to support the war in Algeria and to advocate immigrants' rights in France, as well as periodic attacks on police and military targets in the metropole. Concerned with this political organization and the potential transformation of immigrant workers into enemies within, the French state actively kept watch over Algerian organizations, took measures to disaggregate Algerian settlements and relocate immigrants from shantytowns to newly built housing projects, detained thousands of Algerians in police round-ups, and established curfews specifically for Algerian residents.

This repression of the Algerian immigrant population exacerbated after the early 1961 foundation of the settler Organisation de l'Armée Secrète (OAS), which was opposed to the French government's forthcoming negotiations with the FLN and dedicated to maintaining an Algérie française by all means necessary. Numerous attacks on immigrant workers and their residences followed, alongside an increased campaign of mass detentions of Algerians by the Parisian police under the direction of former Vichy official Maurice Papon, renowned for his previous hardline tactics against nationalists while prefect of Constantine (eastern Algeria) from 1956 to 1958. In protest, the FLN renewed their targeting of police officers, killing eleven and wounding seventeen others during the late summer and early autumn of 1961. During the violent police interventions that followed, numerous Algerians disappeared, their bodies later discovered floating in the Seine. Papon actively encouraged this violence, promising that "for every blow received, we will deliver ten" and ensuring police officers legal impunity should they shoot first. He further declared a new curfew for all Algerian residents of France.

In response to this state violence, the FLN sought to regain public opinion, ended their campaign of metropolitan attacks, and organized a massive nonviolent demonstration in Paris for the evening of October 17, 1961. The protest was violently suppressed by the French police, who brutally beat the unarmed protesters trying to enter Paris or march along the boulevards. By the night's end, at least ten thousand Algerians had been arrested and two hundred killed, although official reports listed only two casualties and subsequent parliamentary inquiries were systematically blocked. The memory of the massacre has been a touchstone for subsequent Algerian politics in France and has been repeatedly memorialized in the writings and actions of subsequent generations of political actors.[6]

In the years following the Algerian war, the institutional structuring of the Algerian community in France was subsumed under the activities of the Amicale des Algériens en Europe and its parallel youth organization, the Union National de la Jeunesse Algérienne (UNJA), official organs of the ruling FLN party. The Amicale and the UNJA sought to be the primary mediator between Algerians in France and at home, centralizing all documentary procedures for maintaining Algerian citizenship status while abroad (as pertaining to property rights, local voting privileges, military service, etc.), directing all Arabic language and Islamic religious instruction for children of immigrants, and arranging all transfers of immigrant corpses back for burial in Algeria. This monopoly was enabled by the series of postwar agreements between Algeria and France and abetted by France's ban on immigrant voluntary associations that remained in effect until the socialists took power under François Mitterrand in 1981.

The Amicale and the UNJA officially propagated the nationalist ideology of the FLN state that presented Algeria as historically Arab and naturally Islamic. During the revolutionary period, the FLN systematically marginalized alternate ideological frameworks from the nationalist movement. In the first place, it rejected the constitutional reform efforts of the secularist Union Démocratique du Manifeste Algérien (UDMA) of Ferhat Abbas, which sprang from the Jeunes Algériens student movement of the 1920s. Second, it actively battled the Messalist MNA in a veritable "war within the war,"[7] which resulted in hundreds of casualties on both sides and most notably the massacre of the pro-MNA village of Mélouza.[8] Third, it systematically excluded, in the name of national unity, those militating for a multiethnic Algerian state, for an Algérie algérienne. During the early days of the uprising, revolutionary songs were composed in Berber, calling upon Kabyle villagers to "Rise up, Berber son!" (*Kker a mmi-s umazigh*).[9] The most extreme of these groups, led by Rachid Ali Yahia, even called for a rejection of any inclusion of Algeria in the larger Arab world, on the basis that Algeria was rightfully Berber in nature.[10] Beginning in 1949, these advocates were successively purged from the nationalist party in what was declared a "Berberist crisis." Kabyle francophone intellectuals such as Mouloud Mammeri and Mouloud Feraoun were condemned for their anachronistic "regionalism" in the nationalist newspapers, and prominent Kabyle leaders within the FLN, most notably Abbane Ramdane and, later, Krim Belkacem, were assassinated.[11]

These tensions between visions of an Algérie algérienne and an "Arab-Muslim Algeria" (Algérie arabo-musulmane) resurfaced after independence in 1962. The Algiers Charter, adopted in April 1964 as Algeria's de facto constitution, declared Algeria to be an "Arab-Muslim country" and decried regionalist identities as "feudal survivals" and "obstacles to national integration." Rejecting this direction in the ruling FLN ideology, the Kabyle war hero Hocine Aït Ahmed founded the first rival political party in independent Algeria, the Socialist Forces Front (FFS), in September 1963 and subsequently led a ten-month guerrilla insurrection throughout Kabylia against the Algerian national army and the "ethnic fascism" of president Ahmed Ben Bella. Although the revolt failed to gain widespread support, the FFS remained a strong oppositional (though unarmed) force to the Algerian regime in both Kabylia and France, even after Aït Ahmed's arrest and flight to Europe in 1965. After 1973, the Boumediene regime carried out further steps of forced Arabization, demonizing Berber identity as simultaneously backward (part of the pre-Islamic *jahiliyya*, or "age of ignorance and barbarity") and colonialist (in that it was supposedly privileged by the French). University courses in Berber linguistics (in place since the colonial period) were eliminated, the public and literary use of Berber was outlawed, and a disproportionate number of Islamic institutes were established in berberophone areas.

The Kabyle intelligentsia in France reacted strongly to these processes of cultural hegemony and, further, rejected the role of the Amicale in controlling Algerian overseas identity production along such Arab-Muslim ideological lines. A group of Paris-based Kabyle militants, including scholars (among them, Mouloud Mammeri), artists (such as singer Taos Amrouche), and FFS activists (including Bessaoud Mohand Arab), founded the Académie Berbère d'Echanges et de Recherches Culturels, renamed Agraw Imazighen in 1969. Although originally dedicated to the "universal" and "harmonious cooperation between all humanity," the Agraw's goals became increasingly ethnocentric: "to introduce the larger public to the history and civilization of Berbers, including the promotion of the language and culture," as stated in the second article of its 1969 statutes. Adopting the appellation "Imazighen," or "free men," members of the academy worked to standardize Berber language (Tamazight) and develop a neo-Tifinagh script. At the same time, the academy was actively involved in the social life of the Kabyle emigrant community, publicizing Algerian and French policy changes of relevance to the community and pushing its ideology of a "Berber nation" through the medium of *cafés arabes* and the variety of *tajmaâts* transposed onto the French urban landscape.[12] In spite of these efforts, however, the academy maintained its primary presence among Kabyle student groups in the university system.

This intellectual slant of Kabyle expatriate activism was underlined in the 1973 formation of the Groupe d'Études Berbères at the Université de Paris-VIII-Vincennes. Dedicated to teaching Berber language and culture, the organization received national and international recognition, garnering the participation of many sympathetic, non-Kabyle scholars, including such eminent names as Pierre Bourdieu and Ernest Gellner. In 1978, the group formed the *Ateliers Imedyazen*, a publication cooperative in Paris, to diffuse such intellectual debates to a more popular level. Over the course of the next several years, the cooperative published works on linguistics, theater, poetry, and other literature, including translations into Tamazight (of Brecht, among others), grammar manuals, *dossiers de presse* that followed events in Algeria, and political communiqués, including the 1979 FFS party platform. These publications were further paralleled by the growth of a Kabyle recording industry in France, and particularly the invention of the *neo-chanson kabyle* by recording artists (notably Lounis Aït-Menguellet, Idir, Ferhat M'henni, and Lounès Matoub), several of whom were based in Paris. Drawing on the earlier sung poetry of Taos Amrouche and the musical commentary on exile (*lghorba*) by Slimane Azem, these singer-songwriters adopted traditional poetry into "revolutionary songs of struggle" and eventually came to play direct political roles in the struggle for Berber linguistic rights. Given this development of emigrant cultural production, as Salem Chaker has remarked, "it would not be an exaggeration to say that thousands of young Kabyles have learned to read and write in their language from those works published in France."[13]

In addition to the elaboration of Berberist politics in France, Algerian immigrants and their children outlined several other political trajectories in the wake of Algerian independence that challenged the monopoly of the Amicale and the UNJA as well as the efforts by the French state to depoliticize immigrant life. Originally, immigrant workers had been largely excluded from labor unions, as union leaders viewed their temporary presence and often lack of official documentation as a means of employer manipulation and a safety net against organized labor. However, by the 1970s, with their residence in France more firmly established via the arrival of their families and their residence in state housing projects, immigrant workers became more vocal in their demands for better working and living conditions. Algerian membership in the French Communist party and a variety of Trotskyist organizations active in France increased throughout the 1970s, and Algerian workers became active in local union branches of the Confédération Général du Travail (CGT) and the Confédération des Syndicats Libres (CSL). Additionally, Algerian workers founded their own Mouvement des Travailleurs Arabes in Marseille in 1970 and had by the mid-1970s gained support among their compatriots in Paris. This membership translated into concrete forms of protest. In the summer of 1973, workers in Marseille staged a one-day general strike to protest a series of racist killings in the city.[14] Likewise, from 1975 to 1979, residents of the state-run SONACOTRA (Société Nationale de Construction de Logements pour les Travailleurs) foyers for immigrant workers staged a series of sit-ins to protest poor upkeep and obtain expanded social services. During this same period, workers staged punctual strikes at the Renault, Citroën, and Talbot factories near Paris demanding better pay and benefits.[15] These actions set a precedent of militancy for later civil rights activism of the younger generations of Algerians in France.

Alongside these Marxist modes of political organization, forms of Islamic organization burgeoned. If, for the most part, North African Islamic practice is heteroprax in character, allowing for multiple regional forms of Sufism, maraboutic divination and healing, and local pilgrimage, in the setting of immigration and in the absence of a centuries-endowed, evocative sacred landscape, it became increasingly objectified and recentered around communal prayer, group celebration of holy days (particularly the sacrifice of the ʿid al-adha), *halal* food restrictions, and Qur'anic education. In all these areas, the Algerian state, via the Amicale, sought a monopoly of religious organization; yet various local groups challenged the Amicale's dominance and worked to establish autonomous sites of religious practice.

Beginning in the 1960s, a variety of Islamic cultural associations were founded under the leadership of naturalized French citizens or converted French Muslims, thus negotiating the legal barrier to immigrant associations. By 1981, nearly 150 such associations, of various national and denominational bents, were in existence.[16] They provided alternative spaces for group prayer, holy day celebration, and Islamic education. One group, the Association Culturelle Islamique, worked to construct a full-scale mosque that would be independent of the Algerian-controlled Grand Mosquée de Paris. Beginning in 1969, it first established the mosque in the basement of a condemned building, then in a church crypt, and then in an abandoned garment warehouse where it became the most attended mosque in Paris. In 1994, the mosque leadership submitted plans for the building of a twenty-two-hundred-square-foot structure, but the construction was repeatedly delayed due to city logistical concerns and far-Right protests. In the meantime, thousands of other prayer rooms and minor mosques—both official and underground—had been established throughout France, the fruits of protracted worker and resident strikes in the mid-1970s to force employers and housing officials to open such spaces in automobile factories and SONACOTRA foyers.[17] Many of these associations and prayer spaces would later become rallying points for a variety of Salafi and other reformist Islamist movements that burgeoned in Algeria in the 1980s in protest against the Algerian state's direction of Islamic training and worship.

Beur Movement

These three modes of Algerian immigrant politicization—Islamist, Berberist, and Marxist—found themselves represented in various forms in the civil rights protests of the younger generation of Algerians and other Maghribis born and/or raised in France known colloquially as *les Beurs*. In 1981, newly elected President Mitterrand rescinded the 1939 ban on immigrant associations. In the wake of these changes, hundreds of second-generation cultural associations formed throughout France in the early 1980s, focusing on a variety of social and cultural issues, from grassroots urban development (e.g., Association Gutenberg of Nanterre and Vivons Ensemble [Living Together] of Val-Fourré), to antiracist politics (e.g., SOS-Racisme), to youth politics (e.g., Association de la Nouvelle Génération Immigrée, or ANGI, of Aubervilliers), to cultural activism (e.g., Association de Culture Berbère, or ACB, of Ménilmontant). These associations further became sites for Beur cultural production, establishing newspapers (*Sans Frontières* [Without Borders]), publishing houses (Éditions Arcantère and Agence Im'media in Paris), and radio stations (Radio Gazelle in Marseille and Radio Beur in Paris), and home to a burgeoning complement of Beur novelists, musicians, and actors. These individuals and groups—in coordination with the mass political demonstrations of the 1983 Marche des Beurs, the 1984 Convergence, and the 1985 March for Civic Rights—constituted what would become known throughout France as "the Beur movement."

In general, the Beur movement, in its various actions and productions throughout the 1980s, emphasized the "second generation" of Maghribi immigrants as a particular, multicultural political subject distinct from their Algerian, Moroccan, or Tunisian forebears and French neighbors. In publications such as *La Beur génération*,[18] Beur activists and writers celebrated the arrival of a new "hybrid" (*métis*) population in France, endowed with their own politicians, academics, and artists. Claiming to occupy, in the words of Beur novelist Leila Sebbar, a subject position "between Algeria and France,"[19] Beur cultural producers sought to represent a generation in all its diversity. Novels written by Beur authors employed dialogical techniques of code switching and heteroglossia to portray Beur cultural in-betweenness. Likewise, Beur musical groups mixed Algerian *cha'abi* and *raï* musical styles with Arabic and Kabyle lyrics into Euro-American genres such as rock (e.g., Les Rockin' Babouches), rhythm and blues (e.g., Carte de Séjour), and electronic pop (e.g., Djurdjura).

Beurs thus presented themselves as the ultimate *bricoleurs*, combining multiple codes into their own language and styles particular to their daily lives in the French *cités* of the early 1980s. Cobbling their identity from referents beyond the Mediterranean, some, such as Nacer Kettane, president of Radio Beur, saw themselves as the rejects of a globalizing world—"mutants torn from the McDonald's couscous-steak-fries society."[20] Others imagined the Beurs as the vanguard of a particular postcolonial space that linked North Africa and France via the media of American Beat authors and soap operas: "From Santa Barbara to Tamanrasset by way of Dunkerque,[21] Carthage and Marrakech, they will soon be speaking not of Greenwich Village, but of Beur Village, where the Ahmed Ben Kerouacs, Aïcha MacCullers and Abderrahman Burroughs will be sweeping away the fluff [of society] (*balaieront la pâte de guimauve*)."[22] As either the globalized rejects or the avant-garde, the Beurs presented themselves as the generation of the future, of the "year 3000," if not earlier.[23]

In highlighting this multiculturality—in having, as the colloquialism went, their "ass between two chairs"—Beur authors and activists presented themselves as the ultimate cultural and political mediator between Algeria and France, as a new embodiment of the pan-Mediterranean *homme frontière* (border man) of French colonial discourse.[24] Beur leaders attempted to chart a "third route" (*troisième voie*) between the French state's schemas of integration and the ongoing attempts by the Amicale and the UNJA to resuture immigrant political life to the other side of the Mediterranean.[25] In this logic of independence, the "new generation" had to separate itself from both French and Algerian political and cultural institutions and establish its own means of intervention. As Saleiha Amara, the president of the ANGI, explained, groups like hers saw their primary goal of preserving the "autonomy" of the demands of immigrant youth from being co-opted by existing political parties or Algerian governmental bodies.[26]

In spite of these attempts at generational autonomy, the Beur movement remained deeply connected to Algerian transpolitics. For instance, Radio Beur, in addition to serving as the major promoter of North African music in France, was a major node in the dissemination of information back and forth across the Mediterranean, particularly during the April 1980 and October 1988 protests in Algeria, when, in the face of a dearth of reliable coverage from the mainstream media, the station interrupted its normal programing to provide a news and debate forum for those directly and indirectly affected. For all of their focus on everyday life in the *cités*, Beur activists and cultural producers took a great interest in educating themselves about Maghribi history and culture in an attempt to get beyond the reified, nationalist versions presented by Algerian state organs, and, in founding cultural associations, they served as the prime intermediaries of this vernacular cultural history to their younger siblings and even their uneducated parents.

Moreover, Beur activists remained closely tied to various Marxist, Islamist, and Berberist political currents. Many Beur militants began their activism in the French Communist party and various Trotskyist organizations that had been active in the various housing and factory strikes by immigrant workers during the late 1970s,[27] and in many cases they maintained their ties to these political groups. Several weeks after the conclusion of the 1983 Marche, North African auto workers in the Talbot plant in the Parisian suburb of Poissy staged a sit-in, protesting discriminatory wages and promotion practices. Radio Beur, demonstrating its solidarity, proclaimed that "we are all the *bougnoules*[28] of Talbot," and a number of Beur militants joined the striking workers inside the factory. Whereas the 1983 Marche had been heralded by the ruling Socialist party, the Talbot strikes were dismissed as "not part of the French reality," and the Beur strikers were called "traitors" by their former governmental supporters, including Georgina Dufoix, then minister of social affairs and once considered the "fairy godmother of the Beur Movement."[29]

The ongoing participation in such forms of labor politics divided the Beur movement. For some Beur militants, participation in the formal political sphere was considered highly illegitimate, an index of individual political careerism. Other Beur activists, however, came to view Marxist ideology as an antidote to the generational parochialism of Beur concerns, as a means to open up the movement to the "universal." One former Beur activist I interviewed in 1995 began his political career in the SONACOTRA and later the Talbot-Poissy strikes and went on to found a French wing of the Britain-based Socialist Workers' party. By 1986, he had grown disenchanted with the Beur movement, which "was driving a wedge between children of immigrants, their parents, and proletarian struggles more generally." He declared, "I built Socialisme Internationale in order to bring together my identity struggles with those of my father in the factories. Socialisme Internationale was a means to fight the growth of ethnic and religious movements in the *cités* that were a capitalist 'lure' (*leurre*) away from the real issues of marginalization."

In addition, Beur activism encompassed a growing Islamic public sphere in France. Alongside the growth of neighborhood improvement and vernacular cultural associations, the 1981 reforms paved the way for the florescence of Islamic immigrant associations, with over 450 founded in the first four years after the ban was rescinded.[30] Although the majority of Beur activists were avowedly secular, most supported larger community demands for the building of prayer rooms and mosques in and around the *cités*. Furthermore, some key figures in the Beur movement—among them Toumi Djaidja, an association leader from Les Minguettes (Lyon) and one of the organizers of the 1983 Marche—later adopted more fundamentalist forms of Islam. In general, however, Muslim organizers emerging from the Beur movement tended to advocate the elaboration of an Islamic identity and practice attuned to everyday life in France—an Islam *of* France rather than simply an Islam in France—and thus ended up lining up closer to the theological reforms suggested by Tariq Ramadan, among others.

Finally, the Beur movement also drew on the precedent of Kabyle activism in France. These transgenerational ties were reinforced by the events of March–April 1980, colloquially known as the "Berber Spring" (or *Tafsut*). Following the cancellation, by the governor of the wilaya of Tizi-Ouzou, of a lecture on ancient Berber poetry, which was to have been given at the University of Tizi Ouzou on March 10 by Mouloud Mammeri, students occupied the university. When security forces arrived, violent confrontations broke out, lasting two weeks and culminating in widespread student demonstrations, a general strike throughout the region, and the eventual injuring of hundreds of protesters when the newly installed president Chadli Benjedid called in the military. These events not only concretized the previously amorphous Berber Cultural Movement (MCB) and initiated Berberism as a political force in postcolonial Algeria[31] but also reinforced the ties between

Kabylia and the berberophone Algerian community in France. The events themselves were well covered in the Kabyle immigrant media, particularly as published by *Imedyazen*. The nascent Ateliers de Culture Berbère (now the ACB), formed in 1979 by dissident members of the Groupe d'Études Berbères, organized a protest in front of the Algerian embassy in Paris.

Arguably, Tafsut had a significant effect of politicizing Kabyle Beurs in France, those born away from the quotidian realities of Berber cultural life. A disproportionate number of their interventions adopted particularly Berber signs to express this identification as cultural mediators. Many of the Beur theater troupes (e.g., Kahina),[32] musical groups (e.g., Djurdjura),[33] radio stations (e.g., Radio Tiwizi),[34] and novelists (e.g., Tassadit Imache) devoted themselves to popularizing artistic genres deemed native to Kabylia and drew political inspiration from the annals of Kabyle resistance leaders. Indeed, certain Kabyles within the Beur movement even claimed that the very appellation "Beur," though generally considered today a syllabic reversal of "Arab," was an acronym for "Berbers of Europe."[35]

Most important, this period witnessed a proliferation of Kabyle cultural associations in France: the ACB and the Association Berbère des Recherches, Information, Documentation et Animation (ABRIDA) in the Paris region, Afus deg Wfus (Hand in Hand) in Roubaix, Assiren in Lyon, and a number of subsidiary branches of the ACB formed throughout the country.[36] Throughout the 1980s and 1990s, these associations sponsored talks on Berber history and culture, taught courses in Tamazight, served as electoral bases for Kabyle political parties, functioned as community centers for local immigrant populations (offering day care and after-school tutoring services), and staged public celebrations of Kabyle holidays. These latter festivities, through their accompanying slide shows of Algeria, dance demonstrations, and musical performances, functioned as primers in Berber culture for the younger generation born in the diaspora.

Schoolyard Secularism and Cultural Difference

The years following the Berber Spring in Algeria and the Beur movement in France witnessed a radicalization of transpolitics across the Mediterranean. In the mid-1980s, both Algeria and France underwent severe economic crises, which had their most bitter repercussions for their urban youth and immigrant populations who experienced, in the *cités* on the outskirts of Paris, Lyon, and Algiers, disproportionately high rates of unemployment, drug use, and petty crime. In Algeria, a situation of "stagflation" was precipitated by an unprecedented 60 percent drop in hydrocarbon prices (Algeria's main industry, representing 98 percent of total exports) in 1986. Double-digit inflation was accompanied by an estimated 25 percent general unemployment, with figures as high as 60 percent for workers under twenty years of age. In the French suburban *cités*, unemployment figures for 1989 reached from a minimum of 30 to as high as 85 percent for workers under twenty-four years of age, well over twice the national average.[37] The significance of these figures lies in the numerical growth of this population, with the under-twenty category amounting to more than 50 percent of the Algeria's total population in the period in question. This situation of extreme marginalization contributed to an atmosphere of unrest that produced a number of confrontations in both countries opposing French *cité* youth or Algerian *hittistes*[38] to the respective government forces. Although the generalized demonstrations of October 1988 and the corresponding military repression in Algeria[39] certainly overshadow the localized violence of 1989–91 in Vaulx-en-Velin, Satrouville, and Mantes-la-Jolie (France), both sets of events were part of a single transpolitical process in which a marginalized groups of social actors (urban, sub-proletariat, youth, ethnoracial minorities) was responding to its systematic exclusion from a national project and its material fruits.

One of the cruxes of the conflict in both countries concerned the general dissatisfaction over the role of the state education system as a mechanism of integration qua assimilation, of the "Frenchification" or "Arabization" of its inhabitants. In fact, a two-tiered system had developed in both Algeria and France by which extant socioeconomic divisions were reproduced rather than erased. In Algeria, despite successes in the "generalization" of education since independence, its "democratization" remained a myth due to the continued employment preference for francophone diplomas and the relative exclusion of women from upper levels of education.[40] In France, similarly, despite special educational funding advanced to a number of suburban areas,[41] high numbers of Algerian immigrant children were routinely tracked to vocational diplomas (BEP, CAP) rather than the more valorized, university-preparatory baccalaureate.

The response of student activists in both countries to this situation of exclusion has been twofold: On the one hand, student strikes in the Paris region in 1990 and 1997 amounted to calls for pragmatic reforms, increased numbers of teachers, and a democratization of the curriculum; on the other hand, activists in both countries militated for the introduction of "cultural difference" into the national education systems. In France, a decade of debates over the introduction of a multicultural curriculum (the teaching of

Arabic, North African history, Maghribi art forms, etc.) came to a head in the "headscarf affair" of 1989 and subsequent mini-affairs that led to the 2004 *laïcité* law banning religious signs from French public schools.[42] The affair largely centered around the intrusion of religion into French public spaces, what was perceived by French spokesmen from across the political spectrum as a direct challenge to France's particular version of "state secularism" (*laïcité*).[43]

If the exclusion of the young women and the proposed legislation were generally derided throughout the larger Muslim world as an "attack on Islam," Muslim immigrant groups in France had more mixed reactions. From the beginning, the banning of the *hijab* was strongly supported by Franco-Algerian feminist groups like Ni Putes Ni Soumises (Neither Whores nor Downtrodden). Gisèle Halimi, one of the outspoken feminists in France and, at the time of the 1989 affair, French ambassador to UNESCO, decried the headscarf as the "the flag of fundamentalism,"[44] and Khalida Messaoudi, a Kabyle feminist living in exile in France, likewise compared it to the yellow stars worn by Jews during the Holocaust.[45] The ban was also supported by certain antiracist groups emerging from the Beur movement, such as SOS-Racisme and France-Plus, although others, such as the Mouvement contre le Racisme et pour l'Amitié entre les Peuples (MRAP), were more reticent. French Islamic associations were similarly split on the issue. Although the Mosquée de Paris was among the ban's strongest advocates, other major umbrella groups of French Islamic associations, such as the Fédération Nationale des Musulmans de France (FNMF), were cautious in their support, and still others, including the Union des Organisations Islamiques en France (UOIF) and the Parti des Musulmans de France (PMF), vigorously opposed it.

In direct opposition to these last groups (which were roundly denounced by many French commentators as "fundamentalist"), Berberist groups in France have been among the most vocal supporters of hardline *laïcité*. In April 1995, the Parisian wing of the MCB, under the auspices of the ACB, addressed an open letter to the candidates in the French presidential elections of the following year, emphasizing that the Republican school system, the "principal instrument of integration and social promotion," needed to be protected against Islamist "manipulation." Appealing to a democratic image of Kabylia, the letter urged the institutional encouragement of *berberité* as the true cultural "soul" of North African youth in France as the key to their future "integration." Likewise, the 2004 ban garnered equivalent support among French Berberists. In a letter published by the Amazigh press across the globe, the president of the Fédération des Associations de la Culture Amazighe en France (FACAF), Areski Sadi, congratulated Jacques Chirac on behalf of all "the Berbers of France" for his decision to press for a legal ban on the "veil" in public schools. Claiming that religion is an "affair of individual conscience and spirituality," Sadi championed the proposed law as protecting young women against the "pressure of politico-religious groups" and schools against the "rampant plague (*fléau*) of Islamic fundamentalism (*intégrisme*)." Sadi specifically underlined the distinction between his position and the *intégrisme* of the most outspoken opponent of the proposed law, Tariq Ramadan—whose fundamentalism was further emphasized in an op-ed article in *Libération* sponsored by the ACB.[46] Rather, Sadi claimed that the identity of Berbers in France could not be reduced to a "simple religious subjectification (*asujettissement*)," and ended his letter with an evocation of the spiritual assimilation of French Imazighen: "Because France is our country, her interests are ours and our interests are hers."

Moreover, such a solicitation of *berbérité* as consonant with *laïcité* and an identity diacritic alternate from Islam for immigrants in France, was equally supportive of a simultaneous movement in Kabylia that has focused directly on the Arabic-based educational system in its struggle for the recognition of Tamazight as an official and national language of Algeria. A series of student strikes in 1994 culminated in a school boycott for the entire 1994–5 academic year, touching all levels of education (from grammar to medical schools). The boycott was strongly supported by Kabyle associations in France and was the focus of their April 1995 annual celebrations of the anniversary of Tafsut. The festivities were held in auditoria decorated with banners displaying slogans such as *Tamazight di likul* (Tamazight in the schools) and *Tamazight ass-a azekka* (Tamazight, today, tomorrow), Amazigh flags flying, participants wearing military uniforms signifying a Kabylia at war, and heated debates over the effectiveness of the boycott and the political divisions within the MCB that it had made evident. Although the actual strike was almost entirely limited to Kabylia and opposed by many even there, the international popularization of this event did nonetheless result in the government's creation of a High Amazigh Commission (Haut Commission à l'Amazighité) to examine the strikers' demands.[47]

In France, meanwhile, the incorporation of vernacular languages in the school system has received mixed support. In November 1992, the Council of Europe adopted the European Charter on Regional or Minority Languages. The charter provided for the official recognition of and financial support for regional and immigrant languages represented on the European territory, including providing for their teaching in the national education systems. In the case of France, this included not only Breton, Occitan, Catalan, Basque, Flemish, and Alsatian but also Arabic and Tamazight. Although the socialist-led French government ratified thirty-nine of the ninety-one resolutions of the charter in May 1999, the charter was later rejected wholesale by the Constitutional Council on the basis that it violated France's basic constitutional principle regarding the indivisibility of the French Republic. In spite of this setback, however, Berber activists have succeeded in obtaining some level of recognition and support for Tamazight on French soil. Beginning in 1995 and in the wake of the school boycott in Kabylia, Tamazight was accepted as an optional subject on the French baccalaureate examination. Within a few years, it became the second most demanded optional language after Arabic. This success bred further concessions from the French government, as Berber activists' outspoken support for the 2004 *laïcité* law was quickly rewarded with a promise from the minister of education for the proximate offering of Tamazight courses within selected public schools.[48] This promise was heralded by Amazigh militants throughout North Africa. In this respect, the education system has become one of the main grounds on which contemporary Algerian transpolitics is being contested.

The Algerian Civil War

Alongside these contests over the direction of public education, the most direct interface between demands for ethnic or religious representation in Algeria and immigrant cultural politics in France occurred in the context of the "second" Algerian war, which began after the military coup in 1992 following the success of the Islamist Front Islamique du Salut (FIS) in the first round of the aborted 1991 parliamentary elections and resulted in at least 125,000 deaths by century's end. The daily fighting between government and Islamist forces in the mid- to late 1990s forced citizens of Algeria and Algerian immigrants in France to express openly their solidarities, lest their silence make them victims of the growing chaos. In Algeria, feminists and Berber intellectuals were among the main targets of violence generally attributed to one or more Islamist military faction, evidenced by the assassination of the journalist and playwright Tahar Djaout, the kidnapping and later assassination of the political singer-songwriter Lounès Matoub, and the death threats levied against Khalida Messaoudi and many other women's rights activists. Threatened and actual lethal violence resulted in the flight of many public figures abroad. Car bombings and reciprocal massacres periodically struck poorer urban areas and the villages of the central Mitidja plains, particularly in 1997, victimizing hundreds of thousands and forcing many civilians into pragmatic alliances with locally powerful militias. In Kabylia, prolonged demonstrations in April 1995, July 1998, and April 2001 pitted young Kabyle men against government forces, demonstrations that in many cases turned violent. This violence resulted in the increased presence of police, gendarme, and military forces in the region, the combined effect of which was, ironically, to heighten a general sense of insecurity.

Given this violence, civil war politics in Algeria tended to operate as a dual classification system, following a strict binary logic that alternately opposed Islamists and Berberists to the state and to each other.[49] These binary oppositions took on a recursive character, with rival political parties and military factions within both the Islamists and the Berberists opposing each other. In Kabylia, the Rassemblement pour la Culture et la Démocratie (Rally for Culture and Democracy, or RCD), founded in 1989 following the multiparty liberalization reforms, explicitly challenged the hegemony of the FFS. The FFS consistently espoused a position of reconciliation with the outlawed FIS as the only possible means to resolving the civil war. The party was a cosignatory with the FIS of the 1995 Sant'Egidio platform that called for a negotiated, multiparty solution and a civil peace; it boycotted the 1995 presidential elections and consistently refused to take part in the various military governments in power since 1992. In contrast, the RCD took part in national elections in 1995 and 1999 and participated in the coalition government under Abdelaziz Bouteflika, who became president in 1999. More significantly, the RCD advocated a hardline (*éradicateur*) position that rejected any dialogue with Islamist forces. In its literature, it consistently opposed any "Middle Eastern or Afghan identity" for Algeria, supposedly proffered by the "peons of the Islamist International," and instead called upon Kabyles to rise up in "resistance" following the "spirit of independence" of the "eternal Jugurtha."[50] Moreover, it brought this discourse to action, supporting the government's formation of Self-Defense Groups—civilian militias armed by the state and charged with protecting local populations from Islamist incursions, universally referred to as "patriots" in Kabyle villages. Although these "patriot" groups may have produced a sense of agency for certain Kabyles, they often resulted in an increase rather than decrease of violence, as they have been specifically targeted by Islamist militias and have been employed in local operations of vengeance.[51]

Obviously, any absolute political distinctions between the RCD and the FFS are idealtypic and belie the complex reality of civil war politics, where brothers and sisters found themselves on opposite sides of the Islamist/Berberist split, not to mention the FFS/RCD one. Nonetheless, popular perceptions of political differences, coupled with the mutually opposed party platforms, divided Amazigh activists in both Kabylia and France and resulted in the fragmentation of the MCB into factions aligned with each party, making concerted political action difficult. Indeed, although the 1994–95 school boycott did result in the creation of the HCA, it broke down prematurely—without meeting its original objectives of forcing the officialization and nationalization of Tamazight—due to internal strife between the MCB factions. Subsequent popular mobilizations against the state likewise found themselves bifurcated and weakened by the constant doubling of organizational committees, marches, and demands. As a result, the two parties were increasingly discredited, particularly after their inability to bring an end to the violence of the April 2001 "Black Spring" demonstrations in Kabylia—giving rise to a new umbrella organization, the Coordination des Aarouch, Daïras, et Communes (CADC).

In France, the Algerian civil war clearly politicized immigrant cultural activism along similar lines of binary opposition to those in Algeria. As with the Algerian war of independence, the civil war played itself out on French soil in political assassinations (the 1995 assassination of FIS leader Imam Sahraoui), terrorist attacks (the summer 1995 bombings of underground railway stations and markets in Paris and Lyon, attributed to the Algerian Armed Islamic Group, al-jama'a al-islamiyya al-musallaha/Groupe Islamique Armé, or GIA), and the increased militarization of immigrant neighborhoods.[52] At the same time, with the failure of the Beur movement and the rise of a French neoracism (most visible in the electoral gains of Jean-Marie Le Pen's National Front) that appropriated the Beurs' claims of a "right to difference" in order to justify policies of exclusion and "national preference," more and more Franco-Maghribis became alternately attracted to Islamist and Berberist movements. Both offered visions of identity and belonging that, though often posed in strict opposition to one another, shared the common trait of presenting an alternative to official (but, as ever, ambivalent) French policies of assimilation or integration. Both sought to resuture these children of immigrants, deemed to be in a state of social and cultural disarray, to larger imagined worlds—whether an Islamic *umma* or a Berber Tamazgha—that extended across the Mediterranean and beyond.

Nowhere were these divisions more evident than in the events surrounding the 1995 Algerian presidential elections. Contrasting directly with the paucity of turnout for the 1991 legislative elections that nearly brought the

FIS to power, 620,000 immigrant voters, or more than a third of the estimated Algerian nationals in France, turned out to vote, with a remarkable number of the younger generation exercising their double nationality.[53] In discussions at the polling places, young Franco-Algerians explained to me that their decision to vote was motivated by two factors: a desire to end the violence in Algeria and a hope to one day immigrate to a postwar Algeria for work because there was "nothing left" for them in France. Although 65 percent of voters in Algeria and France voted for the ruling Gen. Liamine Zéroual, the remaining 35 percent were split between the Berberist RCD and the "moderate" Islamist Mouvement pour une Société Islamique (Movement for an Islamic Society, Haraka lil-mujtama' al-islami).

As immigrant politics became increasingly factionalized between Islamist and Berberist tendencies, so too was French Kabyle politics divided along RCD/FFS lines. In the 1995 elections, both parties engaged in heavy electioneering, with the RCD pushing its candidate Said Sadi, and the FFS joining the FIS and the FLN in publicly calling for a boycott. Moreover, these political divisions came to map onto Berber cultural associations in France, with the ACB serving as the de facto French headquarters of the RCD, other groups such as Paris-based Tamazgha remaining close to the FFS, and yet others, such as MCB-France, remaining purposively unallied. With both the FFS and RCD simultaneously having official "immigration" wings, it is clear that the diaspora has become more than ever a central locus of Kabyle politics.

Within this context of diasporic civil war politics, the RCD (via the ACB) has proved particularly apt at playing the French state's game, consistently expressing an anti-Islamist position that dovetails with France's official policy of state secularism (laïcité). In its 1995 celebration of Tafsut, the ACB plastered the walls of the conference and reception rooms with laminated newspaper clippings recounting recent political assassinations by the GIA. The anniversary began with a moment of silence observed at the beginning for these "martyrs" of the recent struggle, whose memories were juxtaposed and held as equivalent to those casualties of the original Berber Spring. Further, as an American, I was on several occasions personally berated for my country's harboring of "Islamic terrorists."

Nonetheless, there is a sense in which the RCD has been left behind in the involution of Algerian transpolitics. Beginning in the mid-1990s, Berber associations worldwide united in the foundation of a World Amazigh Congress (Congrès Mondial Amazigh, or CMA). First meeting in Tafira (Canary Islands) in August 1997, the CMA brought together hundreds of militants from Algeria, Morocco, Tunisia, Libya, France, Belgium, Spain, Sweden, Canada, and the United States. If the internal organization of the CMA mapped onto the national origins of the militants, its activities and meeting places nonetheless pointed to wider transpolitical predicaments—from Touareg rights in Niger to ongoing battles with the state gendarmerie in Kabylia to Berber educational rights in the diaspora—which Berbers faced worldwide. In this sense, the Algerian civil war and its repercussions have extended not only across the Mediterranean but also into a greater transpolitical space.

The New Europe

Indeed, the outlining of Franco-Algerian transpolitics has not been solely limited to the Mediterranean region. Algerian activists in France in the years since the Beur movement forged working alliances with other minority ethnic, linguistic, and immigrant groups throughout France and, more generally, Europe. In particular, in the 1990s there occurred a burgeoning interaction of the transnational Algerian-Berber cultural movement and the localized Breton and Occitan militant organizations, with both groups allying their demands for equal cultural and linguistic expression (intimated as a "universal right") and together petitioning European administrative bodies. Such an interaction points to how challenges to the integrity of the French nation-state itself, to its capacity of managing immigrant ethnoracial and religious difference, have been intimately tied to a transnational sphere of activity linking France to Algeria, and from Algeria back to the European Union.

Beginning in the late colonial period, indigenous elites in peripheral areas in France appropriated objectified portrayals of ethnolinguistic identity to articulate various political critiques of Parisian "internal colonialism," thus forging symbolic ties with colonial peoples in search of national liberation. The 1980s saw a continuation of the close proximity between regional and immigrant demands, as Breton and Occitan activists benefited like Beur militants from the tentative government support for multiculturalism.[54] However, unlike the latter group, they remained sharply critical of the French nation-state even during this period, and instead of acquiescing to the government's national, social, and economic integration projects, instead sought direct ties with other ethnic and linguistic minority populations via flourishing European supranational bodies.

These avenues of transregional and transnational unity that defy the limits of state national territory have only increased in the last fifteen years. Although in the 1980s immigrant and regional groups in France largely forged connections with spatially distant others as defined generally in terms of (real or fictive) kinship (Beurs and Berbers, Bretons and Welsh), by the mid-1990s, the connections had transcended such considerations, with highly disparate immigrant and regional groups conjoining their efforts against extreme nationalist incursions. These efforts were abetted by the growth of supranational European bodies such as the European Court or the European Parliament, the conventions of which have sought, in the name of human rights, to protect the rights of immigrant and refugee populations. These European institutions have provided forums for immigrant communities themselves to initiate change. Already in 1994, under the guise of the "13th Nation," non-European immigrant groups throughout Europe jointly appealed to the European Parliament for independent representation.[55]

More recently, Berber groups based in Europe, representing populations throughout North Africa and the diaspora, have likewise addressed letters, petitions, and speeches to the United Nations, UNESCO, and the European Parliament demanding the official recognition and teaching of Berber culture in individual countries such as Algeria and France. Notable is the success of the umbrella group called Mediterranean in organizing a special session of the European Parliament on Berber (Amazigh) culture in June 1997. In preparation for this session, the organizers solicited specific proposals using the various Internet discussion groups, Amazigh-Net and www.kabyle.com, which have since the early 1990s served as forums for political and cultural debate among Berber populations resident throughout the world—thus forging a virtual transnational solidarity regardless of any actual political developments.

If Algerian immigrant groups in Europe appear to have followed the inspiration of the French regionalist movement in utilizing Europe as a court of appeals against individual nation-states, such a tactical overlap has been by no means incidental. Beginning in the 1980s, immigrant issues in France became directly united with larger European ones of minority populations, as witnessed in the Charter on Regional or Minority Languages, which, in its initial French ratification, provided official recognition for Arabic, Tamazight, and Yiddish alongside Breton, Occitan, and Catalan. Since its inception in the early 1980s, the yearly musical Fête du Peuple Breton (Festival of Breton People) organized by the Breton Democratic Union (UDB) has invited artists and artisans from other French regions, from across the Channel, and from former North African colonies.[56] Moreover, the related

Breton Douarnenez film festival has focused since 1978 on one or more regional European linguistic or ethnic groups (Bretons, Basques, Celts, etc.), the 1994 and 1996 festivals devoted to "Berbers" and "Immigrant Communities" respectively. The 1996 event featured films produced by Algerians in France, Turks in Germany, and Pakistanis in Britain, offered lectures and debates animated by prominent leaders within the respective immigrant communities, and provided space for immigrant organizations to promote their causes and interact among themselves. Although Breton films were still shown in these festivals, they took a peripheral place to the focus group's endeavors.

Immigrant groups in France have similarly begun to open their conferences and festivals to regional minority groups in Europe. During its 1996 commemoration of Tafsut, the Argenteuil-based Berber cultural association, MCB-France, composed primarily of Franco-Kabyles in their twenties, invited two Occitan scholars/activists to participate in a roundtable discussion concerning the "Amazigh Question in 1996." Although the room was decked with Kabyle flags and maps, and the majority of interventions addressed aspects of Berber identity and the place of Tamazight (Berber language) in France and Algeria, the Occitans attempted to relate these questions to the larger issue of minoritized languages in the French metropole. In particular, Jean-François Blanc, director of the one the oldest Occitan cultural organizations, the Institute of Occitan Studies, centered his discussion on a critique of the nation-state as an instrument of homogenization. Warning the Berber activists about the initial support of the interim Algerian government for the teaching of Tamazight, Blanc concluded that "the [Occitan] experience with regards to the central State shows that we cannot count on it." Just as Occitan activists took heed of Algerian revolutionaries during the wars of decolonization, so now are they returning the favor of experience in the postcolonial period.

In this way, the joint action of noncommensurable "minority" groups in France has largely predicated itself on a critique of the nation-state as an agent of homogenization and cultural destruction. In a tract distributed five months after the conference, on the eve of the referendum of an Algerian constitution, which, as Blanc had predicted, betrayed the Berber populations by once again reiterating the "Algeria, Arabic, Islam" national triad, the MCB-France levied its definitive disavowal of traditional state structures: "The rupture with the concept of the nation-state, 'one language, one culture, one school,' elsewhere paradoxically defended until now by a large number of militants, is today a necessity." What remained was to work through larger, more decentralized bodies, such as the imagined Berber homeland (Tamazgha), or, alternately, a more unified and egalitarian Europe.

Conclusion

In this chapter, I have indicated the parameters of Algerian transpolitics within the ongoing French and Algerian nation-states' management of ethnoracial, religious, and linguistic difference, within their general disavowal of subnational categories of identity in favor of homogenizing criteria of national unity and belonging. Since the Algerian war, there have been a series of shifts in the imagination of internal and external boundaries, as the contours of the French political imaginary have shifted from a colonial empire to a unified Europe, as Algeria has sought to transform itself from an authoritarian single-party state, through a militarized civil war scenario, to a regime of transparency and human rights. For the Algerian immigrant community, these changes have outlined new possibilities for the enactment of transnational politics and civil society. From electioneering to jointly petitioning the Council of Europe, Franco-Algerians have been able to articulate an identity politics that reaches beyond the confines of "assimilation" to French Republican norms and points to a cultural involution by which internal modalities of community organization and imagination have become heightened and objectified. Although this transnationalization has on occasion abetted the growth of religious or ethnic extremism, of dogmatic forms of Islamism and Berberism, it has as often encouraged the expansion of minority rights and tolerance.

In other words, processes, events, and institutions such as the headscarf affair, the Algerian civil war, the Charter for Regional and Minority Languages, and the World Amazigh Congress need to be understood as total social phenomena that simultaneously have political, cultural, and socioeconomic dimensions. They inhabit and operate in a *transnational* space of discourse and practice that unites France and Algeria, Europe and North Africa. Nonetheless, while operating within such conditions of cross-border flows and fluxes (of ideas, commodities, and people), these processes have contributed to the production of sets of national and intranational (religious, ethnic, linguistic) categories that have largely conditioned the constitution of political subjectivities within the Algerian community in France. As such, in both their functioning (in a transnational space) and demands (for infranational particularity), instrumentalized Franco-Algerian identities and solidarities call into question the unitary authority of the nation-state to monolithically couple people, territory, and power. However, since the challenge exists only in dialectical relation with transformations within French and Algerian state structures, one must see the contemporary contestation in large part within the logic of the nation-states' own processes of cultural involution. In what Zygmunt Bauman has termed the "ambivalence of modernity,"[57] France and Algeria each find themselves forced to reevaluate and concomitantly transform their own ideological and structural balance between national particularism and civic universalism, between nation and state.

Notes

1. Riva Kastoryano, *Negotiating Identities: States and Immigrants in France and Germany* (Princeton, N.J.: Princeton University Press, 2002); Yasemin Soysal, *The Limits of Citizenship: Migrants and Post-National Membership in Europe* (Chicago: University of Chicago Press, 1994).

2. For a discussion of involution as a process of agricultural transformation in colonial and postcolonial Indonesia, see Clifford Geertz, *Agricultural Involution* (Berkeley and Los Angeles: University of California Press, 1963).

3. Abdelmalek Sayad, *La Double absence: Des illusions de l'émigré aux souffrances de l'immigré* (Paris: Seuil, 1999); Abdelmalek Sayad, "Les trois 'âges' de l'émigration algéreienne en France," *Actes de la Recherche en Sciences Sociales* 15 (1977): 59–79; Karima Direche-Slimani, *Histoire de l'émigration kabyle en France au XXe siècle: Réalités culturelles et réappropriations identitaires* (Paris: Harmattan, 1997); Mohand Khellil, "Kabyles en France: Un aperçu historique," *Hommes et Migrations* 1179 (1994): 12–18; Mohand Khellil, *L'Exil kabyle* (Paris: Harmattan, 1979); Claude Liauzu, "Prétoires, mémoires, histoire: La guerre d'Algérie a eu lieu," *Temps Modernes* 606 (1999): 11–12; Claude Liauzu, *Histoire des migrations en méditerrané occidentale* (Brussels: Complexe, 1996); Abdelmalek Sayad and Alain Gillette, *L'Immigration algérienne en France* (Paris: Maspero, 1984); Larbi Talha, *Le Salariat immigré devant la crise* (Paris: Éditions du CNRS, 1989); Ahsène Zehraoui, *L'Immigration: De l'homme seul à la famille* (Paris: CIEMI/Harmattan, 1994).

4. Paul A. Silverstein and Chantal Tetreault, "Urban Violence in France," *Middle East Report Online*, November 2005, http://www.merip.org.

5. Ali Haroun, *Le Septième wilaya* (Paris: Seuil, 1986).

6. For an authoritative account of the October 17, 1961, massacre and larger political context in which it occurred, see Jean-Luc Einaudi, *La Bataille de Paris: 17 octobre 1961* (Paris: Seuil, 1991). See also Mogniss H. Abdallah, "Le 17 octobre 1961 et les médias: De la couverture de l'histoire immédiate au "travail de mémoire," *Hommes et Migrations* no. 1228: 125–33 (November–December 2000); Étienne Balibar, *De Charonne à Vitry. Les frontières de la démocratie* (Paris: La Découverte, 1992); Haroun, *Septième wilaya*; Liauzu, "Prétoires, mémoires, histoire"; Paulette Péju, *Ratonnades à Paris* (Paris: François Maspero, 1961); Benjamin Stora, *La Gangrène et l'oubli: La mémoire de la guerre d'Algérie* (Paris: Éditions La Découverte, 1991); Pierre Vidal-Naquet, *La Torture dans la République* (Paris: Minuit, 1972); "17 Octobre 1961: Contre l'Oubli," Web site of the Association, http://17octobre1961.free.fr/.

7. Stora, *Gangrène et l'oubli*.

8. John Ruedy, *Modern Algeria: The Origins and Development of a Nation* (Bloomington: Indiana University Press, 1992), 164.

9. Salem Chaker, "Berbérité et emigration kabyle," *Peuples Méditerranéens* 31–32 (1985): 218.

10. Mohammed Harbi, "Nationalisme algérien et identité berbère," *Peuples Méditerranéens* 11 (1980): 33.

11. Mostefa Lacheraf, "*La Colline oubliée* ou les consciences anachroniques," *Le Jeune Musulman*, February 13, 1953; Mohammed C. Sahli, "La colline du reniement," *Le Jeune Musulman*, January 2, 1953.

12. Salem Chaker, *Imazighen ass-a (Berbères dans le Maghreb contemporain)* (Algiers: Éditions Bouchene, 1990), 44.

13. Chaker, "Berbérité et emigration kabyle," 222.

14. Driss El Yazan, "Les Beurs entre la mémoire et le débat," in *La Beur Génération*, edited by Farid Aïchoune, 8 (Paris: Sans Frontières/Arcantère, 1985).

15. Adil Jazouli, *Les Années banlieues* (Paris: Seuil, 1992), 27.

16. Gilles Kepel, *Les Banlieues de l'Islam* (Paris: Seuil, 1991), 229–42.

17. Jocelyne Cesari, *Etre musulman en France: Associations, militants et mosques* (Paris: Karthala/IREMAM, 1994), 175.

18. Farid Aïchoune, ed., *La Beur Génération* (Paris: Sans Frontières/Arcantère, 1985). On Beur writing, see Alec Hargreaves, *Immigration and Identity in Beur Fiction: Voices from the North African Community in France* (New York: Berg, 1997).

19. Kacem Basfao and Jean-Robert Henry, "Le Maghreb et l'Europe: Que faire de la Méditerranée?" *Vingtième Siècle* 32 (1991): 51.

20. Nacer Kettane, *Droit de réponse à la démocratie française* (Paris: La Découverte, 1986), 19.

21. This formulation inverted Charles De Gaulle's famous defense of an imperial France "from Dunkerque to Tamanrasset."

22. Mustapha Ammi, "Paroles de Beurs," in Aïchoune, *Beur Génération*, 90.

23. Ibid.

24. Paul A. Silverstein, "France's *Mare Nostrum*: Colonial and Post-Colonial Constructions of the French Mediterranean," *Journal of North African Studies* 7, no. 4 (2002): 1–22.

25. Saïd Bouamama, Hadjila Sad-Saoud, and Mokhtar Djerdoubi. *Contribution à la mémoire des banlieues* (Paris: Éditions du Volga, 1994), 99.

26. Ibid., 56.

27. Jazouli, *Années banlieues*, 27.

28. A derogatory term for an Algerian, likely from the slang expression for a coal miner (*bougna*) used in the north of France, where many Algerians previously labored. For Radio Beur's role in reporting on the October 1988 events in Algeria, see Radio-Beur, *Octobre à Alger* (Paris: Seuil, 1988).

29. Ahmed Boubeker and Mogniss H. Abdallah, *Douce France: La saga du mouvement Beur* (Paris: Im'media, 1993), 45–46.

30. Kepel, *Banlieues de l'Islam*, 229–42.

31. Chaker, *Imazighen ass-a*, 51–64; Bruce Maddy-Weitzman, "Contested Identities: Berbers, "Berberism" and the State in North Africa," *Journal of North African Studies* 6, no. 3 (2001): 23–47; Hugh Roberts, "Towards an Understanding of the Kabyle Question in Contemporary Algeria," *Maghreb Review* 5, nos. 5–6 (1980): 115–24; Paul A. Silverstein, "Martyrs and Patriots: Ethnic, National, and Transnational Dimensions of Kabyle Politics," *Journal of North African Studies* 8, no. 1 (2003): 87–111.

32. A legendary female Berber chieftain supposed to have led Berber resistance to the Arab conquest in the seventh century.

33. The principal mountain range forming the geographical heartland of Kabylia.

34. Created in October 1987 and later absorbed into the increasingly commercial Radio Beur/Beur FM, Radio Tiwizi's name derives from the collective labor (*tiwizi*) that seasonally marks Kabyle village life.

35. Cf. Aïchoune, *Beur Génération*.

36. In 1991, a large number of these associations were confederated into the Fédération des Associations Culturelles Amazighes de France (FACAF) under the aegis of the ACB and the Algerian Rally for Culture and Democracy (RCD) political party. For a history of Kabyle associational politics in France, see Slimani, *Histoire de l'émigration kabyle*.

37. Zakya Daoud, "Le chomage?" in *Banlieues ... intégration ou explosion?* ed. Catherine Wihtol de Wenden and Zakya Daoud, special edition of *Panoramiques* 2, no. 12 (1993): 75; Kamel Rarrbo, *L'Algérie et sa jeunesse: Marginalisations sociales et désarroi culturel* (Paris: Harmattan, 1995), 11, 131.

38. From the Arabic word for "wall," this popular term designates a subclass of unemployed young males, renowned for passing entire days leaning against the sides of buildings in the urban slums of Algiers and Oran. The term *banlieusard* evokes the same image in lower-class suburban France.

39. Unofficial figures place the number of deaths at over five hundred. Radio-Beur, *Octobre à Alger*, 56.

40. Rarrbo, *L'Algérie et sa jeunesse*, 93–126.

41. For example, the creation of Zones d'Education Prioritaires (ZEP) in 1990.

42. David Beriss, "School, Scarves, and Scapegoating: The Headscarf Affair," *French Politics and Society* 8, no. 1 (1990): 1–13; Paul A. Silverstein, "Headscarves and the French Tricolor," *Middle East Report Online*, http://www.merip.org (January 29, 2004). In 1989, three young Moroccan girls from a Creil grammar school were suspended for refusing to remove their *hijab*s in the classroom. In spite of a subsequent high court decision legitimizing the headscarf when a personal (and neither "ostentatious" nor "prostelytizing") sign of religious identity, every school year witnessed the exclusion of *hijab*-wearing students, leading to the public debates that resulted in the 2004 legislation.

43. In the meantime, multicultural education in France was nearly dealt a further setback, with a 2005 law passed by the National Assembly requiring public schools to teach the "positive effects" of French colonialism. This law, eventually rescinded, was deeply protested in Algeria (as well as in other former and current colonies in the Africa and the

Caribbean), as it was taken as yet another sign of France's refusal to take responsibility for its violent history of colonialism and decolonization that left as many as one million Algerians dead in the war of national liberation.

44. *Le Monde*, November 30, 1989.

45. *Le Figaro*, October 29-30, 1994, 27.

46. Mekboul, Sahra and Arezki Metref. "De l'intégration à l'intégrisme." *Libération*, January 20, 2004, 35.

47. However, the new Algerian constitution, popularly ratified in October 1996, reiterated the designation of previous national charters of Arabic as the sole "official and national language" of Algeria.

48. The teaching of "non-state languages" (notably Tamazight and Kurdish) was among the twenty-six measures recommended by the Stasi Commission, which had been charged by President Chirac in 2003 to draft a proposal of legislation to ensure freedom of belief, the legal equality of religious groups, and the neutrality of the state vis-à-vis religion. Only the proposed ban on "ostensible" religious signs was adopted by the president and later ratified by the National Assembly.

49. Silverstein, "Martyrs and Patriots."

50. RCD-Immigration, communiqué titled "20 avril 1995: 15 ans de lutte ininterrompue." Jugurtha refers to the king of Numidia who challenged Rome in the Punic Wars. He is claimed by Amazigh activists as an antecedent and a model of Berber resistance.

51. Compare José Garçon, "La dérive sanglante des milices en Algérie," *Libération*, April 15, 1998.

52. Extended police round-ups (*rafles*) of suspected Islamist militants occurred after the 1995 bombings, preceding the 1998 World Cup, and, more recently, immediately following the September 11, 2001, attacks. In addition, heavily immigrant-populated *banlieues* (suburban areas of high-density, low-income housing) have become increasingly subject to police and military surveillance. In February 1999, socialist prime minister Lionel Jospin activated thirteen thousand riot police (CRS) and seventeen thousand military gendarmes to patrol several hundred such areas deemed "sensitive urban zones" (*zones urbaines sensibles*). Patricia Tourancheau, "Police de proximité cherche effectifs," *Libération*, February 13-14, 1999.

53. This exercise of double nationality was remarked as "scandalous" by Farid Smahi, president of the integrationist group Arabisme et Francité, who warned that it threatened to transform immigrant France into a series of miniature Gaza Strips. Farid Smahi, "Plaidoyer contre la bi-nationalité," *Le Figaro*, October 20, 1995.

54. See Parti Socialiste, *La France au pluriel* (Paris: Éditions Entente, 1981); Henri Giordan, *Démocratie culturelle et droit à la différence: Rapport présenté à Jack Lang, ministre de la Culture* (Paris: Documentation Française, 1982).

55. Riva Kastoryano, "Mobilisations des migrants en Europe: Du national au transnational," *Revue Européenne des Migrations Internationales* 10, no. 1 (1994): 169-80; Soysal, *Limits of Citizenship*.

56. Maryon McDonald, *"We Are Not French!" Language, Culture and Identity in Brittany* (London: Routledge, 1989), 151.

57. Zygmunt Bauman, *Modernity and Ambivalence* (Ithaca, N.Y.: Cornell University Press, 1991).

Contributors

Ahmed Aghrout is research fellow at the European Studies Research Institute, University of Salford, Manchester, England.

Louisa Aït-Hamadouche is assistant professor of political science at the University of Algiers and Lecturer at the Institute of National Security Studies, Algiers.

Michele Penner Angrist is associate professor of political science at Union College, Schenectady, New York.

Mickael Bensadoun is lecturer in political science at Bar-Ilan University, Ramat Gan, Israel.

Gideon Gera is principal research associate emeritus at the Moshe Dayan Center for Middle Eastern and African Studies, Tel Aviv University, Israel.

Michael Hodd is professor of economics at the University of Westminster, London.

Bruce Maddy-Weitzman is senior research fellow at the Moshe Dayan Center for Middle Eastern and African Studies, Tel Aviv University, Israel.

Robert Mortimer is professor of political science, Haverford College, Haverford, Pennsylvania.

Paul Rivlin is senior research fellow at the Moshe Dayan Center for Middle East and African Studies, Tel Aviv University, Israel.

Paul A. Silverstein is associate professor of anthropology at Reed College, Portland, Oregon.

Benjamin Stora is professor of Maghribi history at the National Institute of Oriental Civilizations and Languages (INALCO), Paris.

Michael J. Willis is Mohamed VI Fellow in Moroccan and Mediterranean Studies, St. Antony's College, Oxford University, Oxford, England.

Daniel Zisenwine is research fellow at the Moshe Dayan Center for Middle Eastern and African Studies, Tel Aviv University, Israel.

Yahia H. Zoubir is professor of international relations and international management at EUROMED MARSEILLE, École de Management, France.

Index

Abbas, Ferhat, 36, 241
Abbasid empire, 53
Abd al-Jabri, Muhammad, 17–18, 20
Abd al-Krim (Muhammad bin Abd al-Krim Khattabi), 54, 55, 56, 57, 58, 68n22
Abdelkader, Emir, 39
Abdennour, Ali Yahia, 118, 130n23
Académie Française, 39
Adda, Abdelkrim Ould, 125
Addi, Lahouari, 49n23
Adekar, 109
Adghirni, Ahmed, 29
Afghanistan, ix, 80, 106, 112, 114, 126, 129n14, 170
Africa, 16, 53, 85, 155
African heritage, ix
African Sahel, 112
African Union, 85
Agadir, 25
Agdz, 25
Aghrout, Ahmad, xi
Aïn Delfa, 112
Aït Ahmed, Hocine, 63, 118, 130n23, 242
Aït-Hamadouche, Louisa, x
Aït-Menguellet, Lounis, 243
Aix-en-Provence, 186
Ajdir (Abd al-Krim's headquarters), 56
Ajdir (Khenifra), 29
Algeria, ix, x, xiin1, 4, 17, 20, 59, 227; agricultural sector, 220; Algerian immigrants in France, 237–39; —politicization of, 238–45; Algerian Muslims, 36; Algiers Charter (1964), 242; Amicale des Algériens en Europe, 241, 242, 244, 246; antiterrorist corps, 81–82; Arab nationalist culture, 37; Armed Islamic Group (Groupe Islamique Armée–GIA), 44, 82, 85, 109, 111, 112, 113, 114, 255; Armed Islamic Movement (MIA), 105–6; Armée Islamique du Salut (AIS), 82, 85, 107, 109, 110, 111; Arms, 91–92; Arab Afghans, 106; Association of Algerian Ulema, 36, 104; Association of Guidance and Reform, 119; attempt to introduce systemic reforms (1989–91), 79; "authoritarian pluralism," 118; banking sector, 225–26, 232n19; Bank of Algeria, 226; Berbers, 6–7, 8, 42, 52, 61–66, 70n50, 76, 86–87, 99n34, 241, 253, 254–55, 257; capital punishment and life imprisonment, 108, 128n4; Charter for Peace and National Reconciliation, 90, 93, 95, 128; civil society, 3; civil rights, 104, 109; civil war, x, 3, 36, 39, 42, 44–45, 46, 47, 79, 94, 107, 113, 120, 175, 253–57; clientism, 78, 79, 87, 94; collapse of Khalifa Bank and Banque Commerciale et Industrielle d'Algérie, 226, 232n24; constitution, 76, 111, 119; constitutional reform of 1989, 38; corruption, 79, 83, 87, 117; culture, 76; *décideurs*, 116, 129n18; Democratic and Popular Algerian Republic (RADP), 37; democratization, 96, 106, 115–16; demography, 1, 78–79, 82, 217–18; Domains Agricoles Socialistes, 220; earthquake, 86, 92; economy, xi, 37, 76–77, 78–79, 80–81, 87, 92–93, 95, 96, 217–31; —global, 226–27; —recovery support plans (PSRE and PCSRE), 222, 229, 231n8; —reforms, 217, 219–23; employment, 217–18; Ennahda party, 106–7, 119, 121, 124, 127; and Europe, 81, 86, 92, 114; and the European Union, 227; extermination of Ouled Riah clan, 40; family legal code, 7, 90–91, 95, 126, 127, 131n40; financial crisis, 221; five-year plan, 93; foreign debt, 221; foreign policy and standing, 37, 92; and France, xi, 36, 39–40, 61, 81, 86, 91, 92, 94, 237, 239–41; French rule in, 39, 76, 103–4; Front de Libération Nationale (FLN), 2–3, 36, 38, 42, 43, 64, 84, 88, 89, 90, 93, 100n44, 105, 118–19, 120, 121, 122, 125, 126, 240, 241, 242, 256; GDP, 79, 218, 220, 225; Front des Forces Socialistes (FFS), 120, 130n23, 242, 243, 254–55, 256; and the G-8 group, 85; the Gendarmerie,

268 / Index

Algeria—*continued*
86; General Union of Algerian Workers (UGTA), 93; Group for the Struggle against the Illicit, 105; history, 52; hydrocarbon, 77, 94, 227, 228, 250; identity and memory, x, 36–48, 75–76, 104; independence, 76, 94; inflation, 219, 223; international relations, 85; Islam, Islamists, 36, 37, 38, 64, 75–76, 80, 85, 88, 89, 90, 95, 100n44, 106, 108–11, 113, 115–19, 123, 128, 152, 156, 185; Islamic League of Daawa and Djihad (LIDD), 109, 111; Islamic Salvation Front (Front Islamique du Salut–FIS) 3, 38, 43, 44, 77, 81, 82, 85, 89, 106, 107, 113, 116, 118–19, 120, 121, 124, 125, 126, 127, 129n14, 159, 161, 162, 253, 256; —Sant'Egidio initiative, 120, 254; Islamist insurgency, 75, 79, 81–83, 85, 90, 92, 94, 95; Islamist movement, x, 3, 103, 106, 108, 126, 171, 254; Islamist Mouvement pour une Société Islamique, 256; Islamist opposition, 7, 77, 105, 106, 108, 111, 113, 117–18, 121–24; *jaz'ara* ("Algerianist"), 115–16, 125, 131n35; Katiba El Khadra (Green Brigade), 112; Katibat Djounoud Allah, 112; Katibat es Sunna, 112; radical Islamism, 80, 105, 111, 119–26; "Jacobin" *rentier* state, 77, 94; Katibat el Islam (Islamic Brigades) 112; Kabylia/Kabylians, 29, 62–65, 71n55, 86–87, 89, 95, 109, 238, 241–42, 249, 254, 251, 252, 255, 257, 263n36; Law on Civil Concord, 85, 108–11, 112; Le Forum des Chefs d'Enterprises (FCE), 225; liberalization, 106, 220, 221, 223; military, 80–81, 83, 84, 87, 88, 89, 91–92, 95; military coup (1992), 253; modernization, 94, 95; and Morocco, xiin1, 15, 92, 132, 204; Mount Chenoua region, 40; Mouvement de la Société pour la Paix (MSP, HAMAS), 89, 90, 95, 106–7, 119–21, 124, 127, 130n23; Mouvement National Algérien (MNA), 240; municipal elections (1990), 3, 107; National Assembly, 120, 121, 126; National Charter, 37, 38, 105, 111, 120; nationalism, nationalist movement, nationalists, 2, 36, 76, 104, 123; National Popular Army (ANP), 36, 78, 109, 110, 124, 127; National Reform Movement (MRN), 119, 121, 122; oil and gas industry, 75, 76, 77, 79, 81, 85, 92, 93, 219, 220, 230; one-party system, 2, 38; opposition strategy of Islamist political militancy, 119, 121–24; parliament, 78, 81, 90, 95; parliamentary elections, of 1991, 3, 38, 81, 107, 161; —of 1997, 83, 88, 120, 123; —of 2002, 88, 121, 123; participation strategy of Islamist political militancy, 119–21; Parti pour le Renouveau Algérien (PRA), 128; political Islam, 103–28; politics, 76, 88–90, 105, 106, 115, 116–19, 127, 220; polygamy, 91; poverty, 229, 230; presidential election, of 1995, 255; —of 2004, 121, 122; press, 91; privatization process, 217, 223, 224–26, 230, 232n23; the public sector, 219, 224, 225, 229; and al-Qa`ida, 112–15, 129n14; El-Qiyam al-Islamiyya, 105; the question of state legitimacy, 2–3; radical Islamist groups, 1, 8, 15; Rassemblement National Democratique (RND), 88, 89, 90, 121; reconciliation of September 2005, 38; referendum of September 1999, 38; revolution of 1954, 44, 47; riots of October 1988, 38, 79, 80, 220; and Russia, 91; Salafist Group for Combat (GSC), 112; Salafist Group for Preaching and Combat (GSPC), 36, 82, 85, 87, 92, 102n69, 109, 110, 111, 112, 113–14; secret police, 77; secularism, 104; Self-Defense Groups, 254; society, 76, 102n73, 117; socialism, 37, 104, 105; socioeconomic conditions, 86, 92, 94, 95; socioeconomic crisis, 78–79, 83, 87, 105, 127; the state, 77–78, 104; terrorism, 8, 110, 111–1, 127; tribe factor, 75; turmoil of the 1990s, 46; unemployment, 79, 86, 92, 95, 222, 229; Union du Manifeste Algérien (UDMA), 104, 241; Union National de la Jeunesse Algérienne (UNJA), 241, 243, 246; and the United States, 85–86, 89, 92, 93, 114; violence, 1, 15, 47, 85, 107, 108, 110, 220, 253–54; Wafa party, 118, 124–26; war (1954–62), 36, 47, 63, 95, 127, 238, 239, 241; welfare state, 105; Western Sahara question, xiin1; women, 7, 40–42, 47, 48, 90–91, 120; Workers' Party (PT), 120; and World Trade Organization, 227; writers and intellectuals, 39

Algiers: Stock Exchange, 224; University of Algiers, 116

Ali (the Prophet Muhammad's son-in-law), 52

Alsatian language, 253

Amara, Saleiha, 246–47

Amazigh (Berber) culture movement, x, 8, 31n1, 33n51, 35n71, 255, 259; the Agadir

Charter, 17; the Administrative Committee of the Institute Royal de la Culture Amazigh (IRCAM), 26, 29, 54; the Amazigh Manifesto (March 2000), 26, 27, 28, 33n51, 34n52, 53–54, 55, 58–59, 61; "Amazigh Spring," 62; and the Arabization of the education system in Morocco, 58; Associations de la Culture Amazigh en France (FACAF), 252, 263n36; communal land rights and traditions, 60; Congrès Mondial Amazigh, 62; and discourse on national identity, 13, 14, 23, 25–30; and France's Moroccan Protectorate, 55–57; High Amazigh Commission (HAC), 252, 255; history of, 53, 61; holidays of Yennayer, 62; identity, 54, 62, 67; Imazighen, 26, 27, 55, 242; and Islam, 52, 53, 54; and King Hasan II, 17–19, 135, 154; Massyle Amazigh dynasty, 66; "memory work/workers," 50–67; political traditions, 54; and Rif rebellion, 55–57; Royal Institute of Amazigh Culture, 140; World Amazigh Congress (CMA), 256–57. See also Berbers
Amnesty International, 108–9, 178
Amokrane, Lt. Col. Muhammad, 59
Amor, Mohamed Belhaj, 176, 177
Amrouche, Taos, 63, 242, 243
Amrouches, Jean, 50; Chants Berbères de Kabylie, 63
Andalusia, 16, 27, 53
Angrist, Michele Penner, xi
Anoual, 55, 58
Aourid, Hasan, 26, 28, 30, 135
Arab, Bessaoud Mohand, 242
Arab Afghans, 106, 113
Arab culture, 103
Arab East, ix
Arab homeland (al-Watan al-`Arabi), 62
Arabic language, 7, 8, 21, 29, 40, 51, 55, 58, 62, 80, 86, 241, 253, 258
Arab Maghrib Union, ix, xii, xiiin1, 204
Arab-Muslim heritage, ix
Arab-Muslim political tradition, 6
Arab nation, 17, 18
Arab nationalism, 2, 3, 5, 16, 17, 28, 62
Arabo-Islamism, 28, 29
Arabs, 52, 61
Arab states, 17, 211
Arab world, 2, 18, 19, 48, 178, 183
Aramaic script, 62, 70n45

Arnobius, 52
Asia, 155, 205, 211
Assid, Ahmed, 30
Atlantic Ocean, 62
Atlas mountains, 25, 29, 57
Aurès Mountains, 62, 65, 71n58, 100n44
Ayadi, Muhammad El, 23
Azaykou, Ali Sidqi, 58, 61, 69n35
Azoulay, André, 15

Babor mountains, 109
Baghaï, 65
Balfour, Sebastian, 57
Barghawata kingdoms, 34n59
Basque language, 253
Basques, 259
Basri, Muhammad Faqih al-, 20, 69n38
Batna, 66, 125
Bauman, Zygmunt, 261
Beghal, Djamel, 129n14
Belgium, 1, 35n79, 125, 237
Belhadj, Ali, 44
Belkheir, Larbi, 85, 87
Ben Ali, Zayn al-Abidin, 3, 156; and civil society, 182–83; cult of personality, 175; and democratization, 178–79; and France, 187; and Islamists, 180–81; and one-party regime, 188–90; opening up the political system, 179–80; and opposition parties, 183–86; and presidential election of 1994, 180; —of 1999, 176–77; —of 2004, 177; and the press, 177–78; and the status of women, 182–83; and the UGTT, 180; and the United States, 187–88, 192n48
Ben Badis, Sheikh Abdelhamid, 36, 38, 104
Ben Barka, Mehdi, 24, 58
Ben Bella, Ahmed, 36–37, 38, 91, 242
Ben Boulaïd, Mostéfa, 71n62
Benbrahim, Melha, 63
Benchikh, Madjid, 49n23
Ben Fadhel, Riad, 178
Benflis, Ali, 88, 89, 90, 96, 100n44, 122
Benhadjar, Ali, 111, 124, 125, 131n35
Benhamouda, Abdelhak, 131n35
Benjedid, Chadli, 3, 37–38, 79, 80, 81, 84, 85, 106, 107, 116, 126, 248
Benjelloun, Omar, 151, 172n2
Bennani, Salma, 135, 143
Bensadoun, Mickael, x

Bentalha, 45
Benyellès, Rachid, 118, 130n23
Benzekri, Driss, 24, 25, 161
Berbers, x, 6, 237, 238, 241, 242–43, 258–60; in Algeria, x, 4, 6–7, 42, 52, 61–66, 70n50, 86–87, 99n34, 241–42, 253, 254–55, 257; the *aarouch*, 64; Académie Berbère/Agraw Imazighen, 53, 62, 242–43; Almohad Berber dynasty, 53; Army of Liberation, 58, 59; Association Berbère de Recherches, Information, Documentation et Animation (ABRIDA), 249; Association de Culture Berbère (ACB), 245, 249, 256; Ateliers de Culture Berbère (ACB), 249; *Ateliers Imedyazen*, 243, 249; Berber culture, 6, 61, 67n5; Berber Cultural Movement (MCB), 248, 251, 255, 259; Berber dialects, 8, 18; Berber heritage, ix, 56, 65; Berber history, 50; Berber identity, 6, 26, 27, 28, 50, 51, 56, 57, 61, 62, 140; Berberist ethos, 6; Berber kings, 26, 54; Berber "spirit," 50; in Morocco, x, 4, 6–7, 17–19, 26–30; —the Agadir Charter, 17; Berber *dahir* (May 1930), 28, 57; Berber mountains, 28; Berber Spring (*Tafsut*), 248, 249, 256, 259; Black Spring, 64, 86; customary law (*izerf*), 57, 60; French Berber policy, 28, 61; and Islam, 52, 53, 54, 56; and the Istiqlal party, 58–60; Kabylian-Berber consciousness, 62–63, 86–87, 99n34; "memory work/workers," 50–67; pan-Berber identity, 62; political and social marginalization, x, 57; Rally for Culture and Democracy/Rassemblement pour la Culture et la Démocratie (RCD), 63, 122, 128, 131n43, 254–55, 256, 263n36; satellite television (BRTV), 64; Tamazgha, 31n1, 62; Tamazight language, 7–8, 18, 28, 29, 31n1, 51, 52–53, 58, 71n58, 86, 89, 242, 243, 249, 252, 253; World Amazigh Congress (CMA), 256–57. *See also* Amazigh (Berber) culture movement
Beur Movement (*les Beurs*), 245–49, 251, 257
Bin Laden, Usama, 113, 184
Blanc, Jean-François, 259
Bosnia, 126
Bosquet, Captain, 39
Bouaza, Moulay, 59
Boudhan, Muhammad, 29, 30
Bougafer, 57

Boukhamkham, Abdelkader, 125, 131n38
Boukous, Ahmed, 30
Boumediene, Houari, 37, 38, 76, 78, 79, 84, 91, 98n13, 101n55, 104, 127, 220, 242
Bourboune, Mourad, 49n23
Bourdieu, Pierre, 243
Bourgass, Kamel, 113
Bourgiba, Habib, 2, 3, 178, 182, 186, 188, 189, 190
Bouteflika, Abdel Aziz, 36, 38, 65, 83, 100n44, 111, 232n18, 254; and Benflis, 88, 89, 96; biography and vision, 83–85; first term of, 75, 85–88, 125; and the Kabylian question, 87; Law on Civil Concord, 108, 110; "Little Big Man," 84; reelection and second term, 75, 88–94, 95, 110, 111, 116, 121, 122
Bouteflika, Said, 84
Bouyali, Mustapha, 105–6
Breton Democratic Union (UDB), 258
Breton language, 253, 257, 258
Bretons, 259
Bretton Woods institution, 224
Britain, 17, 113; Socialist Workers' party, 248; Warwick University, 168
Brotherhood (*zawiyat*), 21
Burgat, François, 22
Bush, George W., 187

Caliphate, 168
Camau, Michel, 184, 185
Canada, 129n14
Canary Islands, 62
Capitalism, 15, 21
Carte de Séjour, 246
Carthaginans, 52
Casablanca, 8, 151, 203; repression of riots (1965), 24; suicide bombing attacks (2003), 29, 136, 137, 142, 145, 150, 154, 162, 164, 166, 169, 170, 174n45
Catalan language, 253, 258
Chafik, Mohamed, 18, 26, 33n51, 52, 53–54, 57
Chaker, Salem, 63, 71n58, 243
Chalabi, El-Hadi, 49n23
Chaouia, 62, 65, 66
Chechnya, 126
Chelf, 112
Cherchell, 40
China, 202

Chirac, Jacques, 86, 264n48
Christianity, 27, 34n59
Citroën factory, 244
"Clash of civilizations," 21, 113
Cold War, 15, 20, 155
Collective identity, x, 6
Collective memory, 24, 52
Committee of Victims of the 1958 Walmas Events, 58
Committee to Protect Journalists (CPJ), 177–78
Congress of Fidelity (1991), 125
Constantine, 240
Council of Europe, 252, 260

Dar al-Islam/dar al-harb, 126
De Gaulle Charles, 84, 88, 262n21
Demnati, Meryam, 29
Democracy, 15
Dihya/the Kahina, 52, 54, 63, 65, 68n13, 249
Dilem, Ali, 64
Djaballah, Abdallah, 106, 121, 122
Djaidja, Toumi, 248
Djaout, Tahar, 253
Djebar, Assia, 39–42, 47; *L'Amour, la fantasia*, 39–41, 47; *La femme sans sepulture*, 41; *La Nouba des femmes de Mont Chenoua* (film), 48n8; *La soif*, 42; *Vaste est la prison*, 41–42
Djeddi, Ali, 125, 131n38
Djender, Mahiedine, 52
Djouadi, Yahia (Yahia Abou Amar), 112
Djurdjura, 63, 109, 246, 249
Dufoix, Georgina, 247

École Nationale des Beaux-Arts d'Alger, 65
Economist, The, 176
Economy, 8, 9; globalized economy, ix, 180, 226–27; world economic system, 2. See also under specific countries
Edinburgh, 113
Egypt, 62, 80, 152, 171; demography, 197; pharoanic Egypt, 52
Eizenstat, Stuart, 227
England. *See* Britain
Essaouira (Mogador), 15
Étienne, Bruno (*L'Algérie, Cultures et Révolution*), 37
Europe, 16, 17, 161; and Algeria, 81, 114; and the Maghrib, 1, 2; European heritage, ix; and Morocco, 159; North African immigrant population, ix, xi, 1, 4–5, 237; radical Islam in, 112
European Charter on Regional or Minority Languages, 252–53, 258, 260
European colonialism, 51
European Court of Human Rights, 57, 258
European imperialism, 51
"European Marshall Plan" for North Africa, 5
European Parliament, 258
European Union (EU), 1, 4, 5, 86, 92, 238; and Algeria, 227; Common Agriculture Policy, 213; and Morocco, 146, 204, 205; Muslim population, 86, 237; North African immigrant population in, 205; and Tunisia, 190n11, 210

Fassis, 27
Féraoun, Mouloud, 63, 242
Fête du Peuple Breton, 258
Fez (city), 136
Flemish language, 253
France, 17, 24, 45, 58, 61, 71n58, 129n14; and Algeria, xi, 36, 39–40, 61, 81, 86, 91, 92, 93, 103, 237, 239–41; Amazigh activists, 255; L'Amitié entre les Peuples (MRAP), 251; anticolonial activities against, 2; Association Culturelle Islamique, 244; Association de Culture Berbère (ACB), 245, 249; Association de la Nouvelle Génération Immigrée (ANGI), 245, 247; Association Gutenberg of Nanterre and Vivons Ensemble, 245; and Britain, 113; Communist party, 244, 247; Confédération des Synndicats Libres (CSL), 244; Confédération Général du Travail (CGT), 244; Fédération Nationale des Musulmans de France (FNMF), 251; France-Plus, 251; Islamic immigrants associations, 248; and Islamic terrorism, 113; Kabyle intelligentsia in, 242; as a key site of Algerian transpolitics, 239–40; *laïcité* law, 251; and the Maghrib, 2; military, 78; Mouvement pour la Triomphe des Libértés Démocratique (MTLD), 240; National Assembly, 263n43; National Front, 255; North African population in, 1, 237; Organisations Islamiques en France (UOIF), 251; Parti des

France—*continued*
  Musulmans de France (PMF), 251; protectorate over Morocco, 28, 55–57, 60; and Rif rebellion, 56, 57, 58; and Russia, 91; Société Nationale de Construction de Logements pour les Travailleurs (SONACTORA), 244, 245, 248; SOS-Racisme, 245, 251; and Tunisia, 175, 187; Vichy regime, 238; violence (October–November 2005), 239
  —Algerian immigrants, 237–39, 249–253, 260; and the Amicale des Algérien en Erope, 241, 243; "arab café," 239, 243; Beur Movement (*les Beurs*), 245–49, 251; *cités*, 239, 246, 247, 248, 249, 250; Étoile Nord-Africaine (ENA), 239; in French Communist party, 244, 247; in Islamic organizations/associations, 244; marginalization of, 239; Organisation de l'Armée Secrète (OAS), 240; politicization of, 238–45; Parti du Peuple Algérien (PPA), 239–40; repression of, 240; *tajmaâts*, 239, 243; in Trotskyist organizations, 244, 247; unemployment, 250
Freemasons, 21
French language, 8, 22, 40
Fukuyama, Francis, 15

G-8 group, 85
Geisser, Vincent, 184, 185
Gellner, Ernest, 243
Gera, Gideon, x
Germany, 1, 57, 113, 125, 237
Géze, François, 45
Ghallab, Abd al-Karim, 68n22
Ghannouchi, Rachid al-, 184–85
Ghazi, Halima, 26
Ghemmati, Abdelkrim, 125
Glasgow, 113
Glawi, Thami al-, 55
Globalization, ix, 16, 19, 51, 179, 180
Great Britain. *See* Britain
Greater Middle East, ix
Greeks, 52
Grenada, 27
Guantánamo Bay, 113
Guellila, Ahmed (Abou Hafs), 112
Guemazi, Kamel, 125, 131n38
Guenaiza, Abd al-Malik, 91
Gulf Emirates, 84

Gulf states, 205
Gulf War (1991), 19–20, 156, 184

Habibi, Injaz Abdallah, 61
Hachani, Abdelkader, 125
Haddam, Anouar, 131n37
Hadj, Messali al-, 36, 239, 240, 241
Hagan, Helene, 53
Halima, Abdelmounaïm Mustapha (Abu Bassir), 112
Halimi, Gisèle, 251
Hamrouche, Mouloud, 129n17, 220, 221
Hani, Abd al-Rahman al-, 190n3
Harbi, Mohammed, 49n23
Hasan I, King of Morocco, 26
Hasan II, King of Morocco, 3, 13, 14, 15, 16, 17, 23–24, 25, 28, 34n58, 132, 136, 146, 214; and Abdessalam Yassine, 151, 165, 172n7; and the Amazigh movement, 17–19; *Amir al-Mu'minin*, 153, 173n24; attempts on his life, 155; coup d'état against, 59; funeral of, 132; and Islam/Islamists, 22, 155, 156, 158; and the political left, 153; and the private sector, 203; repression of political dissidents and human rights, 141–42, 133, 141
Hattab, Hassan, 109, 112
Hijab, 251
Hijra calendar, 54
Hodd, Michael, xi
Holland, 35n79; North African immigrant population, 1
Holocaust, 251
Houti, M'hamed (Abou Othba), 112
Human rights, 15, 24, 25, 140, 155
Human Rights Watch, 178
Huntington, Samuel, 19, 20; *Clash of Civilizations*, 20

Iberia, 53
Ibn Khaldun, Abdul Rahman, 51, 126
Ibn Tumart, 53
Ibrahimi, Ahmed Taleb, 118, 124
Idir, 243
Idris I, 52
Idrissi, Rachid, 54, 55
Imadghacen, 65
Imilchil, 25
India, 202

International Day in Support of Victims of Torture, 24
International Monetary Fund (IMF), 81, 187, 197, 198, 199, 213, 214, 220, 221, 222, 224, 226
International terrorism, ix, 112–15
Internet, 17
Iran, ix; Islamic Revolution (1979), 22, 80
Iraq, ix, 19, 160, 170; Kurds, 30; Persian Gulf War, 81
Islam, 14, 15, 16, 19, 22, 23, 26, 27, 34n59, 37, 51–52, 53, 56, 75; political Islam, 15, 37, 103–28
Islamic culture, 103
Islamic fundamentalism, 20, 21, 252
Islamic history, 51
Islamic law. *See* Shari`a
Islamic opposition movements, ix
Islamist movements, x-xi ,3, 6, 8, 9, 13, 14, 19–22. *See also specific movements*
Islamist movements: Armed Islamic Group (Groupe Islamique Armé - GIA), 44, 82, 85, 109, 111, 112, 113, 114, 255; Armed Islamic Movement (MIA), 105–6; Armée Islamique du Salut (AIS), 82, 85, 107, 109, 110, 111; Islamic League of Daawa and Djihad (LIDD), 109, 111, 124, 131n35; Islamic Salvation Front (Front Islamique du Salut–FIS) 3, 38, 43, 44, 77, 81, 82, 85, 89, 106, 107, 113, 116, 118–19, 120, 121, 124, 125, 126, 127, 129n14, 159, 161, 162, 253, 256; —Council of Coordination, 125; —Delegation overseas, 125; —EFE, 125; Katiba El Khadra (Green Brigade), 112; Katibat Djounoud Allah, 112; Katibat es Sunna, 112; Muslim Brotherhood, 80; Al-Qa`ida, 92, 93, 102n69, 112–14; El-Qiyam al-Islamiyya, 105; Salafist Group for Preaching and Combat (GSPC), 36, 82, 85, 87, 92, 102n69, 109, 110, 111, 112, 113–14; Salafist Group for Combat (GSC), 112
Israel, 23, 188
Israeli-Palestinian peace process, 16, 20, 169, 187
Israeli-Palestinian violence, 169
Istislam, 51
Italy, 1, 113, 237

Jama`a, 61
Jerba, 8; El Ghriba synagogue, 212
Jettou, Driss, 139

Jihad, jihadist groups/movements, xi, 8, 22, 29, 107, 126
Jijel, 109
Joffé, George, 96
Jordan, 210
Jospin, Lionel, 264n52
Juba I, 27, 34n58, 52
Juba II, 26
Judaism, 27
Jugurtha, 27, 34n58, 42, 63, 67n5, 264n50

Kalaa M'Gouna, 25
Kartali, Mustapha, 124
Kassimi, Muhammad al-, 59
Kastoryano, Riva, 238
Kebir, Rabah, 125
Kepel, Gilles, 171, 172
Kettane, Nacer, 246
Khadra, Yasmina (Mohammed Moulessehoul), 39, 42–47; *À quoi rêvent les loups*, 39, 42–43; *L'Automne des chimères*, 46; *Wolf Dreams*, 43–44, 46, 47, 49n13
Khatib, Abdelkrim, 157, 163, 173n23
Khenchela, 65
Khenifra, 29, 59, 60
Khomeini, Ayatollah Ruhollah, 80
Krim, Belkacem, 63, 242
Ksentini, Farouk, 110
Kurdish language, 264n48
Kurds, 30

La Beur generation (Aïchoune), 246, 262n18
Lamari, Gen. Muhammad, 82, 89, 91, 100n47, 111, 121
Language, 7–8. *See also* Alsatian language; Arabic language; Basque language; Breton language; Catalan language; European Charter on Regional or Minority Languages; Flemish language; French language; Kurdish language; Latin (language); Occitan language; Paris: Centre de Recherche Berbère at Institut National des Languages et Civilisations Orientales (INALCO); Tamazight language
L'Association Aurès El-Kahina, 65
Latin America, 155
Latin (language), 29
Lebanon, 35n79, 152

Leicester, 113
Le Journal (weekly), 25
Le Matin du Sahara (daily), 24, 25, 26, 66
Le Monde (daily), 45, 47
Le Monde Amazigh (monthly), 26, 53, 54, 57, 60, 69n35
Le Pen, Jean-Marie, 255
Les Rockin' Babouches, 246
Leveau, Rémy, xi
Libération (daily), 252
Libya, xiin1, 1, 188, 204
Lmrabet, Ali, 143
London, 113; Finsbury Park, 113
Los Angeles International Airport, 129n14
Louis-Philippe, 41
Lyon, 239, 248, 249, 255; Assiren (cultural association) in, 249

Madani, Abassi, 44, 89, 109, 111, 119, 125, 126
Madani, Tawfiq al-, 52
Maddy-Weitzman, Bruce, x
Madrid, 150, 154
Mammeri, Mouloud, 50, 63, 65, 241, 242, 248
Manchester, 113
Manjra, Mehdi el-, 20
Mantes-la-Jolie, 250
Marseille, 239; Mouvement des Travailleurs Arabs, 244; Radio Gazelle, 245
Martinez, Luis (*La guerre civile en Algérie, 1990-1998*), 47
Marxism, 23, 244, 245, 247
Marzouki, Moncef, 186, 190n3
Mascara (department in western Algeria), 112
Mashriq (Arab East), 6
Masinissa/Massinissa (king of Numidia), 27, 34n58, 52, 63, 66, 67n5
Massinissa, Guermah, 64
Matoub, Lounès, 50, 64–65, 243, 253
Mauritania, xiin1, 1
McDougall, James, 66
Médéa, 112
Mediterranean civilization, 52
Mediterranean Sea, ix, xi, 1, 2, 86, 92, 227, 237, 246, 247, 257
Mehenni, Ferhat, 65, 243
Mellah, Salima, 45, 49n23
Mélouza, 241
"Memory community," 50

"Memory sites" (*lieux de memoire*), 50
Menguillet, Ait, 63
Merzouki, Ahmed, 24
Messaoudi, Khalida, 251, 253
Mexico, 202; Institutional Revolutionary Party, 175
Mezrag, Madani, 110, 124, 125
Middle East, 4, 16, 55, 204. *See also* Near East; specific countries
Mitterrand, François, 241, 245
Mogador. *See* Essaouira
Montagne/adrar, 63
Morocco, ix, x, xiin1, 227; agriculture, 202, 213; and Algeria, xiin1, 15, 92, 132, 204; *alternance* government, 137–38, 139, 145; Amazigh (Berber) culture movement, x, 8; anti-Western and anti-Zionism feelings, 19–22, 23; Association Agreement with the European Union, 204; balance of payments, 201; Berbers, 4, 6–7, 8: —the Agadir Charter, 17; —Royal Institute of Amazigh Culture, 140; "caravans of truth," 25; "clash of civilizations" in, 21; civil liberties, 141, 142; collective identity, x; collective memory, 24, 28; Conseil Consultatif des Droits de l'Homme, 15; constitution, 163; decolonization process, 17, 21; democracy, 133; democratization and liberalization, 134; demography, 1, 197–98, 202; discourses on national identity, 13, 14, 17–23, 25–30; economy, xi, 144, 161, 197–205, 213–14; economy reforms, 198–202, 205; educational system, 23, 138; elite, 161; emigration to the EU, 205; and the Euro-Mediterranean partnership, 16; family law, 91, 136–37, 144–46; and the EU, 146, 204; and Europe, 159; First Congress on Birth Control, 23; foreign direct investment (FDI), 205; Forum Justice et Vérité, 24, 25; French protectorate, 28, 55–57, 60; GDP, 199;-201, 203; Hasan II Development Fund, 140; history, 51–52; human development index (HDI), 212–13; human rights, 15, 23, 24, 25, 140, 141–42, 155; the Idrisid dynasty, 52; independence, 152; industry, 200; inflation, 201; Instance Equité et Reconciliation (IER), 25, 140, 141, 142; al-Islah wal-Tajdid/al-Tawhid wal-Islah, 157, 158, 166, 172nn9, 10; Islam, Islamists, 14,

15, 19, 26, 51–52, 136, 142, 155–58; Islamist movement/groups, x–xi, 18, 21–22, 23, 139, 150–72; Islamist movement/groups, and discourse on national identity, 13, 14, 19–22, 30 ; Islamist movement/groups, and the Gulf War (1991), 19–20; and the Israeli-Palestinian peace process, 16, 20; Istiqlal party, 2, 17, 21, 28, 30, 58–60; Jews, 16, 23; Justice and Development Party (PJD), 22, 30, 138, 150, 151, 154, 158, 159–64, 166, 171, 172n10, 174n45; —agenda and objectives, 167–68; —Fifth Congress, 163; —radicalization of, 168–70; Justice and Spirituality movement (al-Adl wal-Ihsan), 22, 150, 151, 152, 154, 156–57, 158, 159, 164–167, 171, 172n4, 173n29; —agenda and objectives, 168; —Guidance Council, 165; —Majlis al-Shura, 165; —radicalization of, 168–70; labor force, 197, 198; liberalization of the political sphere, 13, 24, 154–55; and Libya, 204; *makhzen*, 14, 17, 18, 24, 26, 27, 31n2, 53, 54, 55, 56, 59, 138, 140, 147n8, 146; manufacturing output, 200; military coups, 24, 29, 59; monarchy's co-optation, 13; Moroccan Constitution, 14; the Moroccan Spring, 23–25, 64; Mouvement National Populaire, 69n37; Mouvement Populaire, 59, 69n37; Mouvement Populaire Démocratique et Constitutionnel (MPDC), 157–58, 160, 162; municipal elections (2003), 172n1, 174n45; national history, 23; nationalist movement, 28, 128n1; nationalism, 28, 55, 104; new interest in recent history, 24–25; NGO, 139; opposition parties, 19, 137, 160–61, 138; pan-Arabists, 19, 20; parliament, 135, 136, 137, 140, 150, 159, 161, 162; parliamentary elections: —of 1997, 137, 138, 139; —of 2002, 138–39, 160, 161, 162; Parti du Progrès et du Socialisme (PPS), 139; personal status code (Moudawwana), 7, 144–46; phosphates, 200, 202; pluralism, 133, 153; political changes and reforms, 132, 133–34, 136–37, 146, 155–58, 161, 171; political entity, 75; the private sector, 203–4; proportional representation (PR) electoral system, 161; question of state legitimacy, 3–4; press freedoms, 141, 142–44; radical Islamist terrorism, 1, 134, 136, 142, 145, 150, 162, 164, 166, 169, 170, 174n45; radical Left, 22; radical Jihadist groups, xi, 22, 29; reforms, x, 134, 198–202; Rif rebellion (1921–26), 55–57; Rif region, 18, 25, 28, 58; royal *dahir* ("edict") of January 7 2004, 25; al-Shabiba al-Islamiyya (Islamic Youth), 151, 152, 157, 158, 172n2; and the Shah of Iran, 23; sharifian rule, 16; *siba*, 27; social problems, 228–30; society, 134, 136, 144, 146; state fundamentalism, 22–23; and the State of Israel, 23; status of women, 7, 134, 136, 143, 144–45; and Tunisia, 204; unemployment, 202–3; Union Nationale des Forces Populaires (UNFP), 59; Union Socialiste des Forces Populaires (USFP), 3–4, 17, 138, 139, 145, 160, 162; and the United States, 146, 159, 204; vocation as a bridge between Islam and the West, 16, 19, 22; Wahabbism, 23, 30; Western Sahara question, xiin1, 14, 24, 30, 132, 143; years of lead (*les années des plomb*), 24

Mortimer, Robert, x
Mouha U Hamou Zayani, 60
Moulay Ismail, Sultan, King of Morocco, 26, 34n58
Moulessehoul, Mohammed. *See* Khadra, Yasmina
Mounib, Muhammad, 57
Moutawakil, Abdelwahed El, 168
Mouti`, Abdelkrim, 151, 157, 172n4
M'sa`adi, Abbas, 58
Muhammad, the Prophet, 54, 112, 153, 165, 168, 173n30
Muhammad V, King of Morocco, 26, 34n58
Muhammad VI, King of Morocco, x, 7, 13, 14, 23, 25, 27, 29, 56, 57, 147, 158, 163; and Abdessalam Yassine, 165; accession to the throne, 132, 154; and Algeria, 132; and the "years of lead," 133; "commander of the Faithful," 132; family law reform, 136–37, 144–46; human rights and press freedoms, 141–44; and Islamist terrorism, 136–37; "king of the poor," 135; marriage of, 135–36; and Morocco's economic problems, 133; "new concept of authority," 134–35; reforming the political system, 132, 133–34, 136, 137–40, 146, 155; social initiatives, 139–40; style of leadership, 134–37; and Western Sahara question, 132
Munson, Henry, 153

Murphy, Emma C., 181–82, 185, 191n11
Muslim Brotherhood, 80, 119, 120
Muslim *umma*, 6, 21, 22, 255
Muslim world, 19, 48

Nahnah, Mahfoud, 106, 119, 120
Naimi, Hamed, 143
Napoleon, 84
Nationalism, 26, 28, 36
Nationalist movements, 2. See also specific movements
Nation-state, 5, 6, 26
NATO. See North Atlantic Treaty Organization
Nazis, 238
Near East, 28. See also Mideast; specific countries
Netherlands, 237
North African history, 50
North African society and politics, x
North America, 112
North Atlantic Treaty Organization (NATO), 92
Nuhayan, Shaykh Zayid bin Sultan Al, 84

Occitan language, 253, 257, 258
Occitans, 259
October 1973 Arab-Israeli war, 239
Oil, in Algeria, 75, 76, 77, 79, 81, 85, 92, 93, 219, 220, 230; Arab oil embargo, 239
Omar, Abdelkader, 131n38
Omnium Nord Africain (ONA), 203–4
Orientalism, 23
Othmani, Saad-Eddine, 159, 162, 163, 168
Oufkir, GenMuhammad, 59–60, 69n38
Oujda, 6, 84
Ouyahia, Ahmad, 88

Palestine, 170
Palestinian territories, 152
Papon, Maurice, 240
Paris, 41, 65, 88, 129n14, 239, 249, 255; Académie Berbère/Agraw Imazighen, 53, 62, 242–43; Association Berbère de Recherches, Information, Documentation et Animation (ABRIDA), 249; Ateliers de Culture Berbère (ACB), 245, 249, 252; *Ateliers Imedyazen*, 243, 249; attacks on immigrant workers in, 240; Centre de Recherche Berbère at Institut National des Languages et Civilisations Orientales (INALCO), 62; École Normale Supérieure, 41, 42; Éditions Arcantère and Agence Im'media (publishing house), 245; FLN 's nonviolent demonstration (1961), 240–41; Grand Mosquée de Paris, 244–45; Groupe d'Études Berbères, 249; Groupe d'Études des Berbères de L'Université de Paris–VIII, 62, 243; Radio Beur, 245, 246, 247
Pélissier, Colonel, 40
Pelletreau, Robert, 114
Perrault, Gilles (*Notre ami le roi*), 14–15
Persian Gulf, 62, 93, 120, 206
Poissy, 247, 248
Polisario, 143
Pontecorvo, Gillo, and *The Battle of Algiers* (film), 48
Powell, Colin (secretary of state), 187

Qaddafi, Mu`ammar al-, 192n48
Qaid, GenSalah Ahmad al-, 91
Al-Qa`ida, 92, 93, 102n69, 112–14, 129n14
Qatar, 89
Qutb, Sayyid, 80

Rabat, 19, 132, 156
Raha, Rachid, 26
Raissouni, Ahmed, 173n24
Ramadan, Tariq, 248
Ramadane, Abbane, 63,
Ramid, Mustapha, 163, 167
Rashidun Caliphs (first four Caliphs), 54
Relizane, 112
Renault factory, 244
Ressam, Ahmed, 129n14
Rivlin, Paul, xi
Romans, 52
Rome, 120
Rosen, Lawrence, 66
Roubaix: Afus deg Wfus (cultural association) in, 249
Russia, 91, 230. See also Soviet bloc; Soviet Union, collapse of

Sadi, Areski, 252
Sahara, 92; natural gas in, 2; Touareg Berbers, 62; Western Sahara question, xiiin1, 14, 30, 143, 227

Sahnoun, Ahmed, 116
Sahraoui, Imam, 255
Saïda, 112
Salafism, 17, 21, 28, 125, 245
Sans Frontières (newspaper), 245
Satour, Khaled, 49n23
Satrouville, 250
Saudi Arabia, 19
Sebbar, Leila, 246
Secularism, 23
Shah of Iran, 23
Shari`a, 6, 57, 21, 60, 105
Sheshounk I, 53
Sidi Bel Abbès, 112
Silverstein, Paul A., xi
Skikda, 122
Smahi, Farid, 264n53
Smith, Anthony, 50, 51
Socialism, 37
Souaïdia, Habib (*La sale guerre: Le témoignage d'un ancient officier des forces spéciales de l'armée algérienne, [1992-2000]*), 45
Soummam, 125
Soussi, Mokhtar, 55, 68n27
South Korea, 202, 210
Soviet bloc, 2
Soviet Union, collapse of, 15. See also Russia
Soysal, Yasemin, 238r
Spain, 18, 113, 205, 237; golden age of Muslim Spain, 16; North African immigrant population, 1; Islam, 53; and Rif rebellion, 55-57, 58
St. Augustine, 52
Stora, Benjamin, x, xi, 24, 64
Straits of Gibraltar, ix, 2
Sufism, 151, 152, 154, 165, 166, 244
Susser, Asher, xi
Switzerland, 84

Taliban, 112
Taiwan, 202
Talahite, Fatiha, 49n23
Talbot factory, 244, 247, 248
Tamazight language, 7-8, 18, 28, 29, 31n1, 51, 52-53, 58, 71n58, 86, 89, 242, 243, 249, 252, 253, 258, 259, 264n48
Tariq Bin Ziyad, 53
Tazmamart, 24, 25

TelQuel (weekly), 25, 142-43
Temmar, Abdelhamid, 224
Terentius, 52
Tertullianus, 52
Tetouan, 57
Third World, 37, 38, 202
Tifinagh script, 29, 242
Tissemsilt, 112
Tizi-Ouzou, 248
Tlemcen, 6, 12
Tlili, Abderrahmane, 176, 177
Touati, Maj. Gen. Mohamed, 130n29
Toumi, Khalida (Messaoudi), 128, 131n43
Trofimov, Yaroslav, 185
Tunisia, x, xi, xiin1, 4, 42 128n1, 172, 203, 227, 238; agriculture, 181, 207, 208, 213; army, 188, 189; Association Agreement with the European Union, 210; balance of payment, 210-11; civil and political organizations, 182-86; constitution, 177; Council for National Security, 189, 193n 61; Democratic Forum for Work and Freedom, 190n1; democratization, 175, 178; demography, 1, 197-98, 208; economy, xi, 178, 186, 190n11, 197-98, 206-12, 213-14; emigration to the EU, 205; Ettajdid, 190n1; and the European Union, 190n11, 210, 211; and France, 175, 187; GDP, 178, 206-7, 208, 209, 212; human development index (HDI), 212-13; human rights, 178, 179, 191n26; Human Rights League, 191n26; Islamic Tendency Movement (MTI), 183; Islamists, 152, 179, 182, 183; and the Israeli-Palestinian peace process, 187; labor force, 197, 198; Left, 186; Liberal Socialist Party, 190n1; and Morocco, 204; Movement of Democratic Socialists, 190n1; Multi-fiber Agreement (MFA), 210, 211; National Pact (1988), 179; "medical" coup (1987), 3; en-Nahda party, 183-86; —Ezzeitouna TV, 184, 185; National Council on Liberties in Tunisia, 191n26; nationalism, nationalists, 104; Neo-Destour party (*see* Rassemblement Constitutionelle Démocratiqe, *below*); one-party regime, 175, 188-90; opposition parties, 176, 183-86, 190n1, 191n29; parliament, 176; parliamentary elections: of 1994, 176; —of 1999, 176; —of 2004, 176; political entity,

Tunisia—*continued*
75; political and civil rights, 175; polygamy, 91; political pluralism, 178, 179; Popular Unity Party, 176, 190n1; presidential elections: of 1994, 180; —of 1999, 176–77; —of 2004, 177, 183; press and media, 177–78; the private sector, 208–10; Progressive Democratic Party, 190n1; question of state legitimacy, 3; Rassemblement Constitutionelle Démocratiqe (RCD), 2, 175, 178–79, 182, 183, 184; Right, 186; security apparatus, 179, 188, 189; social forces, 179–82; terrorism in, 212; tourism, 212; unemployment, 207, 210, 211; Unionist Democratic Union, 176, 190n1; Union Générales Travailleurs Tunisiens (UGTT), 180; and United States, 187–88, 192n48, 210; urban middle-class women, 181–82; women's rights and status, 178, 182–83; workers, 179, 181; and World Trade Organization, 190n11

Turkey, 19, 171; Justice and Development party (AKP), 167

Umed, Sidi Muhammad, 59
Umma, 51, 55
Ummayad empire, 53
United Kingdom. *See* Britain
United Nations (UN), 229; Committee for the Elimination of Racial Discrimination (CERD), 62; Development Fund, 212; Development Program, 230; General Assembly, 84; human development index (HDI), 212; Security Council, 85; UNESCO, 65, 251, 258
United States, 120, 162, 258; and Algeria, 85–86, 89, 93, 114; Clinton administration, 114; foreign policy, 15; and global war on terrorism, 176; Greater Middle East Initiative, ix; and the Maghrib, 2, 227; Pan-Sahel Initiative, 92; and Morocco, 146, 159, 204; and al-Qa'ida, 113; September 11 events, 20, 85, 112, 126, 169, 184, 187; and Tunisia, 187–88, 192n48, 210

Vaulx-en-Velin, 250

Wahabbism, 23, 30
West, 16, 19–21, 22; Islamic West, 28; Judeo-Christian West, 20, 22
Westernization, 19
Western policy makers, ix
Willis, Michael J., x
Women, status of: in Algeria, 7, 40–42, 47, 48, 90–91, 120; in Morocco, 7, 134, 136, 143, 144–45; in Tunisia, 182–83
World Bank, 198, 199, 209, 212, 213, 222
World Trade Organization, 190n11, 227
World War I, 36, 238

Yahia, Rachid Ali, 241
Yakouren, 109
Yassine, Nadia, 143, 166
Yassine, Shaykh Abdessalam, 21, 22, 143–44, 151–152, 154, 156, 157, 158, 164–67, 168, 172nn4, 7, 173n12
Yatim, Muhammad, 172n9
Yazghi, Muhammad El, 162
Yiddish, 258
Yones, Imam, 43
Yous, Nesroulah (*Qui a tué à Bentalha? Chronique d'un massacre annoncé*), 45, 46
Youssoufi, Abderrahman, 138

Zaoui, Ahmed, 131n37
Zarhuni, Nur El-Din "Yazid," 84, 88, 111
Zayan tribe, 60
Zeroual, Gen. Liamine, 83, 108, 256
Zionism, 19, 20, 21, 23
Zisenwine, Daniel, x
Zouabri, Antar, 109
Zoubir, Yahia H., x, xi, 131n37

www.ingramcontent.com/pod-product-compliance
Lightning Source LLC
Chambersburg PA
CBHW031431160426
43195CB00010BB/686